For one generation,

Margaret and Nick

and another,

Carlotta and Cameron

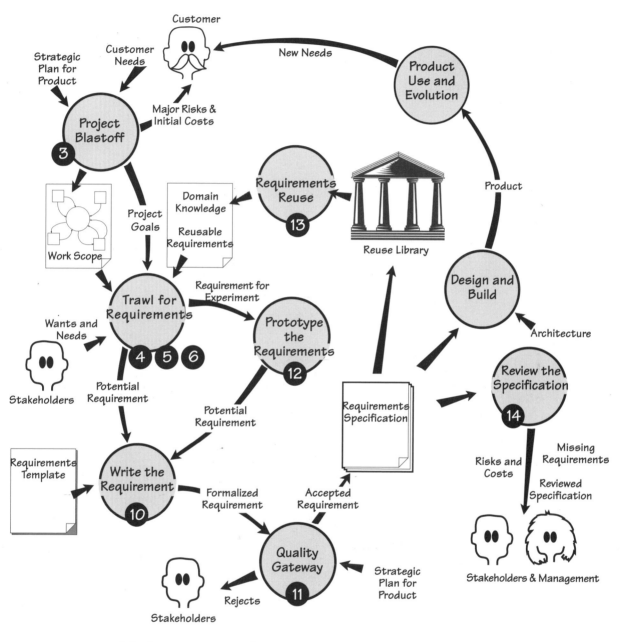

Volere requirements process

Mastering the
Requirements Process

Second Edition

Mastering the Requirements Process
Second Edition

 Suzanne Robertson
James Robertson

Addison-Wesley

Upper Saddle River, NJ • Boston • Indianapolis • San Francisco

New York • Toronto • Montreal • London • Munich • Paris • Madrid

Capetown • Sydney • Tokyo • Singapore • Mexico City

Many of the designations used by manufacturers and sellers to distinguish their products are claimed as trademarks. Where those designations appear in this book, and the publisher was aware of a trademark claim, the designations have been printed with initial capital letters or in all capitals.

The authors and publisher have taken care in the preparation of this book, but make no expressed or implied warranty of any kind and assume no responsibility for errors or omissions. No liability is assumed for incidental or consequential damages in connection with or arising out of the use of the information or programs contained herein.

The publisher offers excellent discounts on this book when ordered in quantity for bulk purchases or special sales, which may include electronic versions and/or custom covers and content particular to your business, training goals, marketing focus, and branding interests. For more information, please contact:

> U.S. Corporate and Government Sales
> (800) 382-3419
> corpsales@pearsontechgroup.com

For sales outside the United States please contact:

> International Sales
> international@pearsoned.com

 This Book Is Safari Enabled

The Safari® Enabled icon on the cover of your favorite technology book means the book is available through Safari Bookshelf. When you buy this book, you get free access to the online edition for 45 days.

Safari Bookshelf is an electronic reference library that lets you easily search thousands of technical books, find code samples, download chapters, and access technical information whenever and wherever you need it.

To gain 45-day Safari Enabled access to this book:

- Go to http://www.awprofessional.com/safarienabled
- Complete the brief registration form
- Enter the coupon code XTHN-UQII-LKJY-AZID-N9SN

If you have difficulty registering on Safari Bookshelf or accessing the online edition, please e-mail customer-service@safaribooksonline.com.

Visit us on the Web: www.awprofessional.com

Library of Congress Cataloging-in-Publication Data
Robertson, Suzanne.
  Mastering the requirements process / Suzanne Robertson, James Robertson.—2nd ed.
      p. cm.
  Includes bibliographical references and index.
  ISBN 0-321-41949-9 (hardcover : alk. paper)
  1. Project management. I. Robertson, James. II. Title.

TA190.R48 2006
005.10684—dc22

                                                                2005036027

ISBN 0-321-41949-9

Text printed in the United States on recycled paper at Courier Westford in Westford, Massachusetts.

4th   Printing   December 2007

Contents

9   Fit Criteria   203

*in which we show how measuring a requirement makes it
unambiguous, understandable, and, importantly, testable*

10   Writing the Requirements   223

in which we turn the requirements into written form

Preface to the Second Edition

In the six years since we published the first edition of this book, the world's knowledge of requirements has grown, and more people have a job called "business analyst," "requirements engineer," or something similar. The Volere Requirements Specification Template has been downloaded countless times. The Volere Requirements Process is in use by thousands of people who are engaged in the activity of successful requirements gathering. They, in turn, have given us feedback over the years about what they needed to know, and what they are doing when gathering requirements.

This book is a reflection of the feedback we have received, and of the way people have made use of the first edition.

The requirements activity has moved away from wanting to be seen as an engineering discipline, to the realization that it is a sociotechnical activity. Requirements analysts now see their role first as one of communication, and second as a technician adding rigor and precision to the results of the human communication.

As a result, we have updated and expanded the project sociology analysis section of the book. In a similar vein, we have added the appropriate rigor to the technicalities of recording and measuring the requirements.

Perhaps the greatest change to come along since the first edition has been the arrival of agile methods, accompanied by some wonderful technological advances. Agile methods have influenced the way people develop software, with the result being that greater emphasis is placed on close customer relationships, and less emphasis is placed on documentation. We heartily applaud this advance. However, we have also seen too many people, who, in the name of agility, rush to a solution without first understanding the real business problem to be solved.

This, then, is the role of requirements in the agile world: to ensure that we hear not only one customer's voice, but also the voices of the other stakeholders—those with some value to add to the requirements for the product. Agile requirements analysts ensure that the work is considered, not just the product, and that the nonfunctional requirements are studied, not left to the whim of the programmer.

Agile methods have brought with them a healthy disdain for documentation. We agree with this view. Throughout this second edition we urge you to consider the benefit before committing anything to writing. But while we suggest sometimes you can develop software successfully without formally written requirements, we never suggest you can do it without understanding the requirements.

The emphasis on iterative development means that the requirements "phase" is no longer completed before building begins. The drive toward short, sharp release cycles means requirements analysts get feedback on their requirements efforts more quickly. Stakeholders receive positive reinforcement when they see the time they invest in requirements paid back with progressive versions of working software that does what they expect, and what they need.

For the convenience of the reader, throughout this book we have used "he" to refer to both genders. The authors (one male and one female) find the use of "he or she" disruptive and awkward.

Technological advances have changed requirements gathering. Blogs and wikis mean that requirements analysts can gather their requirements informally and iteratively using the convenience of networking with their stakeholders. Desktop videoconferencing and instant messaging mean closer, quicker communication with stakeholders, which is, of course, necessary for good requirements gathering.

The gap between what we wrote in 1999 and what we found ourselves doing when gathering requirements gradually grew wider, until we knew it was time to update our book. The volume that you hold in your hands is the result of the last few years of our work and teaching. We trust you find it interesting, enlightening, and useful.

Foreword to the First Edition

It is almost ten years now since Don Gause and I published *Exploring Requirements: Quality Before Design*. Our book is indeed an exploration, a survey of human processes that can be used in gathering complete, correct, and communicable requirements for a software system, or any other kind of product.

The operative word in this description is "can," for over this decade the most frequent question my clients have asked is, "How can I assemble these diverse processes into a comprehensive requirements process for our information systems?"

At long last, James and Suzanne Robertson have provided an answer I can conscientiously give to my clients. *Mastering the Requirements Process* shows, step by step, template by template, example by example, one well-tested way to assemble a complete, comprehensive requirements process.

One watchword of their process is "reasonableness." In other words, every part of the process makes sense, even to people who are not very experienced with requirements work. When introducing this kind of structure to an organization, reasonableness translates into easier acceptance—an essential attribute when so many complicated processes are tried and rejected.

The process they describe is the Volere approach, which they developed as an outcome of many years helping clients to improve their requirements. Aside from the Volere approach itself, James and Suzanne contribute their superb teaching skills to the formidable task facing anyone who wishes to develop requirements and do them well.

The Robertsons' teaching skills are well known to their seminar students as well as to fans of their *Complete Systems Analysis* books. *Mastering the Requirements Process* provides a much-requested front end for their analysis books—or for anyone's analysis books, for that matter.

We can use all the good books on requirements we can get, and this is one of them!

> *Gerald M. Weinberg*
> *www.geraldmweinberg.com*
> *February 1999*

READING

Gause, Donald C., and Gerald M. Weinberg. *Exploring Requirements: Quality Before Design*. Dorset House, 1989.

READING

Robertson, James, and Suzanne Robertson. *Complete Systems Analysis: The Workbook, the Textbook, the Answers*. Dorset House, 1998.

Acknowledgments

Writing a book is hard. Without the help and encouragement of others, it would be nearly impossible, at least for these authors. We would like to take a few lines to tell you who helped and encouraged and made it possible.

Andy McDonald of Vaisala was generous with his time, and gave us considerable technical input. We hasten to add that the IceBreaker product in this book is only a distant relation to Vaisala's IceCast systems. The Vaisala User Group, of which E. M. Kennedy holds the chair, also provided valuable technical input.

Thanks are due to the technical reviewers who gave up their time to wade through some fairly incomprehensible stuff. Mike Russell, Susannah Finzi, Neil Maiden, Tim Lister, and Bashar Nuseibeh all deserve honorable mentions.

We would like to acknowledge our fellow principals at the Atlantic Systems Guild—Tom DeMarco, Peter Hruschka, Tim Lister, Steve McMenamin, and John Palmer—for their help, guidance, and incredulous looks over the years.

The staff at Pearson Education contributed. Sally Mortimore, Alison Birtwell, and Dylan Reisenberger were generous and skillful, and used such persuasive language whenever we spoke about extending the deadline.

For the second edition, Peter Gordon provided guidance and persuasion at exactly the right times. Kim Boedigheimer, John Fuller, and Lara Wysong were invaluable at steering us through the publishing process. Jill Hobbs tamed our faulty grammar and punctuation, and made this text readable. The technical input of Ian Alexander, Earl Beede, Capers Jones, Chuck Pfleeger, and Tony Wasserman goes far beyond valuable. Thank you, gentlemen, for your insights. And we hasten to add that any remaining technical errors are ours and ours alone.

And finally we thank the students at our seminars and our consulting clients. Their comments, their insistence on having things clearly explained, their insights, and their feedback have all made some difference, no matter how indirect, to this book.

Thank you, everybody.

James and Suzanne Robertson
London, January 2006

What Are Requirements?

in which we consider why we are interested in requirements

The most useful products are those where the developers have understood what the product is intended to accomplish for its users and how it must accomplish that purpose. To understand these things, you must understand what kind of work the users want to do and how the product will affect that work and fit into the organization's goals. What the product does for its users and which constraints it must satisfy in this context are the product's requirements. Apart from a few fortuitous accidents, no product has ever succeeded without prior understanding of its requirements. It does not matter what kind of work the user wishes to do, be it scientific, commercial, e-commerce, or word processing. Nor does it matter which programming language or development tools are used to construct the product. The development process—whether agile, eXtreme Programming, prototyping, the Rational Unified Process, or any other method—is irrelevant to the need for understanding the requirements. One fact always emerges: You must come to the correct understanding of the requirements, and have your client understand them, or your product or your project will fail.

This book discusses how to discover the requirements and determine their precise nature. Moreover, it explains how you will know that you have found the correct requirements and how to communicate them.

Any important endeavor needs some kind of orderly process. Moreover, the people who are active in the process must be able to see why different parts of the process are important, and which parts carry particular significance for their particular project. This book presents *Volere*—a process, a requirements specification template, and a set of techniques for gathering, confirming, organizing, and documenting the requirements for a product. This process and template can be—indeed, have been—used for any kind of

> ❝ . . . *even perfect program verification can only establish that a program meets its specification. The hardest part of the software task is arriving at a complete and consistent specification, and much of the essence of building a program is in fact the debugging of the specification.* ❞
>
> Source: Fred Brooks, *No Silver Bullet: Essence and Accidents of Software Engineering*

product or project. Since the first version of Volere was released in 1995, it has been used by thousands of projects in hundreds of countries.

The requirements process, as we describe it here, is a thorough exploration of the intended product with the intention of discovering—in some cases, inventing—the functionality and behavior of the product. The output of this requirements process is a written description of the requirements to be used as input to the design of the product.

Requirements are not meant to place an extra burden on your project. Instead, they are there to make your project run more smoothly. There is little point in attempting to construct a product unless you know what you are trying to build. This does not mean that your understanding must always be perfect before you start construction, and it does not mean that all the requirements have to be written down. But it does mean that if you intend to deliver useful and usable products at the lowest cost to your organization, you must pay attention to requirements.

This book discusses how you can come to an understanding of the requirements and how you might write them down so that the constructors, and the future generations of maintenance people, can understand them.

Requirements are expressed in a technologically neutral way so as to intentionally avoid influencing the design of the solution.

Requirements are usually expressed as an abstraction. That is, they are expressed in a technologically neutral way so as to intentionally avoid influencing the design of the solution. The requirements are a pure statement of business needs, without any implementation bias. The role of product design is to translate the requirements into a plan to build some physical reality that will, in the real world, do what is needed. Product design determines which devices are to be used, which software components are necessary, and how they are to be constructed. It is important to the success of the product that final design decisions are not taken before the relevant requirements are known. It is equally important to note that a well-organized requirements process means that requirements, design, and implementation can be done as a number of iterative loops. Each iteration produces some usable functionality. Figure 1.1 depicts the requirements process as part of the ongoing development life cycle.

Requirements for a product are not frozen the moment that it is built.

Once the product is built, it is used, and immediately begins to evolve. Users demand more functionality, and the product must be able to grow to accommodate the new demands. If you are using an agile process where new functionality is delivered frequently, the partial product has an effect on the work practices. For example, it may trigger new, previously unforeseen requirements, some of which may change the delivered product. The evolution of the product and its requirements is a process that we cannot control or prescribe, but it is one that we must accept. Requirements for a product are not frozen the moment that it is built. Instead, they evolve over a period of time, and any requirements process must take this fact of ongoing change into account.

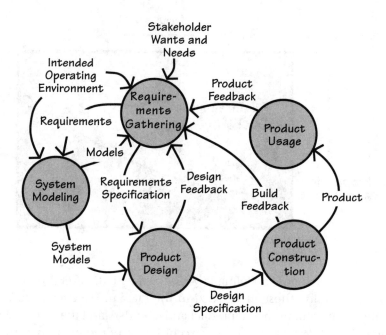

Figure 1.1

The diagram illustrates the role of requirements in the development life cycle. The *Requirements Gathering* process studies the work and then specifies the product that most helps with that work. As an outcome of this process, the *Requirements Specification* provides a complete description of the needed functionality and behavior of the product. *System Modeling* produces working models of the functions and data needed by the product, as well as models of the work to support the requirements process. *Product Design* turns the abstract specification into a design suitable for the real world. Once built, the product is used, and this real-world experience inevitably provides more new requirements. This diagram should be read as iterative. That is, the complete *Requirements Specification* does not have to be produced before design and construction begin. In fact, if you are working in an agile environment, you will produce a minimal set of requirements components and use those as a guide to planning iterations.

Requirements Gathering and Systems Modeling

Requirements gathering and systems modeling have a significant degree of overlap—the requirements gatherer uses models to help find the requirements, and the modeler uses the requirements to help model the functionality and data. Both produce artifacts used to understand and specify requirements.

In the beginning, the requirements-gathering activity is dominant. The only models being built are a context diagram and perhaps an exploratory data model and a stakeholder map. The requirements analysts are busy discovering the business goals, the stakeholders, the work (or business domain), and the desired outcome.

As the knowledge of the work increases and the business use cases evolve from fuzzy intentions to known quantities, the models become more precise and provide valuable feedback to the requirements gathering. Similarly, the growing knowledge of the requirements feeds the modeling process, enabling the modeling to be more productive. This relationship is illustrated in Figure 1.2.

Models can be used to specify the product, or at least its functionality. Provided that the model is complete and is supported by a data dictionary and any needed process descriptions or scenarios, it makes a suitable alternative to the textual specification.

Figure 1.2

The overlap between *Requirements Gathering* and *Systems Modeling* varies as the development of the product progresses. Initially, very little modeling is done, and the majority of the effort focuses on gathering and verifying requirements. As development continues, the modeling activity expands to occupy a continually greater proportion of the effort.

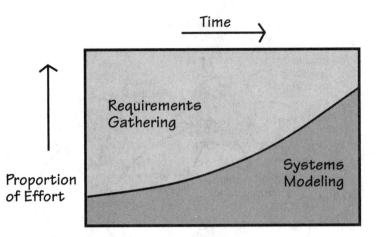

READING

Robertson, James, and Suzanne Robertson. *Complete Systems Analysis: The Workbook, the Textbook, the Answers.* Dorset House, 1998.

Jacobson, Ivar, et al. *Object-Oriented Software Engineering: A Use Case Driven Approach.* Addison-Wesley, 1992.

The craft of systems modeling is well documented. Several books cover this area, including those mentioned in the margin. We encourage you to build models of your proposed product and to understand the work by building models of it. We will not cover, except in a very rudimentary way, how to build these models. That is for you to explore. We will, however, bring you to a complete understanding of what a requirement is, how to write one, and how requirements connect to models.

Agile Software Development

Since the first edition of this book was published, the agile approach to developing systems has become popular, and rightly so. *Agility* refers to product development where the team's development process is based on the principles of the Agile Manifesto. We reproduce it here and, throughout this book, will show its relevance to the requirements activity.

Manifesto for Agile Software Development

We are uncovering better ways of developing software by doing it and helping others do it. Through this work we have come to value

- *Individuals and interactions over processes and tools*
- *Working software over comprehensive documentation*
- *Customer collaboration over contract negotiation*
- *Responding to change over following a plan*

> *That is, while there is value in the items on the right, we value the items on the left more.*
>
> Kent Beck, Mike Beedle, Arie van Bennekum, Alistair Cockburn, Ward Cunningham, Martin Fowler, James Grenning, Jim Highsmith, Andrew Hunt, Ron Jeffries, Jon Kern, Brian Marick, Robert C. Martin, Steve Mellor, Ken Schwaber, Jeff Sutherland, Dave Thomas.
> © 2001, the above authors. This declaration may be freely copied in any form, but only in its entirety through this notice.

Sadly, like many advances, some followers and acolytes have overhyped this manifesto and misapplied its sensible principles. The important point to keep in mind is that there is no conflict between discovering the right requirements and engaging in agile development. No matter which method you use to build your product, you have to build the right product. The only effective way of doing so is if you correctly understand what the product has to do, how it will be used, by whom it will be used, how it fits into the larger picture of the organization, and so on. These things are the requirements. Unfortunately, some proponents of agile development believe that agility and requirements are not compatible. This view is both wrong and dangerous.

Let's consider the Agile Manifesto and the values it proposes.

● Individuals and interactions over processes and tools

In Chapter 3, Project Blastoff, we show you how to determine the stakeholders for your project. Stakeholders are people who have an interest in the product, and they are your sources for requirements. In Chapter 5, Trawling for Requirements, we discuss techniques for determining the requirements. All of these techniques involve some kind of personal interaction with the appropriate stakeholders. Requirements come from humans, so the better you are at interacting with humans, the better you will be at gathering requirements. There is no tool or process that, as far as we can see, will ever replace the effectiveness of the requirements analyst and the stakeholder sitting down eyeball-to-eyeball and talking about what is needed. The skill of the requirements analyst here is to introduce tools, models, and other measures that can help the stakeholder discover and explain his needs.

● Working software over comprehensive documentation

All too often, the requirements process is seen as a long-winded process that eventually delivers an unreadable (and often unread) specification that the client is asked to sign off. We urge you not to see it this way. In Chapter 2, The Requirements Process, we discuss iterative development of products

READING

For more on the Agile Manifesto, refer to *www.agilemanifesto.org*.

READING

Cockburn, Alistair. *Agile Software Development.* Addison-Wesley, 2001.

and consider how the requirements for just the next release are gathered and implemented. It is only when there is a need for a complete specification—such as when you are outsourcing your technical design and programming—that we would advocate building a complete specification before beginning construction. Otherwise, the delivered version of the *correct* software is the best way of satisfying the client's needs.

> ● *Customer collaboration over contract negotiation*

READING

Highsmith, Jim. *Adaptive Software Development: A Collaborative Approach to Managing Complex Systems.* Dorset House, 2000.

Beck, Kent, and Cynthia Andres. *Extreme Programming Explained: Embrace Change* (second edition). Addison-Wesley, 2004.

We speak often in this book about the need for collaboration with the stakeholders. A collaborative approach is by far the most effective way of determining the needs for the product and ensuring the stakeholders understand what they are asking for. Sometimes, however, there is a need for a contract—outsourcing or complying with departmental responsibilities are examples that spring to mind—and you cannot avoid creating a contractual requirements specification. The courts are jammed with lawsuits between software suppliers and clients where the source of disagreement is not whether the software works, but whether it does what is needed. Astonishingly, in many of these lawsuits, the requirements specification is sketchy and vague, and in some cases it is nonexistent.

Do not ask the client to sign off on the requirements; instead, ask the client to sign on to them and make them a collaborative effort.

You are not writing the requirements to serve as a contract with your client. Rather, you are writing them to ensure that both of you share the same, and demonstrably correct, understanding of what is needed. Do not ask the client to sign off on the requirements; instead, ask the client to *sign on* to them and make them a collaborative effort.

> ● *Responding to change over following a plan*

READING

Boehm, Barry, and Richard Turner. *Balancing Agility and Discipline: A Guide for the Perplexed.* Addison-Wesley, 2003.

The first thing you have to ask about change is why it happens. Our experience is that most change comes from software being delivered and the users discovering that it fails to do what they need. This happens even when the users acknowledge that what is delivered is what they asked for. Good requirements practices encourage change as early as possible in the cycle, when the changes are cheapest to make. By using interactive models such as scenarios and prototypes, the requirements analyst encourages the stakeholder to make changes before building the software.

There is every reason to make your requirements activity as agile as possible. We say "as possible" because in some situations the degree of agility is compromised by factors beyond your control. For example, you may be developing software using contracted outsourced development. In this case, there is a clear need for a complete requirements specification.

To help you relate to the agile way of thinking, we have devised agility ratings to represent your situation. We will use these ratings as we proceed through the chapters. The intention is to help you decide how you would undertake each of the activities in such a way as to be as agile as you can, and get the correct result.

Rabbit—the most agile of projects. You are a rabbit when you have the luxury of frequent iterations, with each iteration delivering a small increment to the working functionality. Rabbit projects will not spend a great deal of time writing the requirements—that is *not* the same thing as not learning the requirements—and probably will use scenarios and prototypes for delivering the requirements to the developers. In a rabbit project the sources of domain knowledge are colocated with the developers. Rabbit projects, like their namesake, have relatively short lives.

Horse—fast, strong, and dependable. Horse projects are probably the most common corporate projects. There is a need for some documentation, because requirements likely must be handed from one department to another. Horse projects usually involve more than a few stakeholders (often in a variety of locations), thus necessitating the need for some consistently written documentation. The organization in this case has a culture that expects a degree of formality, or order, in its development process. If you cannot categorize your own project, think of it as a horse. Horse projects have medium longevity.

Elephant—solid, strong, long life, and a long memory. The elephant project has a need for a complete requirements specification. This can happen when you are undertaking some contractual arrangement such as outsourcing. It also happens in certain industries, such as pharmaceuticals or aircraft manufacture, where regulators demand that not only full specifications be produced, but also the process used to produce them be documented and auditable. Elephant projects typically have a long duration, and they involve many stakeholders and stakeholder representatives in diverse locations. There is also a large number of developers, necessitating more formal ways of communicating.

The authors of this book are well aware that we are not the first to use animals to categorize agility. Barry Boehm and Richard Turner refer to elephants and monkeys in their excellent book, *Balancing Agility and Discipline: A Guide for the Perplexed*. Todd Little uses a menagerie that includes skunks in his article for *IEEE Software*. Each author, including the current ones, categorizes agility by looking at different aspects of product development and using an animal to represent each category. We do not claim the idea of using animals as an original one, but we persist with it, as we believe it to be a simple indicator of your aspirations for agility.

A confession: We chose the rabbit as the most agile symbol because of its misleading association with agility. Several years ago Steve Martin had a play on Broadway called *Picasso at the Lapin Agile,* the latter being a bar in Paris where Picasso meets an imaginary Albert Einstein. Anybody who has eaten *lapin* at a restaurant knows it is rabbit; French speakers also know that *agile* means "active," not "agile." Despite the discrepancies, the idea of an agile rabbit was too attractive to resist.

Projects vary according to their sociology and organizational framework. If you are guided by the agile principles, you will avoid doing things just because they are prescribed and you will look for opportunities to deliver useful functionality more quickly. Throughout this book, we will point out the relevancy of parts of each chapter to rabbits, horses, and elephants. In other words, we will guide you to select the parts of the requirements process that return the best value for the effort expended. The intention is to give you the opportunity to be as agile as possible.

Over the years we have discovered that good requirements practices simply make agile development more effective. Our goal in this book is to provide you with a structure for discovering and managing requirements so that you can make choices about how much requirements work you need to do before you can deliver your product.

> *If you are guided by the agile principles, you will avoid doing things just because they are prescribed and you will look for opportunities to deliver useful functionality more quickly.*

Why Do I Need Requirements?

The product is whatever you want to construct. You might want to produce it from scratch, buy it ready-made, install it for free using open source components, or acquire it in some other way. For the sake of simplicity, we will use the term "constructing" the product. It stands to reason that the product's requirements must be understood before its construction begins. The correct requirements come from understanding the work that the product is intended to support. Only when you know the correct requirements can you design and build the correct product, which in turn enables the product's users to do their work in a way that satisfies their business needs.

Sadly, the requirements are not always correctly understood. Both Steve McConnell and Jerry Weinberg provide statistics that show that as many as 60 percent of errors originate with the requirements activity. Clearly, although developers of products have the opportunity to almost eliminate the entire largest category of error, they choose—or, even worse, their managers choose—to rush headlong into constructing the wrong product. As a result, they pay many times the price for the product than they would have if the requirements and analysis had been done correctly in the first place. Poor quality is passed on. It is as simple as that.

If you are working in an agile shop doing pair programming (this means you are developing a rabbit project), you still need to understand requirements. Programming is constructing the *solution* to the problem. Sure, you

READING

McConnell, Steve. *Code Complete* (second edition). Microsoft Press, 2004. Weinberg, Jerry. *Quality Software Management. Volume 4: Anticipating Change.* Dorset House, 1997.

can turn out many iterations of a solution in a week—but they are still solutions. Without an understanding of the fundamental *work* the user needs to do and of the broader ramifications of introducing your solution into the work environment, your solution can be no better than the user's perception of a fix to the current problem. There is no conflict between agile development and requirements, just a difference in the way you discover and manage the requirements.

The cost of good requirements gathering and systems analysis is minor compared to the cost of poor requirements. But you have bought this book, so we shall not preach to the converted any longer. If you need more justification for installing a quality requirements process, do this: Measure the cost to your organization of repair to substandard products, the cost of cancelled projects that suffered requirements breakdown (no one could agree on the requirements), and the cost of the opportunity lost by not having the correct products at the correct time. If this wastage is insignificant, then stop reading this book. You already have your requirements process under control.

Otherwise, read on.

> *First of all, failing to write a spec is the single biggest unnecessary risk you take in a software project.*
>
> Source: Joel Spolsky, *Joel on Software*, Apress/Springer-Verlag, 2004

What Is a Requirement?

A requirement is something the product must do or a quality it must have. A requirement exists either because the type of product demands certain functions or qualities or because the client wants that requirement to be part of the delivered product.

Functional Requirements

A functional requirement is an action that the product must take if it is to be useful to its users. Functional requirements arise from the work that your stakeholders need to do. Almost any action—calculate, inspect, publish, or most other active verbs—can be a functional requirement.

Functional requirements are things the product must do.

> The product shall produce an amended de-icing schedule when a change to a truck status means that previously scheduled work cannot be carried out as planned.

This requirement is something that the product must do if it is to be useful within the context of the customer's business. In the preceding example, the customers for the product are the counties and other authorities that have responsibility for dispatching trucks to spread de-icing material on freezing roads.

Nonfunctional Requirements

Nonfunctional requirements are properties, or qualities, that the product must have. In some cases, nonfunctional requirements—these describe such properties as look and feel, usability, security, and legal restrictions—are critical to the product's success, as in the following case:

Nonfunctional requirements are qualities the product must have.

> *The product shall be able to determine "friend or foe" in less than 0.25 second.*

Sometimes they are requirements because they enhance the product:

> *The product shall be recognizable as an Atlantic Systems Guild product.*

Sometimes they make the product usable:

> *The product shall be able to be used by travelers in the arrivals hall who do not speak the home language.*

Nonfunctional requirements are usually—but not always—determined after the product's functionality. That is, once we know what the product is to do, we can determine requirements for how it is to behave, what qualities it is to have, and how fast, usable, readable, and secure it shall be.

Constraints

Constraints are global requirements. They can be constraints on the project itself or restrictions on the eventual design of the product. For example, this is a project constraint:

Constraints are global issues that shape the requirements.

> *The product must be available at the beginning of the new tax year.*

The client for the product is saying that the product is of no use if it is not available to be used by the client's customers in the new tax year. The effect is that the requirements analysts must restrict the requirements to those that deliver the maximum benefit within the deadline.

There may also be constraints placed on the eventual design and construction of the product, as in the following example:

> *The product shall operate on a 3G mobile telephone.*

Providing that this is a real business constraint—and not just a matter of opinion—any solution that does not meet this constraint is clearly unacceptable. This leads us to say that constraints are simply another type of requirement.

Constraints are simply another type of requirement.

Evolution of Requirements

At the beginning of a project, the requirements analyst is concerned with understanding the business the product is intended to support. We call this business area "the work." At this stage, the analysts are working with scenarios and other models to help them and the stakeholders come to an agreement on what the work is to be. You can think of these as "high-level requirements"; however, we find the term "high-level" to be subjective and hence fairly meaningless, so we avoid using it.

As the understanding of the work progresses, the stakeholders decide on the optimal product to help with the work. Now the requirements analysts start to determine the detailed functionality for the product and write its requirements. The nonfunctional requirements are derived at about the same time and written along with the constraints. At this point, the requirements are written in a technologically neutral manner—they specify what the product is to do for the work, not which technology is used to do it.

You can think of these requirements as "business requirements," meaning that they specify the product needed to support the business. Once they are adequately understood, they are given to the designer, who adds the product's technological requirements before producing the final specification for the builders. This process is illustrated in Figure 1.3.

The Template

It is easier to write requirements, and far more convenient, if the requirements analysts have a guide to writing them. Appendix B of this book provides the Volere Requirements Specification Template, which sets out a complete description of the product's functionality and capabilities. This template, which is a distillation of literally hundreds of requirements specifications, is currently used by thousands of organizations all over the world.

Requirements can be categorized into several useful types. Each of the template's sections describes a type of requirement and its variations. Thus, as you discover the requirements with your stakeholders, you can add them to your specification, using the template as a guide to necessary content.

Figure 1.3

The requirements evolve as development of the product progresses. They start out as fairly vague ideas as the analysts and stakeholders explore the work area. As the ideas for the product emerge over time, the requirements become precise and testable. They remain technologically neutral until the designer becomes involved and adds those requirements needed to make the product work in its technological environment.

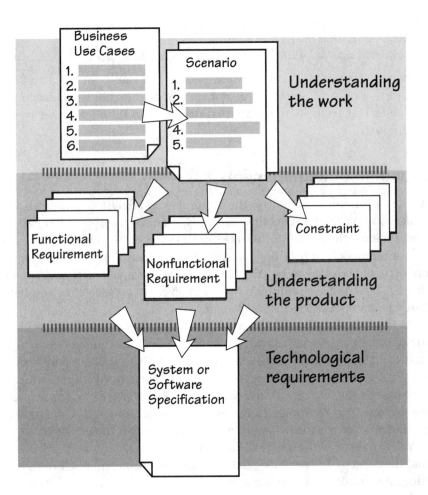

The complete Volere Requirements Specification Template is in Appendix B.

We do not intend that you should complete the requirements specification before starting on any construction of the product. The template is not provided for that purpose. Rather, it is designed to serve as a sophisticated checklist, providing you with a list of things to write about, and suggestions on how to write about them. For example, if you are working on a project with active business/development collaboration and the opportunity for iterative delivery, then you should use the first eight sections of the template as your guide for building your foundation. The table of contents for the template is reproduced on the next page, and we will discuss each section in detail later in the book. Consider carefully which sections apply to your current project.

Project Drivers—reasons and motivators for the project

1 **The Purpose of the Project**—the reason for making the investment in building the product and the business advantage that we want to achieve by doing so

2 **The Client, the Customer, and Other Stakeholders**—the people with an interest in or an influence on the product

3 **Users of the Product**—the intended end users, and how they affect the product's usability

Project Constraints—the restrictions on the project and the product

4 **Requirements Constraints**—limitations on the project, and restrictions on the design of the product

5 **Naming Conventions and Definitions**—the vocabulary of the project

6 **Relevant Facts and Assumptions**—outside influences that make some difference to this product, or assumptions that the developers are making

Functional Requirements—the functionality of the product

7 **The Scope of the Work**—the business area or domain under study

8 **The Scope of the Product**—a definition of the intended product boundaries and the product's connections to adjacent systems

9 **Functional and Data Requirements**—things the product must do and the data manipulated by the functions

Nonfunctional Requirements—the product's qualities

10 **Look and Feel Requirements**—the intended appearance

11 **Usability and Humanity Requirements**—what the product has to be if it is to be successfully used by its intended audience

12 **Performance Requirements**—how fast, big, accurate, safe, reliable, robust, scalable, and long-lasting, and what capacity

13 **Operational and Environmental Requirements**—the product's intended operating environment

14 **Maintainability and Support Requirements**—how changeable the product must be and what support is needed

15 **Security Requirements**—the security, confidentiality, and integrity of the product

16 **Cultural and Political Requirements**—human and sociological factors

17 **Legal Requirements**—conformance to applicable laws

Project Issues—issues relevant to the project that builds the product

18 **Open Issues**—as yet unresolved issues with a possible bearing on the success of the product

19 **Off-the-Shelf Solutions**—ready-made components that might be used instead of building something from scratch

20 **New Problems**—problems caused by the introduction of the new product

21 **Tasks**—things to be done to bring the product into production

22 **Migration to the New Product**—tasks to convert from existing systems

23 **Risks**—the risks that the project is most likely to incur

24 **Costs**—early estimates of the cost or effort needed to build the product

25 **User Documentation**—the plan for building the user instructions and documentation

26 **Waiting Room**—requirements that might be included in future releases of the product

27 **Ideas for Solutions**—design ideas that we do not want to lose

Browse through the template before you go too much further in this book. You will find a lot about writing requirements, plus much food for thought about the kinds of requirements to be gathered.

Throughout this book, we will refer to requirements by their type—that is, by one of the types as shown in the template's table of contents.

The Shell

Individual requirements have a structure. There are a number of components for a requirement, each contributes something to your knowledge, and you need them all to understand the whole requirement.

The components are all used, and all have a contribution to make. Although they may at first glance seem rather bureaucratic, we have found that their value repays the effort used to gather the information. The components will be described as we work our way though the process.

The requirement shell is completed progressively, because it is not practical to find all components of one requirement before moving on to the next. For this reason, we have the shell printed onto cards, and then we use the cards when we are interviewing stakeholders, quickly scribbling each requirement as we discover it, and completing the card as we learn more about the requirement. (See Figure 1.4.)

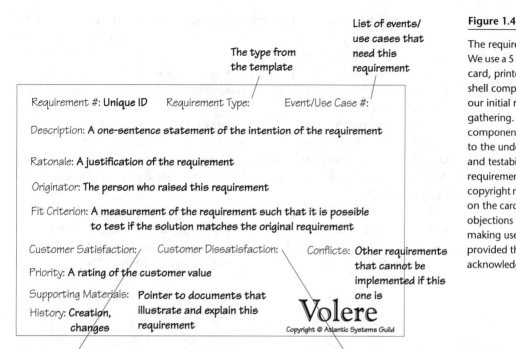

The type from
the template

List of events/
use cases that
need this
requirement

Requirement #: **Unique ID**   Requirement Type: Event/Use Case #:

Description: **A one-sentence statement of the intention of the requirement**

Ratonale: **A justification of the requirement**

Originator: **The person who raised this requirement**

Fit Criterion: **A measurement of the requirement such that it is possible
to test if the solution matches the original requirement**

Customer Satisfaction: Customer Dissatisfaction: Conflicts: **Other requirements
that cannot be
implemented if this
one is**

Priority: **A rating of the customer value**

Supporting Materials: **Pointer to documents that
illustrate and explain this
requirement**

History: **Creation,
changes**

Volere
Copyright © Atlantic Systems Guild

Degree of stakeholder happiness if
this requirement is successfully implemented.
Scale from 1 = uninterested to
5 = extremely pleased.

Measure of stakeholder unhappiness
if this requirement is not part of the
final product.
Scale from 1 = hardly matters to
5 = extremely displeased.

Figure 1.4

The requirements shell.
We use a 5 inch by 8 inch
card, printed with the
shell components, for
our initial requirements
gathering. Each of the
components contributes
to the understanding
and testability of the
requirement. Although a
copyright notice appears
on the card, we have no
objections to any reader
making use of it
provided the source is
acknowledged.

This low-tech approach gives us an initial flexibility and does not hinder us as we gather the requirements at the stakeholders' place of work. We usually keep the cards grouped according to the business event/product use case to which they belong (see Event/Use Case # in the upper right of Figure 1.4), as that makes it easier to find individual cards in the deck. When we think that the requirements for a product use case are well formed, we store them using an automated tool.

A number of automated tools are available for recording, analyzing, and tracing requirements.

The Volere Requirements Process

This book describes a process for successfully discovering, verifying, and documenting requirements. Each chapter covers an activity of the process, or some aspect of requirements gathering that is needed to complete the activity.

Volere is the Italian word for "to wish" or "to want."

As you learn more about the process, keep in mind that it is meant to be a guide for producing deliverables. What you do with the process is driven by

What you do with the process is driven by the relevant deliverables, not by the procedures.

the relevant deliverables, not by the procedures. We would like you to think of the process as a list of things that have to be done (to some degree of detail) for successful requirements projects, rather than as a lock-step procedure that must be followed at all costs. As you read about each part, think about how you would perform that part of the procedure given your own structural and organizational setup.

To understand the process, it is not necessary to read the book in the presented order—although you may encounter some terminology that assumes knowledge from previous chapters. Chapter 2 gives an overview of the requirements process, and you can find a complete and detailed model of it in Appendix A.

Your requirements needs will naturally differ from those of other readers, so you will therefore be interested in exploring some aspects of the process before others. Once you are familiar with the basic outline of the process, feel free to plunge in wherever you feel it will be most valuable.

The Requirements Process

in which we look at a process for gathering requirements and discuss how you might use it

The requirements process described in this book is the product of our experience. We developed the Volere Requirements Process and its associated specification template from the activities and deliverables we have found effective over years of working on projects and consulting with our clients. The result of this experience is a requirements-gathering and specification process whose principles can be applied to almost all kinds of application types in almost all kinds of development environments.

We want to stress from the very beginning that while we are presenting a process, we are using it as a vehicle for finding requirements. That is, we do not expect you to wave the process around and tell your coworkers that this is "the way to do it." We do expect you will find many useful things to do within the process that will help you to gather requirements more productively and accurately. We are sure of this fact, because we have personally seen hundreds of companies adapt the process to their own cultures and organizations, and we know of thousands more that have done so.

A requirements process is not just for waterfall development. Our clients use XP, RUP, and many other acronyms, as well as traditional waterfall, incremental, and all flavors of agile development processes. Over the years they have agreed with us: If the right product is to be built, then the right requirements have to be discovered. But requirements don't come about by fortuitous accident. To find the correct and complete requirements, you need some kind of systematic process.

The Volere Requirements Process Model in Appendix A contains a detailed model of all of the activities and the connections between them. The model is very detailed. Rather than getting involved in that kind of

> *Whether you are building custom systems, building systems by assembling components, using commercial off-the-shelf software, accessing open source software, or making changes to existing software, you still need to explore, understand, capture, and communicate the requirements.*

See Appendix A for the complete Volere Requirements Process.

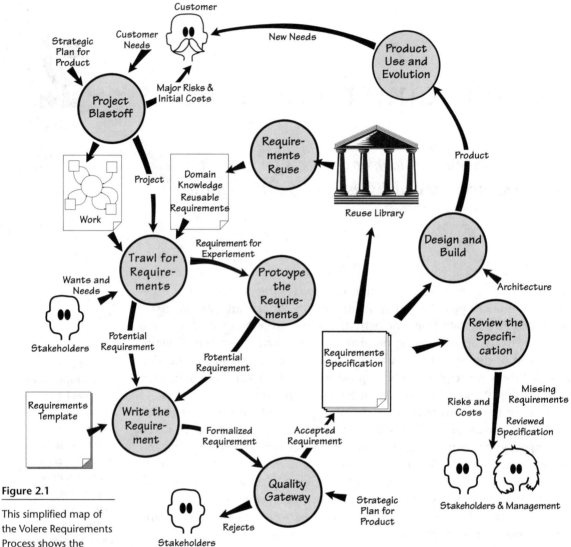

Figure 2.1

This simplified map of the Volere Requirements Process shows the activities and their deliverables. We have used a stylized data flow notation. When you are looking at this diagram, keep in mind that the process is iterative and evolutionary. Each activity (the bubbles) and its deliverables (arrows or documents) are explained in the text.

detail and complexity right away, let's stand back and take a simpler view of the overall process. This simplified view is shown in Figure 2.1.

This simplified version of the process model will reappear at various places throughout this book. For the most part, the simplified version is faithful enough to the complete version in Appendix A. Sometimes, for the sake of making an explanation simpler or clearer, we will make minor changes to the model or show only part of it. Please be aware of this and use the detailed model for any of your important implementation decisions.

Figure 2.1 shows all of the main activities in the Volere Requirements Process, including how they are linked by their deliverables. The deliverables are shown as moving from one activity to the next. For example, the *Trawling for Requirements* activity would probably gather the requirements for one business use case at a time. The requirements would be *written* to demonstrate that they have been correctly understood and agreed, and then passed to the *Quality Gateway* for testing prior to being included in the *Requirements Specification.* Any rejects would be sent back to the originator, who probably would take them back to the trawling activity for clarification and further explanation. Don't take this apparent waterfall approach too literally—the activities usually iterate and overlap before producing their final output. As we go through this process in detail, we will explain where and how iteration and incremental delivery can be used.

Agility Guide

When referring to development processes, *agility* is normally taken to mean the absence of a set process that must be followed regardless of the product being developed. However, it does *not* mean the absence of all process. Agile development means selecting the appropriate process, or parts of a process, that are appropriate for the product and the project.

Not all projects can be as agile as others. Large numbers of stakeholders, the need for documentation, scattered development teams, and other factors will inevitably dictate the degree of agility that can be applied by the project team. As a consequence, you must determine the degree of agility appropriate to your current project. In Chapter 1, we introduced symbols to represent your aspirations for agility. These symbols are intended to guide you as you select the most appropriate way to use the information in this book.

Rabbit projects are those where circumstances allow for the highest degree of agility. They are typically, but not necessarily, smaller projects where close stakeholder participation is possible. Rabbit projects usually include a smaller number of stakeholders.

Participants in rabbit projects may think it odd to consider using any kind of process at all for requirements. However, as you look at the process in this chapter, think not of a process that delivers a *requirements specification*, but rather of a process that delivers a requirement, or at least requirements, one use case at a time. If you are using eXtreme Programming (most likely with rabbit projects), the fastest way to learn your customer's and (importantly) his organization's requirements is not at the keyboard but at the whiteboard. Pay particular attention to the part that prototyping and scenarios play in the process and to the idea of *essence* of the system. It is crucial that you understand the difference between a requirement and a solution.

The fastest way to learn your customer's and his organization's requirements is not at the keyboard but at the whiteboard.

Rabbit projects are iterative. They gather requirements in small units (probably one business use case at a time) and then implement the solution piecemeal, using the implementation to get feedback from the stakeholders. However, we stress that this feedback should not be used to find out what the stakeholders wanted in the first place. That is the role of requirements, and it is far more effective and efficient if done using requirements methods. Read on.

Horse projects are the "halfway house" of agility. They use as much agility as possible, but have constraints imposed by the project and the organization. Horse projects should use most of the process we are about to describe, keeping in mind that you could easily use an iterative approach to requirements gathering. That is, the requirements for one unit of work—probably one business use case—are gathered and then the designers start work on those requirements. This strategy needs the overall architecture to be in place before it can work. The advantage is that while the requirements analysts are gathering the requirements for one business use case, the developers are busy building a solution for the requirements from the previous business use case.

The sections on trawling, writing, and the Quality Gateway will be of great interest to horse projects. If these activities are done correctly and iteratively, your project can achieve a considerable effectiveness without becoming bogged down in its own process.

Elephant projects are the least agile, but—like their namesake—are large, are dependable, and have long memories. In such a case, your aspirations toward agility may be limited by the organization of the project—for example, you may have a large number of scattered stakeholders—or the need to produce formal requirements documentation such as for pharmaceutical or aeronautical projects, projects that entail some contractual obligation, or projects where you are outsourcing some tasks to another organization.

Most of the elements of the requirements process outlined in this chapter are used by elephant projects. But always be on the lookout for opportunities in your project to increase your agility by gathering requirements in an iterative manner.

Requirements Process in Context

Just as the product evolves on its own, so you may choose to make it evolve by building the early versions with a minimal amount of functionality, and later augmenting it by a planned series of releases

There is no end to the requirements process. When a product, or partial product, is delivered and your users start using it, evolution kicks in. As people use the product, they discover new needs and uses for it, and they then want it to be extended. This raises new requirements that, in turn, go through the same requirements process. Just as the product evolves on its own, so you may choose to make it evolve by building the early versions with a minimal amount of functionality and later augmenting it by a planned series of releases. The Volere Requirements Process is designed with evolution in mind.

The people around the periphery of the process play an important part in it. These people supply information to the process or receive information from it. They are some of the *stakeholders*—the people who have an interest in the product, but not necessarily a financial one. They participate in the requirements process by providing requirements and receiving deliverables from the process. Additionally, some stakeholders do not show up on Figure 2.1—the consultants and other interested parties who have knowledge needed to gather the requirements for the product. As we discuss the requirements process throughout this book, we also discuss the different stakeholder roles and responsibilities.

The Process

The requirements process is not applicable just to new products you are developing from the ground up. Most product development that is done today is aimed at maintaining or enhancing an existing product or at making a major overhaul to an existing product or suite of products. A lot of today's development involves commercial off-the-shelf (COTS) products, open source products, or other types of componentware. Whatever your development method, understanding the requirements for the final outcome is still necessary.

The requirements process is not applicable just to new products.

Let's look briefly at each of the activities. Subsequent chapters cover them in more detail. The intention of this chapter is to give you a gentle introduction to the process, its components, its deliverables, and the ways that they fit together. If you want more detail on any of the activities, feel free to jump to the relevant chapter before completing this overview.

As we go through the process, we describe it as if you were working with a brand-new product—that is, starting from scratch. We take this tack simply to avoid becoming entangled in the constraints that are part of all maintenance projects. For the latter kind of project, look ahead to Chapter 15, Whither Requirements?, where we discuss projects that are already under way and projects where the requirements are changing.

A Case Study

We shall explain the Volere Requirements Process by talking you through a project that uses it: The IceBreaker project is to develop a product that predicts when and where ice will form on roads, and that schedules trucks to treat the roads with de-icing material. The product will enable road authorities to be more accurate with their predictions, schedule road treatments more precisely, and thus make the roads safer. The road authorities also anticipate they can reduce the amount of de-icing materials used.

> " The likelihood of frost or ice forming is determined by the energy receipt and loss at the road surface. This energy flow is controlled by a number of environmental and meteorological factors (such as exposure, altitude, road construction, traffic, cloud cover, and wind speed). These factors cause significant variation in road surface temperature from time to time and from one location to another. Winter night-time road surface temperatures can vary by over 10 °C across a road network in a county. "
>
> Source: *Vaisala News*

Project Blastoff

Blastoff is also known as "project initiation," "kickoff," "charter," "project launch," and many other things. We use the term "blastoff" to describe what we are trying to achieve—getting the project launched and flying.

FOOTNOTE 1:
Andorra is a tiny principality in the Pyrenees mountains between France and Spain. It became famous in the 1960s for having a defense budget of $4.50, a tale that has become the stuff of legend. Today Andorra's defense budget is zero.

Refer to Chapter 3 for a detailed discussion of project blastoff.

The project blastoff deliverables are the first of eight sections of the Volere Requirements Specification Template in Appendix B.

Imagine launching a rocket. 10 – 9 – 8 – 7 – 6 – 5 – 4 – 3 – 2 – 1 – blastoff! If all it needed was the ability to count backward from ten, then even Andorra[1] would have its own space program. The truth of the matter is that before we get to the final ten seconds of a rocket launch, a lot of preparation has taken place. The rocket has been fueled, the course plotted—in fact, everything that needs to be done before the rocket can be launched.

The blastoff meeting prepares the project and ensures its feasibility before launching the detailed requirements effort. The principal stakeholders—the client, the main users, the lead requirements analyst, technical and business experts, and other people who are crucial to the success of the project—gather to come to a consensus on the crucial project issues. For the IceBreaker project, Saltworks Systems is the developer of the product, and its employees are aiming for worldwide sales. Northumberland County Highways Department has agreed to be the company's first customer, and it is helping with the requirements. Naturally, key Northumberland people are present at the blastoff meeting.

In the blastoff meeting, the principals work together until they have achieved the blastoff's objectives. That is, they gather enough facts to ensure the project has a clearly defined scope and a worthwhile objective, is possible to achieve, and has commitment from the stakeholders.

It is usually more convenient to define the scope of the business problem first. The lead requirements analyst coordinates the group as they come to a consensus on what the scope of the work is—that is, the business area to be studied—and how this work relates to the world around it. The meeting participants draw a context model on a whiteboard to show the functionality included in the work, the items they consider to be outside the scope of the ice forecasting business, and the connections between the work and the outside world. This model is illustrated in Figure 2.2. Later, as the requirements activity proceeds, it will reveal the optimal product to help with this work.

Once they have reached a reasonable agreement on the scope of the business area to be studied, the group identifies the stakeholders. The stakeholders are the people who have an interest in the product, or who have knowledge pertaining to the product, and thus have requirements. The group identifies the various people who have some interest in IceBreaker: the road engineers, the truck depot supervisor, weather forecasting people, road safety experts, ice treatment consultants, and so on. They do so because if they don't identify all of the stakeholders, the requirements analysts won't find all of the requirements. The context diagram usually identifies many of the stakeholders. We look at how this identification occurs in Chapter 3.

Figure 2.2

The context model is used to build a consensus among the stakeholders as to the scope of the work that needs to be studied. The eventual product is used to do part of this work.

The blastoff also confirms the goals of the project. The blastoff group comes to an agreement on the business reason for doing the project, and it derives a way to measure the advantage the new product will bring. The group also must agree that the product is worthwhile, and that the organization is capable of building and operating it.

It is sensible project management practice at this stage to produce a preliminary estimate of the costs involved for the requirements part of the project. This can be done by using the information contained in the model of the scope of the work. It is also sensible project management to make an early assessment of the risks that the project is likely to face. Although these risks may seem like depressing news, it is always better to get an idea of the downside of the project (its risk and cost) before being swept away by the euphoria of the benefits that the new product is intended to bring.

Finally, the group members arrive at a consensus on whether the project is worthwhile and viable. This is the "go/no go" decision. We know from bitter experience that it is better to cancel a project at an early stage than to have it stagger on for months or years consuming valuable resources with no chance of success. The group must carefully consider whether the product is viable and whether its benefits outweigh its costs.

Alternatively, if many unknowns remain at this point, the blastoff group may decide to start the requirements investigation. It can then review the requirements in a month or so and reassess the value of the project.

The relevant part of the Volere Requirements Process model (Appendix A) is Project Blastoff (Diagram 1).

It is always better to get an idea of the downside of the project (its risk and cost) before being swept away by the euphoria of the benefits that the new product is intended to bring.

READING

DeMarco, Tom, and Tim Lister. *Waltzing with Bears: Managing Risk on Software Projects.* Dorset House, 2003.

Yourdon, Ed. *Death March* (second edition). Prentice Hall, 2003.

Refer to Chapter 4 for a detailed discussion of business events and use cases, and an exploration of how to use them.

Refer to Chapter 5 for details of the trawling activity.

Trawling for Requirements

Once the blastoff is completed, the requirements analysts start trawling for requirements. They learn the work being done by the business area identified by the blastoff. For convenience and consistency, they partition the work context diagram into business use cases. Each business use case is the functionality needed by the work to make the correct response to a business event. A requirements analyst is assigned to each of the business use cases (the analysts can work almost independently of one another) for further detailed study. The analysts use techniques such as apprenticing, scenarios, and use case workshops, among many others, to discover the true nature of the work. These techniques are described in Chapter 5, Trawling for Requirements, and are favored because they involve the stakeholders closely in capturing their requirements. Once they understand the work, the requirements analysts work with the stakeholders to decide the best product to help with this work. That is, they determine how much of the work to automate or change, and what effect those decisions will have on the work. Once they know the extent of the product, the requirements analysts write its requirements. See Figure 2.3.

When they are trawling to discover the requirements, the analytical team members sit with the hands-on users as they describe the work that they do and the work that they hope to do. Some of the team members act as apprentices to the users: They learn how to do the work and, along the way, develop ideas about how improve it. The requirements analysts also consult with other interested stakeholders—usability people, security, operations, and so on—to discover other requirements for the eventual product.

Perhaps the hardest part of requirements gathering is discovering the

Figure 2.3

The blastoff determines the scope of the work to be studied. The business use cases can be formally derived from the scope. Each of the business use cases is studied by the requirements analysts and the relevant stakeholders to discover the desired way of working. When this is understood, the appropriate product can be determined and requirements written for it.

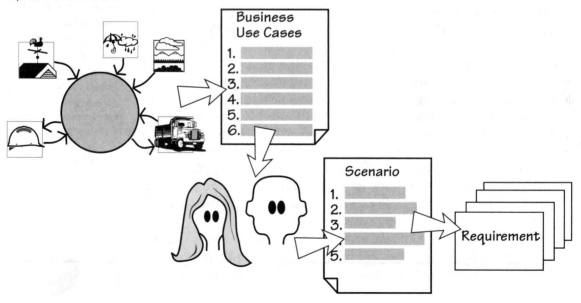

essence of the system. Many stakeholders inevitably talk about their perceived *solution* to the problem. The essence, by contrast, is the underlying business reason for having the product. Alternatively, you can think of it as the *policy* of the work, or what the work would be if there were no technology (that includes people). We will have more to say about essence in Chapter 5, Trawling for Requirements.

The IceBreaker product must not be simply the automation of the procedures that are done at the moment. To deliver a truly useful product, the analytical team should help to invent a better way to do the work, and build a product that helps with this better way of working. With this goal in mind, they hold creativity workshops where the team members use creative thinking techniques and creative triggers to generate new and better ideas for the eventual product.

Prototyping the Requirements

Sometimes requirements analysts get stuck. Sometimes there are requirements that are not properly formed, or the user can't explain them, or the requirements analysts can't understand them. Or maybe the product is so groundbreaking that nobody really knows the requirements. Or the analysts and stakeholders just need to work with something more concrete than a written requirement. This is when prototypes are the most effective requirements technique.

A *prototype* is a quick and dirty representation of a potential product— probably only part of the product. It is intended to present the user with some kind of simulation of the requirements. There are two approaches to building requirements prototypes: High-fidelity prototypes use specialized software tools and result in a partially working piece of software, and low-fidelity prototypes use pencil and paper, whiteboards, or some other familiar means, as shown in Figure 2.4. Teams generally like using the low-fidelity prototypes because they can generate them quickly and the users enjoy the spontaneous nature and inventiveness of these prototypes.

Scenarios

Scenarios are stories. The analysts use them when working with stakeholders to arrive at an understanding of the functionality of a use case. The scenario shows, step by step, how a business use case or a product use case is performed. The analysts find that scenarios are a useful neutral language for talking to the relevant stakeholders about the use cases. The scenarios, once they are agreed upon, form the foundation for the requirements.

READING

Robertson, Suzanne, and James Robertson. *Requirements-Led Project Management.* Addison-Wesley, 2005.

Maiden, Neil, Suzanne Robertson, Sharon Manning, and John Greenwood. *Integrating Creativity Workshops into Structured Requirements Processes.* Proceedings of DIS 2004, Cambridge, Mass., ACM Press.

We look at innovative products in Chapter 5, Trawling for Requirements.

Prototyping as a requirements-gathering technique is fully explained in Chapter 12, Prototyping the Requirements.

This part of the process is shown in detailed model form in Prototype the Requirements (Diagram 5) in the Volere Requirements Process model in Appendix A.

Refer to Chapter 6, Scenarios and Requirements, for a detailed discussion of scenario modeling.

Figure 2.4

A low-fidelity prototype built on a whiteboard to provide a quick visual explanation of some of the requirements, and to elicit misunderstood or missing requirements.

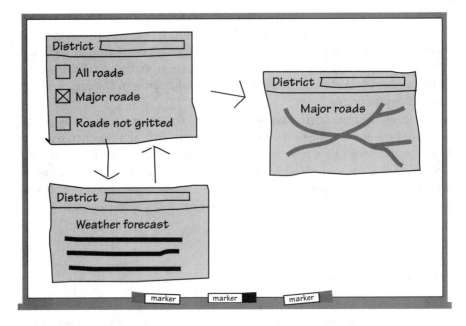

Writing the Requirements

A major problem in system development is misunderstood requirements. To avoid this dilemma, the analysts must write their requirements in a testable manner and ensure that the originating stakeholder understands and agrees with the written requirement before it is passed downstream. In other words, the analysts are writing the requirements to ensure that all parties have achieved the identical understanding of what is needed. Although the task of writing down the requirements may seem an onerous burden, we have found it is the only way to ensure that the essence of the requirement has been captured and communicated, and that the delivered product can be tested. (See Figure 2.5.)

The requirements analysts are writing for the stakeholders. That is, the requirements are the business requirements, and they must be written using business language so that the nontechnical stakeholders can understand them and verify their correctness. Of course, the requirements also need to be written so that the product designers and other technicians can build precisely what the client wants. To ensure this correctness, and to make the requirement testable, the analysts add a *fit criterion* to each requirement. A fit criterion is a quantification or measurement of the requirement so the testers can determine precisely whether an implementation meets—in other words, fits—the requirement.

Chapter 9 describes fit criteria in detail.

I want it easy enough so my mother could use it.

The programmer doesn't know your mother. How about "A truck driver shall be able to select the correct route within 90 seconds of the first use of the product"?

Figure 2.5

The requirements are captured in written form so as to communicate effectively between the stakeholders and the analysts. Only by writing them down can the team ensure that the required product is built.

The analysts use two devices to make it easier to write a specification. The first device, the requirements specification template, is an outline of a requirements specification. The analysts use it as a checklist of which requirements they should be asking for and as a guide to writing their specification documents. The second device is a shell, also known as a snow card. Each requirement is made up of a number of components, and the shell is a convenient layout for ensuring that each requirement has the correct constituents.

See Appendix B, the Volere Requirements Specification Template.

Of course, the writing activity is not really a separate activity. In reality, it is integrated with the activities that surround it—trawling, prototyping, and the Quality Gateway. However, for the purposes of understanding what is involved in getting the correct requirements in a communicable form, we have chosen to look at it separately.

An alternative to writing functional requirements is building models. Numerous kinds of models are available, and we do not intend this book to describe how to build all of them. While we encourage the use of models for requirements work, we must issue a caution about the tendency of some modelers, and some models, to leap straight into a solution without firstly demonstrating an understanding of the problem. Also bear in mind that models do not specify the nonfunctional requirements. As a result, any models you build must be augmented by written requirements for the nonfunctional requirements.

Refer to Chapter 10 for a detailed discussion of writing the requirements.

Lastly, we must consider the primary reason for wanting written requirements. The point is not to *have* written requirements (although that is often necessary), but rather to *write* them. The act of writing the requirement, together with its associated fit criterion, means the analyst has to correctly understand the requirement. If the requirement is not correctly understood, and agreed to by the relevant stakeholders, then any attempt to write it will result in a nonsense—one that is quickly detected when the requirement reaches the Quality Gateway.

The Quality Gateway

Requirements are the foundation for all that is to follow in the product development cycle. It therefore stands to reason that the requirements must be correct before they are given to the designers/developers. The Quality Gateway (Figure 2.6) tests the requirements. It is a single point that every requirement must pass through before it can become a part of the specification. Quality Gateways are normally set up so that one or two people, probably the lead requirements analyst and a tester, are the only people authorized to pass requirements through the gateway. Working together, they check each requirement for completeness, relevance, testability, coherency, traceability, and several other qualities before they allow it to become part of the specification.

The Quality Gateway is detailed in Diagram 4 of the Volere Requirements Process model in Appendix A.

One of the tasks of the Quality Gateway is to ensure that each requirement has a fit criterion attached to it. The fit criterion is a measurement of the requirement that makes it both understandable and testable. The understandability is for the benefit of the client, who has on several occasions said, "I am not going to have any requirements that I do not understand, nor will I have any that are not useful or that don't contribute to my work. I want to understand the contributions that they make. That's why I want to measure each one."

We discuss measurements for requirements in Chapter 9, Fit Criteria.

Figure 2.6

The Quality Gateway ensures a rigorous specification by testing each requirement for completeness, correctness, measurability, absence of ambiguity, and several other attributes before allowing the requirement to be added to the specification.

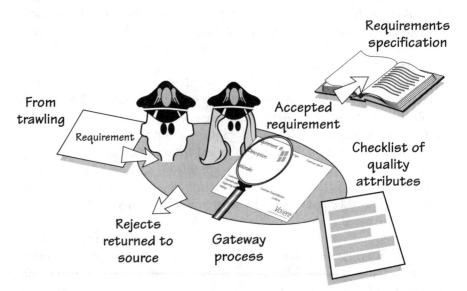

The requirements analyst has a different, but complementary reason for measuring and testing requirements: "I need to ensure that each requirement is unambiguous; that is, it must have the same meaning to both the client and the developer. I also need to measure the requirement against the client's expectations. If I can't put a measurement to it, then I can never tell if we are building the product the client really needs."

Another reason the project has a Quality Gateway is to prevent *requirements leakage*. Just as water seeps into a leaky rowing boat and you cannot tell where it is coming from, requirements sometimes seem to leak into the specification without anyone really knowing where they came from or what value they add to the product. By ensuring that the only way for requirements to get into the specification is through the Quality Gateway, the project team is in control of the requirements, and not the other way around.

Chapter 11 describes how the Quality Gateway tests the requirements for these qualities.

Reusing Requirements

Requirements for any product you build are never completely unique. We suggest that before starting on any new requirements project, you go through the specifications written for previous projects and look for potentially reusable material. Sometimes you may find dozens of requirements you can reuse without alteration. More often you will find requirements that, although they are not exactly what you want, are suitable as the basis for some of the requirements you will write in the new project.

For example, in the IceBreaker project, the rules for road engineering do not change between products, so the requirements analysts do not have to rediscover them. They also know that the business of vehicle scheduling does not radically change every year, so their trawling process can take advantage of some requirements from previous projects. Similarly, on many projects within an organization, the nonfunctional requirements are fairly standard, so analysts can start with a specification from one of the previous projects and use it as a checklist.

See Chapter 13 for more on reusing requirements.

The point about reusing requirements is that once a requirement has been successfully specified for a product, and the product itself is successful, the requirement does not have to be reinvented. In Chapter 13, we discuss how you can take advantage of the knowledge that already exists within your organization and how you can save yourself time by recycling requirements from previous projects.

This topic is the subject of Diagram 7 of the Volere Requirements Process model in Appendix A.

Reviewing the Specification

The Quality Gateway exists to keep bad requirements out of the specification. But it does this one requirement at a time. When you think your requirements specification is complete, you should review it. This final review

See Chapter 14 for more on reviewing the specification.

checks that there are no missing requirements, that all the requirements are consistent with one another, and that any conflicts between the requirements have been resolved. In short, the review confirms that the specification is really complete and suitable so that you can move on to the next stage of development.

This review also offers you an opportunity to reassess the costs and risks of the project. Now that you have a complete specification, you know a lot more about the product than you did at blastoff time. Once the requirements specification is complete, you have a precise knowledge of the scope and functionality of the product, so this is the time to remeasure its size. From that size, and from your knowledge of the project's constraints and solution architecture, you can estimate the cost to construct the product.

You also know at this stage which types of requirements are associated with the greatest risks. For example, the users may have asked for an interface that their organization has not built before. Or perhaps they want to use untried technology to build the product. Does the developer have the people capable of building the product as specified? By reassessing the risks at this point, you give yourself a better chance to build the desired product successfully.

Iterative and Incremental Processes

One common misconception in the requirements world is that you have to gather *all* the requirements before moving on to the next step of design and construction. In some circumstances this is necessary, but not always. On the one hand, if you are outsourcing or if the requirements document forms the basis of a contract, then clearly you need to have a complete requirements specification. On the other hand, providing the overall architecture is known, construction can often begin before all the requirements are gathered. We suggest that you consider this point when working on your own requirements projects.

Let's go back to the IceBreaker project. The developers are ready to start building the product, so right after the blastoff meeting the key stakeholders select a few (let's say three or four) of the highest-priority business use cases. The requirements analysts gather the requirements for only those business use cases, ignoring the remainder for the meantime. It is feasible to ignore them because there is always a minimal functional connection between the business use cases, so the analysts do not interfere with one another's work. Then, when the first tranche of requirements have successfully passed the Quality Gateway, the developers can start their work. The intention is to implement a small number of use cases as early as possible to get the reaction of the stakeholders. If there are to be nasty surprises, then the IceBreaker team members want to get them as early as possible. While the first use cases are being developed and delivered, the analysts are working on the requirements for the next-highest-priority ones. Soon they have established a rhythm for delivery, with new use cases being delivered every few weeks.

Requirements Retrospective

You are reading this book about a requirements process, presumably with the intention of improving your own process. Retrospectives are one of the most effective tools for discovering the good and bad of a process, and suggesting remedial action. Retrospectives for requirements projects consist of a series of interviews with stakeholders and group sessions with the developers. The intention is to canvas all the people involved in the process and ask tough questions:

- What did we do right?
- What did we do wrong?
- If we had to do it again, what would you do differently?

By looking for honest answers to these questions, you give yourself the best chance of improving your process. The idea is very simple: Do more of what works and less of what doesn't.

Keep a record of the lessons learned from your retrospective. The next project can then use that record as a starting point, so the lessons learned from previous projects are passed along.

Your retrospective can be very informal: a coffee-time meeting with the project group, or the project leader collecting e-mail messages from the participants. Alternatively, if the stakes are higher, it can be formalized to the point where it is run by an outside facilitator who canvases the participants, both individually and as a group, and publishes a retrospective report.

The most notable feature of retrospectives is this: Companies that regularly conduct retrospectives consistently report significant improvements in their processes. Retrospectives are probably the cheapest investment you can make in your own process.

> *"If we did the project again tomorrow, what would we do differently?"*

Your Own Requirements Process

The itinerant peddler of quack potions, Doctor Dulcamara, sings the praises of his elixir, which is guaranteed to cure toothache, make you potent, eliminate wrinkles and give you smooth beautiful skin, destroy mice and bugs, and make the object of your affections fall in love with you. The rather fanciful libretto from Donizetti's opera *L'Elisir d'Amore* points out something that, although very obvious, is often disregarded: There is no such thing as the universal cure.

We have distilled our experiences from a wide variety of projects to provide you with a set of foundation activities and deliverables that will apply to any project.

READING

Brooks, Fred. "No Silver Bullet: Essence and Accidents of Software Engineering" and "'No Silver Bullet' Refired." *The Mythical Man-Month: Essays on Software Engineering* (twentieth anniversary edition). Addison-Wesley, 1995.

We really would like to be able to present you with a requirements process that has all the attributes of Doctor Dulcamara's elixir—a process that suits all projects for all applications in all organizations. But we know from experience that every project has different needs. At the same time, we have learned that some fundamental principles hold good for any project. Thus, instead of attempting to provide you with a one-size-fits-all magic potion, we have distilled our experiences from a wide variety of projects to provide you with a set of foundation activities and deliverables that will apply to any project.

We are using a process here to describe the things that have to be done to successfully gather requirements, and the deliverables that are the foundation for any kind of requirements activity. As you read this book, think of adapting them to your own culture, your own environment, your own organizational structure, and your own chosen way of product development.

For instance, projects using eXtreme Programming are not supposed to produce a requirements specification, but there is still a clear need to understand the requirements. This understanding cannot be achieved effectively by writing code. To invest in writing an individual requirement, complete with its fit criterion, remains the fastest way of understanding that requirement. (Writing code is building a *solution* to satisfy the requirement, and it does not guarantee that the real requirement is ever discovered.) In the Volere Requirements Process, we provide scenarios as a way of modeling the functionality of the use case. This is almost always a quicker way to discover requirements, particularly when you start to consider the exceptions and alternatives for a use case. For a nonfunctional requirement, writing it down, complete with its fit criterion, remains the fastest way of understanding it.

Defining the scope of the business area affected by the product is still the most effective way of keeping the requirements and the development work focused. Learning about the work, and not just the product, is the best way of building a relevant product. Of course, we do not intend that you use the Volere process straight out of the box. Instead, we urge you to adopt the most beneficial practices, adapting the process as necessary to make it relevant to your project and your organization.

To adapt this process you need to understand each of the deliverables it produces—the rest of this book will discuss these in detail. Once you understand the content and purpose of each deliverable, ask how each one (provided it is relevant) would best be produced within your project environment using your resources:

● What is the deliverable called within your environment? Use the definitions of the terms used in the generic process model and identify the equivalent deliverable in your organization.

- Is this deliverable relevant for this project?
- How much do you already know about this deliverable? Do you know enough to be able to avoid devoting additional time to it?
- Who produces the deliverable? Understand which parts of the deliverable are produced by whom. Also, when several people are involved, you need to define the interfaces between them.
- When is the deliverable produced? Map your project phases to the generic process.
- Where is the deliverable produced? A generic deliverable is often the result of fragments that are produced in a number of geographical locations. Define the interfaces between the different locations and specify how they will work.
- Who needs to review the deliverable? Look for existing cultural checkpoints within your organization. Do you have recognized stages or phases in your projects when peers, users, or managers must review your specification?

The generic model describes deliverables and procedures for producing them. You decide how to use them.

In Conclusion

We have described—rather briefly—a process for gathering and verifying requirements. The remainder of this book describes the activities in detail, along with their deliverables. Feel free to jump to any chapter that is of immediate concern—we wrote the chapters in more or less the order in which you would arrive at the activities, but you don't have to read them that way.

Keep in kind that the model in Appendix A is a complete record of the Volere Requirements Process.

Project Blastoff

in which we establish a solid foundation for the requirements, and ensure that the members of the project team all start rowing in the same direction

The Project Blastoff is a burst of activity to launch a requirements project. It assembles enough information to get your project off to a flying start and to ensure it is viable and well founded. A blastoff might last a few hours or several days—it all depends on the size of the project and the amount of uncertainty.

The blastoff (see Figure 3.1) identifies the work area the product is to become a part of, and determines the purpose the product is to fulfill. It also identifies the stakeholders, who, it will turn out, are a vital ingredient to any requirements project. Other deliverables from the blastoff qualify the project and are used as inputs to subsequent requirements-gathering activities.

You might know this activity as project kickoff, project initiation, or launch, among many other names. Whatever you call it, its purpose is to lay the groundwork so your requirements activity is efficient and effective.

A number of deliverables result from the blastoff. Please look through the following list and consider those appropriate to your project. For each deliverable, look at its effect. Think of this outcome as payback for taking the time to collect or write it. The typical blastoff deliverables are as follows:

- *Purpose of the project.* This is a short, quantified statement of what the product is intended to do and what advantage it brings to the business. This purpose statement explains why the business is investing in the project along with the business benefit it wants to achieve. It justifies the project and serves as a focus as the requirements gathering proceeds.

- *The scope of the work.* The work is the business area affected by the installation of your product. You need to understand the work to specify the most appropriate product.

> *The loftier the building, the deeper must the foundation be laid.*
>
> Source: Thomas Kempis

35

Figure 3.1

The blastoff activity lays
the foundation for the
requirements-gathering
activities to come. You
can find a complete
model of the blastoff
process in Diagram 1 of
the Volere Requirements
Process model in
Appendix A.

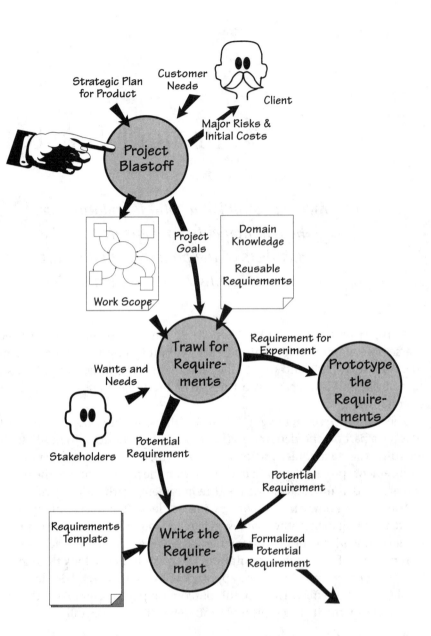

● *The stakeholders.* These people have an interest in the product. They
include the client—the person paying for the development of the product;
the customer—the person or people who buy the product; the users who
operate the product; and all the other people with some influence, or
knowledge needed to gather the requirements for the product.

● *Constraints.* Are there any design solutions that must be used? How much time and money are available for the solution?

● *Names.* Is any special terminology used by this part of the organization?

● *Relevant facts and assumptions (where applicable).* Are there any special facts people need to know? Are assumptions being made that may affect the outcome of the project?

● *The estimated cost.* Deliverables from the blastoff provide input to the estimating process and help project management take advantage of the requirements as input to project planning. This is not really a requirements issue, but as the requirements deliverables are prime input, your project management will thank you for it.

● *The risks.* The deliverables may possibly include a short risk analysis to reveal the main risks faced by the project. Someone skilled at risk assessment should handle this analysis.

● *A first-cut low-fidelity prototype.* You might consider sketching a very quick mock-up of one of the major screens or features of the product.

Taken together (see Figure 3.2), these deliverables give you enough information to make the final deliverable from the blastoff:

● *Go/no go decision.* Is the project viable, and does the cost of producing the product make it worthwhile? Do you have enough information to proceed with the requirements activity, or should you ask for more time to learn more?

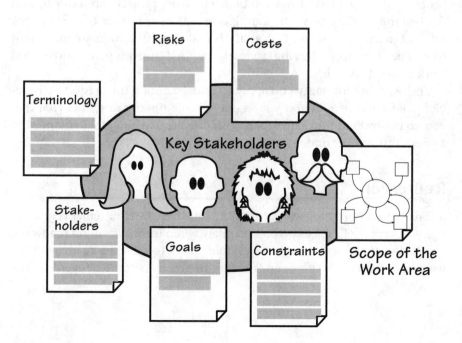

Figure 3.2

The blastoff activity assembles enough information to ensure that the project can proceed smoothly. It also verifies that the project is viable and worthwhile. Most of the outputs build the foundation for the trawling activity to come. The risks and costs are used by project management. You can find a complete model of the blastoff process in Diagram 1 in the Volere Requirements Process model in Appendix A.

Agility Guide

The blastoff deliverables are necessary for all projects regardless of their aspirations for agility. For example, even the most agile of projects must consider the scope of the work if it is to avoid wandering aimlessly because nobody knows which parts of the work are relevant. The differences between agility indicators here focus on the degree of formality used to record the deliverables.

Rabbits should have a sketch of the work scope model pinned to their walls, the list of stakeholders in a blog, and the project goals written with a broad marker pen on the project war room wall. Rabbits will probably have only a brief meeting at best, with most of the consensus on the blastoff coming from blogs, phone calls, and other informal interactive means. Despite the relative informality, we cannot stress enough the importance of documenting the work scope and ensuring you are thinking about the *work,* and not just the intended product.

Horses should be more formal and hold a blastoff meeting. They then communicate the blastoff results to the appropriate people, including all the stakeholders. Deliverables are recorded and distributed. Horse projects are likely to benefit from sketching a first-cut, low-fidelity prototype to ensure all stakeholders understand where the project is headed.

Elephants have a lot to lose by not having the blastoff deliverables firmly in place before proceeding. In most cases, the deliverables are discovered during meetings with the key stakeholders, and the results are recorded and distributed. Elephants should take the additional step of having the QA people test their blastoff deliverables. Elephant projects are critical, and costly if they make errors. The foundation of the requirements must be rock solid, and proved to be so. Risk analysis and cost estimation are important to elephant projects. Having a clearly defined and properly understood work scope is crucial.

The degree of formality you apply to understanding the blastoff deliverables will vary depending on your agility profile. In any case, it is vital that you do understand the deliverables. This chapter explains what you need to achieve this level of understanding.

IceBreaker

IceBreaker is a case study we have built to illustrate the requirements process. It uses a variety of data to predict precisely when ice will form on roadways, and it uses these predictions to schedule trucks to treat the roads with de-icing material (a salt compound) before the roads become dangerous. The

IceBreaker case study uses subject matter knowledge from the many ice forecasting and road de-icing systems, and other products produced by Vaisala (U.K.) Ltd. and Vaisala Worldwide. We acknowledge Vaisala's permission to use its material and the company's kind cooperation. See Figure 3.3 for an illustration of a weather station used by IceBreaker.

Imagine IceBreaker is your project. You work for Saltworks Systems, and you are responsible for producing the requirements specification. Your customer is the Northumberland County Highways Department, which will be providing information and requirements. Northumberland is a county in the northeast of England, tucked up under the border with Scotland. The Highways Department is responsible for keeping the roads free of ice during winter when freezing conditions are likely to cause accidents.

Figure 3.3

This weather station transmits data about the weather and road surface conditions to IceBreaker, which uses the information to predict ice formation. These predictions are used to dispatch trucks to treat the roads with de-icing material. (Photo of Vaisala Weather Station ROSA courtesy of Vaisala, *www.vaisala.com*.)

Scope, Stakeholders, Goals

To start at the beginning: Your project has to build a product—usually this is some software and sometimes hardware—to help people to do their work. And if your product is to be truly useful, then it must improve that work. Moreover, the cost of the product and its operation must be such that a net benefit is to be gained by building it.

We are talking about the work people do. To build the right product, you have to understand the work, the people who do or influence the work, and the end they are trying to achieve. We call this the trinity of *stakeholders—goals—scope* (SGS). See Figure 3.4.

The *scope* is the extent of the business area affected by the product. The *stakeholders* are all the people who have an interest in or an effect on the success of the project. The *goal* is the improvement the business wants to experience when the product is installed.

There is no particular order to these factors (in fact, you iterate around the SGS circle until you have stabilized the deliverables), but scope is usually the most convenient place to start.

Setting the Scope

The scope you are interested in at the beginning of the requirements project is the scope of the work for which the product is to be used. *Work* here means the business activity for which the user needs the product. It can be a commercial activity, some scientific or technical work, currently automated or manual work, or any combination of these or any other types of work. In some cases it can be work that does not yet exist and will be realized only at the end of the project. So long as it involves some processing activity and

Figure 3.4

The scope, stakeholders, and goals are not decided in isolation from one another. The scope of the work indicates which people have an interest in the outcome of building the product— the stakeholders—and they, in turn, decide what they want that outcome to be—the goals.

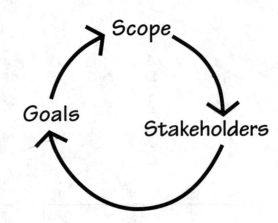

some information, we call it work. The reason for being interested in the work is that if, and only if, you understand the work can you build a product that can help to support it.

You set the scope by dividing the work you are about to study from the work that surrounds it. To do so, you must keep in mind that every piece of work you ever study is connected to other pieces of work. Consider, for example, the work you do as a business analyst, or programmer, or whatever it is you do. Your work is not isolated from the rest of your organization. When you do your work, you produce output. Let's say it is a requirements specification. You transmit your output—by paper or verbally or electronically—to some other person or organization or system or, as we use the term here, some other work. These two pieces of work are connected by one or more flows of information. In fact, the flows of information that enter and leave a piece of work actually define its scope.

The information that enters and leaves a piece of work defines what that work does.

In the preceding example, your output was a requirements specification. Assuming your specification is not a work of pure fiction—you didn't sit down and dream up the whole thing—then you must have had information coming into your work from various sources. Thus we can define your work as processing the information and transforming it into a requirements specification. This important idea of defining work and its boundaries by defining the inputs and outputs will be revisited several times in this book.

Setting the scope of the work means that you determine what work you are about to study, what other pieces of work surround it, and what flows of information make up the connections. When you set the scope, you are deciding how much of the work you will study and what you will not study. The product you build will become a significant part of the work. Thus there is a need to study the work and become familiar with it so as to understand what product you can build to best help with that work. The pieces of work you do not need to study—the *adjacent systems*—are outside your scope. You can safely restrict your study to understanding the details of the connections to the adjacent systems.

Setting the scope of the work means you determine what work you are about to study, what other pieces of work surround it, and what flows of information make up the connections.

For example, the work of IceBreaker is to predict the time that ice will form on a road so a truck can be scheduled to treat the road—as close as possible to freezing time—and prevent the ice from forming. To accomplish this, the IceBreaker work needs data about the weather and the condition of the road. It gets this data from sensing devices that measure the atmospheric conditions as well as the temperature and water content of the road surface. The sensing devices' work, in turn, is connected to another piece of work—the weather. The weather is connected to the slope of the earth's axis as it orbits the sun, which is itself connected to the work of the galaxy. You can only say that there is no more connecting work when you reach the edge of the universe, but usually you can stop a little short of that. In your requirements work, you make a decision on how much you intend to study and how much can safely be declared to be outside your scope.

When you set the scope, you are deciding how much of the work you will study and what you will not study.

The decision as to what is inside and what is outside is not made capriciously. It is based on what you need to know, and for that we can look to domains of interest.

Domains of Interest

A domain is a subject matter area, and because it is "of interest," it is a subject matter area you need to know something about. Naturally, domains can be very large—for example, "insurance" or "banking" or "weather"—so usually your domains of interest are parts of larger domains.

Let's consider the domains of interest for the IceBreaker work. The customer has told you:

> "Roads freeze in winter, and icy conditions cause road accidents that kill people. We need to be able to predict when ice will form on a road so we can schedule a de-icing truck to treat the road in time. We expect a new system to provide more accurate predictions of icy conditions. This will lead to more timely de-icing treatment than at present, which will reduce road accidents. We also want to eliminate indiscriminate treatment of roads, which wastes de-icing compounds and causes environmental damage."

Look through this statement, paying attention to the *subjects* you need to know about. For example, the statement begins with the word "roads." *Roads* is likely to be a domain, as any work that predicts freezing roads will need knowledge of roads—their geography and topography, their surface material, and anything else that helps predict when it will freeze.

"Icy conditions . . . We need to be able to predict when ice will form on a road" suggests a domain that covers the subject of temperature and, if the work is to make predictions, the behavior of temperature. This is the domain of *weather*.

"Schedule a de-icing truck" suggests that *scheduling* is a domain, as the product needs to have knowledge of how to schedule, or the aspects of scheduling that are common to any scheduling product.

The description of the work also mentions trucks, which suggests a domain of trucking or transportation. This domain would include information about what trucks can do, information about what they can't do, their carrying capacities, their speeds and ranges, and so on. The work needs to know these things if it is to manipulate a fleet of trucks and their drivers. Let's call this domain *trucking*.

This exercise gives you four domains:

1 Roads
2 Weather

3   Scheduling

4   Trucking

You are trying to determine the scope of the work you need to study. Clearly, you cannot study everything to do with all of the domains. You need to separate what is feasible and profitable to study from what you consider to be outside the scope of the work. We can highlight this division of study by building a context model that shows the work and its connections to the surrounding adjacent systems.

Let's start by looking for adjacent systems—the works that surround the work. The domains of interest that you have identified act as input to discovering your adjacent systems.

For each domain, ask if there are physical entities that somehow represent the domain. Consider the domain of weather. Yes, there are physical things like wind and rain and clouds, but they are probably too far removed from our problem area to be useful. Instead, there is a *weather forecasting service* that can supply the work with information about the weather. Your client is always able to help with identifying these physical entities. As the work is involved in predicting to a great degree of accuracy where ice will form on roads, it needs more precise information than it can get from a weather forecast. The *weather stations* measure this kind of information and can transmit it to the IceBreaker work. However, weather stations are expensive and the client is anxious not to install thousands of them throughout Northumberland, so he tells you *thermal map suppliers* can provide information about temperature differentials for each yard of a road between the weather stations.

Each of these physical entities is potentially an adjacent system. We say "potentially" because we have to examine them before committing to any decisions. For each entity, we ask if it forms part of the work or if it lies outside the project's authority and should not be considered as part of the work. For example, forecasting the weather is something we are not keen to be involved in, particularly when we can buy forecasts from the weather forecasting service. Similarly, the weather stations and the thermal mapping supplier are things we can safely exclude from our study—the IceBreaker Company does not own them and has no interest in altering them in any way. Thus we consider them to be adjacent systems.

Not all domains have a physical presence. Some domains, for example, are purely policies the work has to adopt. For example, the scheduling domain is a policy domain: The rules for scheduling, optimizing truck usage, manipulating a fleet of vehicles, and so on have no physical presence. Nevertheless, this policy must be part of the work but does not appear as an adjacent system on the context model.

A physical entity represents the domain of roads—a department called *Road Engineering*. These people build and maintain the roads, so it is appropriate they inform the ice-predicting work about the roads. It seems unlikely you would have any desire or need to change Road Engineering, so there is probably an adjacent system called Road Engineering. The work communicates with it through one or more flows of data.

The client says the *truck depot* is the adjacent system that represents the domain of trucking. One of the main reasons for the work's existence is to schedule the trucks, so we would expect to see flows of this nature between the work and the truck depot (which is another physical entity).

First-Cut Work Context

Using our knowledge of the work's responsibilities and the information from the domains given previously, we can build a model showing the work in its context. This model appears in Figure 3.5.

Figure 3.5

The work context diagram identifies the scope of the work that we intend to study. It shows the work as a single, as-yet-uninvestigated process, surrounded by the adjacent systems. The named arrows represent the data that flows between the work and the adjacent systems. The adjacent systems are the physical representatives of the domains. The *Truck Depot* represents trucking. The *Weather Station,* the *Weather Forecasting Service,* and the *Thermal Mapping Supplier* represent the weather domain. *Road Engineering* is the physical representation of the roads domain. The remaining domain, scheduling, is represented by policy inside the work and has no external connection.

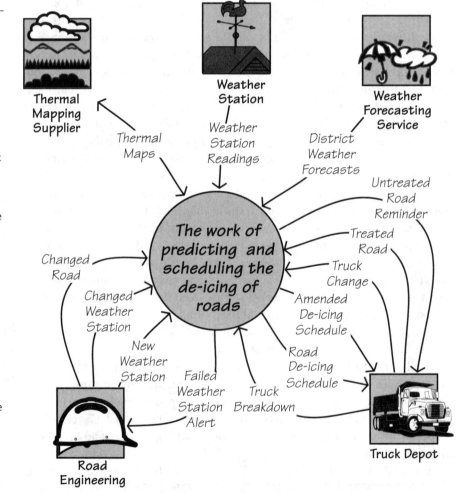

The work context shows where the responsibilities of the work and the responsibilities of the adjacent systems start and end. The flows of data between these entities identify what is done by the work and what must be done by an adjacent system. For example, the flow called *Truck Change* advises the work about changes to the de-icing trucks—new trucks added to the fleet, trucks taken out of service, modifications to trucks that would affect the way that they are scheduled. Why is this flow there? The work needs to know about trucks because it allocates trucks to roads when it produces the de-icing schedule. But what if we changed this responsibility? What if the depot became responsible for determining which truck was allocated to which road? The flow would be different. In fact, the Truck Change flow would not appear on the work context diagram at all, as there would be no need for it.

Flows around the boundary of the work are the clearest indication of its responsibilities. By defining these flows, we define the precise point at which one area of work ends and another starts.

One problem commonly arises in setting the context: Often we see product-centric contexts that contain only the intended software product. Remember that you are investigating some work, and the eventual product will become part of that work. To specify the best possible product, you must understand as much of the work as possible. In most cases, projects that restrict their study to what they think the product will contain build less useful products and often miss important functionality that could well have been included in the eventual product. If you do not have any human beings inside your work context, then chances are that your work context is too narrow.

Also consider the possibility that by enlarging the scope of the work you will find other potential areas for automation or other types of improvements. All too often, before we understand the work, we think of an automation boundary, and we never rethink it. Of course, then the "hard stuff"—the work that we did not intend to automate—is not considered. But by casting our nets wider, we can very often find aspects of the work that would benefit from automation, and in the end turn out to be cheaper than we thought. The moral of the story: First understand the work, then decide which product best supports that work.

> *The work context shows where the responsibilities of the work and the responsibilities of the adjacent systems start and end.*

> *The moral of the story: First understand the work, then decide which product best supports that work.*

Stakeholders

The next part of the trinity is the stakeholders. Stakeholders include anyone with an interest in, or an effect on, the outcome of the product. For example, you are a stakeholder because you have an interest in the requirements. The users of the product are stakeholders because they have an interest in having a product that does their work correctly. A security expert is a stakeholder who is interested in ensuring a secure product is built. In the same way,

> *Stakeholders are the source of requirements.*

READING

For more on stakeholder analysis, refer to Alexander, Ian, Neil Maiden et al. *Scenarios, Stories, Use Cases Through the Systems Development Life-Cycle.* John Wiley & Sons, 2004.

Figure 3.6

This stakeholder map shows the organizational rings surrounding the eventual product, and the classes of stakeholders who inhabit these areas. Use this map to help you determine which classes of stakeholders are relevant to your project and which roles you need to represent them.

potentially dozens of stakeholders exist for any project. The importance attached to stakeholders comes from the fact that they are the source of all your requirements.

The stakeholder map (christened an *onion diagram* by Ian Alexander) in Figure 3.6 identifies common classes of stakeholders that might be represented by one or more roles in your project. Here is how you interpret the map.

At the center of the stakeholder map is the *intended product.* Notice that it has a cloud-like shape, which is appropriate: It indicates that at the start of the requirements activities you should not be sure of the exact boundaries of the product. Surrounding the intended product is a ring indicating the *operational work area.* Stakeholders who will have some direct contact with the product inhabit this space. In the next ring, the *containing business,* you find stakeholders who benefit from the product in some way—even though they are not in the operational area. Finally, the outer ring, the *wider environment,* contains other stakeholders who have an influence on or an interest in the product. Note that the detailed and multiple involvement of the *core team members*—analysts, designers, project manager, and so on—is emphasized by the fact they span all the rings.

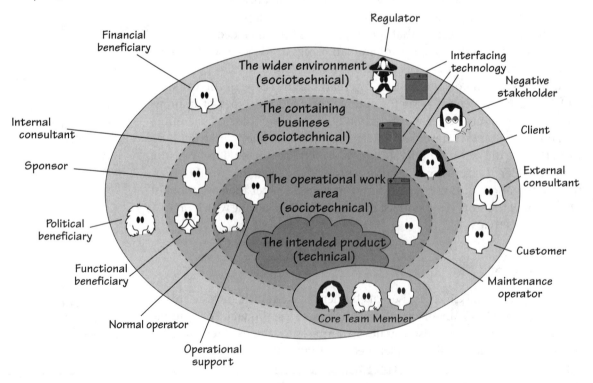

Because there are so many classes of stakeholders, it is helpful if we discuss some of the major categories and then formalize all of them with a detailed stakeholder analysis template.

The Client

Developing a new product is expensive. Someone has to pay for it? Let's assume that you work for an organization that is about to launch into the development of a new product. Let's further assume that the development effort will involve, in total, 50 people from different parts of the organization. Who pays for their time? Whose budget is about to carry the cost of some, if not all, of the people and effort shortly to be expended?

Whoever it is, that person is your *client*. On the simple basis that money talks, the client, by paying for the development, has the last say in what that product does, how it does it, and how elaborate or how sparse it must be.

The client pays for the development of the product.

The client—this stakeholder class is sometimes known as the *sponsor* or *executive sponsor*—is most likely present at the blastoff meeting. (You should be a little worried if the client is not there.) Consider some possible roles to represent the class of client:

- *User Management.* If you are building a product for in-house consumption, the cost of construction is most likely borne by the manager of the users who will be the ultimate operators of the product. Their department, or their work, is the beneficiary of the product, so it is reasonable that their manager pays for it.
- *Marketing Department.* If you build products for sale to people outside your organization, the marketing department may assume the role of client. In other words, it is the marketers you have to satisfy.
- *Product Development.* If you build software for sale, the budget for its development might be with your product manager or strategic program manager.

Consider your own organization. What is its structure? Which role (or roles) in your organization represents the class of client? Who pays for product development? Who reaps the benefit of the business advantage that the product brings? Who do you have to satisfy with your product? That is your client. If the investment resources come from several sources, then you need to decide who takes responsibility as the client and coordinates the sources of investment.

Let's assume the client for the IceBreaker project is Mack Andrews, the chief executive of Saltworks Systems. Mr. Andrews has made the commitment to invest in building the product. You write this agreement into your requirements specification:

> *The client for the product is Mack Andrews, the chief executive of Saltworks Systems. Eventually the client would like to sell the product to customers in other countries. The client has agreed that he is responsible for approving changes in the scope of the product.*

For more details on usability, adaptability, productization, and other types of requirements, refer to the template in Appendix B.

There are several things to note here. First, you name the client. It is now clear to everyone on the project that Mack Andrews takes responsibility for investing in the product. Second, other information is provided about the client that is used as the project progresses and may have a bearing on some of the requirements—particularly, the usability, adaptability, and productization requirements.

The client is recorded in section 2 of the specification. See the Volere Requirements Specification Template in Appendix B for an explanation of the sections and their contents.

The Customer

The customers buy the product. You have to understand your customers well enough to specify a product they will buy and find useful and pleasurable.

The customers buy the product once it is developed. Perhaps you already know the names of your customers, or perhaps they are hundreds or thousands of unknown people who might put down their money and walk out of the store with your product under their arm. In either case, you have to understand them well enough to specify a product they will buy and find useful and pleasurable.

Sometimes the customers are also the end users of the product. This happens when the product is sold via retail channels and aimed at domestic or small-office users. In other cases, your customers may buy your product for use by others. For example, you may be developing a new intranet product. In this case, your customers are the office managers who buy multiple copies of your product and expect their office staff to use it.

Even if you are developing open source software, you still have a customer. The difference is simply that no money changes hands.

You must know what appeals to your customers. What requirements will they pay for? What will they find useful? What window-dressing features are attractive, and what is downright trivial? Answering these questions correctly makes a huge difference to the success of your product.

For the IceBreaker product, the Northumberland County Highways Department has agreed to be the first customer.[1]

FOOTNOTE 1:
The original Vaisala de-icing prediction system was built for the Cheshire County Council. The designers of the product were Thermal Mapping International and The Computer Department. The product is now installed by all counties in the United Kingdom and has thousands of customers overseas. *www.vaisala.com*

> *The customer for the product is the Northumberland County Highways Department, represented by director Jane Shaftoe.*

As there is a single customer (at this stage), it would, of course, be advisable to invite her to participate as a stakeholder in the project. This kind of out-reach results in the customer being actively involved in selecting which requirements are useful, choosing between conflicting requirements, and making the requirements analysts aware of her problems and aspirations.

Saltworks Systems has further ambitions for the IceBreaker product. The company suspects that a successful ice forecasting system could be sold to road authorities in other counties and other countries. If you plan to build the product with this aim in mind, then your requirements specification should include an additional customer statement:

> Potential customers for the product include all counties in the United King-dom as well as northern parts of North America and Europe. A summary of the requirements specification will be presented to the Highways Depart-ment managers of selected counties, states, and countries for the purpose of discovering additional requirements.

It is clear that the customer should always be represented on the project. Where many potential customers exist, there is a need to have a customer representative. This representative can be a member of the marketing depart-ment, a representative from a user group, a senior user from one or more of your key customers, or a combination of domain and usability experts from within your organization. The nature of your product, the structure of your organization, your customer base, and possibly several other factors will decide which roles on your team represent the customer stakeholder class. For consumer products or shrink-wrapped software, you might consider using a *persona*. The decision to use a persona should be made here. We have more on personas in Chapter 5, Trawling for Requirements.

The Users: Get to Know Them

When we talk about users, we mean the people who will ultimately operate your product. The stakeholder map (Figure 3.6) refers to them as *normal oper-ators* to emphasize that we are concerned with people who will have direct contact with the product. For in-house products, the users are usually the people who work for your client. For external products, the users and the cus-tomers may be the same people.

Identifying the users is the first step in understanding the work they do. After all, your product is intended to help with this work. Additionally, you have to know what kind of people they are so you can write the correct usa-bility requirements. You have to bring about a product that the users can and will use. The more you know about the users, the better the chance you have of specifying a suitable product.

The purpose of identifying the users is so that you can understand the work that they do.

READING

Don Gause and Jerry
Weinberg give a wonderful
example of brainstorming
lists of users in their book:
Gause, Don, and Gerald
Weinberg. *Exploring
Requirements: Quality Before
Design.* Dorset House, 1989.

Different users will make different demands on your product. For example, an airline pilot has very different usability requirements from, say, a commuter buying a ticket on a rail system. If your users are commuters, then a "person without cash" and a "person with only one arm free" would raise their own usability requirements.

There are always too many potential users, and too many that might be forgotten or overlooked. We recommend that you build a checklist of the categories of people who might conceivably use your product. List their role or work title, or describe their job. Add any abnormal or unusual attributes, such as users who would use your product while driving or simultaneously with another product. Also consider the user's physical location—outside, on an aircraft, in a public place.

The consideration of potential users is vital for agile development. Too often we see only one user asked to supply the requirements for a product, and little or no consideration given to what will happen when the product is released to a wider audience. We strongly urge you to always consider the broadest spectrum of users and, at the very least, to choose user stakeholders from both ends.

For each of the user categories that you have on your list, identify the particular attributes that your product must cater to:

- People with disabilities: Consider all disabilities. This, in some cases, is a legal requirement.
- Nonreaders: Consider people who cannot read and people who do not speak the home language.
- People who need reading glasses: This is particularly near and dear to one of the authors.
- People who cannot resist changing things like fonts, styles, and so on.
- People who will probably be carrying luggage, large parcels, or a baby.
- People who do not normally use a computer.
- People who might be angry, frustrated, under pressure, or in a hurry.

For the users, write a section in your specification to describe, as fully as possible, all known and potential users and their attributes. For their attributes, consider these possibilities:

- Subject matter experience: How much help do they need?
- Technological experience: Can they operate the product? What technical terms should be used?
- Intellectual abilities: Should tasks be made simpler? Or broken down to a lower level?

- Attitude toward the job: What are the users' aspirations?
- Education: What can you expect your user to know?
- Linguistic skills: Not all your users will speak or read the home language.

We realize that writing all this stuff down seems like a chore. However, we have found that taking the time to write something down so other people can read it is one of the few ways for you to demonstrate that you understand it. The users are so important to your cause that you must understand what kind of people they are and what capabilities they have. To wave your hands and say, "They are graphic designers," falls short of the minimum level of understanding.

Another class of stakeholder in the operational work area is maintenance operators. From these people you will discover the appropriate maintainability requirements.

Operational support is another source of requirements relating to the operational work area. Roles that are sources of these requirements include help desk staff, trainers, installers, and coaches.

At this stage, any users you identify are potential users. That is, you do not yet precisely know the scope of the product—you determine this later in the requirements process—so at this stage you are identifying the people who could *possibly* use, maintain, and support the product. Remember that people other than the intended users might end up using your product. It is better to identify superfluous users than to fail to find them all.

> *People other than the intended users might end up using your product. It is better to identify superfluous users than to fail to find them all.*

Other Stakeholders

There are more people you have to talk to so that you can find all the requirements. Your contact with these people might be fleeting, but nevertheless necessary. Any of them may potentially have requirements for your product.

The problem that we often face is that we do not know who all the stakeholders are, and thus we fail to consider them. This results in a string of change requests when the product starts being used, and has an adverse effect on people we overlooked. When any new system is installed, somebody gains and somebody loses power. This shift may be a subtle gain or loss, or it may be a wholesale change. People may find that the product brings them new capabilities, or people may not be able to do their jobs the way they used to do them. The moral of the story is clear: Find everyone who will be affected by the product, and find their requirements.

We list our stakeholders in section 2 of the Volere Requirements Specification Template. This list acts as a checklist, pointing the requirements analysts to the right people for gathering their requirements.

Let's consider some other stakeholders by looking at some candidate categories. You can also see most of these illustrated as classes on the stakeholder map (Figure 3.6).

> *" Every context is composed of individuals who do or do not decide to connect the fate of a project with the fate of the small or large ambitions they represent. "*
>
> Source: Bruno Latour, *ARAMIS or the Love of Technology*

Consultants

Consultants—both internal to your organization and external—are people who have some expertise you need to help you uncover the right requirements. Consultants might never touch or see your product, but their knowledge is nevertheless part of it. For example, if you are building a financial product, a security expert will be one of your stakeholders. The security expert might never see your product, but his stake in the matter is that the product is secure.

Management

Consider any category of management. These groups show up on the stakeholder map as classes like *functional beneficiary, political beneficiary,* and *financial beneficiary.* Does the board of directors have any interest in the product? Is it a strategic product? Do any managers other than those directly involved have a stake?

Product managers and program managers are good sources of requirements. They might also be considered the client for the project. Project managers or leaders who are responsible for the day-to-day management of the project effort likewise have contributions to make.

Subject Matter Experts

This constituency, represented by the classes of internal and external consultants, may include domain analysts, business consultants, business analysts, or anyone else who has some specialized knowledge of the business subject. As a consequence, these experts are a prime source of information about the work.

Core Team

The core team is the people who are part of the building effort for the product—the product designers, programmers, testers, systems analysts, systems architects, technical writers, database designers, and anyone else who is somehow involved in the construction. It is not necessary to have all these people at the blastoff meeting, as some of them will be involved for only part of the construction.

You can also consider the open source community as stakeholders because they have knowledge about new technological trends. You can contact these people via open source forums. They are usually very enthusiastic and ready to share their knowledge with you.

When you do know the people involved, record their names. Otherwise, use this section of the template to list the skills and duties that you think will most likely be needed to build the product.

Inspectors

Consider safety inspectors, auditors, firefighters, technical inspectors, and possibly government inspectors. It may well be necessary to build inspection capabilities into your product.

Market Forces

The marketing department of your organization probably represents this constituency. When building a product for commercial sale, trends in the market are a potent source of requirements. As an example, note how quickly new technology is built into personal computers and their software. Any new product in this arena that does not include the latest technology is likely to be consigned to the "also-ran" category by the marketplace.

Legal

Consult your lawyers, or possibly the police, for legal requirements. Also include in this constituency any standards that are relevant to your product. You will have to determine who your organization's standard bearers are, because they are stakeholders as well.

Negative Stakeholders

Negative stakeholders are people who do not want the product. Although they may not be the most cooperative individuals, you would be wise to consider them. You may find that, if the requirements are different from the commonly perceived version, the opposition may turn into supporters.

Industry Standard Setters

Your industry may have professional bodies that expect certain codes of conduct to be followed or certain standards to be maintained by any product built within the industry or created for use by the industry.

Public Opinion

Do any user groups for your product exist? They will certainly be a major source of requirements. For any product intended for the public domain, consider polling members of the public about their opinion. They may make demands on your product that could spell the difference between acceptance and rejection.

Government

Some products rub up against government agencies for reporting purposes, or they receive information from the government. Other products have requirements that necessitate consulting with the government. Although the government may not assign a person full-time to your project, you should nevertheless nominate the agency as a stakeholder.

Special-Interest Groups

Consider handicapped-interest groups, environmental bodies, foreign people, old people, gender-related interests, novices, or almost any other group that may come in contact with your product.

Technical Experts

Technical experts do not necessarily build the product, but they will almost certainly consult on some part of it. For the stakeholders from this constituency consider usability experts, security consultants, hardware people, experts in the technologies that you might use, specialists in software products, or experts from any technical field that the product could use.

Cultural Interests

This constituency is more applicable to products intended for the public domain. For example, is it possible in these politically correct times that your product could offend someone? Might religious, ethnic, cultural, political, or other human interests be affected by your product? Consider inviting representatives from these groups to be consultant stakeholders for the project.

Adjacent Systems

The adjacent systems on your work context diagram are the systems, people, or work areas that directly interface with the work you are studying. Carefully examine each adjacent system and then start asking questions: Who represents its interests, or who has knowledge of it? When the adjacent system is an automated one, find out if it has a project leader or maintainer. Otherwise, you may have to spend some time looking at its specifications to discover whether it has any special demands created by interfacing with your product. For each adjacent system you should discover one or more stakeholders.

Finding the Stakeholders

There is a paradox here: The stakeholders are identified by the blastoff, but the blastoff is often run as a meeting of the main stakeholders. It will be necessary to have a short session to identify the key stakeholders before the blastoff.

During the blastoff, you normally hold a brainstorming session and inspect your context model to identify all possible stakeholders. You do not have to start from scratch. We have constructed a spreadsheet with many categories of stakeholders, along with the kind of knowledge you need from each person. This spreadsheet cross-references the stakeholder map (Figure 3.6) and provides a detailed specification of your project's sociology. Once you have identified the stakeholder, add that person's name to the list. Have a look at Appendix D, Project Sociology Analysis Templates, for a compressed version of the template. The complete spreadsheet is available as a free download at *www.volere.co.uk*.

You will be talking to the stakeholders, so at this stage it pays to explain to them why they are stakeholders and why you need to consult them about requirements for the product. Explain specifically why their input will make a difference to the eventual product. It is polite to inform stakeholders of the amount of their time you require and the type of participation that you have in mind. A little warning always helps them to think about their requirements for the product. The greatest problem concerning stakeholders is the requirements that you will miss if you do not find all the stakeholders or if you exclude stakeholders from the requirements-gathering process.

Goals: What Do You Want to Achieve?

When you are working with your stakeholders on detailed requirements, it is very easy to go off track and either spend time on irrelevant details or miss requirements that are important.

Your client is making an investment in a project to build a product. You need to understand the reason behind this investment by determining the precise benefits the project is to deliver. You also need a guide to help you steer your efforts toward those requirements that will make the greatest contributions to the expected business advantage.

In other words, you need to know the goal of the project. You can think of the project goal as the highest-level requirement. All of the detailed requirements must make a positive contribution toward reaching that goal.

Your effort will pay handsome dividends if you spend a little time during the blastoff to reach a consensus on the goal of the project and to write it clearly, unambiguously, and in a measurable way so it quantifies the benefits of the project. This measurement also makes the goal testable.

Usually at the beginning of a project, unless you have very good ongoing collaboration with your strategic planners, the purpose of the project is vague or is stated in terms that almost any solution could satisfy. How do you make it clearer? Start with a statement of the user problem or background to the project. (We make this problem statement the first part of all our specifications. See the template in Appendix B for a suggested format.)

Appendix D, Project Sociology Analysis Templates, includes a compressed version of the template. The complete stakeholder analysis spreadsheet is available as a free download at www.volere.co.uk.

The greatest problem concerning stakeholders is the requirements that you miss if you do not find all the stakeholders, or if you exclude stakeholders from the requirements-gathering process.

The project goal is the highest-level requirement.

Those stakeholders who represent the user or business side of the organization should confirm that you do, indeed, understand the problem, and that your problem statement is a fair and accurate one.

The customer has given you this background:

"Roads freeze in winter, and icy conditions cause road accidents that kill people. We need to be able to predict when a road is likely to freeze so that our depot can schedule a de-icing truck in time to prevent the road from freezing. We expect a new system to provide more accurate predictions of icy conditions by using thermal maps of the district and the road temperatures from weather stations installed in the roads, in addition to the weather forecasts. This will lead to more timely de-icing treatment than at present, which will reduce road accidents. We also want to eliminate indiscriminate treatment of roads, which wastes de-icing compounds and causes environmental damage."

Once you and your blastoff group know and can articulate the business problem, you can concentrate on discovering the requirements that will make the greatest contribution toward solving the problem.

The problem appears to be road accidents due to ice on the roads, and the solution to the problem is to treat the roads to prevent the ice from forming (and presumably to melt the ice if it has already formed). Thus you can write the purpose for this project as follows:

> *You can use "purpose, advantage, measurement" (PAM) as a mnemonic to help you discover and analyze the goals.*

Purpose: To accurately forecast road freezing times and schedule de-icing treatment.

The purpose of the project should be not only to solve the problem, but also to provide a business advantage. Naturally, if there is an advantage, you must be able to measure it.

> *The purpose of the project is not only to solve the problem, but also to provide a business advantage.*

The business advantage is the reduction—ideally the elimination—of accidents due to ice. The road authorities (the customers) are particularly interested in reducing the accident rate. You have been told:

"The new system will lead to more timely de-icing treatment than at present, which will reduce road accidents."

Thus you can define the advantage the business would like to get from the project as follows:

Advantage: To reduce road accidents by eliminating icy road conditions.

Is this advantage measurable? Yes. The success of the product you build can be measured by the reduction in the number of accidents where ice is a contributing factor:

> *Measurement: Accidents attributed to ice shall be no more than 15 percent of the total number of accidents during winter.*

You have stated a measurable goal, and monitoring the accidents for a winter or two is reasonable. As accident statistics and police reports are already collected, you should have no trouble establishing whether the product you build is successful.

But is this a reasonable goal? Is the elimination of most of the accidents due to ice worth the cost and effort of building the product? And where did "15 percent of the total" come from, anyway? The Northumberland County Highways Department representative at the blastoff assures you that this is a target figure set by the county. If it can be achieved, the County Council will be happy, and they are prepared to spend money to achieve the target. Note that at this stage if there was no concrete goal or if the effort (we will deal with estimating the effort shortly) was too great given the business advantage, then now is the time to call a halt.

Is this goal feasible? Can a "timely de-icing treatment" lead to a reduction in accidents? And to as little as 15 percent of the total? One reason for having the key stakeholders present at the blastoff is to answer questions like this one. One of the stakeholders (see the description elsewhere in this chapter of how stakeholders are selected) is from the National Road Users Association. She assures you that this group's research shows ice treatment is effective and the expected reductions are realistic.

Is this goal achievable? The stakeholders representing the product designers and builders, the technical experts from the hardware side, and the meteorologist all assure the blastoff participants that the technology is available, or can be built, and that similar software problems have been solved previously by the team.

Note the major aspects of the project goal:

- *Purpose:* What should the product do?
- *Advantage:* What business advantage does it provide?
- *Measurement:* How do you measure the advantage?
- *Reasonable:* Given what you understand about the constraints, is it possible for the product to achieve the business advantage?
- *Feasible:* Given what you have learned from the blastoff, is it possible to build a product to achieve the measure?

● *Achievable:* Does the organization have (or can it acquire) the skills to build the product and operate it once built?

Sometimes projects have more than one purpose statement. Look at the customer's statement:

"We also want to eliminate indiscriminate treatment of roads, which wastes de-icing compounds and causes environmental damage."

This reveals another purpose for the project:

> *Purpose: To save money on winter road maintenance costs.*

The advantage stemming from this purpose is that accurate forecasts reduce the cost of treatment because only roads in imminent danger of freezing are treated. Additionally, by preventing ice from forming on road surfaces, damage to roads is reduced. (When ice forms in cracks in the surface, it expands as it freezes and forces the crack to expand. Eventually, this process results in significant holes in the road surface.)

The advantage is straightforward:

> *Advantage: Reduced de-icing and road maintenance costs.*

The measurement of "reduced costs" is usually expressed in monetary terms:

> *The cost of de-icing shall be reduced by 25 percent of the current cost of road treatment, and damage to roads from ice shall be reduced by 50 percent.*

Naturally, you need to know the current costs and damage expenditures so that you will know when they have been reduced by 25 percent and 50 percent, respectively. If there is supporting material available, then cite it in your specification:

> *Supporting Materials: Thornes, J. E. Cost-Effective Snow and Ice Control for the Nineties. Third International Symposium on Snow and Ice Control Technology, Minneapolis, Minnesota, Vol. 1, Paper 24, 1992.*

The engineers also know that applying too much salt compounds to roads damages the environment. By having a more accurate treatment, less material finds its way to the environs of the roads, and less damage results. This means that more accurate forecasts give you another advantage:

> *Advantage: To reduce damage to the environment by unnecessary application of de-icing compounds.*

This advantage can be measured by comparing the amount of de-icing material used by the product with that used at present:

> *Measurement: The amount of de-icing chemicals needed to de-ice the authority's roads shall be reduced by 50 percent.*
>
> *Supporting Materials: Thornes, J. E. Salt of the Earth. Surveyor Magazine, 8 December 1994, pp. 16–18.*

Note that the purpose statements result in an advantage and a measurement. If you cannot express an advantage for the purpose, or the advantage is not measurable, then it should not be part of your specification. For example, suppose the purpose of a project is something vague:

> *Purpose: To improve the way we do business.*

The advantage here is unclear. Do we want the business to make more money, or do we want the business process to function more smoothly? Or something else? The discipline necessary to give the purpose an advantage and a measurement means that fuzzy or ill-defined purposes are far less likely to find their way into your specifications.

You cannot build the right product unless you know precisely what the product is intended to do and how the product's success is to be measured. Whether the using organization achieves the target set by the product purpose may depend on the way that it uses the product. Obviously, if the product is not used as intended, then it may fail to provide the advantages for which it was built. Thus the statement of project purpose must assume that the resulting product will be used as intended.

You cannot build the right product unless you know precisely what the product is intended to do and how the product's success is to be measured.

Keeping Track of the Purpose

Once you have established the purpose, you also need to keep the project aimed toward it. It is always possible that the project purpose will be forgotten as the requirements analysts and the users explore the work and the proposed product. As more and more requirements are discovered, and more and more exciting new ideas are proposed, the product might wind up being formed so that it no longer meets the original purpose of doing the project, and thus the original advantages are not realized.

Our approach is to write the project purpose, advantage, and measurement (PAM) on some large medium and have it at all meetings with stakeholders. Make sure it is visible and everyone is aware of it; treat it as a target that you are all aiming to meet. This approach helps to keep everyone aware of the purpose.

See Chapter 11, The Quality Gateway, for more on using the project purpose as a test for relevancy. The Quality Gateway runs each requirement through a series of tests, including relevancy. If a requirement is not in some way relevant to the purpose, it is rejected.

When you write the purpose, you should make the point that all decisions about the project are driven by this purpose. Make sure everyone understands that if the purpose changes during the project then you will need to review the scope, stakeholders, and any requirements that have been defined.

Requirements Constraints

Requirements constraints are usually global requirements. Because they are restrictions, they help to determine which subset of requirements can be included in the eventual product. Constraints affect decisions about the scope of the product: Perhaps they limit the amount of time or money that may be spent on the project, or perhaps they are pre-ordained design decisions that limit the way the problem is solved. You can think of constraints as a special type of requirement that provides some guidance on where to focus your requirements-gathering efforts. Your management, your marketing colleagues, or your client probably already knows the constraints. The task at blastoff time is to elicit and record these limitations.

Section 4, Mandated Constraints, of the Volere Requirements Specification Template provides a complete description of how you record constraints. You can find the template in Appendix B.

Solution Constraints

Your specification should describe any mandated designs or solutions to the problem. For example, you may be told that the only acceptable solution is one that will run on a mobile phone. Your management or some other party may have other expectations about the eventual design, such that no other design is allowable. While we warn you against designing the solution before knowing all the requirements, it may be that for some overriding reason—marketing, cultural, managerial, political, expectations, or financial—only one acceptable design solution exists. If this is the case, it must be part of your specification.

Any partner or collaborative applications should also be brought to light and recorded at the blastoff. Partner applications are those other applications or systems with which your product must cooperate. For example, your product may have to interact with existing databases, reporting systems, or Web-based systems. Thus the interfaces to those systems become constraints on your product. Mandated operating systems should also be included here.

Commercial off-the-shelf (COTS) and open source applications, if they are to be used, are recorded under the Constraint heading. It may be that your product must interact with COTS or open source software, or perhaps your product must incorporate COTS/open source software in the eventual solution. There may be good reasons for mandating this cooperation—but then again, there may not. The blastoff is the ideal opportunity for you to reach a consensus with the stakeholders as to whether the decision to incorporate ready-built software is appropriate for your situation.

Project Constraints

The project constraints section of the specification contains information about the schedule and financial budget on the project. These parameters should be known at blastoff time, because they affect the requirements that you gather later. If you have a $500,000 budget, there is no point in collecting the requirements for a $1 million product.

Time constraints can be imposed to enable the product to meet a window of opportunity, to coincide with coordinated releases of associated products, to meet the scheduled start-up of a new business venture, or to satisfy many other scheduling demands. If this type of constraint exists, then you and your team must be aware of it. Keep in mind that a time constraint is not the same thing as an estimate of the time necessary to complete the project.

Financial constraints indicate how elaborate the product may be, and they give you a good idea if the product is really wanted. If the budget is impossibly small, it may indicate that no one really wants the product. Impossibly small budgets and impossibly short deadlines almost always cripple projects. There is no reason to think yours will be different.

Financial constraints indicate how elaborate the product may be, and they give you a good idea if the product is really wanted.

Naming Conventions and Definitions

Names are important. Good names convey meaning; poor names do just the opposite. We have found that every project has names particular to it, and they should be recorded for the sake of communication and future understanding. During the blastoff you begin to collect and record the names, along with their agreed-upon meanings.

Record the names in section 5, Naming Conventions and Definitions, of the specification template. This glossary serves as a reference point for the entire project. We are always amazed at how many misunderstandings occur simply because no central glossary is available, and how effective good names can be at communicating meaning. It is worth expending effort in this area to ensure smooth communication later on in the project.

For example, the IceBreaker project team added the following definition to its glossary during the blastoff:

> *Weather Station: A collection of hardware capable of collecting and transmitting road-temperature, air-temperature, humidity, and precipitation readings. Weather stations are installed in eight locations in Northumberland.[2]*

Starting to define terminology at blastoff time has a distinct advantage: You make the words visible. The stakeholders can then discuss them and change them to reflect the consensus of the meaning.

Starting to define terminology at blastoff time has a distinct advantage: You make the words visible. The stakeholders can then discuss them and change them to reflect their consensus of the meaning. Subsequent development activities build on the glossary and use it as the basis for building a complete data dictionary.

How Much Is This Going to Cost?

At this point in the blastoff, you have a lot of information on which to base your estimates of cost and effort. The needed effort is usually proportional to the amount of functionality contained within the work area. This relationship makes sense: The more functions done by the work area, the more effort needed to study it and devise a solution. At this stage you do not know the size of the product—how much functionality it will contain—but you do know the size of the work area. That is, at least you do if you measure it.

The easiest way to measure the size or functionality of the work area is to count the number of adjacent systems on the context model as well as the number of inputs and outputs. While more accurate ways to measure size have been devised, counting the inputs and outputs is fast and gives you a far better idea of size than merely guessing. If your context has more than 30 inputs and outputs, then it falls into the "average cost per input/output" range of estimating. Simply put, your organization has an average cost for gathering the requirements for one input or output. You can determine this cost by going back to previous projects, counting the number of inputs and outputs on the context, and dividing this number into the total cost of that requirements investigation.

A more accurate estimate comes from determining the number of business events that affect the work. We discuss this approach fully in Chapter 4, Event-Driven Use Cases. For the meantime, if you accept that the business events can be derived from the context model, then their number is the determining factor in the cost of the requirements effort. It is, of course, necessary to know the cost to your organization of analyzing the average business event. You can learn this cost by looking at previous projects or, if necessary, running a benchmark. Multiply the cost per event by the number of events to give a reasonably accurate price you will pay for requirements gathering.

More accurate still is function point counting. At this stage you need to have an idea of the data stored by the work, and this information can usually be identified in a short time if your team includes some experienced data modelers. Function point counting measures the amount and the complexity of the data processed by the work—the inputs and the outputs from the context model—along with data stored within the work. Enough is known about function points to enable you to find figures for the average cost per function point of requirements investigation.

A brief overview of function point counting appears in Appendix C, Function Point Counting: A Simplified Introduction.

The key consideration is not so much that you use a particular estimating system at this stage, but rather that you use a system based on measurement, not hysterical optimism. Too much risk is courted by not measuring. If you do not make even the most basic of measurements, then any predictions you do make will be based on nothing more than guesswork. Guesswork and optimism usually lead to unrealistic project schedules, and these in turn force developers to cut corners and scrimp on quality. Inevitably, the project gets into trouble when the shortcuts turn out to cause longer delivery times (it always happens), and the users lose confidence in the integrity of the product and its developers. There is too much evidence of the downside of not measuring, and too much known about measuring, to have any excuse for not doing it.

READING

Garmus, David, and David Herron. *Function Point Analysis: Measurement Practices for Successful Software Practices.* Addison-Wesley, 2001.

Risks

We face risks every day. Just leaving your home to go to work involves some risk—your car won't start, the train will be late, you will be assigned to share an office with the boring person with body odor problems. But still we go to work each day, because we know the risks and consider the outcome to be worth the risk.

However, once we are at work, we might well plunge into situations where we have no idea of the risks involved, and thus no idea whether the outcome is worth braving the risks.

Pop quiz time: Have you ever worked on a project where nothing went wrong? No? Something always goes wrong. Now, did you ever try and figure out ahead of time what could go wrong, and do something to prevent it going wrong, or at least allow for the mishaps by budgeting for them? This, in its simplest sense, is risk management.

Your blastoff process should include a short risk analysis. Such an assessment is probably outside the remit of the business analyst, and should be done by a competent risk-assessment person. The job is to assess the risks that are most likely to happen and the risks that will have the greatest impact if they do, in fact, become problems. The deliverables from your blastoff provide input for the risk assessor to identify risks. For each identified risk, the assessor determines the probability of it becoming a problem, along with its cost or schedule impact. At the same time, the assessor determines the early-warning signs—the happenings that signal a risk is coming to fruition. In some cases where the risks are considered serious, a risk manager is assigned to monitor for the telltale signs that some risks are turning into full-blown problems.

Risk management is common-sense project management or, in the words of our partner Tim Lister, "project management for adults." If your organization is not doing it, then you should prepare for the budget or time overruns that are coming your way. The most noticeable effect of doing risk analysis is that it makes the risks visible to all stakeholders. Once aware of the risks, they can contribute to risk mitigation. Similarly, the risk assessor makes management aware of the risks and their impact if they become problems.

READING

DeMarco, Tom, and Tim Lister. *Waltzing with Bears: Managing Risk on Software Projects.* Dorset House, 2003.

To Go or Not to Go

The deliverables you produce during the blastoff provide the basis for assessing the viability of your project. When you take a hard look at what these deliverables are telling you, you can decide whether it makes good business sense to press the button and launch the requirements project.

Consider your deliverables:

READING

Tockey, Steve. *Return on Software: Maximizing the Return on Your Software Investment.* Addison-Wesley, 2004.

● Is the product goal clear and unambiguous? Or does it contain fudge words?

● Is it measurable? That is, will it give a clear indication you have successfully completed the project?

● Does it indicate a benefit to the organization?

● Is it viable? Is it possible to achieve the objectives of the project within the allotted time and budget?

● Have you reached agreement on the scope of the work?

● Do some risks have a high probability of becoming problems?

● Is the impact of these risks such that it makes the project unfeasible?

● Is the cost reasonable given the product's benefit?

● Are the stakeholders willing to be involved?

- Do you have sufficient justification to invest in the project?
- Do you have enough reasons not to invest in the project?
- Is there any further investigation that you should do before launching the requirements project?

The point is to make an objective decision based on facts, not on boundless enthusiasm or giddy optimism. For some reason it is always very difficult to stop a project once it is under way and has consumed some resources. Ed Yourdon refers to these doomed ventures as "death march" projects—they stagger along for years when most of the people involved know that they were never viable enough to have been started in the first place. A little consideration at this stage can prevent poor projects from being started and give good projects a flying start.

Blastoff Alternatives

We have suggested in this book that the stakeholders get together for a couple of days and derive all of the blastoff deliverables. We understand that in a lot of organizations this type of meeting, despite its merit, is simply not possible. But, there are other ways.

While coming together is important, it is the deliverables that really matter. Some organizations come up with these items in other forms—a lot of companies write a business plan or some similarly named document that covers many of the topics we advocate. This is fine as long as you have an objective, quantifiable plan and it is circulated and agreed to by the stakeholders.

Some organizations use feasibility studies as a way of getting their projects started. Of course, the feasibility study must honestly look at the costs and risks as well as the benefits from the product. Provided the study delivers realistic numbers, it will serve. We make the proviso that all the key stakeholders must have seen and commented on the accuracy of the feasibility study. You don't have to have a meeting, but you do need to know all the facts that the meeting would deliver.

You don't have to have a meeting, but you do need to know all the facts that the meeting would deliver.

Summary

The project blastoff is about knowing. Knowing what you want the product to do for you, and what it will cost to build it. Knowing the scope of the work that is to be studied so as to gather the requirements for the product. Knowing which people will be involved in the project, and having them know what is expected of them. Knowing the users, which in turn will lead you to knowing the usability requirements for the product.

The project blastoff is about knowing.

Knowing the constraints on the project—how much money have you got to spend, and how much or how little time do you have to deliver the product? Knowing the words to be used on the project.

Knowing whether you can succeed.

The blastoff delivers knowledge. What is better, it delivers it at a time that it is most useful—at the beginning of the project when crucial decisions have to be made.

The blastoff deliverables will reappear later in this book. Some of them are used as input to the mainstream requirements activities. None of them is wasted.

Event-Driven Use Cases

*in which we discuss a fail-safe way of
partitioning the work into use cases, and along
the way discover the best product to build*

The blastoff process establishes the scope of the work. This scope—ideally shown graphically as a context diagram—defines a business area, part of which is to be automated by the intended product. However, this work scope is probably too large to be studied as a single unit. Just as you cut your food into small bites before attempting to eat it, it is necessary to partition the work into manageable pieces before studying it to find the product's requirements.

In this chapter we lay out a set of heuristics to guide you in finding the most appropriate use cases. Almost as a by-product of this effort, you will arrive at the most useful product that you can build.

Never eat anything bigger than your head.

Source: B. Kliban

Agility Guide

Rabbits should pay particular attention to this chapter. We discuss here how we look at the work—not just the product—to determine the use cases. Agility cannot come at the expense of getting the right product, and looking at the work from the outside is the best and fastest way of getting it right. No extra documentation is required when using our approach to use cases.

For horses and elephants, we recommend that you consider partitioning the work area using business events as we describe them in this chapter. Your documentation may well include the scenarios we suggest here.

Understanding the Work

The product you intend to build must improve your client's work. Your product will be installed in the client's area of work and will do part of (sometimes all of) that work. It does not matter what kind of work it is—

commercial, scientific, embedded real-time, manual, or currently automated—you always have to understand it before you can decide what kind of product will best help with it. By "work," we do not mean just a computer system (either the current system or an anticipated one); instead, we mean the system for doing business. We include the human tasks, the computers, the machines, and the low-tech devices like telephones, photocopiers, manual files, and notebooks—in fact, anything that is used to produce your client's goods, services, or information. Until you understand this work and its desired outcomes, you cannot know which product is the optimal one to build.

Figure 4.1 presents an overview of how we intend to proceed. You might wish to refer back to this figure as you read the text, as it will help smooth the way.

Figure 4.1

The scope of the work is agreed to by all parties at the blastoff. It defines both the work area to be studied and the adjacent systems that surround it. The adjacent systems supply data to the work and/or receive data from it. Business events happen in the adjacent systems—usually the event is a demand for a service provided by the work. In addition, time-triggered business events occur when it is time for the work to provide some information to the adjacent system. The response the work makes to the business event is called a business use case. It includes all of the processes and data needed to make the correct response. The requirements analysts study the functionality of the business use case with the help of the appropriate stakeholders. From this study, they determine the optimal product to build and construct a product use case scenario to show how the actor and the product will interact. Once agreement is reached on this product and scenario, the requirements analysts write the requirements for the product.

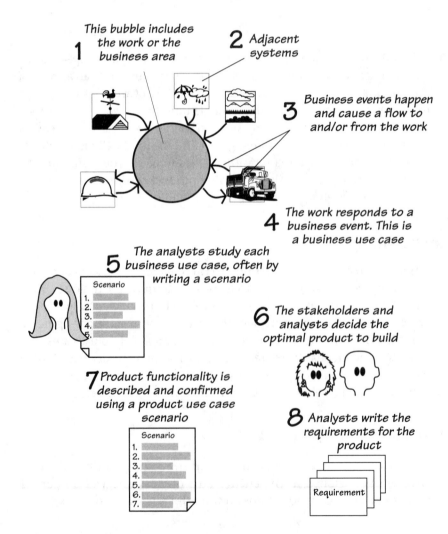

While it is necessary to understand the work, the scope of this work is likely too large to be digested in its entirety. If we attempt to treat the work as an indivisible whole, the requirements analysts and designers will fail to understand it, and the stakeholders will have little chance of explaining it to them. By finding smaller parts of the work, you have a better chance of finding stakeholders who are specialists in that part of the work and can give you a more comprehensive explanation of it. Thus the work must be partitioned into smaller pieces. For the purposes of requirements gathering, we are looking for pieces that meet the following criteria:

- They are "natural" partitions—each one makes an obvious and logical contribution to the work.
- They have minimal connectivity to other parts of the work.
- They have a clearly defined scope.
- They have rules for defining their scope.
- They have boundaries that can be observed and defined.
- They can be named using names that are recognizable to stakeholders.
- Their existence can be readily determined.
- They have one or more stakeholders who are experts for that part of the work.

Use Cases and Their Scope

The term *use case* was coined by Ivar Jacobson to describe an amount of work to be done. He chose to break the system into smaller units, as he felt that object models were not scalable. Thus, to conquer the complexity and largeness of modern systems, Jacobson said it was first necessary to partition them into convenient chunks, and that these chunks should be based on the user's view of the system.

However, Jacobson leaves us with some loose ends. For example, his definition of a use case does not indicate precisely where or how a use case starts and ends. In fact, Jacobson's definition of a use case must have left some ambiguity. Others have written about use cases—in fact, more than 40 published definitions of "use case" exist and, predictably, few of them agree. This chaos is unfortunate. Jacobson also uses the term *actor* to mean a user role, or perhaps another system, that lies outside the scope of the system. The *system* in this usage is presumed to be the automated system. This point leads to a question: How can we know the automated system before we understand the work for which it is to be used?

Think about this: If the responsibilities of the actor and the system are established at the *beginning* of the analysis process, and the requirements gathering focuses on the automated system, how could you ever understand

READING

Jacobson, Ivar, et al. *Object-Oriented Software Engineering: A Use Case Driven Approach*. Addison-Wesley, 1992.

If the responsibilities of the actor and the system are established at the beginning of the analysis process, and the requirements gathering focuses on the automated system, how will we ever understand the work the actor is doing or the work the automated product could be doing for the actor?

the work the actor is doing, or the work the automated product might be doing for the actor? Without understanding the actor's true task—which surely happens if you exclude the actor from the analysis study—you run the risk of missing opportunities for automation or automating where a non-automation would be a better solution. You also could be guilty of building products that are not as useful as they might be as well as running the risk of constructing interfaces that ultimately do not satisfy the user.

So let us instead first establish the scope of the work. This work scope must include the intended actors and the work they are doing. Once you have established a satisfactory scope for the work, you will partition it into smaller pieces. These pieces are the use cases—both business use cases and product use cases.

Let's look at how to handle this task. Keep in mind that it probably takes longer to describe each of the steps than it does to actually complete most of them.

The Work

READING

Beyer, Hugh, and Karen Holtzblatt. *Contextual Design: Defining Customer-Centered Systems.* Morgan Kaufmann, 1998. Beyer and Holtzblatt have some wonderful insights into work and ways that we should look at it. This book is highly recommended.

The work is the business activity of your client/customer. Whatever this activity is—selling shoes, controlling aircraft, administering a hospital, transmitting television signals, or any other form of activity—the automated product you intend to build is a tool that helps with the work. This product automates or streamlines some of the existing processes, or it changes the work by adding new capabilities. Either way, the product is simply a tool to help with the work. Clearly, it is imperative to understand that work.

The Context of the Work

To understand the work, you must first know how it relates to the world outside it. The work exists to provide services to the outside world. To provide those services, the work must receive information and signals from the outside world and send messages to it. This world is made up of the adjacent systems, which are the automated systems, people, departments, organizations, and other parties that place some kind of demand on, or make some kind of contribution to, your work. To locate your work in the outside world, you must be able to demonstrate its context—how the work connects to the adjacent systems. In other words, your context model shows how your work relates to its business environment.

The most convenient and useful way to show the work's connections to the outside world is to use a context diagram. Figure 4.2 provides the context diagram for the work of predicting when roads are due to freeze and scheduling trucks to treat them with de-icing material. (This diagram also appeared in

Chapter 3.) The work is surrounded by adjacent systems that are supplying data necessary for this work or receiving services and information from the work.

The work to be studied must include anything that can be affected by your product. For example, if you are building a product intended to automate part of some existing work, then the study context should include those parts of the existing work—human activities, together with any existing computer systems—that could potentially influence the eventual product. For embedded systems, there may be no human activity in your work, but the work context must include any devices that can be changed by the current development. Even if you are building an electro-mechanical device, such as an automated teller machine (ATM), and most of the human participation is outside the product boundary, your work context must still include the work that the human will be doing with the device.

> *The work to be studied must include anything that can be affected by your product.*

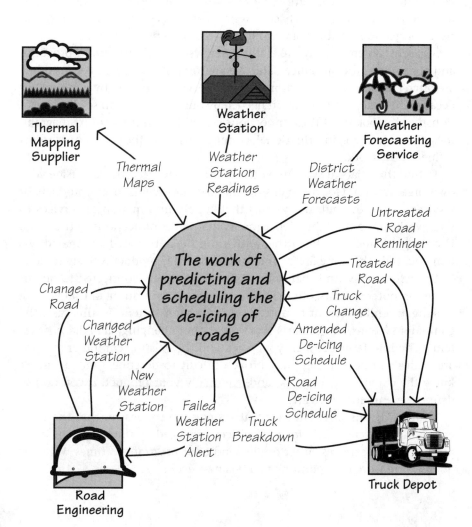

Figure 4.2

The context diagram showing the scope of the work. The central area of the diagram represents the work you are about to study. The product you eventually build becomes part of this work. The outside world is represented by the adjacent systems—*Weather Station, Truck Depot*, and so on. The named arrows represent flows of information between the adjacent systems and the work.

RULE OF THUMB

The work context includes anything that you are permitted to change, and anything that you need to understand to decide what can or should be changed.

RULE OF THUMB

The farther away from the anticipated automated system you look, the more useful and innovative your product is likely to be.

Do not be limited by what you think might be the limits of a computer system. Instead, try to find the farthest practical extent of any influence on the work.

While we are talking about the context, note the limited, but nevertheless useful, aim of the model. This model shows only the flows of information. It does not attempt to show the constraints upon the work, although these may be inferred from the model. It does not explicitly show who or what is doing the work, although these, too, might be inferred. Like most models, the context model shows a single view. In this case, by illuminating the flows of information, we are able to make better use of the model for determining the business events affecting the work. But first, let's look at one part of the context model in more detail: the outside world.

The Outside World

On the surface, the context diagram shows the work area to be studied and its informational connections to the outside world. However, this diagram bears much closer examination, particularly in the area of the adjacent systems. As noted earlier, the adjacent systems are those parts of the world that have connections to the work and have an important effect on it.

Adjacent systems behave like any other systems: They contain processes and consume and/or produce data. We are interested in them because they are often customers for the information or services provided by our work, or because they supply information needed by our work. You can see these relationships by looking at the connections established in the context diagram. It is through these informational connections that the adjacent systems influence the work.

To find the adjacent systems, you sometimes have to venture outside your own organization. Go to the customers for your organization's products or services. Go to the outside systems that supply information or services to your work. Go to the other departments that have connections to the work. Use the guideline that the farther away from the anticipated automated system you look, the more useful and innovative your product is likely to be.

You will usually find that your work is also closely connected to one or more computer systems, often within your own organization, or that you are making an enhancement to an existing computer system. In this case, the computer systems, or the parts that you are not changing, are adjacent systems. The interfaces between your work and the existing computer systems are critical. Although they may prove difficult to describe, you can never know the extent of your work, and eventually your product, if you do not define these interfaces clearly.

Think of it this way: The adjacent systems are the reason that the work exists; they are customers for the services produced by the work. The work produces these services either on demand or at prearranged times. When it does so, the work is responding to a business event.

Business Events

Any system or piece of work responds to things that happen outside it. It's that simple. For the sake of clarity, because we are discussing your customer's work or business, we shall call these happenings *business events*.

Let's look at one. Suppose you bought this book in a bookshop. You found it on the shelf, thought it was useful and interesting, and approached the cash desk. That moment, the instant you signaled your intention to buy the book, is the business event. The sales assistant responded to this business event by scanning the bar code, asking you for the cover price plus any applicable tax, perhaps asking the credit card company for authorization, ringing up the sale at the cash register, and putting the book in a bag before handing it to you. That, or something similar, is the bookshop's preplanned response to that particular business event. We call this response to the business event a *business use case*.

When you pay your credit card bill at the end of the month, it is a business event as seen from the point of view of the credit card company. The credit card company responds to this event (its business use case) by checking that your address has not changed and then recording the date and amount of your payment.

In both examples—when you commit to buy the book and when you decide to pay your monthly bill—you cause a business event to happen. The piece of work that you affect—selling books or recording payments—is a business use case, which is the work's preplanned response to the event. You do not own or control either the bookshop or the credit card company. Nevertheless, in both cases you do something to make them respond by doing some processing and manipulating some data. Think of it this way: Those pieces of work have a preplanned business use case, which is activated whenever an outside body (the adjacent system) initiates a business event. Figure 4.3 illustrates this idea.

READING

McMenamin, Steve, and John Palmer. *Essential Systems Analysis.* Yourdon Press, 1984. McMenamin and Palmer were the first authors to use events as a way of partitioning systems. Their words on the essence of the system are well worth reading.

Figure 4.3

A business event takes place outside the scope of the work. The work learns that it has happened through the arrival of an incoming flow of information. The work contains a business use case to respond to this business event.

When a business event happens, the work responds by initiating a business use case.

Note that business use cases are triggered by the arrival of an information flow—the book and your payment at the cash desk, and your payment slip and check at the credit card company—from an adjacent system. As a consequence, the responsibility for triggering the business use case lies outside the control of the work. We will return to this point shortly. First, however, let's look at another kind of business event.

Time-Triggered Business Events

Time-triggered business events are initiated by the arrival of a predetermined time (or date). For example, your insurance company sends you a renewal notice shortly before the anniversary of your policy. Your bank sends you a statement on the fifteenth day of every month (or on whatever day you have arranged to have it sent). "The arrival of a predetermined time" may also mean that a certain amount of time has elapsed since another event happened. For example, a computer operating system may check the available memory 2.4 microseconds after the last time it checked, or you may be sent a reminder that you borrowed a library book six weeks ago.

The usual response to a time-triggered business event is to produce some information and send it to an adjacent system. Consider the example depicted in Figure 4.4.

Once the predetermined time for the event arrives, the work's response is to do whatever is necessary to produce the output. This almost always involves the retrieval and manipulation of stored data. Once again, we use the response to the time-triggered business event—the business use case—as our unit of study.

Figure 4.4

A time-triggered business event happens when a prearranged time is reached. This is based on either a periodic occurrence (for example, the end of the month, or 5 P.M. each day), a fixed time interval (three hours since the last occurrence), or a certain amount of time elapsing since another business event (30 days after sending out an invoice). The normal response is to retrieve stored data and send some information to an adjacent system.

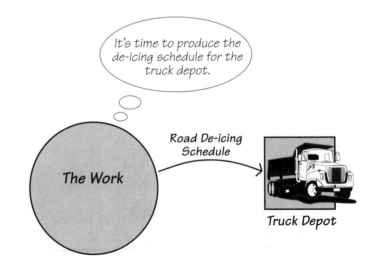

Why Business Events and Business Use Cases Are a Good Idea

We may seem to be going to a lot of trouble to describe something that may, at first glance, seem fairly obvious. But this care with the subject is certainly warranted: Our experience has amply demonstrated the value of having an objective way of partitioning the work, and the value of understanding the work itself, before plunging into the solution. The result is that we discover the real requirements, and we discover them more quickly.

You can partition your work in a nonsubjective way by identifying responses to outside stimuli. After all, that is how your customers see your business. The internal partitions, whatever they may be, hold no interest for outsiders. Similarly, the current partitioning of any system is based on technological and political decisions taken at the time the system was built. Those decisions may no longer be valid—at the very least, you should question them and avoid perpetuating them just because they are there. By looking not at the inside, but from the outside, we get a far clearer idea of the most functional way of partitioning the work.

> *By looking not at the inside, but from the outside, we get a far clearer idea of the most functional way of partitioning the work.*

A business event points out which things belong together, and as a result, delivers cohesive partitions with minimal interfaces between the pieces. This partitioning, in turn, leads to chunks of work that act as vehicles for the detailed requirements investigation. The fewer the dependencies that exist between the pieces, the more the analysts can investigate the details about one piece without needing to know anything about the others.

But perhaps the overriding reason for using business use cases is to further the investigation of what is happening at the time of the business event. In many of the texts available today, the existence of a "system" is assumed. That is, the author assumes the boundary of the automated system and begins the use case investigation by looking at the actor and the interaction with the automated system, completely ignoring the work surrounding this interaction.

To do so is dangerous and wrong. This product-centric way of looking at the problem means that you miss seeing opportunities for improving your product by branching into other parts of the work. It also discourages analysts from asking, "But why is this like it is?" This failure, in turn, leads to "technological fossils" being carried from one generation of a product to the next.

> *The product-centric way of looking at the problem means that you miss opportunities for improving your product by branching into other parts of the work. It also discourages the analyst from asking, "But why is this like it is?" This failure, in turn, leads to "technological fossils" being carried from one generation of a product to the next.*

Consider this example: "An insurance clerk receives a claim from a policy holder and then enters the claim into the automated system." This view encourages the requirements analyst to study the work of the clerk entering the details of the claim. However, if you spend a few moments looking at the real business being done here, you will see that the claim is simply the insurance company's implementation—it is the *accident* that initiates this piece of business. Why is this understanding important? If you start your business investigation at the real origin of the problem, you build a better product. For example, perhaps it would be feasible to build a product that processes the claim in real time at the scene of the accident. Think of the originator of the business event. In this case, it is the driver or owner of the vehicle. What are his aspirations or goals here? He wants to have the vehicle repaired as quickly and effortlessly as possible. His goal is *not* to fill in claim forms and wait for them to be approved.

Another example: "A caller contacts the help desk. The help desk person initiates the use case by asking the caller for details of the problem and logging the call." The use case is the logging, and the actor is the help desk person. Again, this product-centric view misses the real business event—the happening that started it all. In this case it is the initiation of the call to the help desk. Why is viewing this way important? If you think of making the call as the business event, the correct response is to log the call, use caller ID to identify the caller's equipment, retrieve information on the equipment, and provide it for the help desk person. You might also decide that the real business event is the malfunctioning of the caller's equipment. If you think of it this way, you also think of the equipment making the call for help itself. Or perhaps a better understanding of the reasons underlying the malfunction might result in your new product giving the help desk operator historical information that will facilitate him in answering the call. People often don't ask for these sorts of requirements because they are thinking only of the supposed product. It is the duty of the requirements analyst to look beyond that, which means understanding the intentions of the adjacent system when it initiates the business event.

A security system this time: "The actor receives the shipment and logs it in." Nope. The real business event is the *dispatch* of the shipment. The business use case should log the shipment from its inception and monitor its transit and arrival.

If you become too immersed in the current technology and the way the business works at the moment, it is sometimes harder to see the business events. To overcome this difficulty, we suggest an informal process for discovering them.

The requirements analyst must look past the obvious, which means understanding the true nature of the work.

Finding the Business Events

Business events are things that happen and, in turn, make the work respond in some way. They may occur outside the scope of the work or because it is time for the work to do something. In either case, a communication from the outside—represented by the adjacent systems—must let the work know that the event has happened, or a flow to the outside world must occur as the outcome of a time-triggered event. The resulting communication appears as an information flow on the context diagram.

Figure 4.2 provided the context diagram for the de-icing project. Take a look at it and note the information flows that connect the adjacent systems to the work. Some of these you have already seen when we discussed business events. For example, the flow called Changed Road is the result of the event that occurs when the Road Engineering department makes changes to a road. These personnel then advise the work of the change so that the scheduling work can update its own stored data about roads. The flow called Road De-icing Schedule is the outcome of a time-triggered business event: When it is time, the work produces a schedule of the roads to be treated and sends it to the truck depot.

Each of the flows that enters or leaves the work is the result of a business event and/or the resultant business use case. There can be no other reason for an external communication to exist. If you look at each flow, you can determine the business event or business use case that caused it. In some cases, several flows may be attached to the same business use case. For example, when the truck depot advises that a scheduled truck has broken down or will be withdrawn from service for some other reason (the input flow is Truck Breakdown), the work responds. Because one of the trucks is now out of service, the other trucks have to be rescheduled to compensate for the shortfall, and the resultant outgoing flow is the Amended De-icing Schedule.

Each of the flows that enters or leaves the work is the result of a business event.

Look at the list of events and their input and output flows shown in Table 4.1. Compare it with the work context diagram shown in Figure 4.2, and reconcile the business events with the data that flows to and/or from the work.

EVENT NAME	INPUT AND OUTPUT
1. Weather Station transmits reading	Weather Station Readings (in)
2. Weather Bureau forecasts weather	District Weather Forecasts (in)
3. Road engineers advise changed roads	Changed Road (in)
4. Road Engineering installs new weather station	New Weather Station (in)
5. Road Engineering changes weather station	Changed Weather Station (in)
6. Time to test Weather Stations	Failed Weather Station Alert (out)
7. Truck Depot changes a truck	Truck Change (in)
8. Time to detect icy roads	Road De-icing Schedule (out)
9. Truck treats a road	Treated Road (in)
10. Truck Depot reports problem with truck	Truck Breakdown (in) Amended De-icing Schedule (out)
11. Time to monitor road de-icing	Untreated Road Reminder (out)

Table 4.1

Business Events and Their Associated Input and Output Flows for the Road De-icing Work

READING

Robertson, James, and Suzanne Robertson. *Complete Systems Analysis: The Workbook, the Textbook, the Answers.* Dorset House, 1998.

Admittedly, you need some knowledge of the work to figure out the business events. To this end we advise you to start the process of determining business events during blastoff, when the key stakeholders are present. In most situations, you will find the business events are known to the stakeholders; in general, they can be observed when you look at the work.

Each flow in the context diagram is attached to a business event, but it is the work's *response* to the event that is of interest to the requirements analyst. Let's investigate that topic next.

Business Use Cases

The business use case is the most convenient unit of work to study.

For every business event, there is a preplanned response to it, known as a *business use case.* The business use case is always a collection of identifiable processes, data that is retrieved and/or stored, output generated, messages sent, or some combination of these. In other words, the business use case is a unit of functionality. This unit is the basis for writing the functional and nonfunctional requirements (we will talk about these requirements in more detail in Chapters 7 and 8).

You can identify one or more stakeholders who are expert in each business use case.

You can readily isolate the work of a business use case, because it has almost no connections to other business use cases. As a consequence, different analysts can investigate different parts of the work without the need for constant communication between them. In fact, the only overlap between business use cases is their stored data. The relative isolation of each business use case means you can identify one or more stakeholders who are expert in that part of the work, and they (with your help) can describe it precisely and in detail. They describe both the normal cases, where everything goes according to plan, and the exceptional cases, where almost nothing goes to plan. You can also observe the business use case. After all, business events are known to the stakeholders, and they can show you how the organization responds to any of them. For example, it would not be hard to find someone in your favorite bookshop who can take you through the process of selling a book, or someone in your insurance company who can show you how they process a claim. We discuss trawling techniques for this kind of investigation in Chapter 5.

The processing for a business use case is continuous. That is, once it is triggered, it processes everything until there is nothing left to do that can logically be done at that time. All the functionality has been carried out, all the data to be stored by the business use case has been written to the data stores, and all the adjacent systems have been notified. You can see an example of this processing in Figure 4.5.

The requirements for the product you are specifying contribute to the work done by the business use case. Your product does not change the real nature of the work; it just changes the way it is done. But before you can

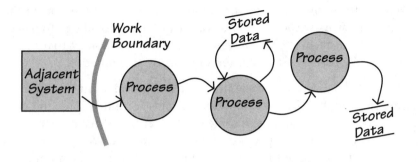

Figure 4.5

The work's response to the business event is to continue processing until all active tasks (the processes) have been completed and all data retrieved or stored. You can think of the response as a chain of processes and their associated stored data. Note that the processes are surrounded by a combination of data stores and adjacent systems.

design the optimal product, you must understand the work it supports. Most importantly, you must understand your client's desired outcome of the work. So for the moment, forget the details and technicalities of the business use case, and instead look outside the organization to see what kind of response is needed, or wanted, by the organization's customers and suppliers.

Let's start our look outside the organization by examining the systems that are adjacent to the work that you are studying.

The Role of Adjacent Systems

The adjacent systems are those pieces of work that supply your work with information or that receive information and services from your work. An adjacent system might be an organization, an individual, a computer system or some other piece of technology, or a combination of any of these. It is also the customer for the business use case. Examine the adjacent system and consider what it really wants from that business use case. Perhaps the adjacent system may want to do more than passively supply information to, or receive a service from, the work. Consider the type of service or information your organization would provide if the adjacent system participates in some of the activities that make up the business use case.

An adjacent system might be an organization, an individual, a computer system or some other piece of technology, or a combination of any of these.

For example, when an adjacent system initiates a business event, what possibilities do you have to involve that adjacent system more closely in your business?

The intentions of the adjacent system may be disguised by the technological limitations of the products currently in use by the work.

- What are the technological capabilities of the adjacent system? Is it capable of interacting with the product? Is it human? Does it have some interactive technological capability? Could it use, say, a mobile phone or a text message to initiate the business event?

- What is the desired outcome from the point of view of the adjacent system? What are its aspirations at the time of triggering the business event? Keep in mind that the intentions of the adjacent system may be disguised by the technological limitations of the products that are currently in use by the work.

What is the desired outcome from the point of view of the work? What is it that the work wishes to provide or is capable of providing? To meet this demand satisfactorily, you have to ignore the technology that the work used in the past as well as current organizational limitations.

We are trying to discover the intentions of the adjacent system when it started the event. What outcome does it have in mind? Does the current work scope place restrictions or some burden on the adjacent system? If the adjacent system is a customer of the work, how can the work provide a better service when it responds to this event? Does the adjacent system want to participate in the business use case by performing some of the work or by exerting more control over the work? If you could get inside the brain of the adjacent system, what would you find?

The scope of the product you build—that is, the functionality you include in the product—is largely shaped by the adjacent systems. We need to understand the adjacent systems and their potential role in the work. Let's look more closely at the characteristics and capabilities of adjacent systems, by categorizing them.

Active Adjacent Systems

Active adjacent systems behave dynamically. They can interact with or participate in the work because they are usually humans. When they initiate events, they have some objective in mind. They can collaborate with the work or the product by exchanging data, responding to questions, indicating choices, and providing other signals, until their objective is satisfied. Figure 4.6 shows an example of an active adjacent system—a bank customer interacting with the bank

In this example, an active adjacent system interacts with the work. This interaction can occur face to face, by telephone, with an automated teller machine, or over the Internet. For the moment, let's ignore the technology being used. Instead, let's look a little more closely at the nature of the active adjacent system:

RULE OF THUMB

Active adjacent systems are humans. They initiate business events with an objective in mind.

- You (the requirements analyst or product designer) can predict the adjacent system's behavior within reason.

- You can expect the adjacent system to respond to signals from your work. As long as there is some perceived benefit to the adjacent system, it will obey (more or less) instructions from the work. For example, if a person is checking in for a flight, he is likely to respond correctly about bags and seat allocations.

- The adjacent system will respond in a suitably short time. It is reasonable to say that the adjacent system will act promptly so as not to delay the transaction any more than necessary.

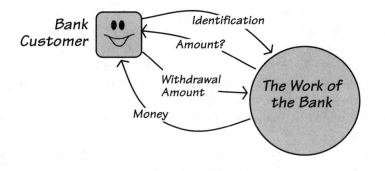

Figure 4.6

An active adjacent system interacting with a bank. The bank customer initiates a business event, and then supplies information or does whatever is needed until he achieves the desired outcome. In this instance, the business use case is everything the bank does when a customer wants to withdraw money from his account. The precise nature of the flows between the work and the adjacent system depend on the technology used by the bank.

What can we make of that list? First, because the active adjacent system can interface directly with your work, you should consider it to be part of the work, not just an inert outside body. Of course, you must understand the desires and motivations of the active adjacent system. This knowledge always opens up a rich area of product innovation.

As an example, let's consider a bank customer using an automated teller machine. Don't think of the ATM as an automated product, but rather as the boundary of the bank's work. The customer is currently outside the work. Now imagine that this bank customer—the adjacent system—is a woman taking a lunch break from her office. She approaches your ATM. But what does she really want when she goes to the ATM? Just cash? To see her balance? If that is all you are prepared to give her, then you may fall sadly short of the mark.

Get inside the brain of the adjacent system. Why does the bank customer want the cash? Does she intend to pay her electricity bill on the way back to her office? If so, why not offer her the opportunity to pay it at your ATM— or to top up her phone card, or to buy a bus/train ticket? Does the customer want the cash to buy something? Then why not extend the ATM card to act as a debit card in retail outlets so she doesn't have to go to the ATM in the first place? Does the customer just want to look at her account balance? Why not give her the facility to do so on her mobile phone?

While we are looking into the brain of this lady, what else does she want? Does she want the bank to identify each cash withdrawal so that her monthly statement tells her which members of her family made each of the withdrawals? Does she want a limit on withdrawals made by her children? Does she want to go to an ATM at all? Would she rather handle most of these tasks at home— or while she is shopping at the supermarket, or, more pleasantly, at a café?

Note that, for the purposes of understanding the business, we are ignoring the technology currently being used. While this omission may seem cavalier, it is only by taking a view that ignores current technology and its limitations that we become able to see the opportunities for providing products closer to the innermost needs and wants of our customers.

Consider whether you can change the scope of your work to provide a better service to the adjacent system. Does allowing the adjacent system to participate in the work mean that it will receive a greater benefit from your work?

For example, business event number 10 in the list of business events given in Table 4.1 is called "Truck Depot reports problem with truck." From time to time, trucks salting the road break down, slide off the road, or somehow get into a situation where they cannot complete the treatment of their allocated roads. They then radio the depot, and the supervisor tells the de-icing work. The work responds by rescheduling trucks so as to disperse the broken truck's allocation among the remainder of the fleet. Seems straightforward enough (see Figure 4.7) .

The aim of getting into the brain of the adjacent system is to produce a better product.

Let's look more closely at the adjacent system to see what is going on. The supervisor has, like many automated system users, been using the existing de-icing product in a way not intended by its builders. The original designer of the product reasoned that trucks would break down when they were in active duty, but not while they were parked in the garage. The supervisor is using business use case 10, "Truck Depot reports problem with truck," not only to handle breakdowns, but also to take trucks out of service for maintenance. This causes the supervisor a certain amount of inconvenience. However because it is the only way he can prevent his trucks from being scheduled so that he can maintain them, he puts up with it.

Why did this happen? No one looked closely enough at the work of this adjacent system when the original requirements were gathered. By scrutinizing this adjacent system more rigorously, you learn more about its needs: You learn that the supervisor needs to schedule truck maintenance. At first glance, this need appears to call for the definition of a new business event, "Supervisor withdraws a truck for maintenance." However, you should consider whether the product itself could do that. Given that the product has data about each truck's activity, it should be straightforward enough for it to schedule their maintenance via a temporal event, called something like "Time to withdraw trucks for scheduled maintenance."

The result of getting into the brain of the adjacent system is a product that fulfills more of the requirements that exist in the world surrounding it—in other words, a better, more useful product.

Figure 4.7

Business events are initiated by the truck depots. Because they wish to be more closely involved with the product, we can make the supervisors into active adjacent systems. This choice will probably result in part of the automated product being located in the truck depots so that the supervisors can have direct interaction with it.

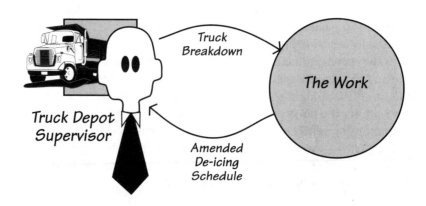

Autonomous Adjacent Systems

An autonomous adjacent system is some external body, such as another company, a government department, or a customer who is not directly interacting with your work. It acts independently of, or unconstrained by, the work being studied, but has connections to it. Autonomous adjacent systems communicate through one-way data flows.

For example, when your credit card company sends you a monthly statement, you (the card holder) act as an autonomous adjacent system. When you receive your paper statement, you have no interaction with the credit card company: You are acting as a sink for the information your card company sends you. You make no immediate response to the statement: You wait until such time as it is convenient for you to pay the bill. Thus you are acting independently or autonomously as seen from the viewpoint of the work of the credit card company.

Similarly, when you do eventually pay your credit card bill, you are again an autonomous adjacent system from the point of view of the work of the credit card company. You send your check by post, and you have no expectations about participating in the response the work makes upon the arrival of your check.

Another example of an autonomous adjacent system is a weather station that sends a reading to the work of predicting and scheduling the de-icing of roads (see Figure 4.8). The weather stations are programmed to transmit readings of the air and road-surface temperatures and moisture content periodically. The business event happens when the weather station decides it will transmit a reading. In response to this event, the business use case records the time and values of the reading. The transmission is one way: No signal is sent back to the weather station in acknowledgment, nor does it interact with the work. Thus the weather station acts autonomously from the work.

Autonomous adjacent systems use a one-way communication, either because of their technology or because of their preference. However, be careful

RULE OF THUMB

An autonomous adjacent system sends and/or receives a one-way data flow to or from the work.

Figure 4.8

When a weather station transmits information, its readings arrive as a complete packet of data. The work accepts this data and processes it according to a preplanned policy. The work does not interact with the weather station—there is no reason to do so. Indeed, it is not possible for the weather station and the work to have any kind of interaction.

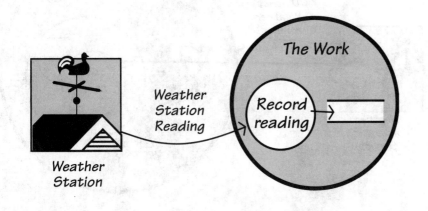

Weather Station

Weather Station Reading

The Work

Record reading

Weather Station

to determine that this mode of communication really is the choice of the adjacent system, not a result of your own business's past technological decisions. If an autonomous system is your customer, then it may well prefer to be connected directly to your product—in other words, become an active adjacent system—and not deal remotely.

When considering the nature of adjacent systems, bear in mind that the same physical entity can be any of several different types at different times. For example, when you send a check to pay a bill, you are autonomous; in contrast, when you go to that business in person and make an inquiry, phone it, or interact with it over the Internet, you are an active adjacent system.

Let's look at another example of a business event involving an autonomous adjacent system, as shown in Figure 4.9. The Weather Forecasting Service sends the District Weather Forecasts by fax. When we ask the service, we find that it cannot, or will not, send the data to the work any other way. Thus its one-way transmission of data makes the service an autonomous system. Faxes are not a suitable medium for any automated product to utilize directly, so we must employ clerks to act as interpreters of the faxes and enter the weather data into the IceBreaker product. Thus the only available boundary for our product is one that interfaces with the clerks rather than with the autonomous Weather Forecasting Service.

An autonomous adjacent system does not involve itself in the response to the business events that it triggers. Similarly, when it acts as the receiver of the output of a business use case, such as a report or invoice, then it is a passive receiver of the output and makes no attempt to respond immediately.

While it appears there are few opportunities to involve autonomous adjacent systems in the work, you must be certain the adjacent system actually *chooses* to be autonomous, and is not forced to be so by your work's technology. For

Figure 4.9

The autonomous adjacent system uses a transmission medium that makes it impractical for the product to receive it directly. We must therefore install some other process—in this case, a human clerk—to manually transcribe the data for the product.

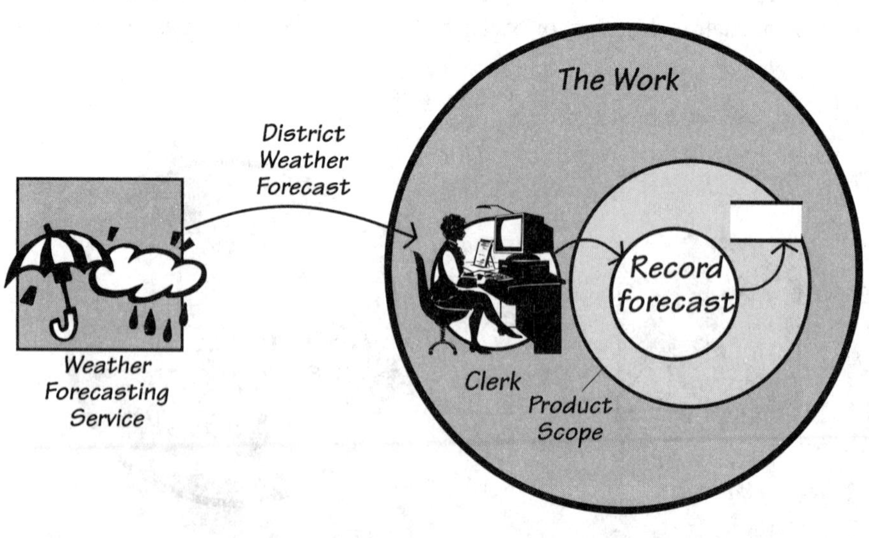

example, our bank forces us to fill in forms whenever we need a new service from it. That makes us, as customers, autonomous. We would much prefer to initiate any appropriate business use case with some direct interaction—telephone, the Internet, or face-to-face meeting—and thereby give the bank the information it needs. That way, the bank could make use of the information it already holds about us, and not ask us to fill in yet again our name, address, account number, and so on.

There are many opportunities to make better products by involving the adjacent systems. We will revisit this idea in Chapter 5, Trawling for Requirements. For the moment, simply note that you must be familiar enough with the autonomous adjacent system that you understand precisely the desired interface between it and the work. If there is no real desire for, or limitation to, one-way communication, then take the opportunity to expand the scope of the product to involve the adjacent system in the work.

Cooperative Adjacent Systems

Cooperative adjacent systems can be relied on to behave predictably when called upon. They cooperate with the work during the course of a business use case. This is almost always done by means of a simple request–response dialog. A cooperative adjacent system might be another automated product containing a database that is accessed or written to by the work, an operating system, or any other system that provides a predictable and immediate service to the work.

RULE OF THUMB
Cooperative adjacent systems are computerized.

An example of a cooperative adjacent system: The Thermal Mapping Supplier provides data used by the de-icing prediction work. In particular, this data is used by the business use case that schedules the trucks to treat the roads. The Thermal Mapping Supplier has the needed data on a database, and it allows the IceBreaker product to access that information. Because the data is fairly volatile, it makes good sense to retrieve current data when it is needed, rather than IceBreaker maintaining its own version of it. We could summarize this situation rather neatly: The product has on-demand access to the Thermal Mapping Database.

This situation involving a cooperative adjacent system is shown in Figure 4.10. When the ice prediction work asks for data from the database, the adjacent system responds with the requested data in an agreed-upon and timely manner. Thus the cooperative adjacent system receives a single input, the district for which it wants the thermal conditions, and produces a single output in response. The response is quick enough that the requesting product is prepared to wait for it.

This immediate and predictable response means that you can think of the cooperative adjacent system as conceptually part of the business use case. In our example, it forms part of the business use case responding to business event 8, "Time to predict icy roads." The processing of the business use case

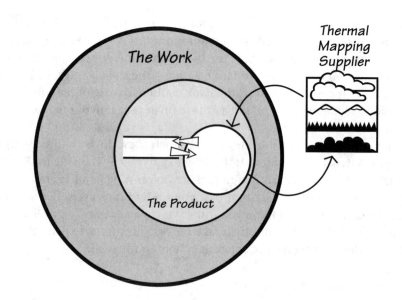

Figure 4.10

An adjacent system maintaining the Thermal Mapping Database is not owned by the de-icing business, but rather is the responsibility of another party. However, the de-icing system may access the data; when it does, it expects to get data quickly.

does not stop when it reaches the adjacent system, as would normally occur with other kinds of adjacent systems; instead, it continues until the desired outcome of the business use case has been reached. For the sake of convenience, we generally include it in our models of the business use case, as illustrated in Figure 4.11.

It is unlikely that you will need—or want—to change the interfaces with the cooperative system. Cooperative systems are black boxes, their services are stable, and there is rarely much to be gained from trying to change them. The only reason to change them is if your product needs a different service or data.

Business Use Cases and Product Use Cases

We have stressed the importance of understanding the work, not just the product. By looking at the larger scope of the work, you ask more questions about the business requirements and build a better product. The following example

Figure 4.11

The processing for a business use case does not stop when it involves a cooperative adjacent system. Even though the adjacent system is outside the scope of the work, it can be considered part of the work due to its ability to respond immediately. The double arrow indicates a special type of adjacent system, in which the data flow "passes through" the adjacent system. This kind of adjacent system does not initiate events, nor does it act as an external sink for information flows.

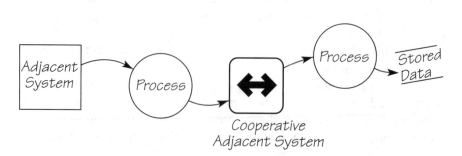

comes from a recent consulting assignment: "The product is to rip a CD into MP3 or some other digital format." When the engineers looked at the technical part of the product (they are engineers, after all), they saw a use case that was triggered by the insertion of the CD and then went on to rip the CD.

However, when we stand back and look at the wider context of the real business being done here—the business use case—we see something else. What is the end user trying to accomplish? What are his aspirations and desired outcomes? We define them as "getting the music from the CD into an MP3 player." Thus the real question is not about the technicalities of ripping CDs and converting to MP3 format, but the remainder of the true business.

For example, the end user wants the track names to appear on his MP3 player. So, when the CD is inserted, one of the early functions of the business use case must be to add the track names—presumably via an automated process that would use the Gracenote database or something similar—and to add the album cover art—again, presumably from one of the many sources on the Internet. Once that operation is complete, the business use case continues by allowing the user to change the order of tracks, delete unwanted ones, and make any other organizational changes to the music.

So what do we have? At the outset, we have the scope of the work being studied. This scope is bounded by the communications with the adjacent systems that surround the work. Business events happen in the adjacent systems when they decide they want some information or service from the work, or they want to send some information to the work. Once the business event has happened and the resulting data flow has reached the work, the work responds. This response constitutes the business use case.

Study the business use case, considering what the work does and what the adjacent system desires or needs. In other words, consider whether the organization is making the correct response to the adjacent system. We will have more to say about how to investigate and understand the work in Chapter 5, where we discuss trawling for requirements, and in Chapter 6, where we present scenarios as a way of documenting your understanding.

Once you understand the correct work of the business use case, determine the scope of the product for that business use case. As part of this effort, consider whether the adjacent system is capable (or desirous) of making a different contribution to the work than it currently does. Do not assume the responsibilities of the product and the adjacent systems at the beginning of the project; instead, derive them from an understanding of the work and from what the external customer considers to be a useful product.

The part of the response handled by the proposed automated system is a product use case. But note how we got to this point: The product use case is simply a part of the business use case, and we found it by examining what the work is and how the work responds to outside demands. The involvement and intentions of the adjacent systems determine—or at least strongly influence—the role the product plays in the work's response.

Figure 4.12

The business event is either some happening or a decision taken by the adjacent system. The resulting information flow notifies the *work* of the event and triggers a response (the *business use case*). After study, the requirements analysts and the interested stakeholders decide how much of the business use case is to be handled by the proposed product (the *product use case*). Whatever is immediately outside the scope of the product becomes the *actor,* who manipulates the functionality of the product use case within the product.

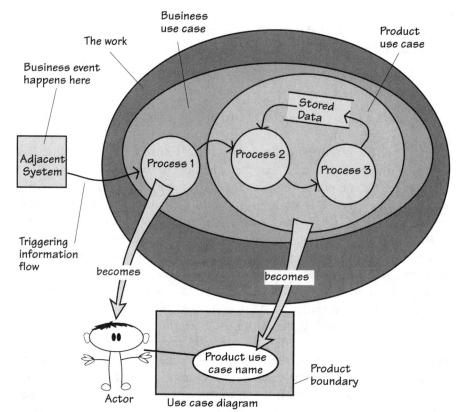

Thus the product use cases are derived from the business events that are the driving force of the work. This relationship is shown graphically in Figure 4.12.

Sometimes, for technical reasons, you might choose to implement a business use case with a number of product use cases. Perhaps you wish to subdivide the work inside the computer into smaller pieces. Or perhaps you have the opportunity to reuse product use cases that have previously been developed for other parts of the product or for other products.

When you are looking to reuse product use cases, keep in mind that linking constructs called <<include>> and <<extend>> are available for this purpose. These constructs are similar enough not to bother with the distinction between them here. What they mean is that one product use case can make use of the functionality of another product use case.

The selection of product use cases is somewhat driven by technical considerations. If the product is to be recognizable and usable by its intended users, however, then the product use cases must be based on the original business events and business use cases.

When you determine the product use cases, you are also selecting the actors who interact with the product.

Actors

Actors are the people or systems that interact with the automated product. In some cases, the actors are adjacent systems that are outside the work or organization that owns the product—for example, the organization's customers. In other cases, you appoint actors from inside the organization, as the adjacent systems. Figure 4.13 shows the product use cases that were selected for the IceBreaker product as well as the actors that operate each of the product use cases.

You can take advantage of the product use cases in many ways:

● They provide a vehicle for discovering and clustering groups of related requirements.

● You can use the product use cases to plan implementation versions.

Figure 4.13

The use case diagram for the IceBreaker product, including the product use cases, the actors involved in each product use case, and the product's boundary. An active actor is represented as a stick figure (you can draw these any way you like). Autonomous actors are shown as houses, and the cooperative one as a rounded square with two-way arrows.

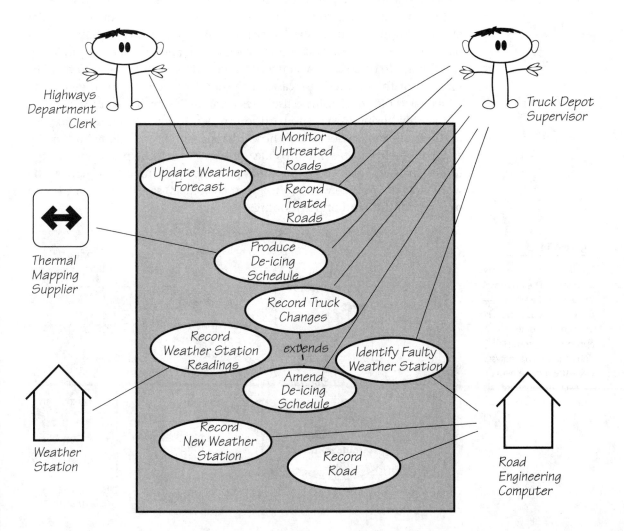

- Testers may use product use cases as input when writing test cases.
- A product use case provides a business-related basis for building simulations and prototypes.
- It is easier to deal with changes because the product use case can be traced back to the business use case and hence the business event.

Summary

Business events and business use cases allow us to carve out a cohesive piece of the work for further modeling and study. By first understanding the effect each of the adjacent systems has on the work, we can come to understand the optimal product to build for that work. We arrive at the product scope by understanding the work in its context, not by presupposing that there will be a user and a computer, or by slavishly following the existing technology.

In some situations, you may not have any idea of the product scope. For example, suppose you are specifying business requirements so that an external supplier or outsourcer can come back to you and describe the product it can supply. To do so, you would write a scenario and then the requirements for each of the business use cases. The supplier would, in turn, determine which parts of those business use cases it can deliver as product use cases.

By using business events to partition the work, you take an external view of the work. You do not rely on how it happens to be partitioned internally at the moment or on someone's idea of how it might be partitioned in the future. Instead, you partition according to the most important view of the work: how the outside world (often your customers) sees it. Figure 4.14 is an overview of this kind of partitioning.

Figure 4.14

The flow of requirements gathering. The response to each business event—the business use case—is examined and an appropriate product determined. The analysts write the requirements for each product use case.

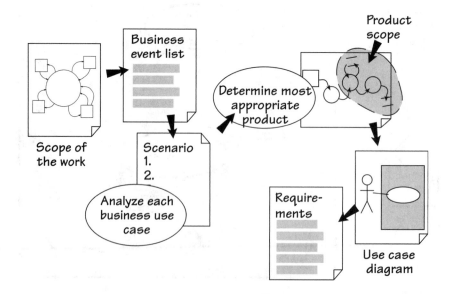

The idea of deriving the use cases from the business events means your requirements are grouped according to how the work responds to the business event. As a consequence, *all* of the response is part of the business use case, regardless of where in the work it happens to be partitioned at the moment. The result is a natural partitioning of the work. The actors are chosen as an outcome of this partitioning, with the end result being a work area and eventually a product that are more responsive to the outside world.

Trawling for Requirements

in which we drag the net through the work area looking for requirements, and discuss some useful techniques for doing so

The term *trawling* comes from our partner Steve McMenamin (a source of many useful and descriptive images). We use it because it evokes the nature of what we are doing here: fishing. Not idly dangling a line while hoping a fish might come by, but rather methodically running a net through the work to catch every possible requirement. With a little experience and good techniques, the skipper of a trawler knows where to fish so that he gets the fish he wants, and not the ones that he doesn't.

This chapter explores the techniques for discovering and determining both the requirements and the people involved in the process. You have two major concerns here: finding all of the requirements and finding the correct requirements. This means, inevitably, you need a variety of techniques so as to find the ones most applicable to the stakeholders who are providing the requirements.

> *Requirements don't litter the landscape out at the customer site.*
>
> Source: Beyer and Holtzblatt, *Contextual Design*

Agility Guide

Let's start with a fundamental truth: Requirements come from people. Your task as a requirements analyst is to talk to people, understand them, listen to what they say, hear what they don't say, and understand what they need. Most of the time you learn requirements from people at work. Here's another fundamental truth: Requirements are not solutions. You need to learn the requirement before you can find the solution. It just won't work the other way round.

One of the cornerstones of agility is the idea of not doing more than you have to. This chapter does not present a prescription or process for determining the requirements. Instead, you are invited to read about the techniques, along with our suggestions on when and how they are used, and determine for yourself what is most appropriate for your stakeholders and your particular project.

Rabbit projects need to be very aware of the section on essence. It deals with separating the idea for an implementation from the real requirements. Too often we see developers rushing for their keyboards as soon as they see the first glimmer of a solution. When you understand the essence of what is being said, your solutions will be far more appropriate, and usually more elegant. The section on electronic requirements is also central to rabbit projects.

Horse projects, due to their larger number of stakeholders, will probably make more extensive use of apprenticing, interviewing, and use case workshops. These techniques give rise to better documentation—in particular, the scenarios that usually emerge from use case workshops.

Elephant projects, due to their larger number of stakeholders, have a need to document their findings as they go about trawling for their requirements. Because of the more extensive set of possibilities for elephant projects, we suggest that you read all of this chapter, paying special attention to the owl recommendations.

Responsibility

The requirements analyst and the users collaborate to gather the requirements.

Trawling is instigated by the requirements analyst. But the analyst does not work alone: Users and other stakeholders collaborate to gather the requirements, as shown in Figure 5.1.

We build products to help us do work. For our purposes, it doesn't matter whether the work is processing insurance claims, analyzing blood samples, designing automotive parts, predicting when ice will form on roads, keeping track of a "things to do" list, controlling a telephone network, downloading music or podcasts, monitoring a household, or one of many other human activities. There are things to do and data to store, and, for one reason or another, you have been asked to build a product that helps with this work.

So let's look at how we go about gathering requirements.

The Requirements Analyst

The analyst is a translator: He has to understand what both the users and the other stakeholders are saying about the work, and then translate that knowledge into requirements for a product. But there is more to it. The requirements analyst acts as a catalyst, injecting something new into the work. In other words, the requirements are not simply the passive interpretation of an existing piece of work, but rather contain inventions that will make the work easier, better, more interesting and more pleasant. Along the way, the requirements analyst must fill several roles:

- *Observe and learn the work, and understand it from the point of view of the user.* As you work with your users, you study their work and question them about what they are doing, and why they are doing it. Each piece of information you hear is treated at several levels simultaneously.

- *Interpret the work.* A user's description of some work should be treated as factual. After all, the user is the expert on that part of the work. However, the analyst must filter the description to strip away the current technology and thereby reveal the essence of the work, not its incarnation.

- *Invent better ways to do the work.* Once the requirements analyst sees the essence, he interprets what the product must do to satisfy that part of the work. At the same time, in conjunction with other stakeholders, he derives a product to improve the work.

- *Record the results in the form of a stakeholder-understandable requirements specification and analysis models.* The analyst must ensure that he and the stakeholders have the same understanding of the product, and stakeholders agree this is the needed product.

Not so easy as it first appears.

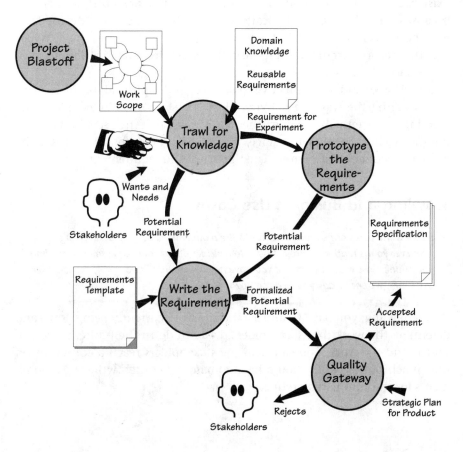

Figure 5.1

The trawling activity is central to the requirements process. It uses the outputs of the project blastoff activity as its starting point for collecting the requirements from the stakeholders. Prototyping runs as a parallel activity. Note that the requirements gathered at this stage are *potential requirements;* they still have to be tested by the Quality Gateway.

This is a long chapter—there is a lot to know about trawling—and we know that not all trawling techniques are applicable to all projects. The owl gives you guidance on whether the technique is applicable to your situation. By all means, read this entire chapter—but realize that you don't need to.

Conscious requirements *are those requirements that are uppermost in the stakeholders' minds; they are often symptomatic of something that the stakeholders want to improve.*
Unconscious requirements *are those that the stakeholders often fail to mention because they know so much about them, and assume everyone else has the same knowledge.*
Undreamed-of requirements *are things that are useful, but the stakeholders don't realize are possible.*

Several techniques are available to help with the task of trawling for requirements. As is the case with any technique, no single one works all the time, so your task is to select the technique that best fits the situation. In our discussions of the techniques, we indicate when and why one would be useful. But don't just take our word for it—try to connect each technique to your own situation, and consider where and when each would be most advantageous.

Consider your stakeholders. They are very conscious of some requirements and bring them up early. Other requirements are "unconscious" requirements—things that are so ingrained into the stakeholders' work that they have forgotten they exist. The techniques that capture the conscious requirements may not necessarily work for the unconscious ones. Then there are the "undreamed-of" requirements—those functions and features the stakeholders are unaware they could have. Undreamed-of requirements exist because the stakeholders do not realize they are possible, perhaps because of a lack of technological sophistication, or perhaps because they have never seen their work in the way that you will show it to them. Whatever the reason, part of your responsibility is to bring these requirements to the surface.

It is cheaper and more effective to uncover and capture all of the requirements during the trawling activity. Those that are not discovered during trawling will eventually be unearthed, probably when the users start operating the product. At the latter stage, it is much more expensive to make the changes necessary to accommodate the newfound requirements.

Trawling and Business Use Cases

Business use cases are so fundamental to the requirements activity that we urge you, whatever your situation or project type, to consider doing your requirements trawling one business use case at a time. If you have not already read Chapter 4, Event-Driven Use Cases, we encourage you to do so now.

When trawling, you have to understand the work currently being done, and determine the work that stakeholders desire to do in the future. Once you understand the work, you can help the stakeholders reach a consensus on how much of that work should be automated. You then write the requirements for the automated product.

The trawling activity uses outputs from the project blastoff activity. The blastoff determines the scope of the work, the goals of the project, and the constraints that apply to any solution. It also identifies the stakeholders involved in the project and the potential users. Naturally, you need to know whom to interview and study to get an understanding of the work.

From the work context diagram, you determine the business events and the resulting business use cases. In Chapter 4, we discussed business events, exploring how happenings outside the work cause a response inside the work. This response is a business use case, and we suggest that you do your requirements analysis one business use case at a time.

The business use case is what the work does in response to a business event. Note that we remain concerned with the work for now, so we are not thinking about the product yet. From the moment the triggering data flow enters the work, the functionality within the work starts to process it. If the triggering data flow arrives via a telephone call, then a person might be there to answer it. Alternatively, an automated telephone system might prompt the caller to identify the nature of the call. But it doesn't matter what or who does it; what matters is *what* is done. This functionality is what you study when trawling, as is illustrated in Figure 5.2.

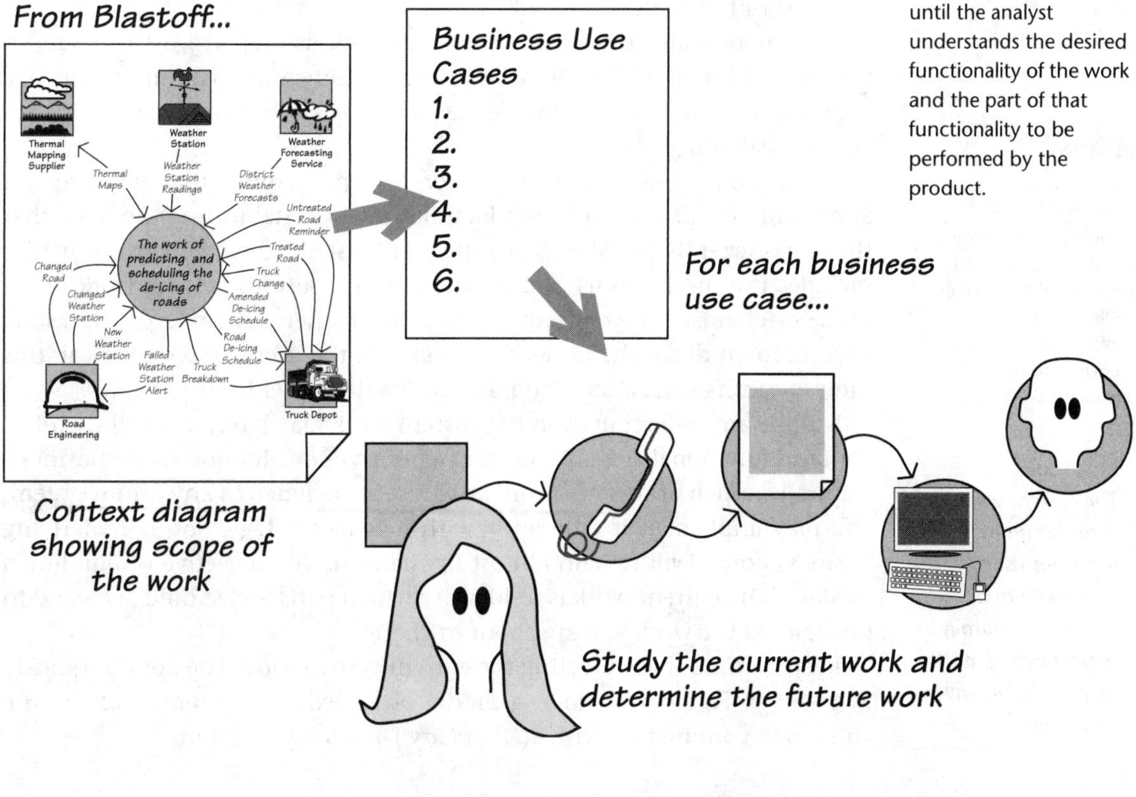

Figure 5.2

Business events are determined using the flows from the adjacent systems on the context diagram. The business use cases are the work's responses to the business events. These are studied until the analyst understands the desired functionality of the work and the part of that functionality to be performed by the product.

From Blastoff...

Context diagram showing scope of the work

Business Use Cases
1.
2.
3.
4.
5.
6.

For each business use case...

Study the current work and determine the future work

The trawling activity entails both a study of the work and improvements to that work. Reflecting this dual nature, you write the requirements for the product once you have achieved a consensus on what the product is to do. Let's look at the trawling techniques available to the requirements analyst.

The Role of the Current Situation

This trawling activity is best done when you need to understand a medium to large work area for which no documentation exists. Moreover, the individual users currently doing the work struggle to give you an idea of how it all fits together.

We have mentioned several times—and probably will several times more—the need to understand the work. This is best done not by being a passive onlooker, but by being actively involved in modeling the work.

You can use models to help you understand the work but, paradoxically, you can't build a model without understanding the work. This paradox follows from the way the modeling activity leads you to ask all the right questions. Models are *working* models, so if your model is not working, you haven't asked enough questions to get enough right answers. By asking the questions prompted by the model, you discover more information and use your new knowledge to refine the model so it reflects your growing understanding of the work.

Your models also record the work and demonstrate, at least to yourself, your understanding of it. Because the model serves as a common language between you and your stakeholders, you can agree that you have the identical understanding of the work.

When you model the current work, keep in mind that you are not attempting to specify a new product, but merely establishing the work that the users currently do. Most likely the users describe their work in a way that includes the mechanisms and technology they use to get the work done. These mechanisms are not requirements for the new system—you must look beyond them to see the underlying policy of the users' system. We call this inner meaning the essence, and discuss it a little later in this chapter.

Despite any bad reputation the current work may have, it is still useful: It contains functionality that is making a positive contribution to the business. Naturally, much of this functionality must be included in any future system. You may implement it differently with new technology, but its underlying business policy will remain almost unchanged. The objective of building a model of the current work is to identify which parts you should keep and to understand the work you are about to change.

Keep in mind that modeling the current system should be done as quickly as possible. Figure 5.3 shows a model of an existing system, built by the authors in conjunction with staff at City University, London.

READING

Robertson, James, and Suzanne Robertson. *Complete Systems Analysis: The Workbook, the Textbook, the Answers.* Dorset House, 1998. This book demonstrates how to build models of current, future, and imaginary work.

The current work contains many functions that contribute to the business. Naturally, these functions must be included in any future work.

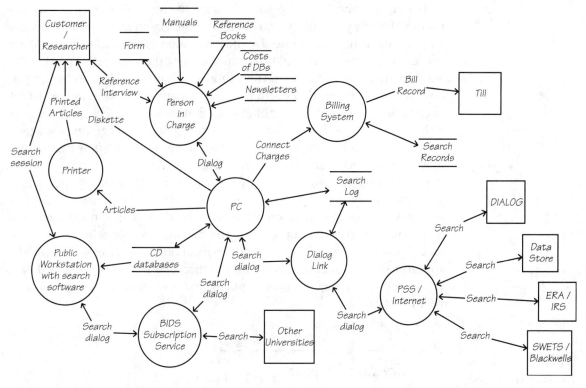

Figure 5.3

City University researchers' process for interrogating commercial databases. This model was built by the authors working with the user of the process. As the user described the work, the authors modeled and demonstrated their understanding. The model took about 15 minutes to complete. This model uses conventional data flow notation. Most process models would do the job equally well, so use whichever model you are most familiar with.

Restrict the amount of detail you include in your models of the current system. There is little point in modeling every tiny facet of something you are about to replace. The ideal model contains enough detail to give you an understanding of the work, and no more. The detail shown in Figure 5.3 is about right. That is, it shows the major parts of the current situation. It allows the user to verify that it is a correct representation of the work that he does, and it gives the requirements analyst places to make further inquiries.

One aspect of the model that should not be restricted is the area of the work covered by the model. Here it is almost—and we stress "almost"—a case of "the more, the merrier." Your models should cover all the work that could possibly be relevant to your product, those parts of the business that could contribute to the new product, and those parts where operational problems have popped up in the past. The other areas worth covering are those where the business is not well understood.

The point of having a large scope for models of the current work is that requirements analysis is really work reengineering. You specify products to improve work; the more of the work you study, the more opportunities to improve things emerge. The greater the scope of your study, the better your understanding and the better your chance of finding areas that will benefit from improvement.

The current model is also used to confirm the work scope. During the project blastoff, you and the stakeholders built a context model to show the scope of the work you intended to study. Any models you build while looking at the current situation should confirm that all of the appropriate parts of the work are included in the context, as shown in Figure 5.4. If at this stage you discover areas that would benefit from your attention, parts of the work that need to be understood, or anything at all that should be included, then now is the time to adjust the context. Such a revision does entail getting the agreement of the stakeholders, but it is better to enlarge the scope now than to end up with a product that lacks important functionality.

One benefit that is generated by building current system models is that you find out where to ask questions (Figure 5.5). As the model develops, it becomes increasingly more obvious what you don't know, how much you don't know, and (sometimes) what the business people don't know. The model points out those areas where understanding is lacking. If your model appears to be dysfunctional, your information about the functions and data is probably incorrect; the model guides you toward where to concentrate your questions.

Figure 5.4

The first-level breakdown shows the processes contained with the context. It is used to confirm the context and to partition the scope into areas of study.

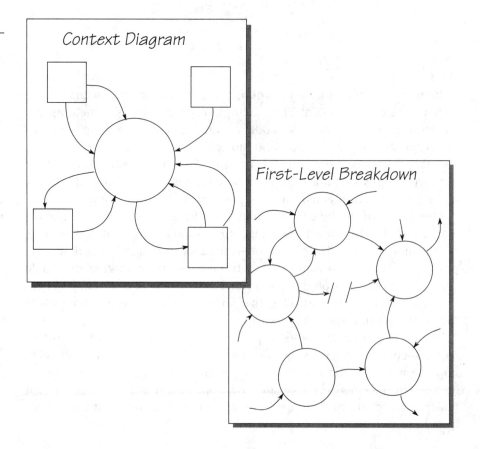

Figure 5.5

Knowing where to ask questions, and which questions to ask, is almost as useful as knowing the answers. If your model has flows going nowhere, processes without inputs, read-only or write-only data stores, or other breaches of the modeling conventions, then you need to ask your stakeholders more questions about those aspects of the work.

It is, of course, impossible to change something without knowing what that "something" is. A study of the current work shows you how to fit something new into, or change, whatever currently exists. The models of the current system ensure that you understand the situation before introducing any improvements to it.

Apprenticing

Apprenticing is particularly useful for in-house work. The underlying assumption for apprenticing is that users are currently doing work, and you, as the requirements analyst, have to understand their work. This work could be clerical, commercial, graphic arts, or almost anything short of brain surgery. Keep in mind you are not attempting to reimplement the work exactly as is. We recommend that all apprentices refer to the section on essence.

Apprenticing—based on the old idea of masters and apprentices—is a wonderful way to observe the real work. In this case, the requirements analyst is the apprentice, with the user as the master craftsman. The analyst sits with the user at the user's place of work, learning the job by making observations, asking questions, and perhaps doing some of the work under supervision.

It is unlikely that many users can explain what they do in enough detail for the developer to completely understand the work and thus capture all the requirements. For example, if you are away from your work, you tend to

READING

Beyer, Hugh, and Karen Holtzblatt. *Contextual Design: Defining Customer-Centered Systems.* Morgan Kaufmann, 1998.

describe it in abstract terms and using generalized cases. An abstraction is useful in one sense, but it does not hold enough detail for it to work every time.

Nor can you expect users to have the presentation and teaching skills needed to present their work effectively to others. Conversely, almost everyone is good at explaining what they are doing while they are doing it. If the user is doing his job in his normal workplace, he can provide a running commentary and provide details that might otherwise be lost. Only while working can the user describe his task precisely, tell you why he is doing things, and explain what exceptions can occur. You will see this process first-hand the first time a user shows you his work-around for special cases.

To have the user describe the work, you must not take him away from it. Rather, the analyst sits alongside the user at the normal workplace and receives a running commentary on the work as it happens. Each action is explained. If the explanation is not clear, the apprentice asks questions: "Why did you do that?" "What does this mean?" "How often does this happen?" "What happens if this piece of information is not here?" Through this process, the analyst eventually sees all the cases and the actions the user takes for each.

Apprenticeship can be combined with current system modeling. As the work is observed and explained, the analyst sketches a model of each task and its connections with the other tasks. Given that several models are suitable here, you should use whichever is most comfortable to you and your user. As the models are built, the analyst feeds them back to the user to obtain confirmation that they are correct and to raise questions about any areas of uncertainty (see Figure 5.6).

> *Nobody can talk better about what they do and why they do it than they can while in the middle of doing it.*
>
> Source: Beyer and Holtzblatt

Figure 5.6

The requirements analyst learns the work while sitting at the user's desk. Sometimes models of the work are built while learning it.

and then I ...

The requirements analyst uses his term of apprenticeship to try out requirements and design ideas. The analyst asks the user if an idea is feasible and if it would improve the work. This communication generates in the user's mind the notion that the analyst is more than an observer—the analyst is there to help improve the work.

The requirements analyst is an interpreter as well as an observer. While observing the current work, the analyst must abstract away from what he sees. He must overcome the user's close connection to the physical incarnation of the work. In other words, the artifacts, the technology, and so on that are currently used must be seen as a product of a previous designer. Someone, some time ago, decided that was the best way to do the work. But times have changed. Today it may be possible to do things that were impossible yesterday. There may now be better ways—ways that take advantage of up-to-date technology, that use streamlined processes, that simplify the work or automate some or all of it.

Thus, while the apprentice is learning the work by seeing the same tasks performed many times, he is also looking past how the user does the work to discern the underlying essence of the work. We will come back to essence a little later.

Observing Structures and Patterns

Structures and patterns are useful when you find a situation where the work is complex, with a probability of overlapping and similar tasks being done. This trawling technique aims to simplify the work, so it has less relevance for smaller projects. The benefits of structure/pattern observation are long term, so don't attempt it if your deadline is very tight.

Now is when you observe and interpret. By seeing the users at work over a period of time, you can determine an abstract structure or a pattern to the work.

The *structure* is a framework for the user to do his task for the normal cases, although it also supports improvisation to handle the exceptions. The structure is most likely invisible to the user—people usually do not consciously note the necessary abstraction and think in terms of work structure.

You are also looking for which skills people use and how they see themselves when they do the work. Which conceptualizations and metaphors do they use?

Once you have observed the structure, look for patterns. Does this structure match, or almost match, another structure? Is there a pattern to the work that recurs elsewhere in the enterprise? The objective is to find similarities that can yield common requirements.

Look for similarities, not differences.

For example, one of our clients, the international section of a bank in London, had 20 different products. The products ranged from letters of credit, to guaranteed foreign bank loans, to guaranteed funds, among others. At first glance, the users appeared to handle each of these products differently. However, a common pattern emerged as we studied the structure of the work—we were looking for similarities, not differences. We observed that each product was, in fact, a different way of guaranteeing that exporters got paid for their goods in foreign countries. The end result: We found a common set of requirements and were able to make a single core implementation, which we could then dress differently for each of the products. In some cases, this different window dressing involved little more than changing a few words and icons on screens.

We suggest building abstract models of the work structure—that is, models that are abstract in the sense that they do not give specific technological names to things or use distinctive terminology that belongs to one part of the organization. Abstract models should not name any particular user or use terminology identified with a particular user. These models are made remote from their source—they use categorizations rather than specifics. Instead of modeling the work the way any single user sees it, they model the *class* of work as all users could see it.

See Chapter 13, Reusing Requirements, for more on patterns.

This kind of abstraction enables you to discover whether the same pattern exists in another part of the organization. It has been our experience that although the names and the artifacts may vary, the same work pattern occurs several times in an organization. We have used the recurrence of patterns first to understand the requirements more quickly, and then to deploy the implementation of one part of the work to suit another part.

Interviewing the Stakeholders

Interviewing is used by almost all projects, as it is really a part of all elicitation techniques. Despite its omnipresence, we suggest that you do not use interviewing as your only technique for gathering requirements. Rather, conduct interviews in conjunction with the other techniques discussed in this chapter.

Interviewing users is the most commonly employed approach to requirements gathering. In this technique the interviewer relies on the interviewee to know, and be able to verbalize, all of his requirements. This procedure may work very well for requirements that people are conscious of, but few people know all their requirements or can think of them all during an interview. For this reason, it is wise to avoid relying on interviews as your sole method of gathering requirements; instead, use them in conjunction with other techniques.

That cautionary note notwithstanding, interviewing skills are highly useful in other contexts. For example, a requirements analysts can "interview" a model or a document. The skill here is knowing which questions to ask of the model or the appropriate stakeholder for the model.

Often requirements analysts may choose to draw up questionnaires in advance. While this preparatory step gives some structure to the subsequent interview, we have found few stakeholders who are motivated enough, or who have time enough, to fill in a questionnaire prior to meeting the analyst. We suggest that you send an agenda of the topics that you wish to cover to your interview subject. This at least gives the interviewee a chance to have needed material close by or to ask subject matter experts to be present.

Stakeholders should not remain completely passive during the interview. Instead, do your best to involve them by building models—business event responses, use cases, scenarios, and so on—during the interview. This approach creates a feedback loop between you and your stakeholders, and it means you can iteratively test the accuracy of what you are being told. Follow these guidelines to make your interviews more effective:

● Set the interview in context. This step is necessary to avoid having your stakeholders talk about something irrelevant to your purpose. It also gives them a chance to withdraw gracefully if they have not prepared for the interview.

● Use business use cases as an anchor for the interview. Users recognize business use cases (although they may not necessarily call them by that name), and it makes for more directed conversations if you talk about their work one business use case at a time.

● Ask a question (more on this in a moment), listen to the answer, and then feed back your understanding.

Feed back your understanding. Build models while you are interviewing the user.

● Draw models and encourage the user to change them. Plenty of models (e.g., data flow diagrams, activity diagrams, sequence diagrams) are available to help you communicate your understanding of a process. You can also construct data models for information, and mind maps to link different subjects.

● Use the stakeholders' terminology and artifacts, both conceptual and real. If the stakeholders do not use their own language, then you force them to make technological translations into terms they think you will understand. This, sadly, usually leads to misunderstandings. By contrast, if you are forced to ask questions about their terminology, you inevitably make new discoveries.

● Keep samples or copies of artifacts. Artifacts are the things the stakeholders use in their daily work. They can be real things: documents, computers, meters, spreadsheets, machines, pieces of software. They can also be conceptual things: status, contracts, schedules, orders. Artifacts will inevitably cause you to raise questions when you examine them later.

● Thank the stakeholders for their time and tell them what you learned and why it was valuable. After all, they have lots of other things to do. Talking to you is not the reason they are employed, and they often view the interview as an interruption.

Thank the stakeholders for their time.

Asking the Right Questions

The technique called neurolinguistic programming (NLP) utilizes a set of models, skills, resources, and techniques for improving communication. One of its resources is a linguistic meta-model for helping interviewers listen to what interviewees are saying and arrive at an unambiguous common understanding. This meta-model consists of a number of patterns together with questions that you can ask to identify potential misunderstandings and clarify meaning.

Suppose that one of your stakeholders says, "We get the sales information . . . ." But what is meant by "we"? Who, specifically, are we talking about? And what about the "sales information"? What is the subject matter of this information? Just in this innocent sentence you uncover two examples of a pattern known as *unspecified noun*. This pattern is characterized by a term that is not defined consistently and might be interpreted differently by two people who are having a conversation, even though those people are nodding and thinking that they agree with each other.

Another pattern leads to further questions: What is meant by "get the sales information"? Who is getting it from where? Does this imply some other activity associated with the sales information? This pattern is referred to as an *unspecified verb*.

Some other useful patterns to listen for and trigger questions follow:

- *Comparison:* When you hear the word "better," ask, "Compared to what?"
- *Judgment:* Who says that it is better? What is the authority?
- *Generalization:* When you hear the words "can't" or "must," then ask: What prevents you? Why must you do it? What would happen if you did not?

READING

For more about NLP, refer to O'Connor, J., and J. Seymour, *Introducing Neurolinguistic Programming.* Thorsons, 1990.

- *Universal Quantifiers:* When you hear "never" or "always," it triggers other questions: Is it really never or does it happen sometimes? Is it really always or are there some exceptions?
- *Nominalization:* In nominalization, a verb that describes an ongoing process is turned into a noun—for example, "Processing renewals over the Internet is better." But what does the speaker mean by "processing"? What activities are implied by the use of that word in this context?

We are often tempted to make assumptions about which meanings people are intending to communicate. In reality, most of the terms we use have a certain amount of elasticity; we can stretch almost any term to accommodate a number of different meanings. As a requirements analyst, you can take advantage of NLP patterns to identify elastic terms and then use those terms as the basis for triggering questions that lead you to a more precise understanding.

Getting to the Essence of the Work

The essence is crucial to all projects, to all work areas, and to all levels of agility. Only by understanding the essence of the problem do we become able to find the correct requirements, and eventually the right solution. In fact, once you have found the essence of a problem, its solution is usually self-evident.

When trawling for requirements, much of what you hear is inevitably a stakeholder's idea for a *solution*, not a description of the underlying problem he is trying to solve. Your task is to interpret what is said, thereby uncovering its *essence*. The essence of the work represents the fundamental reason that the work exists. The fundamental reason for IceBreaker's existence—its essence—is to accurately predict when roads are about to freeze. How it accomplishes this goal—the technology, the instruments, the computers, and the people it uses—constitutes its implementation, and is not part of its essence.

You must be able to separate the essence of the problem from any proposed solution. There are several reasons for doing this. First, it allows you to solve the real problem. You won't achieve that goal if your stakeholder is fixating on some "flavor of the month" solution. Second, it allows you to avoid inadvertently reimplementing past technological decisions. What may have been appropriate several years ago when the current system was built is not necessarily the right thing today. When you discover the essence, it means you understand the real work; in most cases, the essence will then suggest the best solution.

> *You must be able to separate the essence of the problem from any proposed solution.*

Try to imagine the essence as existing separately from its implementation. Consider this: On the one hand, you have technology—machines, electronics, networks, people, paper, and so on. Technology can be used to implement a solution to many problems. A computer doesn't know if you are running a spreadsheet or playing a game—it's just a piece of technology. On the other hand, you have the problem to be solved. The problem is some piece of work, some business policy that can be stated without any attendant technology. The problem would exist regardless of any technological implementation. That is the essence.

> *The essence exists regardless of any technological implementation.*

You can derive the essence from a technological implementation. For example, when you approach an automated teller machine, what is the essential piece of business that you wish to conduct? "Withdraw money from your bank account" would be a logical answer. The actions that you have to take—such as insert a plastic card, enter a PIN, have your retina scanned, and so on—involve interacting with the technology the bank chooses to use. In contrast, the essence is that you access your account and withdraw money from it.

Note how technology-free that statement is: "You access your account and withdraw money from it." Consider it, and now consider how many other

READING

McMenamin, Steve, and John Palmer. *Essential Systems Analysis.* Yourdon Press, 1984. The title refers to "essence."

ways you could "access your account and withdraw money from it." Lots of technological possibilities exist, but only one essence. And that is the point. The requirements you are looking for are the essential requirements. How they are implemented now or in the future is not important to you at the moment.

As a consequence, when you are trawling for requirements, you must look past the current implementation. You must also ignore the future technology, for that matter, however exciting it may be. Instead, focus on the underlying concepts that exist because of the real work.

For example, the current implementation of IceBreaker uses a computer to interpret the electronic signals from the weather stations and record the road-surface temperature and moisture content. The engineers use a PC to run their analyses of the freezing roads. But all those devices are incidental to the essence—they are just the means chosen to carry out the essence. Look past those devices and ask, "What is this activity doing to help the work?" "What policy is being followed by the activity"? That policy—let's call it "the fundamental policy"—is the essence.

Why is this important?

If you write a requirement that contains a technological element, then that piece of technology becomes a requirement. For example, suppose that you have a requirement like this:

> *The product shall beep and put a flashing message on the screen if a weather station fails to transmit readings.*

What's wrong here? The message is now consigned to a screen. Perhaps there are better solutions, such as telephoning the road engineers, sending an e-mail message, or launching a weather station diagnostic application. Now imagine you write the requirement like this:

> *The product shall issue an alert if a weather station fails to transmit readings.*

Because you have described the real, the *essential*, requirement, the designer can now cast about and find the most appropriate solution.

As another example, consider this requirement for a ticket-selling product for a metro train:

> *The traveler shall touch the destination on a map on a screen.*

READING

Robertson, James, and Suzanne Robertson. *Complete Systems Analysis: The Workbook, the Textbook, the Answers.* Dorset House, 1998.

If a requirement contains the means of implementation, then it is a solution, not a requirement.

The stakeholder wanted to employ a touch-sensitive map of the metro network and have the travelers touch their destination station. The product would compute the appropriate fare and, as a bonus, show an illuminated pathway of the fastest route to the destination. This might be a clever implementation, but it is not the essence of the problem. It is not the only way to implement the requirement: Perhaps better ways might be discovered. If the requirement is expressed in its essential form, it looks like this:

> *The product shall accept the destination from the traveler.*

The designer is now free to study the best way to implement the essence, and can use other technologies (within the constraints of the project) to get the traveler's destination into the product. Had the touch screen idea been left as the requirement, it would have resulted in a less than optimal product. Indeed, studies in this case showed that the majority of travelers did not know the rail network well enough to be able to locate their destination quickly enough.

The point is that we should not prejudge the implementation, no matter how well we think we understand the problem, nor how appealing the technology might be.

Letting go of these preconceptions is not always easy, and over the years we have found it one of the hardest concepts to convey to our clients and students. It becomes even harder if you are using eXtreme Programming. This approach, which is aimed at producing solutions, emphasizes getting to the next iteration as quickly as possible. But something is missing here: How do you know if the solution is addressing the real problem? Have you included a brief pause to think about the essence of the problem? Have you carefully scrutinized your enthusiastic customer's ideas about how to solve the problem? Once you do, you may come up with not only the best solution, but also one that will last even after today's technology falls out of favor. When you address the real issues, your solution does not have to be chopped up and changed as successive users tweak it to do the job it should have been doing all along.

When you address the real issues, your solution does not have to be chopped up and changed as successive users tweak it to do the job it should have been doing all along.

Solving the Right Problem

The way of thinking discussed here follows from understanding the essence. This section is relevant to all requirements analysts, regardless of the size of the project or the degree of agility.

You have heard the old joke about the drunk who is looking for his keys under the lamppost at night. The kindly policeman stops to ask if he can help. The drunk tells him he lost the keys a block or so away, but he is looking for them here "because the light is better."

We have seen real-life adaptations of this scenario: The project team sets out to build some whiz-bang product. The product is built but somehow, despite the project team's enthusiastic cheerleading from the sidelines and the expense of building it, the users never seem to put it to use. Why? Because it solved the wrong problem. Why didn't the team build a product to solve the right problem? Because for the problem the team did solve, the "light was better." The team members looked for solutions where the light was brightest, but ignored the shadowy corners where the real problem lurked.

One of our clients, a financial institution, was looking into building a new system that would allow passwords to be reset more efficiently. This task posed a major problem for the organization, as the cost of establishing its customers' bona fides before resetting their passwords was running at several million dollars per year. The proposed new system would reduce some of the cost. But what is really happening here? The system producers are looking where the light is better—a slick new system to establish bona fides more effectively—and not into the dark corners. The real problem—the one they are avoiding—is that *customers forget their passwords.*

Discovering the right problem to solve appears to be harder than building a new system: It's finding a way for customers to remember their passwords. Of course, if you read what we said about essence earlier, you will by now be saying, "Hold it! Passwords are a technology for doing something, not the essence." Passwords are not part of the business problem; they are the bank's chosen technology, and they now appear to be a less than perfect solution.

The right problem to solve is this: Allow customers secure access to their accounts, and do so in a way that does not require prodigious feats of memory on the part of the customers.

We usually set out to solve the wrong problem when we begin a project by thinking about the product and not the work, or by not having a sufficiently large work scope to begin with. By focusing inward, on the proposed product, the project team fails to see the larger world—the one that contains the real problem to solve.

READING

Gause, Don, and Jerry Weinberg. *Are Your Lights On? How to Figure Out What the Problem Really Is.* Dorset House, 1990.

READING

Jackson, M. *Problem Frames: Analyzing and Structuring Software Development Problems.* Addison-Wesley, 2001.

Innovative Products

This section deals with innovative requirements. We contend that the requirements analyst today must be looking for ways to improve his client's work. Improvements usually come about through innovation. Use innovation when you are working with stakeholders who have an existing situation that needs to be improved. Also, use innovation when you are working in a new application area. Naturally, if you work for a software house or something similar, innovation is what keeps you ahead of the pack.

If you want to compete in today's commercial market, or with offshore companies offering to build cheaper software for in-house consumption, or with the vast amount of available off-the-shelf software, or with the rapidly growing catalog of open source software, then innovation is your greatest ally. Software development productivity is fine as far as it goes, but buying off-the-shelf software will always be cheaper (providing it meets requirements). Climbing the CMM (capability maturity model) ladder is also fine, but it won't do you a bit of good if your client, your customers, and your users are not thrilled with your product.

The requirements activity is all too often seen as a "stenographer's task," one where the requirements analyst passively records while the stakeholders state their needs. This view relies on stakeholders knowing exactly what they need and what they want. Our experience has been that, except for rare visionaries, people do not know what they want until they see it. Many of the most useful products that we take for granted today did not come about from the stakeholders' imagination or from people asking for something, but rather emerged from an invention. The mobile phone, text messaging, the World Wide Web, graphic user interfaces, the iPod, and many, many other products and services are inventions—no one asked for these things before they were invented.

Don't rely on your stakeholders knowing exactly what they want and, just as importantly, being able to ask for it. True, much of the product you build is a natural outcome of studying the users' work. However, if all of it is, then you have not improved anything. To make the leap forward, to deliver the product that truly satisfies your client, you have to be inventive.

The first thing to consider is that you cannot invent a better way of working by merely automating yesterday's way of working. Nor can you do it by re-automating yesterday's automation. Only by rethinking the business use cases can you come up with innovative products that will be able to compete in tomorrow's marketplace. That is, for any business use case, you must first understand the essence and ensure that the stakeholders similarly understand it. Once you have achieved that goal, innovations and improvements will follow.

As an example of the kind of innovation we are talking about, consider your customers, the people who consume your product or service. Consumers today are much better informed than they have ever been, and they have ready access to information that previously was denied them. The Internet gives consumers the ability to easily find the best available prices and to make comparisons between almost all goods and services. Geography no longer matters. Consumers can order goods from anywhere in the world for delivery to their home in one or two days. As a result, customer loyalty and brand loyalty are rapidly disappearing, to be replaced by customer demand for better service and convenience. Think about the service and convenience

Our job is to give the client, on time and on cost, not what he wants, but what he never dreamed he wanted; and when he gets it, he recognizes it as something he wanted all the time.

Source: Denys Lasdon, architect

Don't rely on your stakeholders knowing exactly what they want.

requirements for the product you are planning to build. Do the requirements indicate the product will provide better service and greater convenience to your users or your organization's customers? If not, you run the risk of building a product that will be abandoned in short order.

Go back over any business use case concerned with providing anything to the outside world. What level of service and convenience does it currently provide? Can you improve it? Can you eliminate even one step of a buying or ordering business use case? Can you do something for the consumer that previously he did for himself? Note that we are not talking about design here. Ignore for the moment the technology you plan to use, and question the essence by thinking about *what* your business should be doing to provide better service and convenience.

How much control does your customer have over his transactions? People are happy, and in some cases demand, to do some of the work themselves. Supermarkets are introducing—to much acclaim—self check-out. Customers are shopping at home, ordering customized products they have specified themselves using interactive Web sites. People buy shares over the Internet without advice or intervention from a broker or trader. Travelers book their own airline flights over the Internet and check themselves in at the airport. This greater consumer involvement brings benefits to both parties: The airlines, and all other organizations that provide self-service, reduce the cost of the transaction by automating it; the consumer gets greater convenience and feels in control of the transaction.

READING

Peters, Tom. *The Circle of Innovation*. Alfred A. Knopf, 1997.

We love to be connected.

How connected are your customers to your business? Humans seem to have a love affair with connectedness. Drivers risk serious injury by answering their phones while driving. People step into the streets, paying attention only to the text message on the screen of their telephone. For young people in Japan, it is a serious social blunder to leave the phone at home or to allow its battery to run down. People of all ages check their e-mail in the middle of the night. Why? Because we love to be connected. And it can work for you. Customer loyalty cards, frequent-flyer plans, newsletters, branded credit cards, and automatic software updates are all examples of businesses connecting their customers. Think about the requirements for the connection that your product makes to your customers or users. Can you invent a better connection?

Choices and information are important requirements for all innovative products. Work with your stakeholders to find ways of giving the users or customers more and better information, and more and better choices. Keep in mind that consumers today have access to an incredible amount of information, but even so, seem to want more. Give it to them before your competitor does.

A little later in this chapter we talk about techniques for fostering innovation. In particular, we look at creativity workshops, brainstorming, and personas as aids to inventing better requirements.

Naturally, your new product is not completely invented. It must be based on the work that it is to support. However, you cannot simply mark off some existing functionality and automate it. Instead, you must invent a better way to do the work—that is, "better" in that it provides better control for the user or customer, better information, better choices, better connectivity, better service, better response to requests, and probably at a lower cost to your organization.

Business Use Case Workshops

We have found business use case workshops to be useful on most projects. These workshops allow you to work with a smaller number of specialized stakeholders at a time.

In Chapter 4, Event-Driven Use Cases, we discussed what business events are and how they trigger a response by the work, which we called a business use case. We hope that by devoting an entire chapter to this subject, we have unequivocally signaled the importance of partitioning the work according to how it responds to the world outside it.

Of course, having partitioned the work, we need to do something with the pieces. That is the role of the business use case workshop. The workshop is a human activity where the interested stakeholders describe or reenact the work done, or desired to be done, by the business use case. Your task is to record these actions and then use them to derive the requirements for the product that will best help with the work.

But let's start at the beginning.

Each business use case has one or more interested stakeholders—people who are experts on that part of the work, and who have a particular interest in the outcome of the business use case. The workshop transfers knowledge of the business use case from its interested stakeholders to the requirements analyst. These individuals lock themselves away in a JAD (joint application development)–style workshop and construct scenarios to show the actions necessary to make the correct response to the business event. (See Figure 5.7.)

In Chapter 6, Scenarios and Requirements, we talk about scenarios, which involve telling the story of the business use case in a fairly structured way. We propose that you use the business use case scenario as a talking point during discussions with your stakeholders. Feel free to peek into Chapter 6, but for the moment it will suffice if you think of a scenario as a breakdown of the business use case's functionality into a reasonable number of steps.

Refer to Chapter 4, Event-Driven Use Cases, for a complete explanation of business events and business use cases.

READING

Gottesdiener, Ellen. *Requirements by Collaboration: Workshops for Defining Needs.* Addison-Wesley, 2002. Gottesdiener's book covers in detail how to plan and conduct requirements workshops.

See Chapter 3, Project Blastoff, for more on how to discover the relevant interested stakeholders.

Figure 5.7

The business use case workshop records the proposed functionality using scenarios and low-fidelity prototypes. Ideally, the interested stakeholders can communicate effectively and express their understanding, ask questions, and give their aspirations for the work.

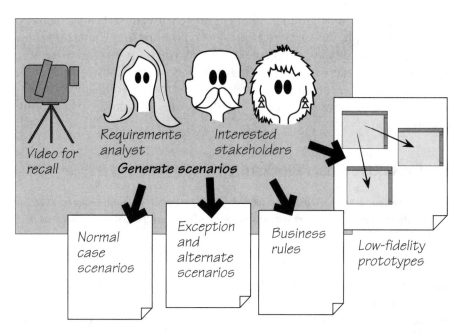

Using scenarios as a communication device, the analyst and stakeholders work together to acquire the knowledge of the business use case:

- The desired outcome for the business use case
- Scenarios describing the work done by the business use case
- Exception scenarios describing what things can go wrong and what the work does to correct them
- Alternative scenarios showing allowable variations to the work
- The business rules applicable to the business use case
- The product use case—how much of the business use case is to be done by the product
- Characteristics of likely users of a product built for this business use case
- Low-fidelity prototypes used to help stakeholders visualize the business use case—these throwaway prototypes are not intended to be kept beyond the requirements phase

Outcome

Think of outcomes, not outputs.

The outcome is what the organization hopes to achieve whenever the business use case occurs. You should think of this result in terms of outcomes, not outputs. For example, suppose the business use case is "Rent a car to a customer." The desired outcome is that the customer drives away in the car of his choice, the rate selected is equitable, the details are recorded, and the transaction is completed with minimal inconvenience to the customer at minimal cost. The outputs of the same business event are the rental document and some recorded data.

Note that the outcome is a business objective, not a way of achieving something. Outcomes are usually expressed from the point of view of the organization or of the organization's customer. The outcome is what you are trying to achieve, which is why it is important. This outcome gives your business use case its reason for existing.

You should be able to write the outcome of the business use case in one sentence: When this business use case happens, what should be achieved when the work for the business use case has finished?

Scenarios

Scenarios describe the work being done by the business use case as a series—usually between three and ten—steps. The scenario is a stakeholder-friendly document used as the focal point of the workshop. The steps are not very detailed, because the intention is not to capture every small part of the business use case, but rather to have a broad-brush picture of the work.

The normal-case scenario shows the actions of the business use case if all goes well and no mistakes are made, wrong actions taken, or any other untoward happening occurs. The intention is for you and your stakeholders to reach consensus on what *should* happen. Other scenarios focus on the exception cases—when unwanted things go wrong—and alternative scenarios—when the people involved in the business use case decide to take some allowable alternative actions.

Chapter 6, Scenarios and Requirements, is a full treatise on scenarios.

The collection of scenarios represents the interested stakeholders' consensus on what the work should do in response to the business event. We stress again the importance of understanding the work, and not just the product. Armed with this understanding, the analyst and the interested stakeholders decide on the optimal product for the business use case. The right product to build usually becomes apparent as the discussion of the work progresses. Once it has been decided, the requirements analyst writes the requirements for the product. We will talk about this task in Chapter 7, Functional Requirements.

Business Rules

The business rules are management prescriptions that transcend and guide the day-to-day business decisions. Naturally, any product you build must conform to the business rules. These rules come to the surface as the stakeholders discuss the work for each business event. Later they are used to guide the functional requirements and to help to discover the meaning of stored data.

There is no set form for the business rules. For most projects you will be able to find, with the help of the interested stakeholders, existing documents that spell out these rules. The business rules eventually become incorporated into the business use case scenarios and the requirements.

Creativity Workshops

Creativity workshops are an outgrowth of the drive for innovative products discussed earlier. Use them when a large number of stakeholders are involved in the invention process. Creativity workshops are also appropriate when you want stakeholders to see the advantages of developing an innovative product, as opposed to just rebuilding the same old system.

There is a growing acknowledgment that creative thinking early in the requirements activities is a powerful way of helping people to think past the current way of doing things. When stakeholders free themselves from the status quo, they can invent new and undreamed-of ideas.

When Eurocontrol decided to investigate the requirements for the air traffic control systems of the future, the organization found it difficult to think past how things are done now. With our colleague Neil Maiden from City University, we developed requirements creativity workshops as a way of encouraging air traffic controllers, pilots, airline representatives, and systems developers to think of innovative requirements for the future. The outcome of the workshops was the invention of several hundred innovative requirements. Participants agreed that the requirements coming from the workshops made a significant, almost startling difference to the final air traffic product. They also agreed that these requirements would never have seen the light of day except for the creativity workshops.

The best time to run a creativity workshop is close to the beginning of the project, before people become too attached to their ideas for a solution. At the same time, it is necessary to have some structure on which to hang the new ideas, because otherwise everything is too intangible and hard to relate to the problem at hand. Here is our technique for planning and running the creative workshops:

1   Set the scope of the investigation, identify the project goals, and run a first-cut stakeholder analysis.

2   Partition the scope of the investigation, using business events to lead to business use cases.

3   Plan the workshop, using a variety of creativity techniques designed to help people to be inventive and to discover new ideas.

4   Run the workshop and use the business events as a focus for clustering the new ideas.

5   After the workshop, summarize the results and feed them back to participants.

Creativity techniques are designed to encourage people to innovate. For example, one technique is to ask an expert in an unrelated field to talk about his work to the group. The group then uses analogies from the unrelated field to trigger ideas for their own field of study. As experts unrelated to air traffic, we have heard from a Hollywood screenwriter, a musician, a textile designer, and a chef. Peter Gordon, the chef at the Providores Restaurant in London, was extremely popular. His talk on ingredients was useful to the air traffic controllers, and his cooking lunch for the workshop participants was a distinct bonus. Susan Rogers, the screenwriter, used an example from the film *Alien* to illustrate how a script is used as the basis for designing and filming a scene. She showed us how the director annotates the script with ideas and uses storyboards as a way of capturing new ideas. Following this presentation, the stakeholders (mostly air traffic controllers) used the film storyboarding techniques as an inspiration and source of ideas for building huge storyboards for the project in their own domain.

Other creativity techniques include combining seemingly disparate ideas to create a new idea. Perhaps the one we are most grateful for happened when Gutenberg combined the coin stamp and the wine press to make a printing press. More recently—and we make no claim as to the virtue of the result—the telephone and the camera have been combined. Perhaps of more practicality is the combination of a GPS-equipped phone and spoken driving or walking directions.

Transformational thinking involves putting an idea into another domain. For example, eBay transformed the traditional auction sale into a Web-based auction sale. Constraint removal is the methodical removal of constraints to explore the possibilities for generating new, different, and potentially useful ideas.

The ideas from the creativity sessions for air traffic controllers were triggered by practices and ideas from another discipline, the inspiration that comes from listening to expert people, the storyboard as a way of generating new ideas, and use of all the ideas as a springboard to leap past the existing and the obvious.

We continue to run the workshops in many different domains and to experiment with new techniques. Many of these techniques make use of the principles of brainstorming.

READING

Maiden, Neil, Sharon Manning, Suzanne Robertson, and John Greenwood. Integrating Creativity Workshops into Requirements Processes. *Proceedings of Designing Interactive Systems Conference,* Cambridge, Mass., 2004.

Brainstorming

Brainstorming is one way of inventing. We recommend that all projects schedule at least one brainstorm session close to the beginning of the project before ideas become fixed. Brainstorming is useful for generating lots of contributions regarding what the scope of the problem should be. It does not mean promoting unconstrained scope creep. Instead, you collect ideas that could lead to a better product without incurring additional expense.

Figure 5.8

A brainstorming session is a gathering of interested people whose task is to generate new ideas for the product.

Brainstorming takes advantage of the group effect. That is, you gather a group of bright, willing people, and ask them to generate as many ideas as possible for the new product (Figure 5.8). Tell them that all ideas are acceptable no matter how crazy they may seem, and that they must not slow the process down by criticizing or debating ideas. The aim is to be as imaginative as possible, and to generate as many ideas as possible, often by using the ideas of others to trigger a different idea of their own.

Here are some simple rules for brainstorming:

- Participants in the brainstorming session should come from a wide range of disciplines, with as broad a range of experience as possible. This mixture of backgrounds brings many more creative ideas to the fore.

- For the moment, suspend judgment, evaluation, criticism, and, most importantly, debate. Simply record requirements as they are generated. The practice of not stopping the flow is the fastest way to develop a creative and energized atmosphere for the brainstorming group.

- Produce lots of ideas. Come up with as many ideas as possible. Quantity will, in time, produce quality.

- Try to come up with as many ideas as you can that are unconventional, unique, crazy, and wild. The wilder the idea, the more creative it probably is, and often the more likely it is to turn into a really useful requirement.

- Piggyback a new idea onto an old one. That is, build one idea on top of another.

- Write every idea down, without censoring.

- If you get stuck, seed the session with a word pulled randomly from a dictionary, and ask participants to make word associations that have some bearing on the product. That is, generate ideas using the word as a springboard.

- Make the session fun. You cannot mandate creativity; you have to let it come naturally. You won't see many ground-breaking ideas if the boss is on the session and says something like, "I only want to hear ideas that are marketable."

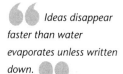

Ideas disappear faster than water evaporates unless written down.

Source: Alex Osborne, the founder of brainstorming

After the brainstorming session, the lead requirements analysts and the client evaluate the ideas. Some of them will be worthless, but they will have served their brainstorming purpose by inspiring other, more useful ideas. Some ideas may need to be merged with others—perhaps two half-formed ideas, when put together, will make some wonderful new idea. Keep the best of the ideas and, providing there is a reasonable chance of implementing them within the project constraints, turn them into requirements.

Some of the ideas might warrant further investigation. Now you can bring into play the other trawling techniques described in this chapter.

Personas

Personas are useful when real users are not available or are too numerous to interview all of them. The persona is a virtual character that substitutes for the human users.

A persona is an invented personality, an imaginary user for whom you are gathering requirements for your product. Why an imaginary character when there are potentially thousands of real users out there? Because, for a mass-market product, you don't know, and can't get to know, all of the real users. But you can know one really well, and that imaginary user's attributes guide your requirements. This is your persona.

You invent your persona, and give him or her characteristics that match the intended audience for your product. Although personas are imaginary, they are an accurate archetype of the many people who would buy and/or use your product.

Why use a persona? When it comes to determining the requirements for the product, it is more effective to have a single, albeit imaginary person as the target user than to try and find all possible requirements for all possible people who might come in contact with the product. Take, for example, the shoes you are wearing at this moment. Unless you are reading this book in a very unusual place, it is likely your shoes not designed with mountain climbing or ballroom dancing in mind. Nevertheless, there are people—and conceivably people who would read this book—who would undertake such activities. So why did the shoe designer design for you and not everybody? Because a shoe suitable for everyone will be suitable for no one.

Now think of a piece of software whose requirements were gathered with a target audience of everyone on the planet. The final product would include so much functionality that finding the actions you want would take most of the day. Its usability requirements would be unbelievably complex and, in the end, ineffectual; its security requirements would drive everyone nuts. Now think of the software you really like to use. You know, that application where it seems the requirements analysts had you in mind—everything works in a manner that seems natural to you, and the functionality does just

READING

Cooper, Alan. *The Inmates Are Running the Asylum: Why High Tech Products Drive Us Crazy and How to Restore the Sanity.* Sams Publishing, 1999. Cooper describes how his product design company uses personas as the driver for specifying new products.

what you want it to. This software does what you want because its requirements were gathered for someone just like you—a persona with your
attributes.

In fact, the book you are reading was written with a persona in mind. Your
authors invented a character: Pam is 34 years old and works for Bank of Scotland IT department, where she has been a business analyst for three years.
She reads a lot, is interested in her job and wants to be better at it, dislikes
people who take too long to say something, enjoys movies and music, is a bit
of a gadget freak (she changes her phone every year), and wants to spend
more time with her six-year-old son. Precision is important when developing
a persona. We found a photograph we thought of as Pam (see Figure 5.9) and
taped it to the wall. Whenever we were stuck when writing some part of this
book, we would imagine what Pam would want to know about the topic. If
you find this book useful and interesting, it is because you have a similar
knowledge, background, and curiosity to Pam's. It is not that we don't care
about you, dear reader—we just don't know you personally. Conversely, we
know our persona intimately and, as it happens, she shares many of your
characteristics.

Figure 5.9

We used a photo of our
persona to help write
this book. (Source: Photo
Dreamstime/pichunter.)

When we talk about requirements for software, we often speak of "user requirements." The problem with this term is that requirements are gathered for *anyone* who could be a user. The result is often too many requirements, many of which conflict with one another, and a product that satisfies none of its intended audience. The way to build a successful product is not to gather requirements that mete out something for everyone, but rather to *thrill* a selected audience.

Define your audience by defining your persona. Don't say, "someone in the acquisitions department"; say, "Bob (always, *always* give your persona a name), 32 years old, has been in the job for 18 months; has a picture of his wife, Terri, in his cubicle, and also has a picture of his hero, Isambard King- dom Brunel; loves baseball and Bruce Willis movies." Find a photograph in a magazine of someone who you and your teammates agree looks like Bob. Now when you are gathering requirements and cannot get interview time with the real users, ask, "Is this a requirement that Bob wants or needs? Is this something he will use? Or is it just another good idea that Bob will ignore?"

Creating more than one persona may prove helpful because it helps you to think about different viewpoints on the importance of specific require- ments. For example, suppose you have another persona called Sally. Sally has ten years experience, is manager of the department, and is very ambitious. She lives in a loft apartment in Docklands and leads a very glamorous social life. She is interested in skiing, opera, and going to restaurants. Do you see how you can already start to know Sally, and recognize that she is not going to agree with all of Bob's requirements? How many personas is it practical to have? We find that a maximum of three personas is manageable and helpful. Any more than that is often an indication that you are trying to please too many people or that you do not yet know the detailed business goals of your project.

Having a persona means that you start to assign priorities early in the project. Once your persona is fully described, your requirements activity focuses on satisfying that persona, with the resultant clarity of purpose and product. The scope is clearer, the usability requirements are sharpened, and it is generally easier to know which requirements you must pay attention to and which can be safely ignored.

After a while, the persona becomes a real person to the team. We worked on a project where the team brought a framed photograph of the persona to every meeting and talked about him as if he were real. That's not unusual. People will refer to Bob in conversation, and the arguments will shift from whether "someone" might use a feature to whether Bob wants the feature. The result is a product with a clarity of purpose and a consistent way of pre- senting that purpose.

READING

Norman, Donald. *The Design of Everyday Things.* Doubleday, 1988. Despite the relative age of this book, Norman's words on clarity of purpose hold true today.

A maximum of three personas is manageable and helpful. Any more than that is often an indication that you are trying to please too many people or that you do not yet know the detailed business goals of your project.

Mind Maps

We use mind maps all the time. We use them for taking notes during interviews, planning projects or actions, summarizing workshops—in fact, any time we need to have a concise and intelligible record. Mind mapping is a skill that will benefit all requirements analysts.

We use mind maps all the time. We use them for taking notes, for planning, for summarizing, for exploring ideas. But let's start at the beginning.

A mind map is a drawing and text combination that attempts to represent information the way that your brain stores it—that is, by making associations. We link each new piece of information to something, or some things, we already know. The mind map imitates this storage mechanism by using lines to link words and pictures that represent the information. Figure 5.10 shows a mind map we drew as notes about Pam, our persona we introduced in the last section.

Mind maps are useful devices for organizing your thoughts. You can see the result of your thinking organized as one diagram—you get an overview and details at the same time—with each of your subtopics teased out to show divergence and connections. The map provides enough information, expressed as keywords and links between those keywords, for you to get the overall picture. You can also decide to follow one of the branches, or make

Figure 5.10

We drew this mind map as we determined the characteristics of our persona, Pam. The mind map breaks down the central subject, Pam, into her major characteristics. Each of these characteristics is then further subdivided. Note how the mind map provides a comprehensive overview of its subject.

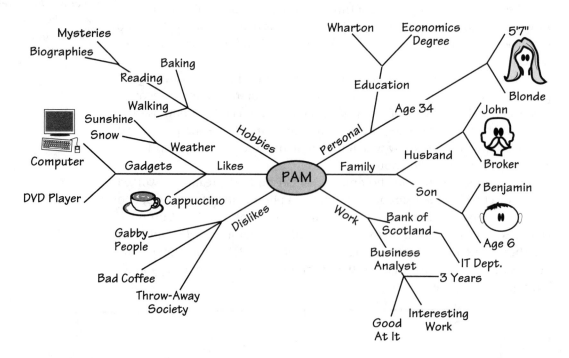

decisions based on having all the information laid out in a convenient format. Any pictures on the mind map help because they can eliminate the need to have as many words and have the advantage of being more easily remembered than words.

If you do not draw mind maps already, then have a go: This is the best way to add them to your toolkit. Have the page in landscape format, and place your central subject in the center of it. The central idea should be a strong image that tells you, or anyone who reads your mind map, what it is about. The first breakdown shows the major concepts, themes, ideas, or whatever subdivisions of your subject you choose. Write these ideas on the lines, using one or two words. Look for strong words that name and describe your ideas. And print rather than using cursive writing; the result will be both more readable and more memorable.

Use lines to make links between the ideas. We remember colors, so use colored lines for areas of the map that contain one theme. The lines can have arrowheads to denote direction, but most of the time the link between ideas is bidirectional.

Mind maps cannot always be built from the center outward. Sometimes you get ideas, or hear things when you are taking notes, that have no connection to anything already in your map. Add it to the map anyway, because you will at some stage find a connection. Your mind map may not end up as organized and pretty as some examples you see, but it still makes sense to your mind—and that is the point.

One last thing on the technique of drawing mind maps: Use the biggest sheet of paper you can find. Borrow a large drawing pad, or flip chart, or anything you can get your hands on. Spread out. Give your mind room to move. Have fun. And be as creative as you can.

You can, of course, buy software for drawing mind maps if you want to have your mind maps on your computer. Your authors never use software because it takes away all the fun of drawing and of using colored pencils. Plus, we like the sheer spontaneity of using paper and pencil.

We use mind maps for note taking when interviewing stakeholders about their requirements. The benefit of using mind maps in these situations is realized when your stakeholder tells you about features and functions of their work and the new product. Some of these are linked, and many are dependent on others. By drawing your interviews in mind map format, you become more likely to see the connections as well as spot connections that the client has not made, but should be explained. Think of the mind map as a more versatile note-taking tool—versatile, because you can replace all the text it takes to establish connections by simply drawing a line.

The best way of learning to draw mind maps is to start drawing mind maps. Use the tips described in this book, or gather examples from the Web to help. But mainly, just start drawing. You will soon see your mind map

READING

Buzan, Tony. *Mind Maps at Work: How to Be the Best at Work and Still Have Time to Play.* Harper Collins, 2004.

Buzan, Tony. *The Ultimate Book of Mind Maps.* Harper Thorsons, 2006.

Russell, Peter. *The Brain Book.* Routledge & Kegan Paul, 1979.

unfold. Draw maps of conversations, meetings, planning sessions, and, most importantly, requirements interviews with stakeholders.

Wallpaper

Wallpaper is perhaps the lowest-tech requirements tool of all. That, and it's free. Do this: Find a corridor, lobby, or some public area where your stakeholders congregate or pass through. Cover the walls with flip chart paper, brown paper, or anything that is both large and able to be written on. Write topics on sections of the wallpaper. Topics are related to the work and/or the product, and are what you want to know about. Wait a few days.

Our experience is that stakeholders start to write their thoughts, and others become encouraged and add their own comments, additions, suggestions, and so on. You can cheat and seed the wallpaper with some of your own material if comments do not start to appear promptly. The end result is a wealth of material, most of it relevant, partly organized, and gained with almost no effort on your part.

One other thing: The Furniture Police (see DeMarco and Lister's *Peopleware* for an explanation) will hate it.

Video and Photographs

A video or photograph is a way of capturing some moments in time so that you can study them later. It is a particularly useful technique if you want to show the current work to people who cannot visit the stakeholders' workplace. Also, we take photos of whiteboards—to show the progression of ideas—and find that we often refer back to these images and include some of them in documents.

Video can be used to codevelop systems. Users and requirements analysts participate in workshops and brainstorms—the proceedings are videoed. Interviews and on-site observations are also videoed. Video is used initially to record, and then confirm, the proceedings. In addition, you can show the video to developers who do not get the opportunity to meet face to face with the users.

Video can serve as an adjunct to interviewing and observing the users in their own workplace. Users have their own ways of accomplishing tasks. They have their own ways of categorizing the information that they use, and their own ways of solving problems that they have found worked well for them in their particular situation. Thus, by using video to capture the users at work, you also capture their ways of doing their jobs, their concerns, their preferences and idiosyncrasies.

Of course, video can also be used in a more structured way. For example, you might select a business use case and ask the users to work through typical situations they encounter while you make a video recording of them. As they work, the users describe the special circumstances, the additional information they use, the exceptions, and so on. The shrugs, grimaces, and gestures that are normally lost when taking notes are faithfully recorded for later playback and dissection.

Obviously, you must ask permission before you begin to video someone. Keep in mind that whoever you are videoing will initially freeze in front of the camera, but subjects usually relax after a few minutes and forget the camera is there. Do not ask any important questions in the first five minutes, as the answers may be given for the benefit of the camera, and not for the benefit of accuracy.

We suggest that you try video in the following circumstances:

- Video users and developers participating in use case workshops and brainstorms.

- Video interviews and on-site observations.

- Video users at work.

- Video a business event. Ask the users to work through their typical response to an event, and to describe how they do their jobs.

If video does not seem practical in your environment, then use photographs. We always carry a small digital camera as part of our requirements analysis kit. During interviews, meetings, and workshops, we take photographs of stakeholders, whiteboards, flip charts, offices, manufacturing plants, and anything else that we think will be useful in helping to discover the requirements. We often include photographs in minutes and progress reports. Photos are an effective way of giving people a detailed review without having to write a huge report.

READING
DeGrace, Peter, and Leslie Hulet Stahl. *Wicked Problems, Righteous Solutions: A Catalogue of Modern Software Engineering Paradigms.* Yourdon Press, 1990. This book has been around for a relatively long time, but it has some relevant ideas on video to pass along.

Wikis, Blogs, and Discussion Forums

These techniques can apply to many types of projects. However, because they require participation from a number of stakeholders, these strategies are most effective for larger projects. Blogs and wikis should be used when developing software for sale.

People love to contribute. The success of wikis and Web logs—see Wikipedia and the tens of thousands of blogs for evidence of their popularity—demonstrates that, given a chance and a forum, people are happy to spend a little time adding their opinions and facts to some public electronic forum. These contributions take many forms—you have probably used several—but for the sake of brevity we shall refer to them all as *wikis*.

The basic idea of a wiki is that anyone—and the point is largely that anyone can do it—can make a post or edit or add to whatever has already been posted. Some forums keep their discussions in threaded form so you can see the discussion unfold; some allow contributors to overwrite or reorganize whatever they find. Additionally, anyone can add hypertext links to other useful sources of information or make any other kind of change.

Wikis rely on technology, but it is technology readily available to all. You can buy or download free hosting solutions to host your requirements wiki. If your organization will not give you the server space, then there are several publicly available sites. If you choose this route, check carefully before you post what could be sensitive commercial information in the public domain.

The Web is a bountiful source for requirements. Search for your domain of interest. You will likely uncover a lot of information on what other people have done in your domain and, if you are lucky, you will find information you can readily convert to requirements for your product.

In this technique, you seed the wiki with an outline of the proposed product and invite stakeholders to add their piece. Once someone posts an opinion on what the product should do, you will no doubt find others chipping in to support or refute the original posting. Others invariably have their say, and before long you have a substantial collection of information and opinions. Anyone can contribute to a wiki. That the contributor is not one of the stakeholders you identified is irrelevant. If a person has something to say, you want to hear it, and you want each of your contributors to see what the others are saying.

And it is free, or can be.

The Web is a bountiful source for requirements. Search for your domain of interest. You will likely uncover a lot of information on what other people have done in your domain and, if you are lucky, you will find information you can readily convert to requirements for your product. At the very least, you will find papers and articles providing valuable information about your domain. And, like wikis, searching the Web is free.

Document Archeology

Document archeology is a technique of searching through existing reports and files for underlying requirements. It is best used when you have some existing or legacy system, and plan on modifying or renewing it.

Document archeology involves determining the underlying requirements by inspecting the documents and files used by the organization. It is not a complete technique, but rather should be used in conjunction with other techniques, and only with caution. Document archeology is reverse-engineering the documents used or produced by the current work. In other words, you dig new requirements out of the material used by the old work. Along the way, you look for requirements that should become part of the new product. Obviously, not all of the old work will be carried forward. But where a current system exists, it will always provide plenty of material that is grist for your requirements mill (see Figure 5.11).

Inspect the documents you have collected (for simplicity's sake, the term "document" means anything you have collected) looking for nouns, or "things." These can be column headings, named boxes on forms, or simply the name of a piece of data on the document.

For each "thing," ask these questions:

- What is the purpose of this thing?
- Who uses it and why?
- What are all the uses the system makes of this thing?
- What business events use or reference this thing?
- Can this thing have a value? For example, is it a number, a code, or a quantity?
- If so, to which collection of things does it belong? (Data modeling enthusiasts will immediately recognize the need to find the entity or class that owns the attribute.)
- What is the thing used for?
- Does the document contain a repeating group of things?
- If so, what is the collection of things called?
- Can you find a link between things?
- What process makes the connection between them?
- What rules are attached to each thing? In other words, what piece of business policy covers the thing?
- What processes ensure that these rules are obeyed?
- Which documents give users the most problems?

These questions will not, in themselves, reveal all the requirements for the product. They will, however, give you plenty of background material and suggest directions for further investigation.

Figure 5.11

In document archeology, you start by collecting samples of all documents, reports, forms, files, and so on. Gather anything that is used to record or send information, including regular telephone calls. User manuals are rich sources of material— they describe a way to do work.

When doing document archeology, you search for capabilities from the current work that are needed for the new product. This does not mean you have carte blanche to replicate the old system. After all, you are gathering requirements because you plan to build a new product. However, an existing system will usually have some capabilities in common with its replacement.

But be warned: Because a document is output from a current computer or manual system, it does not mean that it is correct, nor does it mean that it is what is wanted by your client. Perhaps the document serves no useful purpose, or it needs heavy modification before it can be reused successfully.

We suggest that you incorporate document archeology into your data modeling approach, because most of the answers from the questions listed earlier are commonly used in the latter discipline. Of course, some document archeology is used as a foundation for object-oriented development. The current documents, if used cautiously, may reveal the classes of the data. They may also reveal the attributes of data stored by the system, and sometimes suggest operations that should be performed on the data.

As a rule, we always keep artifacts—documents, printouts, lists, manuals, screens, in fact anything that is printed or displayed—from our interviews because we often refer back to them. Make a habit of asking for a copy of any document or screen that is mentioned.

Some Other Requirements-Gathering Techniques

So far in this chapter, we have described a variety of requirements-discovery techniques that we have found useful and successful over the years. Other techniques are less well known, and many more are being developed. We do not want to make this chapter overly long, nor do we want to dump dozens of techniques on you. However, some of the other options contain ideas you might find interesting.

Family Therapy

Family therapists do not set out to make people *agree*. Instead, they aim to make it possible for people to hear and get an understanding of other individuals' positions, even if they do not agree with them. In other words, you should not expect every stakeholder to agree, but you should help them to accept that disagreements, conflicts, and the need for choices and compromises will always arise. Early in the project identify which mechanisms you will use to deal with these situations when they inevitably occur.

The field of family therapy is a rich source of ideas about how to work effectively with a diverse group of people—such as stakeholders in a requirements-trawling process. We use ideas from family therapy as a way of helping us to listen to stakeholders and of providing a feedback loop to help avoid misinterpretations.

Family therapists do not set out to make people agree. Instead, they aim to make it possible for people to hear and get an understanding of other individuals' positions.

READING

Satir, V., J. Banmen, J. Gerber, and M. Gomori. *The Satir Model, Family Therapy and Beyond.* Science and Behavior Books, 1991.

Soft Systems and Viewpoints

Peter Checkland developed a systems thinking approach called *soft systems*. It provides techniques for observing and modeling the world for the purpose of understanding and tackling real-world problems.

READING

Checkland, Peter, and Jim Scholes. *Soft Systems Methodology in Action.* John Wiley, 1999.

The systems thinker can look at an aspect of the world from a number of different viewpoints. When you use viewpoints, you have a better chance of discovering the requirements. Some viewpoints that are particularly useful are listed here:

- *How it is:* the view of the world you are trying to understand
- *What it is:* the view of the meaning or the essence behind how things are done
- *What it will be:* the view of how things will work in the future, or the product you plan to build

Determining What the Product Should Be

This section applies to all projects. Unfortunately, many projects start with a preconception of what the product should be without understanding the work that it is to become a part of. Here we look at things you can do to find the optimal product.

The unspoken, but nevertheless significant task of requirements analysis is to determine what the work should be in the future and how the product can best contribute to that work. The product is the part of the work you choose to change in some way—usually by automating it. The objective is to find the optimal business use case. As business use cases are usually responses to requests from the outside world for the work's service, the optimal response is to provide the most valuable service (from the customer's point of view) at the lowest cost in terms of time, materials, or effort (from your organization's point of view).

Your task is to find the best business use case—that is, to find the best way to achieve the desired outcome for the business use case. The best business use case is always the one closest to the essence of the work. Sometimes it incorporates some invention. Once you have achieved an intimate understanding of the work of the business use case, you decide how much of this work will be done by your product.

Let's look at an example of how we determine how much of the work is to become the product.

Consider the situation depicted in Figure 5.12. In this typical business use case, we see a customer (an adjacent system) ordering groceries over the telephone. Now, what is the best place to put the product boundary? Or, thinking of it another way, what makes the best product?

It is only by first understanding the work, and then automating part of it, that we achieve a seamless fit between our automated product and the work.

Figure 5.12

Once you understand
the complete business
use case, you establish
how much of it will be
done by the product.
The heavy dotted lines in
the figure represent
alternative product
boundaries. The
automation is to be
whatever is to the right
of the dotted line.

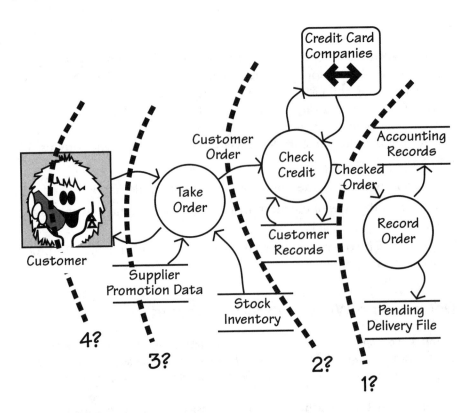

*Getting the right
product scope is
crucial to getting
the right
requirements.*

What about the product that would result from boundary number 1? An operator enters the checked order and the product records the order once the credit card company has authorized it. This approach does not yield a very good product, as it forces the operator to do most of the work.

What about boundary number 2? The user—in this case, the telephone representative—takes the order over the telephone and enters it into the product, which then does the credit card check and records the order. Not bad, but perhaps we could do better.

Boundary number 3 automates order taking. Customers make a telephone call to a product capable of voice recognition or recognizing commands from the telephone keypad. Provided there are no questions or serious responses needed, customers get the advantage of calling 24 hours a day. Alternatively, customers could log on to the grocery company's Web site and enter their own orders online.

Solution number 3 might be convenient for the grocery company, but what about the customer? What does she really want? What service should the grocery company provide to keep her loyalty?

The True Origin of the Business Event

In Chapter 4, when we discussed business events, we suggested you look for the real origin of the event. Almost certainly, the origin does not lie within the operator. The operator is, after all, part of the response to the business event. So the business event does not occur when the operator sits down at a computer to enter some data. Rather, it originates outside the work when the adjacent system does something. In the case illustrated in Figure 5.12, *the true origin of the business event is when the customer became short of groceries.* When the customer became aware of this problem, she probably went around the kitchen counting groceries and determining what she needed to order. Thus the origin of the business event occurred some 30 minutes before she picked up the phone.

From the customer's point of view, the most useful product would count the groceries for her. If the grocery company knew the quantities of grocery items the customer already had and knew her consumption rates, then the customer would not need to make the telephone call. Instead, the company could call the customer, inform her of what she needed, and arrange a suitable delivery time. This scenario extends the product scope until it gets into the brain of the adjacent system, and produces a better—from the service and convenience points of view—product.

> *We extend the product scope until it gets into the brain of the adjacent system.*

Examine your business events, particularly those that are initiated by humans. By this, we do not mean the human operator or user, but rather the human adjacent system. What is the adjacent system doing at the time of the event? Can you extend your product scope to include that activity, whatever it is? For an example of extending the product scope, consider the check-in procedure for passengers flying in Virgin Atlantic's Upper Class. Upper Class (Virgin's first class) passengers are given a limousine ride to the airport (a welcome piece of innovation). Instead of the limo driver dumping the passengers at the terminal and letting them lug their bags to the check-in desk, passengers check in while they are still in the car. The driver phones ahead to the drive-through check-ins that Virgin has installed at some airports and gives the number of bags to be checked. When the car arrives at the drive-through check-in, passengers are handed boarding passes and baggage-claim checks, and then taken to the terminal. All that remains is to walk to the Upper Class Lounge. From this example, we learn that Virgin Atlantic considers the business use case to be triggered when passengers leave home, not when they reach the check-in desk.

> *Find the true origin of the business use case.*

Think about your own business use cases. Do they really begin at the boundary of your work, or do they start well before they reach your organization?

Does Technology Matter?

Technology is important to our study only when it is outside the scope of our work. That is, the technology used by the adjacent systems matters, because it affects the way they communicate with our work. For example, if the adjacent system is a human, then the work must communicate in a human-understandable manner. Achieving this feat might require processing to turn automated data into human-readable form. Likewise, if the adjacent system is automated, there might be requirements to make translations or conversions of the information going to or from that adjacent system.

Imagine that no technology exists inside your work.

But that is a consideration for the technology of the adjacent systems only. The technology used *inside* the work is irrelevant for gathering the requirements. If you are going to gather accurate requirements, you must disregard any technology that currently exists and suppress any thought that you may have about future technology. Here "technology" means humans, paper, and low-tech devices. Imagine for the moment that no technology exists inside your work.

The rationale underlying this approach is simple. Any kind of work contains technology—machines, computers, people, paper, and so on—and procedures. Often the procedures have been set up with a particular technology in mind. If the technology changes, then the procedure is no longer relevant. The implication is that any requirement you gather must not be a technological requirement, but rather a requirement for the work itself. Sometimes this target is easier to think of as "business requirements."

You, or your designer, will employ technology to implement the product. But that technology is the result of the requirements you gather. Even though you have drawn a product boundary, you still have not selected any specific technology. You, as the requirements analyst, are saying, "Here is the amount of work we choose to automate—we call that the product. Here are the requirements for the product. Now select the most appropriate technology for those requirements, both functional and nonfunctional."

To summarize the story so far: You study the work, determine the best product for that work, and then write the requirements for the product without presupposing any technology.

Choosing the Best Trawling Technique

We continue to be more and more ambitious in terms of the size, complexity, fragmentation, and level of human involvement in the products that we build. In similar fashion, the trawling techniques we use continue to develop so that they keep pace with our ambition. With this explosion in the number of techniques available comes a question: Which technique is the best choice in which set of circumstances? There is no simple answer to this question because the choice of technique is driven by the characteristics of the knowledge source, and in most cases that means the characteristics of individual people. As a consequence, a competent requirements analyst needs to be able to use different techniques, and sometimes use techniques in combination.

A lot of this knowledge can come only with experience. Nevertheless, Table 5.1 shows the relative strengths of different trawling techniques.

TRAWLING TECHNIQUES	STRENGTHS	RABBIT	HORSE	ELEPHANT
Business events	Partitions the work according to external demands	★★★	★★★	★★★
Current situation modeling	Examines the legacy system for reusable requirements	★	★★	★★★
Apprenticing	Spends time working with an expert	★	★★★	★★★
Structures and patterns	Identifies reusable requirements	★	★★	★★
Interviewing	Can focus on detailed issues	★★★	★★★	★★★
Essence	Finds the real problem	★★★	★★★	★★★
Business use case workshops	Focuses the relevant stakeholders on the best response to the business event	★★	★★★	★★★
Creativity workshops	Brings the team together to discover innovative requirements	★★★	★★★	★★
Brainstorming	Facilitates creativity and invention	★★★	★★★	★★★
Personas	Uses a composite virtual character to represent the user/customer	★	★★	★★★
Mind mapping	An effective planning/note-taking technique	★★★	★★★	★★★
Wikis	Uses online forums to allow all stakeholders to contribute	★★	★★★	★★★
Scenarios (Chapter 6)	Shows the functionality of a use case	★★★	★★★	★★★
Low-fidelity prototypes (Chapter 12)	Discovers undreamed-of requirements	★★★	★★★	★★
High-fidelity prototypes (Chapter 12)	Discovers usability requirements	★★★	★★	★★
Document archeology	Uses evidence from existing documents and files	★	★★	★★★

Table 5.1

The Relative Usefulness of Trawling Techniques for Rabbit, Horse, and Elephant Projects

Table 5.1 indicates the relative usefulness of techniques depending on your agility ambitions. However, other factors can come into play. The availability of stakeholders to participate in the requirements process is a significant factor in determining how you set about gathering requirements. When stakeholders cannot (or will not) make themselves available, getting their input using a wiki is probably the best technique to use. If that does not work out, then using a persona is the best approach. By contrast, if your stakeholders are willing to participate, business use case workshops and apprenticing are effective.

We also refer you to the owls in the margins, which indicate when particular techniques are most effective.

Lastly, use techniques you and your stakeholders are comfortable with. It is a good idea to invest some time in learning new techniques because they encourage you to question the way that you do things and make you more aware of the sociotechnical nature of requirements work. The best results come when you and the people you are dealing with feel at ease with the way you are gathering requirements. If a technique is not working for you, then try a different one.

Summary

You have two ears and one mouth. I suggest that you use them in that proportion.

Source: G. K. Chesterton

Trawling is concerned with eliciting and discovering requirements. The techniques presented in this chapter are tools intended to help you do something very difficult—extract precise information from another human. And this is the crux of the matter—you have to do this work yourself. No tool has yet been invented that can do it for you.

Of course, we have not covered the most critical tools—the ones attached to either side of your head. *Listening* is the most important technique in requirements gathering. If you can listen to what your client, your user, and your other stakeholders are saying, and if you can understand what they mean, then the tools described in this chapter will be useful. If you do not listen, then you are highly unlikely to discover the product that the user really wants.

The trawling techniques are communication tools. They will help you open a dialog with your stakeholders and provide the feedback that is so essential to good communication. Use them well and watch your requirements come to life.

Scenarios and Requirements

6

in which we look at scenarios as
a way of helping the stakeholders
to discover their requirements

By now you have reached the stage in the requirements process where you have identified the business events, and thereby the business use cases. In Chapter 5, we looked at trawling for the requirements using a variety of techniques. In this chapter, we examine the use of scenarios as a way of discovering and recording business and requirements knowledge. We have found scenarios to be effective, largely because of their ready acceptance by nontechnical stakeholders.

Agility Guide

Let us assume here that your aspirations toward agility have not led you into the treacherous tar pit of hacking with no prior thought for the real requirements, but are (correctly) causing you to question your processes and abandon any that are not giving you the maximum return for effort expended. In this light, we suggest that scenarios give you a handsome return on the effort invested.

Rabbit projects—the most agile ones—use scenarios as a trawling technique to discover their stakeholders' optimal way of working. The requirements analysts and the appropriate stakeholders come together to build a scenario for one business use case at a time. Scenarios are often a faster means to find the normal case and the exceptions and alternatives cases. That is, it is faster to find the required functionality by working with scenarios than it is by coding prototypes. The rabbit scenarios disregard the nonfunctional requirements—these can be discovered later by coding prototypes.

Horse projects *might* consider scenarios as an alternative to writing functional requirements. Certainly they are useful for eliciting requirements. Also, when they have been developed enough, they can serve to inform the developers of the functional needs of the product. However, this approach does not work all the time. If you have complex products, or if you need the functional requirements documented for contractual purposes, then the scenarios are not themselves sufficient.

Elephant projects make use of scenarios as a discovery tool. The meetings with the stakeholders are used to go over the desired way of working for each of the business use cases. When the scenario is complete—that is, when the exceptions and alternatives have been discovered and/or decided—it is used as the basis for writing the functional requirements. Elephant projects should keep their scenarios as part of the documentation. Usually the developers want to see them when they start programming.

Scenarios

The scenario tells the story of a business use case.

READING

For information on many other ways to use scenarios, see Alexander, Ian, and Neil Maiden. *Scenarios, Stories, Use Cases Through the Systems Development Life-Cycle.* John Wiley & Sons, 2004.

❝ *A formal language for talking about work organizes concepts that help people learn to see work.* ❞

Source: Beyer and Holtzblatt, *Contextual Design*

Write your scenarios using between three and ten steps.

Simply put, a *scenario* is a story, albeit one told in a particular format. The term "scenario" is generally used to mean a sketch of the plot of a movie or play, or an outline of a situation. In requirements work, we use this term to mean the plot of a section of the work we are studying. The use of "plot" is intended to imply that we break the work into a series of steps or scenes. By explaining these steps, we explain the work.

We have devoted an entire chapter to business events and business use cases (Chapter 4), so naturally we will make more use of them. From here on, we are talking about using scenarios to tell the story of a business use case.

This makes a certain amount of sense: The business use case is a discrete amount of functionality, it happens in its own continuous time frame, and it can be considered separately from other parts of the work's functionality. For these reasons the business use case is an ideal container for a story.

Business analysts use scenarios to describe a business use case to the interested stakeholders. The scenario is a neutral medium, understandable to all, and the business analyst uses it to elicit agreement on what the work has to do. Once consensus is achieved, the stakeholders can decide how much of that work will be done by the product. An additional scenario describing the user's or actor's interaction with the product might then be produced.

Suppose you have identified a business use case you wish to explore. Good practice indicates that you now identify the interested stakeholders—those with knowledge or expertise in this part of the work. You use the scenario to portray the functionality of the business use case by breaking it down to a series of steps. We suggest that you aim for between three and ten steps.

There is nothing fixed about the range of three to ten steps, and nothing untoward will happen to you if you use more steps than ten. However, if you end up with 126 steps, either you have a gigantic business use case (impossible for normal commercial work) or you are writing your scenario with an unnecessarily meticulous level of granularity. The aim is to keep the scenario simple enough to be readily understandable, and three to ten steps is a guideline for achieving this goal.

Although a formalized template for a scenario exists, your first draft can be simple and informal. As an example, let's leave our IceBreaker case study for the moment and look at something that you are most likely familiar with: a business use case for checking a passenger in for an international flight (see Figure 6.1). Here's Sherri, one of the check-in agents:

"I call the next customer in line. When he gets to my desk, I ask for a ticket. If the passenger is using an e-ticket, I need the booking record locator. Most of the passengers are not organized enough to have it written down, so I ask them their name and the flight they are on. Most people don't know the flight number, so I usually ask for their destination. They must know that!

"I make sure I have the right passenger and the right flight. It would be pretty embarrassing to give away someone else's seat or to send a passenger to the wrong destination. Anyway, somehow I locate the passenger's flight record in the computer. If he has not already given it to me, I ask for the passenger's passport. I check that the picture looks like the passenger and that the passport is still valid.

"If there is no frequent-flyer number showing against the booking, I ask the passenger if he belongs to our mileage scheme. Either he hands me the plastic card with the FF number, or I ask him and if he wishes to join I give him the sign-up form. We can put temporary FF numbers against the flight record so the passenger is credited for that trip.

Figure 6.1

An airline check-in for an international flight. As we go through the scenario for this case, see if it matches your experience of checking in for a flight.

"If the computer has not already assigned a seat, I find one. This usually means I ask if the passenger prefers a window or an aisle seat, or, if the plane is already almost full, I tell him what I have available. Of course, if the computer has assigned one, I always ask if it is okay. Somehow we settle on a seat and I confirm it with the computer system. I can print the boarding pass at this stage, but I usually do the bags first.

"I ask how many bags the passenger is checking and, at the same time, verify that he is not exceeding the carry-on limit. Some people are unbelievable with what they want to carry into a fairly space-restricted aircraft cabin. I ask the security questions about the bags and get the passenger's responses. I print out the bag tags and securely attach them to the bags, and then I send the bags on their way down the conveyor belt.

"Next I print the boarding pass. This means that I have everything done as far as the computer is concerned. But there is one more thing to do: I have to make sure that everything agrees with the passenger's understanding. I read out from the boarding pass where he is going, what time the flight is, and what time it will board. I also read out how many bags have been checked and confirm that their destination matches the passenger's destination. I hand over the documents, and wish the passenger a good flight."

Now sketch out the scenario. Break the story down to the steps that you consider to be the best ones to capture the normal path through the story. There are no hard and fast rules about how you accomplish this—just write whatever seems logical to you. After all, you are going to use the scenario; it might as well fit with your view of the work. It will be adjusted by subsequent activities. Suppose that this is your first draft:

1. Get the passenger's ticket or record locator.
2. Is this the right passenger, flight, and destination?
3. Check the passport is valid and belongs to the passenger.
4. Record the frequent-flyer number.
5. Find a seat.
6. Ask security questions.
7. Check the baggage onto the flight.
8. Print and hand over the boarding pass and bag tags.
9. "Have a nice flight."

Stakeholders are invited to participate and revise the scenario until it represents a consensus view of what the work should be.

Confirm this scenario with the interested stakeholders. It is in plain English—that is intentional—so all stakeholders can be invited to participate and revise this scenario until it represents a consensus view of what the work should be. Once a consensus is reached on the work, start to formalize the scenario. Along the way, you will learn more about the work.

The first part of the formalized scenario identifies it and gives it a meaningful name.

Business Use Case Name: Check passenger onto flight.

Next, you add the start-up mechanism, or trigger, for the business use case. It usually consists of some data or request (often both) arriving from outside your work area. There are also time-triggered business use cases. In this situation, you state the time condition—an hour or a date is reached, an amount of time has passed since another business use case, and so on—that initiates the use case.

Trigger: Passenger's ticket, record locator, or identity and flight.

This is not a perfect situation from the point of view of the work providing a better service. As you are looking at the work, you should be asking whether the business use case could start before the passenger makes it to the desk. For example, could he check in at home, or on the way to the airport, or while standing in line? All of these options are technologically possible and probably offer some business advantage. For the moment, we leave this question as an open issue.

Now you add any preconditions that must exist when the business use case is triggered. Preconditions indicate the state of the work at initiation. Usually this means certain other business events must have occurred before this business use case makes any sense.

Preconditions: The passenger must have a reservation.

The check-in desk is not the place to be if you do not already have a reservation. While it may seem like good service to allow passengers to make a reservation at the check-in desk, the amount of time needed for this transaction would no doubt annoy the rest of the passengers standing in line.

You might consider adding the interested stakeholders to the scenario. These people have an interest in the outcome of the business use case. That is, they will be affected by the manner in which the work is done and what data is produced by it.

Interested Stakeholders: Check-in agent, marketing, baggage handling, reservations, flight manifest system, work flow, security, destination country's immigration.

There are probably more stakeholders, but this list is adequate to show that you are not concerned only with the immediate problem, but recognize that whatever you do here has ramifications on a wider scale.

Active stakeholders are the people or systems that do the work of the business use case. Usually, one active stakeholder triggers the business use case, and then one or more others participate in the work.

Active Stakeholders: Passenger (trigger), check-in agent.

The passenger triggers the business use case by arriving at the check-in desk. He is also the recipient of the business use case's output. The passenger works with the agent to carry out the work of the business use case. Although the agent manipulates any automated product being used, that should be thought of only as the current implementation and has no binding ramifications. The essential business is triggered by the passenger, who, in some future incarnation, might be more closely involved. Self check-in springs to mind here, but (once we have fully understood the work) we should also think of checking in by telephone while on the way to the airport, checking in at the club lounge, using the record locator sent to the passenger's mobile phone by the airline, or any of dozens of possibilities.

Normal Case Scenarios

Now go back over your sketch for the scenario, looking for unanswered questions and ways to improve this work. Change the language to be technologically neutral, which should help you to see any potential opportunities for an improved automated product.

Assume for the normal case that everything works perfectly.

It helps you to consider the details if you deal with the normal case first. Assume for this case that everything works perfectly. Once you have defined the normal case, you can go back over it and add in the alternatives and exceptions.

1. Get the passenger's ticket, record locator, or identity and flight number.

The ticket and the record locator are both constraints on the work. The ticket comes from outside. That is, the passenger has been carrying it up to this point. The record locator is a constraint imposed by the current computer system; in this case, it cannot be changed. However, the ticket and the record locator are merely means to an end—the real work to be done is to find the passenger's reservation. Let's rewrite step 1 to reflect this understanding:

1. Locate the passenger's reservation.

This step could be completed without either a ticket or a record locator. Writing it this way opens up several possibilities for the new product. Perhaps passengers could swipe a machine-readable passport, use a credit card, or use any of several other ways to identify themselves. It remains to be seen if the constraints can be overcome.

Once identified, the work then connects the passenger to his reservation:

2. Is this the right passenger, flight, and destination?

This step focuses on ensuring that the passenger is who he says he is, and that the reservation matches his expectations for the flight. Let's rewrite step 2 accordingly:

2. Ensure the passenger is correctly identified and connected to the right reservation.

Next the scenario checks the passport:

3. Check the passport is valid and belongs to the passenger.

This step is slightly more complex and warrants a few words of explanation. We suggest adding the explanation to the step:

3. Check the passport is valid and belongs to the passenger.
    3.1   The passport must be current.
    3.2   The passport must not expire before the end of the complete trip.
    3.3   The passport must be valid for travel to the destination country.
    3.4   Visas (where needed) must be current.
    3.5   There must be no "refused entry" stamps from the destination country.

Alternatively, you might simply leave this as it was and refer to notes to complete the business rules for the step:

3. Check the passport is valid and belongs to the passenger.
    See procedure guidelines EU-175.

The same technique might be employed for later steps in the scenario. Keep working through it until you and your interested stakeholders agree that it is an accurate, but not yet detailed, portrayal of the work.

Business Event: Passenger decides to check in.

Business Use Case Name and Number: Check passenger onto flight.

Trigger: Passenger's ticket, record locator, or identity and flight.

Preconditions: The passenger must have a reservation.

Interested Stakeholders: Check-in agent, marketing, baggage handling, reservations, flight manifest system, work flow, security, destination country's immigration.

Active Stakeholders: Passenger (trigger), check-in agent.

1. Locate the passenger's reservation.
2. Ensure the correct passenger is connected to the reservation.
3. Check the passport is valid and belongs to the passenger.
   See procedure guidelines EU-175.
4. Attach passenger's frequent-flyer number to the reservation.
5. Allocate a seat.
6. Get correct responses to the security questions.
7. Check the baggage onto the flight.
8. Create and convey to the passenger the boarding pass and bag tags.
9. Wish the passenger a pleasant flight.

Outcome: The passenger is recorded as checked onto the flight, the bags are assigned to the flight, a seat is allocated, and the passenger is in possession of a boarding pass and bag claim stubs.

We add an outcome to the scenario—that is, the desired situation at the successful conclusion of the business use case. Think of it as the stakeholder's objectives at the time when he triggers the use case.

Diagramming the Scenario

Some requirements analysts—and some stakeholders—believe that it is more appropriate to use a diagram to explain the functionality of a business use case. This preference is a matter of personal choice, and it depends largely on whether your audience responds more favorably to either text or diagrammatic scenarios. We leave it to you to experiment and decide which method is right for you.

Several diagrams can be used for scenarios. The UML activity diagram seems to be a particularly popular choice. Figure 6.2 shows the airline check-in example in this form.

In Figure 6.2, note the "swim lanes" that divide the work between the participants. Swim lanes are optional, and they are both good and bad: good because they provide a clear explanation of who is doing what; bad because they tread the dangerous path of inviting readers to believe that they define the way the work must be implemented in the future. Be aware that diagrams like Figure 6.2 are used as explanations. Only after the systems architects and designers have done their work can the swim lanes be taken to mean a specification.

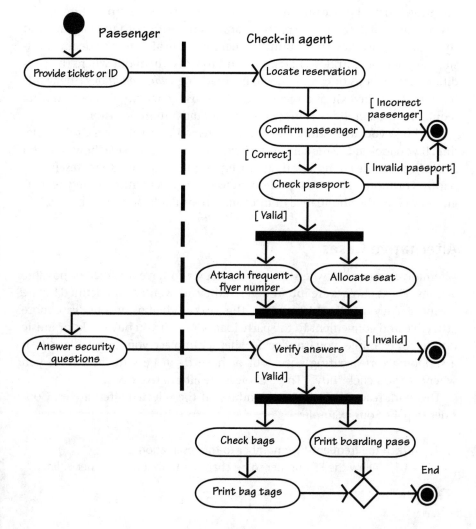

Figure 6.2

An activity diagram showing the passenger checking in for a flight.

The activity diagram shows a certain amount of parallel processing. For example, there is no reason why the "Attach frequent-flyer number" and "Allocate seat" activities cannot be performed in parallel. The text scenario does not show this possibility. However, if you want to point out the parallel nature of these two activities, you could amend the scenario as follows:

The following two things can be done in any order:

4. Attach the frequent-flyer number to the reservation.
5. Allocate a seat.

The activity diagram also shows other control aspects. For example, the diamond at the bottom of the model in Figure 6.2 is called a *merge*. This symbol means that all processing must reach this point before proceeding. In the case of Figure 6.2, the whole process cannot end until both the bag tags and the boarding pass have been printed. Diamonds are also used to denote decisions as they were in flowcharts. We tend to leave them out where the conditions are obvious or can be shown by attaching *guard conditions* (the words in brackets at the exit of an activity). When using activity diagrams during requirements, simplicity is more useful than maximum precision.

The book you are reading makes no claims to be a treatise on UML modeling. If you look at the model and the text scenario side by side, however, you should get the idea of how you can use either models or text to represent scenarios. For more on UML, we refer you to the books mentioned in the margin, as well as the abundance of information available on the Web.

READING

Ambler, Scott. *The Elements of UML 2.0 Style.* Cambridge University Press, 2005.

Fowler, Martin. *UML Distilled: A Brief Guide to the Standard Object Modeling Language* (third edition). Addison-Wesley, 2003.

Pilone, Dan, and Neil Pitman. *UML 2.0 in a Nutshell.* O'Reilly, 2005.

Alternative Cases

Alternative cases arise when there is an intentional choice of user actions.

Alternative cases arise when you wish the user to have a choice of possible actions. These choices are intentional, as they are wanted and defined by the business. They usually exist to make the work of the business use case more attractive and convenient to the participants. When you buy books or music online, for example, you can decide whether to place your selected goods in a shopping cart awaiting check-out or have them be sent directly to you whenever you click "buy." These choices are alternative cases.

The work reacts differently depending on the selected alternatives. Consider step 4 of our example:

4. Attach the frequent-flyer number to the reservation.
    A4.1 Allow the FF number to be changed to that of a partner airline.

You find alternatives by examining each step of the normal case. Look for instances where the step may be carried out differently or the actor can be given a choice. These choices are sometimes interesting from the point of view of improving the work or providing a better service.

4. Attach the frequent-flyer number to the reservation.
    A4.1 Allow the FF number to be changed to that of a partner airline.
    A4.2 Allow the FF number to be changed to that of a family member, or the mileage of the flight to be donated to a charity of the passenger's choice.

Exception Cases

Exceptions are unwanted but acceptable deviations from the normal case. They are unwanted in the sense that the owner of the work would rather that they did not ever happen. However, we know that they will happen on occasion, so we have to cater for them. For example, an end user could enter the wrong data, the passenger might not know the locator number, or the online customer might forget his password.

Exceptions are unwanted but acceptable deviations from the normal case.

The goal of the exception scenario is to show how the work safely handles the exception. In other words, which steps have to be taken to rejoin the path of the normal case? You can write a separate scenario, but in most cases it is more convenient to add the exception steps to your normal scenario.

Consider step 5 as an example:

5. Find a seat.
    E5.1 The passenger's choice of seat is not available.
    E5.1 Record a request for a seat change by the gate agent.

You find the exceptions by examining each step of the normal case and asking questions such as these:

● What happens if this step cannot be completed, or does not complete, or comes up with the wrong or unacceptable result?
● What can go wrong at this step?
● What could happen to prevent the work from reaching this step?
● Could any external entity disrupt or prevent this step, or this business use case?
● Could any technology used to implement this step fail, or be unavailable?
● Could the end user fail to understand what is required of him, or misunderstand the information presented by the product?

- Could the end user take the wrong action—intentionally or unintentionally—or fail to respond?

There are many questions, each of which seeks to find a different potential error. We suggest you make a checklist of the questions pertinent to your particular situation, adding to it each time a new project discovers new questions. We have also seen some successful attempts to use automation to help with this task. Our colleague Neil Maiden at City University in London is having success using the university's ART-SCENE scenario presenter. This tool works with the normal case scenario to automatically generate a list of potential exceptions. It also uses rich-media scenarios where additional information in the form of photographs, movies, sound, and so on is integrated into the scenario.

READING

Details of ART-SCENE can be found at hcid.soi.city.ac.uk/research/ Artsceneindex.html.

The exception questions are intended to prompt the interested stakeholders to discover all the exceptions. Question each step carefully. We know from experience that the exceptions have the potential to necessitate a great amount of remedial rework if they are not found at requirements time. Look for anything that could go wrong. You can ignore the scenario in which the work is struck by a meteor, but almost anything else is possible.

What If? Scenarios

What if? scenarios allow you to explore possibilities.

What if? scenarios allow you to explore possibilities and question the business rules. You ask, "What if we did this?" or "What if we didn't do that?" It becomes easier to find the many possibilities if you think about the constraints. Ask what would happen if the constraint did not exist. As an example, suppose that while going over the scenarios for the flight check-in case, you asked, "What if we took away the constraint of the check-in desk?

This freedom gives rise to all sorts of possibilities. Suppose you wrote your what if? scenario like this:

1. The passenger calls the airline while en route to the airport.
2. Text the passenger and ask if he wants to check in.
3. If yes, get the record locator from the passenger's phone (this was sent at the time of the reservation).
4. Check the passenger onto the flight, and text the seat allocation and passcode (the passenger's phone will be scanned at gates to allow the passenger to move through the airport).
5. Text bag checks (these will activate the automated bag tag printers at curbside).
6. Wish the passenger a pleasant flight.

What if? scenarios are intended to stimulate creativity and guide your stakeholders to come up with more innovative products. However, you must strike a balance between spending too much time and too little looking for innovative solutions.

Misuse Cases and Negative Scenarios

Misuse cases show negative or harmful possibilities, such as someone abusing the work or attempting to defraud it. Examples include users deliberately entering incorrect data, customers using stolen credit cards, and pranksters making fictitious calls or transactions, planting a virus or time bomb, or engaging in any of the myriad other things that can be done to harm the work.

It may be helpful here to think in terms drawn from fiction writing—the protagonist and the antagonist. The protagonist is the hero or main character of the story: the good guy. Think of the protagonist as the normal actor using the product following your normal use case scenario. Winnie the Pooh is the ideal protagonist—he is well intentioned and you want him to win out in the end. But like Pooh, the protagonist might be a klutz and make an unintentional mistake, forget his password, choose the wrong option, get honey on the keys, or any of the many things klutzes can do.

Cast your protagonist as someone who is forgetful, slow, distracted, and not paying attention. (You are bound to know someone like that.) Go through the normal case scenario, and for each step, ask what can be done wrongly. It may be simpler to write a new scenario for each misuse, as the ramifications of a misstep may be complex enough to warrant its own separate story.

So much for the protagonist. The antagonist is the person who opposes the work, seeks to harm it, or wants to defraud it: the bad guy. You have to examine all the steps for the normal case and ask if there is a possibility of someone opposing or misusing that action. In this case, the ramifications upon discovering an antagonist's misuse may be to simply stop the business use case. For example:

> *What if? scenarios are intended to stimulate creativity and guide your stakeholders to come up with more innovative products.*

> " *Maybe 'abuse cases' will always sound jokey, but the idea of the Negative Scenario (e.g., Burglar impersonates householder, Alarm Call Center Operator colludes with Burglar, etc.) is important.* "
>
> Source: Ian Alexander

> *Examine all the steps for the normal case and ask if there is a possibility of someone opposing or misusing that action.*

3. Check the passport is valid and belongs to the passenger.
   M3.1 The passenger produces a passport that is not his.
   M3.2 Call security.
   M3.3 Freeze the reservation.

Whether you annotate the normal case with the misuse steps or write a separate misuse scenario depends on the complexity of the situation and the comfort level of the stakeholders.

Some professions have always made use of what if? scenarios. For instance, chess players routinely think, "What would Black do if I moved my knight to e4?", leading to the minimize–maximize algorithms for game-play. Our governments routinely generate what if? scenarios to plan foreign policy: "What if Lichtenstein invades San Remo?" "What if Switzerland elects a communist government?" "What if Canada closes the St. Lawrence Seaway?" While these examples are obviously fanciful, most governments generate thousands of likely and unlikely scenarios to explore their reactions to possible future events.

When gathering requirements, try generating several what if? scenarios to experiment with the unforeseen. The intention is to turn the unforeseen into the foreseen. After all, the more you know about eventualities before you build the product, the more robust and long-lasting it will be.

Scenario Template

You may, of course, write your business use case scenarios in whatever form you and your stakeholders prefer. The template presented in this section is one we have found useful on many assignments. We suggest it as a fairly good compromise between informality and an overly bureaucratic approach.

Business Event Name: The name of the business event to which the business use case responds.

Business Use Case Name and Number: Give each business use case a unique identifier and a name that communicates the functionality—for example, Record Library Loan, Register New Student Enrollment, Make Benefit Payment, Produce Sales Report. Ideally, the name should be an active verb plus a specific direct object.

Trigger: The data or request for a service that arrives from an external source and triggers a response from the work. The trigger may be the arrival of data from one of the adjacent systems—that is, from outside of the work area that you are studying. Alternatively, the trigger may be the arrival of the temporal condition that causes the use case to activate—for example, the end of the month.

Preconditions: Sometimes certain conditions must exist before the use case is valid. For example, a customer has to be registered before he can access his frequent-flyer statement. Note that another business use case usually takes care of the precondition. In the preceding example, the customer would have registered using the Register Passenger business use case.

Interested Stakeholders: The people, organizations, and/or representatives of computer systems who have knowledge necessary to specify this use case or who have an interest in this use case.

Active Stakeholders: The people, organizations, and/or computer systems that are doing the work of this use case. Don't think about users just yet; instead, think of the real people who are involved in the work of the business use case.

Normal Case Steps: The steps that this use case goes through to complete the normal course of its work. Write the steps as clear, natural-language statements that are understandable to business people related to the project. There are usually between three and ten steps.

Step 1 . . .
Step 2 . . .
Step 3 . . .

Note that a business use case can make use of the services or functionality of another business use case as part of its own processing. However, be careful not to start programming at this stage.

Alternatives: Alternatives are acceptable variations on the normal case of processing. For example, gold cardholders may be given an invitation to the lounge when they check in. Tell the story in the same way:

Alternative step 1 . . .
Alternative step 2 . . .
Alternative step 3 . . .

If the alternative action is simple, you can make it part of the normal case: Step 4. Attach the frequent-flyer number to the reservation.

Alternative 4.1 Issue a lounge invitation if the passenger holds a gold card.

Exceptions: These are unwanted but necessary variations. For example, a customer may have insufficient funds for a withdrawal at an ATM. In this case, the procedure has to offer a lower amount, or offer a loan, or do whatever the stakeholders decide is appropriate. Tag each exception to the appropriate step:

Exception 2.1 . . .
Exception 2.2 . . .
Exception 2.3 . . .

Outcome: The desired situation at the end of this use case. Think of it as the stakeholder's objective at the time when he triggers the use case. For example, the money has been dispensed and taken from the ATM, the customer's account has been debited, and the card has been extracted from the ATM.

Product Use Case Scenarios

The product use case sets out the functionality of the product.

In this chapter, we have discussed writing scenarios for business use cases as a way of understanding, verifying, and questioning the business rules. In Chapter 4, Event-Driven Use Cases, and Chapter 5, Trawling for Requirements, we discussed techniques for deriving the product use cases from the business use cases. In other words, at some stage, you reach a point where you understand enough about the work and its constraints to be able to decide which parts of the work will be carried out by the product. At that point you can write a *product use case scenario*. Recall that the product use case is that part of the business use case for which you decide to build a product.

Chapter 4, Event-Driven Use Cases, and Chapter 5, Trawling for Requirements, contain techniques for identifying the product use case boundary.

What does a product use case scenario look like? Not surprisingly, you can use the same form as you do for a business use case. The difference is that the business use case contains all of the business rules that respond to a business event, whereas the corresponding product use case contains only those business rules to be implemented in the product. Figure 6.3 is a reminder of the connection between the business use case and the product use case. Let's take a look at how we got to the product use case so that we can point the way from there to the atomic requirements.

Determine how much of the business use case is to be implemented as the product. The result is the product use case, which you can describe using a product use case scenario.

To begin, first identify a business event. Then trawl to discover the response to that event—that is, the business use case. You can assess whether you have done sufficient trawling by attempting to write a business use case scenario. As discussed earlier in this chapter, writing the business use case scenario raises many business questions and leads you to formalize the business rules for that business use case. Once you are confident you know enough about the business use case, your next task is to determine how much of the business use case will be implemented as the product. The result

Figure 6.3

This functional model depicts the processes that respond to a business event. The business use case scenario shows the processing steps that respond to the business event. The product use case scenario shows the steps that will be part of the product.

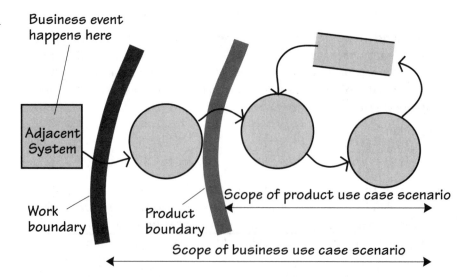

of this determination is the product use case. Naturally, we suggest you describe it using a product use case scenario.

Earlier in this chapter we introduced this business use case scenario:

Business Event Name: Passenger decides to check in.

Business Use Case Name: Check passenger onto flight.

Trigger: Ticket, record locator, or identity and flight.

Preconditions: The passenger must have a reservation.

Interested Stakeholders: Check-in agent, marketing, baggage handling, reservations, flight manifest system, work flow, security, destination country's immigration.

Active Stakeholders: Passenger (trigger), check-in agent.

1. Locate the passenger's reservation.
2. Ensure the passenger is correctly identified and connected to the right reservation.
3. Check the passport is valid and belongs to the passenger. See procedure guidelines EU-175.
4. Attach the frequent-flyer number to the reservation.
5. Allocate a seat.
6. Get correct responses to security questions.
7. Check the baggage onto the flight.
8. Print and convey to the passenger the boarding pass and bag tags.
9. Wish the passenger a pleasant flight.

Outcome: The passenger is recorded as checked onto the flight, the bags are assigned to the flight, a seat is allocated, and the passenger is in possession of a boarding pass and bag claim stubs.

To make decisions about the product boundary for this business use case, we need to define the constraints. We also need input from the stakeholders who understand the technical and business implications and the possibilities for the product boundary along with the business goals for the project.

Let's suppose that you have that information. That is, you and the stakeholders have decided what product to build. The product use case scenario shows what the product is to do:

Product Use Case Name: Check passenger onto flight.

Trigger: Passenger's name + passenger's passport number.

Preconditions: The passenger must have a reservation.

Interested Stakeholders: Check-in agent, marketing, baggage handling, reservations, flight manifest system, work flow, security, destination country's immigration.

Actor: Check-in agent.

1. Locate the passenger's reservation.
4. Attach the frequent-flyer number to the reservation.
5. Allocate a seat.
7. Check the baggage onto the flight.
8. Print the boarding pass and bag tags.

Outcome: The passenger is recorded as checked onto the flight, the bags are assigned to the flight, a seat is allocated, and the passenger's boarding pass and bag claim stubs are printed.

Note the differences between the business use case scenario and its corresponding product use case scenario. For example, the appropriate stakeholders decided that ensuring the correct passenger is attached to the reservation (step 2) is outside the scope of the product. Thus step 2 does not show up on the product use case scenario. Similarly, steps 3 and 6 are defined as being outside the product scope, so they are also omitted from the product use case scenario. (We have retained the same step numbers so that you can compare the business use case and the product use case. In practice, you would renumber the steps of the product use case so they consecutive.)

Note also that, instead of a list of active stakeholders, we identified the check-in agent as an actor. An actor is a person or system that has a direct interface with the product. In other words, the check-in agent will be the hands-on user for this product use case.

Bear in mind that our example product use case scenario reflects a particular set of decisions about the product scope. If the stakeholders had decided on a different product, then naturally the product use case scenario would be different.

As you will see in the next chapters, the product use case is the basis for writing the functional and nonfunctional requirements.

Summary

A scenario is a tool for telling a story. We have discussed how to write scenarios for both the story of the business use case and the story of the product use case.

The business use case scenario is intended to help you and your stakeholders come to a coherent understanding of the business rules that apply to a specific business event. Writing the scenario tests whether sufficient trawling has been done, and whether the requirements analyst needs to ask more questions and investigate further.

The product use case scenario specifies the boundary or scope of the product for a specific business use case. Constraints, goals, and technical and business guidance are necessary input for defining the product use case boundary.

You can use a very similar form of scenario for the business use case and the product use case, providing (for the purposes of communication and traceability) you make it clear which one is which.

Functional Requirements

*in which we look at those requirements that
cause the product to do something*

The functional requirements specify what the product must do. They describe the actions the product must carry out to satisfy the fundamental reasons for its existence. For example, the functional requirement

> *The product shall predict which road sections will freeze within the selected time parameters.*

describes an action the product must take if it is to carry out the work for which it is intended. The intention is to understand the functional requirements and so convey to the developers what the product is required to do for its intended operator.

In Chapter 5, we described how to gather the requirements. In Chapter 6, we described how the requirements analyst uses business use case scenarios to illustrate the functionality for the interested stakeholders, and product use case scenarios to define ideas for the product boundary. When the scenarios have been agreed upon, the requirements analyst writes the functional requirements for the product use cases. This process is illustrated in Figure 7.1.

Chapter 5, Trawling for Requirements, describes how to gather requirements. Chapter 6, Scenarios and Requirements, explores how to use scenarios to describe business use cases and product use cases.

Agility Guide

To get the most out of this chapter, it is necessary to understand the difference between a requirement and a solution. It is also necessary to understand that while we are describing how to write requirements, the most important thing is to understand and communicate them in the way that works for your project.

Rabbit projects have short durations between releases, and as much as possible, they avoid writing the requirements before starting to build a product to meet them. The advice in this chapter that applies to rabbit projects is simple: Rushing to a solution before understanding the requirement—note that we did not say "writing the requirement"—generally wastes time. Without knowing the underlying reason for the solution (in other words, the essential requirement), the solution is likely to solve the wrong problem. But, armed with an understanding of the requirements, rabbit projects for the most part bypass writing the atomic requirements and use their scenarios to communicate the functional requirements.

Horse projects usually have a need to write their requirements. Compared to rabbits, horses have longer release cycles and geographically scattered stakeholders. This wider distribution of project participants puts greater emphasis on communicating requirements in a more precise and consistent form. It is vital that team members have a solid understanding of what a functional requirement is and what the functional requirements do for the eventual product. That said, horse projects should maximize the roles that their scenarios and a business class model play in communicating the functional requirements.

Elephant projects need a complete and correct requirements specification. All of the information in this chapter is relevant to them, but the discussion on level of detail is particularly pertinent.

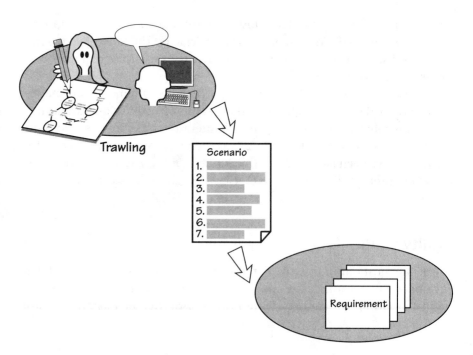

Figure 7.1

The functionality of the work is described during the trawling activity. You usually communicate this functionality back to the stakeholders by writing a scenario. You then write functional requirements by referring to the scenario. The end result is a collection of functional requirements that, taken together, describe the product's contribution to the work.

Functional Requirements

Think of the functional requirements as things the product must do from the point of view of the business. When you talk to business stakeholders, they will describe those actions, which the product must take to complete some part of their work. You can also envision the functional requirements as being independent of *any* technology that might be used. In other words, they are the functional essence of the work.

When it's time to design a solution for the functional requirements, the designer adds technological requirements that are needed by the technology used for the solution. Technological requirements are sometimes lumped together with the business requirements, and the two are collectively referred to as "functional" requirements because they refer to functions of the design or the solution. However, it is more accurate and less confusing to separate technological requirements from functional business requirements. Functional requirements, as we use the term here, describe what the product has to do to satisfy the work or business, and are independent of any technology used by the product.

Functional requirements describe what the product has to do to satisfy the work or business, and are independent of any technology used by the product.

The requirements specification is intended to serve as a contract for the product to be built. Thus the functional requirements must describe in enough detail which actions the intended product will perform. To satisfy this criterion, the functional requirements must contain sufficient detail for the developer to construct the correct product—the one needed by your client—with only the minimum of clarification and explanation from the requirements analyst and the stakeholders. Note we do not say "no additional information." If the developer has absolutely no questions, then you have done too much work and provided too detailed a requirements specification. We explain this point further as we proceed.

Finding the Functional Requirements

Several artifacts reveal the product's functionality. One of the most obvious is the scenario. You arrive at scenarios by partitioning the context of the work using the business events that affect it. For each business event, there is a business use case and, in turn, a product use case. In Chapter 6, we described how to write a scenario for the product use case. This scenario takes the form of a series of steps that complete the functionality of the use case.

The steps in the scenario are readily recognizable to the business stakeholders, because you write them in the stakeholders' language. This means they are probably generalized to encapsulate the details of the product's functions. Think of the details of each step as its functional requirements; your task now is to expose those details by writing the functional requirements. Figure 7.2 illustrates this gradual arrival at the use case's functional requirements.

Figure 7.2

The scenario is a convenient way to work with stakeholders and determine the needed functionality for a product use case. Each of the scenario's steps is decomposed into its functional requirements. The collection of functional requirements reveals what the product has to do to fulfill the product use case.

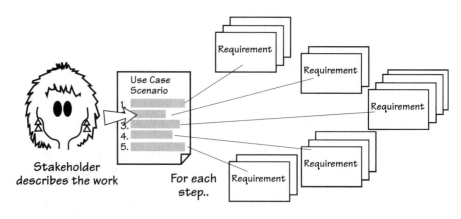

Let's see how this process works by using an example of a product use case scenario. In the IceBreaker road de-icing system, one of the use cases is "Produce Road De-icing Schedule." The actor—the person or thing immediately adjacent to the product, often called a user—for this use case is the Truck Depot Supervisor. He triggers the product to produce the schedule for de-icing the roads in his district. See Figure 7.3.

The product must do several things if it is to achieve the outcome desired by the actor. Here is a scenario to describe for this product use case:

Product use case: Produce road de-icing schedule

1. Engineer provides a scheduling date and district identifier.
2. Product selects the relevant thermal maps.
3. Product uses the thermal maps, district temperature readings, and weather forecasts to predict temperatures for each road section for the district.
4. Product predicts which roads will freeze and when they will freeze.
5. Product schedules available trucks from the relevant depots.
6. Product advises the engineer of the schedule.

Figure 7.3

This use case diagram shows the product producing the road de-icing schedule. It is triggered by the Truck Depot Supervisor. The Thermal Mapping Database is a cooperative adjacent system providing information to the use case upon request.

The steps in this use case are sufficient, in general terms, to do the work. As discussed in Chapter 6, they can be verified with the interested stakeholders. Having a limited number of steps—we suggest between three and ten—in the scenario prevents you from getting lost in the details and keeps the scenario in stakeholder-friendly language.

Once you and your stakeholders have agreed on the steps, for each one ask, "What does the product have to do to complete this step?" For example, the first step in the scenario is

RULE OF THUMB

Three to ten steps in the scenario give a reasonable level of detail, without making it too complex for some business stakeholders.

1. Engineer provides a scheduling date and district identifier.

The first functional requirement to come from this step is fairly obvious:

> *The product shall accept a scheduling date.*

When you ask the stakeholders whether there is anything special about the scheduling date, they tell you that scheduling is never done more than two days in advance. This information suggests another functional requirement:

> *The product shall warn if the scheduling date is neither today nor the next day.*

Another requirement from the first step is

> *The product shall accept a valid district identifier.*

You discover another requirement when you inquire what is meant by "valid." The identifier is valid if it identifies one of the districts for which the engineer has responsibility. It would also be valid if it agrees with the identity of the district that is intended by the engineer. This leads us to two more functional requirements:

> *The product shall verify that the district is within the de-icing responsibility of the area covered by this installation.*
>
> *The product shall verify that the district is the one wanted by the engineer.*

The number of requirements you derive from any step is not important, although experience tells us that it is usually fewer than six. If you uncover only one requirement from each step, it suggests either the level of detail in your scenarios is too granular or your functional requirements are too coarse. If you get more than six requirements per step, either your requirements are too granular or you have a very complex use case. The objective is to discover enough functional requirements for your developers to build the precise product your client is expecting and your actor needs to do the work.

Let's consider another of the use case steps in our example:

4.   Product predicts which roads will freeze and when they will freeze.

This step in the use case scenario leads us to three functional requirements:

> *The product shall determine which areas in the district are predicted to freeze.*
>
> *The product shall determine which road sections pass through areas that are predicted to freeze.*
>
> *The product shall determine when the road sections will freeze.*

Now continue in the same vein, working through each of the steps from the scenario. When you have exhausted the steps, you should have written the functional requirements for the use case. Be sure to test whether you have completed the use case by walking through the requirements with a group of colleagues. You should be able to demonstrate clearly that the use case provides the correct outcome for the actor.

Level of Detail or Granularity

Note the level of detail. The requirements are written as a single sentence with one verb and, where possible, avoid the use of "and." When you write a single sentence, you make the requirement testable and far less susceptible to ambiguity. Note also the form "The product shall . . ."; it makes the sentence active and focuses on communicating what the product is intended to do. It also provides a consistent form for the developers and other stakeholders who need to have a clear understanding of what the product is intended to do.

Incidentally, the word "shall" does not mean that you will definitely be able to find a solution to satisfy the requirement; it simply means that the requirement is a statement of the business intention. The developers are charged with deriving a technological solution to the requirement, and naturally there will be times when they cannot find a cost-effective solution. In the meantime, the requirement clarifies what the business needs the product to do.

One last word on the form employed to write the requirements description: Sometimes people use a mixture of "shall," "must," "will," "might," and so on to indicate the priority of a requirement. This practice results in semantic confusion, and we advise you against doing it. Instead, use one consistent form for writing your requirements' descriptions and use a separate component to identify the requirement's priority.

Use a separate component on your snow card to define the priority rating for each requirement.

The functional requirements we are talking about here are "business" requirements. That is, they indicate what the product has to do to satisfy the organization's business need. The business stakeholders can verify a requirement and tell you whether the functionality is correct. They might also be able to tell you whether you have written enough functional requirements to achieve the intended outcome of the use case. You should probably not hand over the entire collection of functional requirements to the business stakeholders and ask them to verify the accuracy of the complete specification. That is both unfair and pointless. The business stakeholders participate in the development of the scenarios, so their confirmation of the functional requirements should be restricted to those individual requirements that cause problems or raise additional questions. The use of natural language means the requirements are accessible to all stakeholders, but please do not ask them to review the entire requirements specification.

The detail of each requirement is intended to be sufficient for the developers to write the correct software from it. We must qualify this last statement, however, by pointing out that eventually the product designers add the technological requirements. We look at these requirements later in this chapter.

There is more to a requirement than a single "The product shall . . ." statement. Later in this book we look at how to write the other components of a requirement. We also discuss how to make the requirements testable by adding a fit criterion as well as how to test the requirements before they become part of the specification.

Refer to Chapter 10, Writing the Requirements, for the other components; Chapter 9, Fit Criteria, for suggestions on how to make the requirements testable; and Chapter 11, The Quality Gateway, for guidelines on testing the requirements.

Exceptions and Alternatives

Chapter 6 introduced the idea of exception cases for a product use case. Exceptions are unwanted but inevitable deviations away from the normal case caused by errors and incorrect actions. The exception scenario demonstrates how the product recovers from the unwanted happening. The procedure for writing the requirements remains the same: Go through each of the exception steps and determine what the product must do to accomplish that step.

For these requirements, you must make it clear that they become reality only if the exception exists. To do so, you might identify a block of requirements as being attached to a particular exception or write each one to include the exception condition:

> *If there are no trucks available, the product shall generate an emergency request to truck depots in adjacent counties.*

Alternatives are allowable variations from the normal case, which are usually provided at the behest of the business stakeholders. A well-known example is Amazon's 1-Click product. If you have already used a credit card with Amazon, you have an alternative path available to you when buying goods: Instead of going through the normal check-out routine, the goods are recorded as sold as soon as you click on them. The normal case would look like this:

> *The product shall add the selected item to the shopping cart.*

Here is the alternative:

> *If 1-Click is turned on, the product shall record the sale of the selected item.*

Be prepared to create many requirements to handle the exceptions and alternatives. Indeed, these sometimes make up the bulk of the requirements. Given that, as human users of software systems, we are capable of the most bizarre actions, you will need to specify a great deal of recovery functionality.

Avoiding Ambiguity

Whether your source of requirements is written documents or verbal statements from interviews, you should be aware of the enormous potential for ambiguity and the misunderstanding that comes from it. Ambiguity may arise from several sources.

First, the English language is full of homonyms. The language contains an estimated 500,000 words, which have been added to the language and used by many different people over a long period of time. This gradual growth has led to different usages and meanings of the same word. Consider the word "file," which is used so commonly in information technology. In addition to meaning an automated storage place for information, it means a metal instrument for abrading or smoothing; a collection of documents; a row of people, as in "single file"; a slang term for an artful or shrewd person; a verb meaning to rub away or smooth; and more recently a verb used by lawyers, as when they "file suits." Of course, "suit" itself also means the clothing the lawyer wears in court, as well as a set of playing cards such as hearts, diamonds, spades, and clubs. It is difficult to imagine why, when the language contains so many words, so many of them have multiple meanings.

When writing requirements, we have to contend with more challenges than just homonyms. If the context of your product is not clear, then it will also lead to ambiguity. Suppose you have a requirement such as this:

> *The product shall show the weather for the next 24 hours.*

The meaning here depends on the type of requirement and what is near it in the specification. Does the requirement mean the product is to communicate the weather that is expected to happen in the forthcoming 24 hours, or must it communicate some weather and continue to do so until a day has elapsed?

We advise you to group your requirements by product use case. This system of organization will, to some extent, reduce ambiguity. For example, consider this requirement:

> *The product shall communicate all roads predicted to freeze.*

Does "all" refer to every road known to the product? Or just those roads being examined by the user? The use case scenario tells us that the actor has previously identified a district or a section of the district. Thus we may safely say that "all" refers to the geographical area selected. In fact, the meaning of almost any requirements depends on its context. This is quite a good thing, because we do not need to waste stakeholders' time by laboriously qualifying every word of every requirement. While anything has the potential to be ambiguous, the scenario, by setting a context for the requirement, minimizes the risk of ambiguity.

We loved the example erected by the city traffic authority in New York some years ago when it introduced red zones. Red zones were sections of streets where the authorities were particularly anxious that traffic not be impeded. The zones were designated by red-painted curbs and adorned by signs:

> **No Parking**
> **No Stopping**
> **No Kidding**

Although the last directive is ambiguous, the workers at the traffic authority made a reasonable judgment in taking the ambiguity risk. They decided that no driver was foolish enough to think they intended that drivers should not make jokes in their cars or give birth to baby goats. In other words, the authority made a reasonable assessment of how the majority of drivers would interpret the sign.

Similarly, when one of the engineers says, "We want to have the trucks treat the roads before they freeze," it is fairly clear that he does not mean that the roads have to be treated before the trucks freeze. At the very least, the context in which it was said should indicate the meaning.

We record the meaning of special words used by the project in section 5, Naming Conventions and Definitions, of the Volere Requirements Specification Template. We have found that this practice makes inroads into eliminating ambiguity.

You can also reduce ambiguity by eliminating all pronouns from your requirements and replacing them with the subject or object to which the pronouns refer. (Note the potential difference in meaning of the preceding sentence if we had said "they" instead of "the pronouns.")

When you write a requirement, read it aloud. If possible, have a colleague read it aloud. Confirm with your stakeholder that you both reach the same understanding of the requirement. This may seem obvious, but "send the bill to the customer" may mean that the bill goes to the person who actually bought the goods or that the bill is sent to the account holder. It is also unclear whether the bill is sent immediately after the purchase or at the end of the month. And does "bill" refer to an invoice, a bill of materials, or a bill of lading? A short conversation with the appropriate stakeholders will clarify the intention.

Keep in mind that you are writing a *description* of the requirement. The real requirement is revealed when you write the fit criterion. Until you add the fit criterion, a good description is both worthwhile and sufficient.

Technological Requirements

Technological requirements are functionality needed purely because of the chosen technology. In the example of the use case that produces the de-icing schedule, the product interacts with the thermal mapping database. Suppose the designer decides that handling this interaction via an Internet connection is the best option. Because of this technological choice, the product has a need to establish a secure connection. This need is a technological requirement; that is, it arises purely because of the chosen technology. If the designer had selected a different technology to handle this part of the work, the result would be different technological requirements.

The technological requirements are not there for business reasons, but rather to make the chosen implementation work. We suggest that the technological requirements either be recorded in a separate specification or be identified clearly as technological requirements and recorded along with the business requirements. Stakeholders must understand clearly why a requirement appears in the specification, so it is important that the technological requirements are not introduced before the business requirements are fully understood.

Requirements, Not Solutions

Just as there is a difference between business requirements and technological requirements, so there is a difference between a requirement and its solution. It is important to your requirements discovery that you do not write solutions instead of requirements.

The requirements we are discussing here are business requirements—that is, the things needed by the business within the work context regardless of the technology employed. In Chapter 5, we explored the essence of the business, including why it is necessary to understand the essence and not its implementation. We are saying exactly the same thing here: The business requirements are written to reflect the essence, and not any assumed implementation.

Why is this important? Because it is far too easy to hide important functionality by describing an implementation, and far too easy to select the most obvious implementation when better ones may exist. The following, which was taken from an online shopping system, is not a requirement; it's a solution:

> *The product shall display pictures of goods for the customer to click on.*

The requirements analyst has assumed a screen, a picture, and ordering by clicking. Here's the correct way to write this requirement:

> *The product shall enable the customer to select the goods he wishes to order.*

By writing a solution instead of the essential requirement, the analyst precludes the possibility of other implementations, such as ordering by mail, catalogue, mobile or land telephone, or sales representative's visit.

Grouping Requirements

We suggested earlier that you group the functional requirements by use case. The advantage achieved by doing so is that it becomes easy to discover related groups of requirements and to test the completeness of the functionality. Nevertheless, sometimes other groupings may prove more useful.

The word "feature" springs to mind here. The meaning and scope of a feature varies depending on the situation. It could be as small as turning on an indicator light or as large as allowing the user to navigate across a continent. Indeed, the feature itself is often important from a marketing point of view. But different features have different degrees of value to the organization. For this reason, you might find it necessary to discard or radically curtail features. Grouping the requirements by feature makes it easier to manipulate them and to adjust your specification when the market (or the marketing department's request) changes. Bear in mind that a feature will usually contain requirements from a number of different product use cases. Thus, if you are grouping requirements by feature so that you will be able to trace changes from and to the business, it makes sense to be able to group them by product use case as well (as illustrated in Figure 7.4).

It helps to think of the atomic requirements as the lowest level of requirement specification. You group these into a requirements hierarchy for three reasons:

● To be able to involve stakeholders with different depths, breadths, and focuses of interest

● To help you discover the atomic requirements in the first place

● To be able to deal with volume and complexity

A leveled requirements specification meets these expectations as long as you have a nonsubjective traceable path from one level to another. We have

Figure 7.4

A hierarchy of requirements. The work context is the highest-level statement of requirements; it is decomposed into the next level, the business events. The level below the business events comprises the product use cases, each of which is decomposed into a number of product use case steps. The lowest level includes the atomic requirements, each of which you can trace back to the higher-level use case step(s). Another possible hierarchy groups atomic requirements into features; such a grouping is often used by stakeholders from marketing or product version planning.

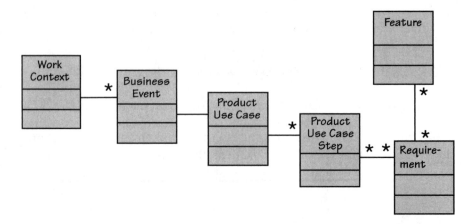

see people run into trouble when they create "high-level requirements" and "low-level requirements" that do not have a formal, nonsubjective link. The practice of attempting to define high- and low-level requirements creates problems and arguments because "high-level" and "low-level" are so subjective. To avoid such conflicts, we recommend that you work with a nonsubjective hierarchy: work context, business event, product use case, product use case step, atomic requirement.

Alternatives to Functional Requirements

We have just taken you through most of a chapter that tells you how to write functional requirements and implies that this is a good thing to do. However, some alternatives to writing functional requirements do exist. The point being made here is not that you have an alternative to understanding the correct functionality of the product before you build it, but rather you might be able to demonstrate and communicate your understanding in a different manner.

We started writing functional requirements with product use case scenarios. If the intended product is routine and the business area well understood, you might consider simply elaborating on the scenario. Add the background processing details that you normally omit when writing a scenario for business stakeholders. Make the steps of the scenario read from the point of view of the product. If the scenario becomes too long or too elaborate, then revert to writing the functional requirements as described earlier. It is also vital that your developers and testers be confident they can write and test the product based on the enhanced scenario.

Do not follow this path if you are outsourcing construction to an external supplier or another department in your organization. In these cases, it is better to avoid the increased potential for misinterpretation by writing the functional requirements. You can always consider a mixture of enhanced scenarios and functional requirements for this type of project.

When you are making use of off-the-shelf (OTS) products or open source products, you do not need to write the requirements for anything other than the extra components needed to make the OTS/open source software work in your environment. Your scenarios should correspond to the OTS/open source capabilities. Once selected, the OTS/open source product becomes a constraint on your project (see section 4 of the Volere Requirements Specification Template), so there is no need to specify its capabilities.

If, as a matter of course, you build process models, then consider whether they, together with their process specifications, can serve as the functional requirements. Many organizations (perhaps that should be "many requirements analysts") prefer to use process modeling as a way of arriving at an understanding of the needed functionality. They find their stakeholders relate more easily to diagrams than to text scenarios.

READING

Robertson, James, and Suzanne Robertson. *Complete Systems Analysis: The Workbook, the Textbook, the Answers.* Dorset House, 1998.

Figure 7.5

An activity diagram
showing the product use
case "Truck Depot
reports problem with
truck."

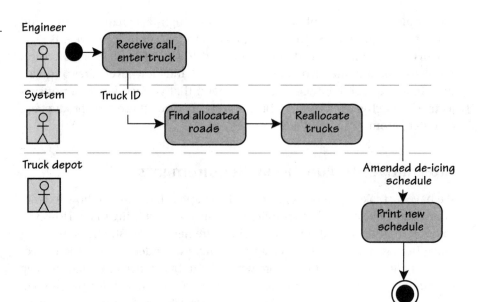

Your process models can use whatever notation you find most convenient. There are few bad notations but, unfortunately, many bad ways of using notations. Probably the most popular techniques are the UML activity diagram (Figure 7.5) and the data flow model of a business use case (Figure 7.6). We have found that analysts have their own preferences when it comes to these diagrams—and these preferences are sometimes expressed with a religious fervor—so we make no attempt to state a preference. Instead, we just ask you to consider them for yourself.

Class models (or data models, as they are also known) can also be rich indicators of the product's functionality. Figure 7.7 shows a class model for the

Figure 7.6

A data flow model of the
product use case "Truck
Depot reports problem
with truck." This
diagram is supported by
process specifications for
each of the processes
shown, and a data
dictionary to define the
data flows and stores.

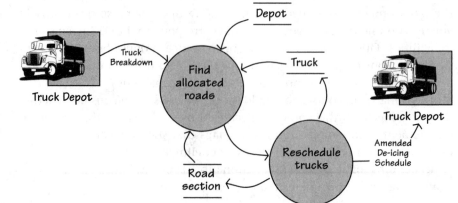

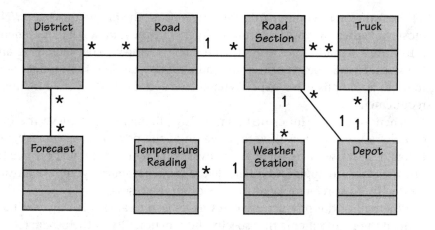

Figure 7.7

A class model showing the stored business data needed to predict the formation of ice on roads. A truck is dispatched to treat a road when the readings from the weather station and the weather forecast indicate the road section is about to freeze.

IceBreaker product. Take a moment to peruse it as we discuss how some of the product's functionality can be derived from this model.

The class model shows the classes, or entities, of data needed by the product to carry out its functionality. There is a strong link between a product's stored data and its functionality. It does not make sense to store data unless some functionality is provided to process it, and functions exist to process data. As the song goes, "You can't have one without the other."

We must mention here that the class model is a stored data model—not a design for a database. Likewise, it does not need to show any implementation details, because they will be added by the database designers.

Let's examine each of the data classes. *Weather Station* is a data representation of the real-world device installed beside a road. The product has to have functionality to record the installation of the sensor and its precise location, and to time-stamp and record the *Temperature Readings* as the weather station transmits them. Similarly, there must be functionality to record, change, and delete the *Roads* and their *Road Sections*, and to know which sections are the responsibility of which *Depots*. The product must know which *Trucks* are attached to a depot, and which are available for scheduling. All of this information, including the scheduling, indicates functionality that must be part of the product.

The data model is not an indicator of the complete functionality. If you routinely build such a model, however, we suggest that it will serve as part of the specification of your functional requirements.

Summary

The functional requirements describe the product's actions—the things it has to do. As such they form a complete, and as far as possible unambiguous, description of the product's functionality.

The functional requirements are derived from the product use cases. The most convenient way we have found to generate the functional requirements is to write a scenario that breaks the product use case into between three and ten steps. Examine each of the steps and ask, "What does the product have to do to accomplish this step?" Whatever it does constitutes the functional requirements.

When you have sufficient functional requirements to achieve the outcome of a use case, it is time to move on to the next one. As you progress through these use cases, you may discover that a requirement you defined for one use case also applies to others. Reuse the requirement you have already written by cross-referencing it to all relevant use cases.

When all of the product use cases have been treated this way, you have defined the requirements that specify the functionality of the product.

Nonfunctional Requirements

in which we look at those requirements that specify how well your product does what it does

How can something called "nonfunctional" be important? Consider this—it really happened. The client rejected some help desk software after it was delivered. The functionality was correct in that the software supported the help desk's activity, but the client didn't want it. Why? Because the users were refusing to use it, preferring to go back to their manual procedures. Why was the product so bad? Because the requirements team ignored the nonfunctional requirements.

Let us explain in more detail. The help desk staff already had nine other applications running on their desktops. The requirement team ignored the users' look and feel requirements, resulting in the new software using a completely different set of icons and screen layouts, which the help desk people rightfully refused to learn. The team also ignored the usability requirements—the new software employed conventions unfamiliar to the users. In addition, the requirements team failed to gather the performance requirements, which should have specified the speeds and volumes of data handled.

The result: A product with a woefully inadequate database, which could not handle the volume of requests made to the help desk. The operational requirements should have set out the operating environment and collaborating products, but didn't. Security was overlooked, and because cultural requirements were not taken into account, the end product contained several icons considered offensive by some members of the help desk. These issues are nonfunctional requirements and, in this unfortunate case, their omission caused the project to fail.

The nonfunctional requirements are the qualities your product must have, or how well it does the things it does. They make the product attractive, or usable, or fast, or reliable, or safe. You use nonfunctional requirements to

171

specify response times, or accuracy limits on calculations. You write nonfunctional requirements when you need your product to have a particular appearance, or be used by nonreaders, or adhere to laws applicable to your kind of business.

These properties are not required because they are the functional activities of the product—activities such as computations, manipulating data, and so on—but are there because the client expects the activities to be performed in a certain manner and to a specific degree of quality.

Agility Guide

On some occasions, the nonfunctional aspects of the product are the prime reason for doing the project. If the users find the existing product difficult to use, slow, or unreliable, then the usability, performance, and reliability requirements could be considered the most important requirements for the new product. Paradoxically, these nonfunctional requirements are often overlooked, and sometimes this neglect leads to the downfall of the project.

Some, though not all, of the nonfunctional requirements should be the earliest to be gathered and understood. They should *never* be assumed, as frequently happens, even when the customers and the developers feel they are obvious.

Rabbit projects should use the requirements specification template (see Appendix B) as a checklist of nonfunctional requirements types. Go through the list (make sure you also check the subtypes) with your key stakeholders and determine which properties are their highest priorities. "All of them" is not an acceptable answer. Keep the project team aware of these high-priority requirements as you work through the use cases.

Horse projects have multiple stakeholders. For this reason, the requirements analysts usually need to take care that they capture the nonfunctional requirements, as well as identify and deal with the conflicts between requirements originating from the different and scattered stakeholders. Horse projects should investigate all the nonfunctional types and their applicability to the product and look for conflicting requirements early.

Elephant projects need to capture all of the requirements in written form, including the nonfunctional ones. This entire chapter is relevant for elephant projects. We suggest you group the nonfunctional requirements by type in the specification (see the requirements specification template in Appendix B). Requirements can be grouped by use case, but as a certain amount of overlap between use cases is common, grouping by type helps prevent duplication.

Nonfunctional Requirements

Let's look at an example. One of the IceBreaker product's functions is to record the road temperatures and moisture levels each time the data is transmitted by the weather stations. Recording data is a functional requirement. Suppose that the data has to be recorded within half a second; once recorded, no one except a supervising engineer is allowed to alter the data. These are performance and security requirements—that is, they are nonfunctional requirements. They are not part of the functional reason for the product's existence, but they are needed to make the product perform in the desired manner.

Nonfunctional requirements do not alter the product's essential functionality. That is, the functional requirements remain the same no matter which properties you attach to them. To confuse matters even more, the nonfunctional requirements might add functionality to the product. For example, the product might have to do something for it to be easy to use, secure, or intuitive. Think of the basis of this functionality: It exists because of the nonfunctional requirements. It exists to make the product have the desired characteristics. Perhaps it is easier to think of the functional requirements as those that cause the product to do the work, and the nonfunctional requirements as those that cause the product to give character to the work.

Nonfunctional requirements make up a significant part of the specification. Provided the product meets its required amount of functionality, the nonfunctional properties—how usable, convenient, and inviting it is (see, for example, Apple's iPod, shown in Figure 8.1)—may be the difference between an accepted, well-liked product and an unused one. Keep in mind that a large part of what people see or feel with your product is there because of the nonfunctional requirements. The usability of a product makes a huge difference to the user's or customer's acceptance of it. The look and feel is important to a significant number of users. The maintainability (or lack thereof) eliminates a lot of frustration for managers of your product. Don't be misled by the name—nonfunctional requirements are as important as any other type of requirement.

Nonfunctional properties may be the difference between an accepted, well-liked product and an unused one.

Every product has a character that separates it from other products. You may have bought your music system because it has a different feel or is easier to use than another. You may prefer the look and feel of one personal computer or operating system to another. You might have bought your electric toaster not because it makes the toast taste any different, but because you thought that the experience of using it would be better, you liked the look of it more than the other toasters on display at the store, or you thought it was safer for children. This experience, or look, or usability is the character of the product. The nonfunctional requirements describe the character, or the way that functions behave. So what nonfunctional requirements do you need for your product?

The nonfunctional requirements describe the character, or the way that functions behave.

Figure 8.1

Apple's iPod music player is a runaway success, largely due to its nonfunctional requirements. The look and feel is simple and elegant, the usability is legendary (no one ever reads the instruction book), and the performance (the capacity of the hard disk, battery life, and so on) is impressive. Not to mention it is downright cool (a nonfunctional requirement). While other music players offer similar functionality, the iPod has won its dominant market share thanks to its nonfunctional qualities. (Photo courtesy Apple Computer, Inc.)

Appendix B contains the Volere Requirements Specification Template.

We went back over the many requirements specifications we have written and extracted a list of the most useful properties for products to have. For convenience, we grouped these into eight major nonfunctional requirement types, and within those, subtypes or variations on the type. You can see these nonfunctional types and their identifying number in the Volere Requirements Specification Template.

There is nothing sacred about the categories we have assigned to the nonfunctional requirements. Feel free to make your own. We identified these particular categories because we have found it makes requirements gathering a lot easier if you have a checklist of the potential types of requirements. Once you are aware of the different types of requirements, you ask questions about them.

Don't spend too much time when it is difficult to precisely categorize a requirement. If in doubt, categorize it with your best guess at the type, or give it both types when it appears to belong to two categories. No harm will come from a few requirements with ambiguous types.

Use Cases and Nonfunctional Requirements

A product use case represents an amount of work the product does when the work is responding to a business event. In earlier chapters, you saw how the scenario breaks the product use case into a number of steps; for each of these steps, you can determine the functional requirements. The nonfunctional requirements, however, do not fit so neatly into this partitioning theme. Some of them can be linked directly to a functional requirement, some apply to the use case as a whole, and some apply to the entire product. Figure 8.2 shows this linking between the functionality and the associated nonfunctional requirements.

The Nonfunctional Requirements

Following are the nonfunctional requirement types we use. The numbers are the identifier allocated to that type of requirement in the requirements specification template.

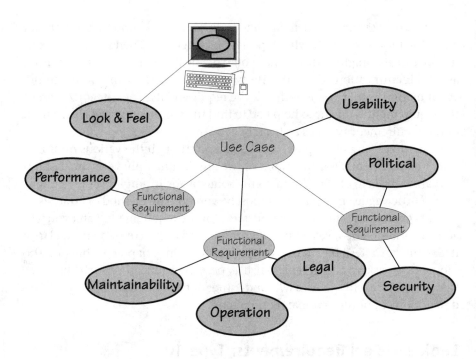

Figure 8.2

Nonfunctional requirements are properties the functionality must have. The functionality can be represented either by a use case or by a functional requirement. In this example, the use case has three functional requirements, each having some nonfunctional properties. The use case as a whole must meet certain usability requirements, whereas the look and feel requirements relate to the entire product.

10 *Look and Feel:* the spirit of the product's appearance

11 *Usability and Humanity:* the product's ease of use, and any special usability considerations needed for a better user experience

12 *Performance:* how fast, how safe, how many, how available, and how accurate the functionality must be

13 *Operational:* the operating environment of the product, and any considerations that must be taken into account for this environment

14 *Maintainability and Support:* expected changes, and the time needed to make them; also specification of the support to be given to the product

15 *Security:* the security, confidentiality, and recoverability of the product

16 *Cultural and Political:* special requirements that come about because of the culture and customs of people involved in the product's operation

17 *Legal:* the laws and standards that apply to the product

We look at each of these categories in more detail later in this chapter. In some cases, the nature of the nonfunctional requirement suggests how you might go about finding any requirements of the type that apply to your product. If nothing suggests itself, there will be a discussion later in the chapter on how to go about eliciting the nonfunctional requirements.

The requirement type is a device to help you to find the requirements; think of it as a checklist.

Later you will add a fit criterion to the requirement to clarify it and make it testable.

As you read though these requirement types, keep in mind that sometimes it is difficult to say exactly what type a requirement is. When this sort of confusion arises, it might indicate that you have several requirements posturing as one. Identification of the precise type is not the most important thing. What matters is that you identify all the requirements. The categorization of the requirement is meant to help you to find the requirements; you can think of the requirement types as a checklist.

One other thing to keep in mind as you go through the various nonfunctional requirements: For the moment, we are dealing only with the description and rationale of the requirement. Some of the examples we give might seem a little vague, ambiguous, or loosely worded. The method of attack is to initially capture the stakeholder's *intention* for the requirement. Later you will add a measurement—we call it a fit criterion—to each requirement to clarify it and make it testable. We discuss fit criteria in Chapter 9, but for the moment we ask you to accept that it is possible to measure such things as "attractive," "exciting," "easy," and other adjectives that appear in the descriptions of nonfunctional requirements.

Look and Feel Requirements: Type 10

The look and feel requirements describe the intended spirit, the mood, or the style of the product's appearance. These requirements specify the intention of the appearance, and are not a detailed design of an interface. For example, suppose you have a look and feel requirement like this:

> *Description: The product shall comply with corporate branding standards.*

This requirement does not say the company logo must be prominent, nor does it talk about the colors to be used. It simply states that the product must comply with whatever branding standards your organization has. These standards are published elsewhere—your own organization has a department or group responsible for these standards—and the designer has access to them. The fit criterion, when you add it, measures compliance with the standards.

Consider the look and feel requirements that you might build into your next product. Among other appearances appropriate for your product, you might want it to have the following characteristics:

- Apparently simple to use
- Approachable, so that people do not hesitate to use it
- Authoritative, so that users feel they can rely on it and trust it
- Conforming to the client's other products
- Attractive to children or some other specific group

- Unobtrusive, so that people are not aware of it
- Innovative and appearing to be state of the art
- Professional looking
- Exciting
- Cool

Software has become a commodity, and the distinction between the functionality of some competing products has largely disappeared. In these cases, the look and feel of one product might give it an edge over a rival. You should also consider the audience for your product (see Figure 8.3). Even when the product will be used in-house, your users have preferences when it comes to the appearance of the software. If your product is for sale, then its appearance is a factor contributing to the customer's buying decision.

Developers of products intended for the Web should place a great deal of emphasis on the look and feel requirements. Your client has in mind the kind of experience he wants visitors to the site to have. Your task is to determine these requirements and to specify them with look and feel requirement descriptions like these:

Developers of Web products should place a great deal of emphasis on the look and feel requirements.

> *The product shall be conservative.*
> *The product shall be intriguing.*
> *The product shall appear authoritative.*
> *The product shall be attractive to an older audience.*
> *The product shall appear simple to use.*
> *The product shall appear state of the art.*
> *The product shall have an expensive appearance.*

Figure 8.3

The intended audience for the product largely determines its look and feel requirements. These requirements make it attractive to the audience and sometimes make the difference between a successful product and one that nobody wants to use.

You might be tempted to describe the required look and feel by using a prototype. However, consider that the prototype does not express the requirement, but rather the result of the requirement. For example, suppose that your client asks for a product "in the company colors." While the prototype may match the required colors, nothing about a prototype tells the designer that the color is important. If the designer chooses to use different colors or a different mix of colors, as well he might, then the requirement for "company colors" will not be met. Thus it is important to write the requirement specifically, and not leave it to someone's interpretation of a prototype. The role of a requirements prototype is to simulate possibilities to help you discover and specify the users' real requirements.

If you know your product will be implemented using software, then some of your look and feel requirements can be described by citing the appropriate interface standards.

> *The product shall comply with the [Aqua/Vista/Motif/etc.] guidelines.*

And here's one other requirement that you should consider:

> *The product shall conform to the established look and feel of the organization's products.*

We repeat: Be careful not to design the interface, because you do not yet know the complete requirements of the product. Designing is the task of the product's designers, once they know the requirements.

Usability and Humanity Requirements: Type 11

Usability requirements make the product conform to the user's abilities and expectations of the usage experience.

For more on how to define your users, refer to the "Stakeholders" section in Chapter 3, Project Blastoff.

Usability requirements are often left out of the requirements specification on the assumption that no sane programmer would build a product that is *hard* to use. At the same time, the product's usability might be one of the key factors that determine whether the intended users actually use it. Do not make the mistake of *assuming* the product will be usable—what is usable to one person could be unfathomable to another. Instead, write the product's usability requirements in a highly specific manner.

The usability and humanity requirements make the product conform to the user's abilities and expectations of the usage experience. Go to section 3, Users of the Product, of your requirements specification and look at your descriptions of the users, along with the classifications of their skill levels. What kind of people are they? What kind of product do they need to do their jobs? The usability requirements ensure that you make a successful product for them. (See Figure 8.4.)

Figure 8.4

Consider the capabilities and knowledge of your intended audience when writing the usability requirements.

The usability of a product affects productivity, efficiency, error rates, and acceptance of the new product. Carefully consider what your client is trying to achieve with the product before writing these requirements.

For example, you might have this usability requirement:

> *The product shall be easy to use.*

At first this requirement may seem vague and idealistic, but remember that you will add a fit criterion to quantify just how "easy to use" the product is for your users. You could, of course, make the requirement much less ambiguous:

> *The product shall be easy to use by members of the public who might not read English.*

You could also revise it for a different user group:

> *The product shall be easy to use by certified mechanical engineers.*

This requirement captures the intention of your client, and for the moment, it is sufficient. However, a designer would be hard pressed to understand exactly what kind of product you want to build. Thus later you must add a measurement so the designer and the client have the identical understanding of "easy to use." We discuss such measurements in Chapter 9, Fit Criteria. For now, simply imagine how you would quantify the requirement for a product to be "easy to use."

"Easy to use" and "easy to learn" are slightly different characteristics. Easy-to-use products are designed to facilitate an ongoing efficiency, so perhaps some training is to be done before using the product. For example, if you were specifying a product to be used in an office by office workers, you would be well advised to make it easy to use. Even if meeting this requirement means training people to use the product, the ongoing efficiency will pay for this extra effort many times over.

Adobe Photoshop is a case in point. Photoshop is a complex product that offers an amazing wealth of options for the manipulation of digital images to its intended audience of graphic artists and photographers. The Photoshop learning curve is a steep one: There is lot to be learned, and we would venture to say that it is not particularly easy to learn (at least it was not for one of your authors). However, once learned, Photoshop's features make manipulating images a straightforward—even easy—task. Given the depth of functionality needed to do the task and its inherent complexity, Adobe has made its product easy to use once you have learned how to use it.

By contrast, easy-to-learn products are aimed at those tasks that are done infrequently and, therefore, may be forgotten between uses—yearly reports, rarely used features of a software product, and so on. Products that are used by the public—and for which no prior training is feasible—must also be easy to learn. For example, telephones in public places and dispensing machines must be easy to learn.

You might describe your requirement as follows:

> *Description: The product shall be easy to learn.*

Alternatively, you might write this requirement:

> *Description: The product shall be easy to use on the first attempt by a member of the public without training.*
>
> *Rationale: Potential users might never before have used this type of product.*

This description might at first glance seem to fall into the "Don't run with scissors" category of obvious advice. But it *is* a requirement: Your stakeholder wants the product to be easy to learn, and the rationale gives some insight into why the stakeholder has included the requirement. Later, when you add its fit criterion, you can quantify "easy to use on first attempt." A suitable fit criterion might be written this way:

> Fit Criterion: Ninety percent of a panel that is representative of the general public shall successfully purchase a ticket from the product within 45 seconds of their first encounter.

We once had a client who asked for the product to be "friendly." Because we could not think of a suitable measurement for "friendly," we felt, naturally enough, that we could not write "friendly" as a requirement. Later on, a little questioning revealed that the product the client had in mind would appeal to the personnel consultants who were to use it. He knew that the consultants would be more productive if they switched to the new product, but he also knew that they would not use it, or would use it badly, if they didn't like it.

So now the requirement began to look like this:

> The personnel consultants shall like the product.

We suggested to the client that we could measure the number of consultants who, after an initial training period, preferred to work with the new product rather than their old way. The client agreed with this plan: He said that he would be satisfied if 75 percent of the consultants were using the product after a six-week familiarization period. He decided to use an anonymous survey to poll the consultants.

Thus we had our usability requirement:

> Description: The product shall provide the preferred way of working for the personnel consultants.
>
> Rationale: To build the consultants' confidence in the product.

We also had the fit criterion:

> Fit Criterion: Seventy-five percent of the consultants shall prefer to use the product after a six-week familiarization period.

Usability requirements can cover areas such as the following:

- Rate of acceptance or adoption by the users
- Productivity gained as a result of the product's introduction
- Error rates (or reduction thereof)
- Use by people who do not speak English (or the language of the country where the product is used)

- Personalization and internationalization to allow users to change to local spelling, currency, and other preferences
- Accessibility to handicapped people (this is sometimes mandated by law)
- Use by people with no previous experience with computers (an important, albeit often-forgotten consideration)

Usability requirements are derived from what your client is trying to achieve with the operability of the product, and from what the users expect. Naturally, the users' characteristics make a difference to their expectations. You, as the requirements analyst, have to discover these characteristics and determine what levels of usability will turn the product into a pleasant and useful experience for them.

Pay particular attention to usability, as it often leads you to discover the differentiating factor between competing products.

Performance Requirements: Type 12

Performance requirements are written when the product needs to perform some tasks in a given amount of time, some tasks need to be done to a specific level of accuracy, or the product needs to have certain capacities.

The need for speed should be genuine. All too often we want things to be done quickly when no real need for speed exists. If a task is to produce a monthly summary report, then there is probably no need to do it quickly. By contrast, the very success of the product may depend on speed:

> *The product shall identify whether an aircraft is hostile or friendly within 0.25 second.*

Capacity is another performance requirement. For example, the client for the IceBreaker product wanted to sell it to road authorities around the world. These authorities are responsible for geographical areas of varying sizes, and the client needed to ensure that the product could handle the largest area covered by any potential client. Initially we would have written the requirement as follows:

> *The product shall accommodate the largest geographical area of any road authority in the world.*

Of course, this is not a practical requirement to hand over to a designer, so eventually we refined it:

> Description: The product shall have the capacity for 5,000 roads.
>
> Rationale: The maximum number of roads in the area of any potential customer for the product.

When you are thinking about performance requirements, consider such aspects as these:

- Speed to complete a task
- Accuracy of the results
- Safety to the operator
- Volumes to be held by the product
- Ranges of allowable values
- Throughput, such as the rate of transactions
- Efficiency of resource usage
- Reliability, often expressed as the mean time between failures
- Availability—the uptime or time periods when users can access the product
- Fault tolerance and robustness
- Scalability of most of the above

Performance requirements include the risk of damage to people or property. If your product is a lawn mower, then there is a genuine need for the product to avoid cutting off the user's toes. And Isaac Asimov included this in his laws of robotics:

> A robot shall not injure a human being.

Hardware is not the only potential source of damage. You should consider whether your software product could cause damage, either directly or indirectly. The IceBreaker product schedules trucks to spread de-icing materials on roads. Because environmental damage from this material can be serious, the requirement covers this issue:

> Description: The product shall schedule de-icing activities so that the minimum necessary amounts of de-icing material are spread on roads.
>
> Rationale: To minimize environmental damage.

In some cases, you may want to specify a performance requirement for the outcome of a use case. For example, we found this performance-related requirement:

> *Description: The product shall schedule de-icing activities so that the rescheduled de-icing truck is estimated to arrive at the breakdown location within 30 minutes of breakdown notification.*
>
> *Rationale: To resume de-icing as soon as possible.*

The performance requirements come mainly from the operating environment. Each environment has its own set of circumstances and conditions. The people, machines, devices, environmental conditions, and so on all place demands on the product. The way your product responds to these conditions—how fast it has to be, how strong, how big, how often—dictates the appropriate performance requirements.

Operational and Environmental Requirements: Type 13

Operational requirements describe the environment in which the product will be used. In some cases the operating environment creates special circumstances that have an effect on the way the product must be constructed.

> *Description: The product shall be used in and around trucks at night and during rainstorms, snow, and freezing conditions.*
>
> *Rationale: This is the environment in which the engineers work.*

Consider the impact if the above requirement had not been written.

Not all products must operate in such an extreme environment—a lot of products are written for personal computers or workstations situated in offices with an uninterruptible power supply. But the seemingly simple environment may be more demanding than it first appears, or it may become more demanding if the operational requirements are not considered carefully.

Figure 8.5 refers to a cargo airline that built its own controller for the high-loader. High-loaders are the machines used to lift the pallets and containers up to the aircraft cargo doors. You have probably watched these devices while staring out the departure gate window waiting for your flight to board. For some reason, the airline's requirements team failed to include the requirement that the product would be used outside for extended periods. The first rainstorm shorted out the electronics of version 1 of the controller.

Operational requirements are also written when the product has to collaborate with partner products, access outside databases, or interface with other systems that supply information. These show up as actors on the product use case diagram, or as adjacent systems on the context model.

Figure 8.5

Will the product work in
its intended operating
environment?

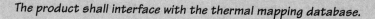

> *The product shall interface with the thermal mapping database.*

To find the operational requirements, look at your product boundary and consider the needs of each of the adjacent systems and/or actors. If necessary, interview each actor or representative of the system to find the requirements resulting from the way that it goes about its product-related work.

You might have to describe the physical environment affecting the users when they use the product. This often means special constraints are placed on the way the product is constructed. For example, if the product will be used by people in wheelchairs or people sitting in an aircraft seat, then you must specify it.

Operational requirements can cover these issues:

● The operating environment

● The condition of the users (Are they in the dark, in a hurry, and so on?)

● Partner or collaborating systems

Portable devices have their own special set of requirements, because you must specify whether the product, or parts of it, will be carried about. For example:

> *The product shall survive being dropped.*
> *The product shall be used in variable lighting conditions.*
> *The product shall conserve battery life.*

If you are building products for sale, you should include any requirements needed to turn the product into a distributable or saleable item. It is also appropriate to describe any operational requirements that relate to the successful installation of the product.

Maintainability and Support Requirements: Type 14

Usually at requirements time you do not know exactly how much maintenance your product will undergo in its lifetime, nor do you always know the type of maintenance that it will need. However, we do have some products where maintenance can, to some extent, be foreseen. Consider whether any expected changes will occur in the following areas:

- Organization
- Environment
- Laws that apply to the product
- Business rules

Might other factors affect your product? If you know or strongly suspect that the product will undergo relatively heavy maintenance due to expected changes, then specify the types of expected changes and the amount of time allowed for those changes.

If you are creating a software product that should be able to run on several different types of operating system, then specify it:

> *Description: The product shall be readily portable to Linux.*
>
> *Rationale: This has been identified as a future growth market.*

Keep in mind that your requirements document is a contract to build the product. You are saying to the developer that you want to be able to port the product to another platform at some point in the future, and that you will hold him accountable for the adaptability of the product to a new machine. When you attach the fit criterion to this requirement, you specify the characteristics of the machine and the expected time or effort necessary to make the transition.

The IceBreaker product had this requirement:

> *The product shall be translated into various foreign languages. As yet, the languages are unknown.*

This requirement had a big effect on the product's designers. They designed the interface in such a way as to make it easy to add new languages.

Also, they took into account the fact that different languages sometimes mean different cultures and different ways of presenting data.

Support requirements are also covered in this section of the requirements specification. In some cases your client may indicate that the product will be supported by the existing help desk, in other cases the product must be entirely self-supporting. By making this point clear at requirements time, you ensure that the designer builds in the appropriate mechanisms for contacting the help desk or providing answers for questions likely to arise with usage.

Security Requirements: Type 15

Security is perhaps the most difficult type of requirement to specify, and potentially the one posing the greatest risk if it is not correct. When you write security requirements, consider the nature of security as it is applied to software and allied products. Shari Lawrence Pfleeger points out that security can be thought of as having three aspects:

- *Confidentiality:* Data stored by the product is protected from unauthorized access and disclosure.
- *Integrity:* The product's data is the same as the source, or authority, of the data.
- *Availability:* The product's data and functionality are accessible to authorized users and can be produced in a timely manner.

Confidentiality

The confidentiality aspect of security means the product's data is not available to anyone except authorized users. You can, of course, achieve this level of security by locking the product in a vault. But if you want people to use it, then you have to provide a key to open the vault and some way to control who or what is allowed to use that key. Locking our products away in vaults is not all that practical, so we tend to use software "locks" that have the same effect. That is, they prevent anyone except keyholders (the authorized users) from accessing the data.

When you write this kind of requirement, you are specify the allowable access—who is authorized, under what circumstances authorization is valid, and what data and what functions are accessible to each authorized user.

> *The product shall ensure that only authorized users have access to the [name of] data (or function).*
> *The product shall distinguish between authorized and nonauthorized users.*

The term "authorized" may also need some further explanation. For example, are all authorized users authorized all the time? Does access depend on the time of day or the location of the user at the time of access? Must a user collaborate with another authorized user to gain access? In other words, is the authorization conditional? If so, write these conditions as a requirement.

It may also be worth considering this requirement:

> *The product shall deliver data in a manner that prevents further or second-hand use by unauthorized people.*

Availability

Availability means that authorized users are not prevented from accessing the data, and the security devices employed do not hinder or delay the users from getting what they want when they want it.

Availability also means the data is, well, available. That is, the product does not keep it in a way that users cannot get at it. Additionally, you must consider requirements for preventing the loss of data and, should the worst happen, recovering lost or corrupted data.

This begins to overlap with the integrity topic, so let's press on.

Integrity

Integrity means that the data held by the product corresponds exactly to what was delivered to the product from the adjacent system (the authority for the data). In our de-icing example, weather stations send data about temperature and precipitation to the IceBreaker product. The weather station originates the data, and thus is the authority for it. Any copies of this data, such as those held by IceBreaker, must be faithful to the weather station's version. Here is the integrity requirement for the IceBreaker product:

> *The product shall ensure its road temperature data corresponds to the data transmitted by the weather station.*

This may seem obvious, but you should also consider several other allied integrity requirements:

- Integrity requirements to prevent unintentional misuse by authorized users. This is the most common form of data corruption.
- Audit requirements to detect improper usage, either by authorized or non-authorized users.
- Requirements relating to proving the integrity of the product after some abnormal happening. These happenings can include such things as a

power failure, an exceptional operating condition, or unusual environmental conditions such as fire, flood, or bombing.

Auditing

You can also consider normal auditing to be part of the security section of your specification. Most accounting products have a requirement to be audited. The goal here is not necessarily to prevent fraud or misuse, but rather to ensure that no mistakes were made and that the results shown by the product are, indeed, correct. Audit requirements are often written such that the product must leave an audit trail. The precise nature of your audit requirements must be negotiated with your own auditors. Naturally, your auditors are stakeholders for your project.

Audit requirements are standard for any product dealing in money or valuables. Their inclusion often results in requirements for the product to retain its records for a given time. It may also mean that the product keeps data on who has accessed what information. The intention of this kind of requirement is that users may not later deny they used the product or had access to its information.

> Description: The product shall retain a journal of all transactions for the statutory period.
>
> Rationale: This is required by the auditors.

. . . And No More

Consider the effect of adding ". . . and no more" to all of your requirements. This phrase means that the product must do no more than the requirement specifies. For example, if the requirement is to find a name and address from a file, then the product must not delete or change the name and address after finding them.

Consider this access requirement:

> The product shall allow access to authorized users.

The ". . . and no more" heuristic yields a complementary requirement:

> The product shall ensure that only authorized users are able to gain access.

For security reasons, you might consider adding an overriding requirement to your specification:

> *The product shall not do anything except that which has been specified as a requirement.*

Sometimes well-meaning product builders make the product perform faster or be bigger than specified, or they add unspecified features. While these properties may be beneficial to a part of the product, they may well have a detrimental effect on the product as a whole or on the security of the product. Use these ideas to ensure that your development team does not build in extra features or properties without first negotiating their inclusion as requirements.

Immunity is also part of the security requirements. Specify requirements for the product to protect itself against malevolent software such as viruses, worms, Trojan horses, and any of the many other variations on the theme of attacking another computer.

Security is important and should be assigned a priority that reflects the value of misusing the product. For example, if your product is for a bank, or if it processes credit card or financial trading transactions, then the value of misuse (in financial terms) is high. Similarly, if your product is intended for the military, then misuse may result in loss of life (perhaps even your own) or loss of a military advantage. Thus, for financial, military, or life-support products, security has a higher priority, and consumes more of the budget, than for many commercial systems.

You should consider calling in a security expert as a consultant stakeholder. Software developers are not usually trained in security, and the security of some functionality and data is so important that the security requirements are best advised by experts.

READING

Pfleeger, Charles, and Shari Lawrence Pfleeger. *Security in Computing* (third edition). Prentice Hall, 2002.

Cultural and Political Requirements: Type 16

Cultural and political requirements are special factors that would make the product unacceptable because of human customs, religions, languages, taboos, or prejudices. These requirements can originate from almost any aspect of human behavior. The main reason for cultural requirements comes when we try and sell a product into a different country, particularly when their culture and language is very different from our own.

The first time your authors went to Italy, looking forward to experiencing the lively Italian atmosphere, we found an elegant, stainless steel coffee bar—the sort of place always full of beautifully dressed people all talking at once. We went to the bar and ordered two cappuccini and two pastries. The barman gave us a lengthy explanation in Italian, shook his head and pointed to the cashier. Thus we discovered a cultural requirement: In Italian coffee bars, it is necessary to first go to the cashier and pay, and only then to go to the bar,

READING

Morrison, Terri, Wayne Conaway, and George Borden. *Kiss, Bow, or Shake Hands: How to Do Business in Sixty Countries*. B. Adams, 1995.

Figure 8.6

Sometimes cultural requirements are not immediately obvious.

hand over your receipt, and place your order (Figure 8.6). At the risk of being deprived of our morning coffee, we soon learned to fit into the culture.

We take our own culture for granted, and we don't give a lot of thought to how other people might perceive our products and ourselves. When we see "before and after" advertising, the "before" is on the left because Western culture reads from left to right. But consider those cultures that read from right to left—unless the "before" and "after" are labeled, they see the advertised product as being detrimental.

Cultural requirements are often unexpected, and at first glance sometimes appear to be irrational. But you have to keep in mind that the reason behind the requirements lies outside your own culture. If your reaction is "Why on earth do they do it like that?", then you have discovered a cultural requirement. You can also consider each requirement and ask yourself, "Is there anything about this requirement that is here purely because of my own culture?" We find that the best way to find cultural requirements is to seek the help of someone from that culture.

If you are building a product that will serve a number of different professions, then you are likely to discover they have different cultural requirements. For example, architects are very conscious of good design, which might spawn requirements about the style of the product. Conversely, these requirements might be irrelevant to the banking profession because its culture is different.

Requirements also exist for purely political reasons. These requirements are the ones for which it is usually impossible to write a coherent rationale. Why is this requirement important to the goals of this project? "Because I say so," "because we have always done it that way," or "because it is company policy" might be the response. While we do not encourage this type of requirement, we accept that they exist and we are pragmatic enough to

READING

Axtell, Roger (editor). *Do's and Taboos Around the World*. John Wiley & Sons, 1993.

If your reaction is "Why on earth do they do it like that?", then you have discovered a cultural requirement.

write them. Subsequent activities, such as using the Quality Gateway, estimating these requirements' cost, or simply making them visible, might eliminate them.

Following are some requirements you might consider cultural or political. Acceptable solutions:

> All software shall be written in the United States.

Unacceptable solutions:

> The product shall include no components supplied by [insert the name of your least favorite country here] companies.

Religious observances:

> The product shall not display religious symbols or words associated with mainstream religions.

Political correctness:

> The product shall not use any terms or icons that might possibly offend anyone on the planet.

Spelling:

> The product shall use American spelling.

Forcing political or cultural alignment:

> The product shall produce all output in ASD Simplified Technical English.

The more we build products for use in different walks of life, by different professions, and for different socioeconomic groups in different countries, the more we need to consider cultural requirements.

Legal Requirements: Type 17

The cost of litigation is one of the major risks for software-for-sale, and it can be expensive for other kinds of software as well. You must make yourself aware of the laws that apply to your kind of product, and write requirements for the product to comply with these laws. Even if you are building software for use inside your own organization, be aware that laws applying to the workplace may be relevant.

Start with your company's lawyers. They have far more experience with the law than you. Here are several things that you can do to facilitate compliance:

- Examine adjacent systems or actors. These are the entities that have contact with your product.

- Consider their legal requirements and rights. For example, are any of the disabled-access laws applicable? Does the adjacent system have any rights to privacy for the data that you hold? Do you need proof of transaction? Or nondisclosure of the information your product has about the adjacent system?

Adjacent systems and actors are defined in Chapters 3 and 4.

- Determine whether any laws are relevant to your product (or to the use case or the requirement). For example, are data protection, privacy laws, guarantees, consumer protection, consumer credit, or "right to information" laws applicable?

A legal requirement is written like this:

> *The product shall comply with the Americans with Disabilities Act.*

You need help from your lawyers to know which law is applicable. The law itself may also specify its own requirements. For example, automated products built for drug development use by the pharmaceutical industry must be self-documenting. The precise nature of this self-documentation varies. Nevertheless, you (or anybody writing requirements for these applications) have to understand that these legal requirements exist and write them into your specification.

You are required by law to display copyright notices, particularly if you are using other people's products. Take a moment to look at the splash screens of software running on your personal computer as an example of how this works.

Products are required by law to display warning messages if there is any danger that some dim-witted user might do the wrong thing with it. For example, a blanket made in a southeast Asian country carries this warning:

> *Warning: Do not use blanket as a hurricane shelter.*

A label on a child's scooter reads:

> *This product moves when used.*

Sarbanes-Oxley Act

The Sarbanes-Oxley Act (SOX; officially titled the Public Company Accounting Reform and Investor Protection Act of 2002) marks a significant change to the U.S. securities laws. This legislation was enacted following a number of large-scale corporate financial scandals involving WorldCom, Enron, Arthur Andersen, and Global Crossing. The act requires all publicly traded companies to report on the effectiveness of their internal accounting controls.

SOX has an indirect impact on the requirements activity. That is, it makes it a criminal offense for CEOs and CFOs to neglect the integrity of the internal controls of their companies. This means that there must be traceability between the source of the information and the company's financial reports. In effect, the executive needs to be able to review your product at some level (presumably not the code) to determine that it presents fair and accurate data about the financial status of the company. To satisfy this need, you may have to present your requirements to the executive. It certainly means that for all internal financial reporting, you must be able to produce the requirements.

Section 404 of SOX is the part most closely tied to IT security. This section aims to strengthen internal controls over financial reporting, thereby minimizing material weaknesses in the reporting process.

Other Legal Obligations

If you are reading this book in the United States, you should also be aware of the Health Insurance Portability and Accountability Act (HIPAA) and the Gramm-Leach-Bliley Act. The former restricts access and disclosure of personally identifiable medical records. That is, not only must you not disclose personal medical information, but also no third party must be able to reengineer statistical data to identify any individual. Gramm-Leach-Bliley applies to financial institutions and likewise prohibits the disclosure of personal information.

In the United Kingdom, the Data Protection Act of 1998 prohibits using data—and this includes disclosing it—in any manner that does not comply with your organization's registration. The act prohibits most personal disclosure, but also provides for an individual's access to personal data held about them.

In all cases, we urge you to consult your organization's lawyers. After all, they are paid to give advice on matters of legal compliance.

Standards

Legal requirements are not limited to the law of the land. Some products must comply with standards. For example:

> *The product shall comply with our ISO 9001 certification.*

Now that we have considered the content of the nonfunctional requirements, let's look at how we find them.

Finding the Nonfunctional Requirements

Like all requirements, the nonfunctional ones can come to light at any time. However, there are places where we can look that give us better opportunities to discover them.

Blogging the Requirements

When you are trying to elicit nonfunctional requirements, blogs and wikis can be immensely useful. Start a blog (or any other form of online collaborative thread) using the template's nonfunctional sections and subsections as headings. That is, don't just say "Usability Requirements"; instead, use the subsections "Ease of Use," "Personalization and Internationalization," "Ease of Learning," "Understandability and Politeness," and "Accessibility." Invite and encourage your team and your stakeholders to contribute what they think are the right properties for the product to have in these categories. You will inevitably receive a number of solutions instead of requirements, but they will provide you with the basis from which to make the abstraction to find the requirement. Do not place any limits on what people can contribute—accept that you will need to analyze the ideas to discover the underlying requirements.

Use Cases

You can consider each use case from the point of its nonfunctional needs. For example, the IceBreaker product has a product use case called "Detect icy roads." This produces the road de-icing schedule showing the roads to be treated and the trucks allocated to them. The relevant stakeholders tell you that the schedule will be used by a junior or medium-grade engineer. For each of the nonfunctional requirements types, interview these stakeholders about the product's needs.

For example—and we list these requirements in the order they appear in the template—the look and feel of the schedule should be such that new engineers (they have a high turnover) can immediately feel comfortable with it:

> Description: The product shall appear familiar to new engineers.
>
> Rationale: We frequently have new junior engineers and want the product to have an appearance that is acceptable to them.

This requirement is slightly more difficult to quantify, but you will be able to write a suitable fit criterion for it after you have read Chapter 9. For the moment, the stakeholders' intention is sufficient.

The usability and humanity requirements for the product use case are next. The stakeholders want the schedule to allow an engineer to easily direct the trucks to the correct roads. The requirement looks like this:

> Description: the product shall produce a schedule that is easy to read.
>
> Rationale: It is important that only the correct roads are treated.

The rationale shows us that the reason for wanting an easy-to-read schedule relates to accuracy of the road treatment. Thus, when you write the fit criterion for this requirement, you would add a quantification to measure that the correct roads have been treated.

Performance requirements focus on issues such as how many, how fast, and so on. In this case, the schedule has to be produced within a few seconds of the engineer wanting it:

> The product shall produce the schedule within 3 seconds of the user's request.

And here's another performance requirement:

> The product shall be able to do ice prediction calculations for 5,000 roads.

Operational and environmental requirements deal with the physical operating environment. In the IceBreaker example, they will be the same for all the product use cases. Naturally, you need write them only once, and they describe the mandated computers, the database, and so on for the product as a whole.

Maintainability and support requirements specify any special conditions that apply to keeping the product up to date or adapting it to another environment. The client for the IceBreaker product intends to monitor roads for different road authorities, so a maintainability requirement is written like this:

> The product shall enable the addition of new road authority areas within two days.

Also, this product use case is usually activated at night:

> *Description: The product shall be self-supporting.*
>
> *Rationale: There is no help desk, nor will other users be available.*

Security requirements deal with access to the product. For the IceBreaker product, the client does not want unauthorized people running the schedule:

> *The product shall allow access only to junior and higher-grade engineers.*

There is also an audit need here, as road authorities must be able to prove they treated the roads correctly:

> *The product shall retain all ice predictions for all occasions the schedule is run.*

Cultural and political requirements are not considered important to this product use case. The client believes the engineers are fairly thick-skinned:

> *The product shall be acceptable to the engineering community.*

And finally we reach the legal requirements. Many road authorities have a statutory obligation to prove that they have exercised due diligence in monitoring and treating the roads under their control:

> *The product shall produce an audit report of all road schedules and their subsequent treatments. This must comply with ISO 93.080.99.*

The Template

Use the template as a checklist of nonfunctional requirement types when interviewing your stakeholders. Go through the template looking at each of the subtypes and probe for examples of each. Refer to the template (found in Appendix B) for more explanation and examples of the nonfunctional requirements.

Prototypes and Nonfunctional Requirements

You can use prototypes to help drive out nonfunctional requirements. The prototype at requirements time is usually a whiteboard sketch, a paper prototype, or some other quick-and-dirty mock-up of what the product *might* be like. The intention is not to design the product, but rather to ensure you have understood the needs by reverse-engineering the requirements from the prototype.

See Chapter 12 for detailed guidance on building requirements prototypes.

In the case of the scheduling product use case, your stakeholders respond favorably to a sketch of a screen showing the roads to be treated in a glowing, cold blue color; the safe roads in green; and the treated roads in yellow. The engineers are delighted they can see the topography of the district and the roads.

> *The product shall distinguish clearly between safe and unsafe roads*
> *The product shall make any unsafe roads obvious.*

You do not yet know that "a glowing, cold blue color" is intuitive—you need some ergonomic input or user surveys for that. But the intention is clear from the prototype.

Go over your own prototypes using the template. For each of the nonfunctional types, which requirements does the prototype suggest? Go through the prototype carefully, and keep in mind that it is not the requirement, but a simulation of the requirement. It is far too risky to hand over the prototype to the developer and expect the correct product to emerge.

The Client

The client for the product may also have expectations that are relevant here. In many cases, the reason for building a new product is to provide a service to the users or to the customers of the business, and the attractiveness of that service depends on one or more nonfunctional qualities. For example, providing portable, or highly usable, or secure functionality may be crucial to the development effort. Alternatively, your client may say that if you cannot provide an interactive and graphic display of the current trading position, then he does not want the product. Thus your client becomes the prime source of the critical nonfunctional requirements.

Once the functional requirements are met, it may be the nonfunctional qualities that persuade a potential customer to actually buy your product. Consider the nonfunctional properties of products that you admire, or you have bought.

Table 8.1 summarizes the questions you should ask for a use case or a functional requirement. Ask your client to what degree these questions are relevant to the product that you are specifying. Your client, or the marketing department, is the source of what will make customers buy the product. Make use of them.

For each use case or the product as a whole, consider the factor in the first column. When you have an adequate knowledge of the factor, use it as a trigger to raise questions about the requirement types in the second column. The numbers in parentheses correspond to the sections in the Volere Requirements Specification Template.

WHO OR WHAT IS (ARE) . . .	DO THEY (DOES IT) HAVE THESE REQUIREMENTS?
The users (3)	Look and Feel (10)
	Usability (11): Are there any special considerations for this kind of user?
	Security (15): Do you have to protect, or protect against, the users?
	Cultural and Political (16)
The operating environment (4, 6, 7, 8)	Operational (13): particularly collaborating products.
	Performance (12): demands made by the environment.
	Maintenance (14): Consider proposed changes to the environment.
The client, the customer, and other stakeholders (2)	Cultural and Political (16)
The adjacent systems (7, 8)	Legal (17): Include special rights for this kind of adjacent system.
	Operational (13)
	Performance (12)

Table 8.1

Finding Nonfunctional Requirements

Don't Write a Solution

We have already mentioned the danger of writing a solution instead of a requirement. But the problem is so widespread (especially with nonfunctional requirements) and potentially so serious that you will forgive us, dear reader, if we mention it again.

Don't presuppose a design solution, or enforce a solution, by the way you write your requirement. By the same token, don't adopt a current solution to a problem and write that as the requirement. For example, if you write a security requirement like this

> *The product shall require a password to access account data.*

then the designer is forced to use passwords. This means that even if a better security device than passwords is available—and there are many to choose from—the product builder may not use it. As you see, this requirement prevents the designer from searching for an alternative, and possibly better, solution.

By writing

> *The product shall ensure account data can be accessed only by authorized users.*

you allow the product designer the freedom to find the most effective solution.

Apart from potentially solving the wrong problem, one of the main concerns with writing a solution instead of a requirement is that technology is constantly changing. Solutions lock you into one technology or another, and whatever is chosen may be out of date by the time the product is built. By writing a requirement that does not include any technological component, you not only allow the designer to use the most appropriate, up-to-date technology, but also allow the product to change and adapt to new technologies as they emerge.

Consider this usability requirement:

> *The product shall use a mouse.*

We can eliminate the technological component by rewriting the requirement:

> *The product shall use a pointing device.*

But the requirement can be even further improved by writing it as follows:

> *The product shall allow the user to directly manipulate all interface items.*

To follow the guideline of not writing solutions, examine your requirement. If it contains any item of technology or any method, rewrite it so that the technology or method is not mentioned. It may be necessary to do this several times before you reach the desired level of technological independence, but the effect on the design of the end product is worthwhile.

Earl Beede suggests a "three strikes" approach to improving the requirement: List three things wrong with the requirement, and then rewrite it to solve those problems. Do this a total of three times. At that stage the requirement is as good as it is ever likely to be.

Figure 8.7

How many nonfunctional requirements does a common household tap have?

Summary

The nonfunctional requirements describe the qualitative behavior, or the "how well" qualities, of the product—whether it has to be fast, or safe, or attractive, and so on. These qualities come about because of the functions that the product is required to carry out.

Even something as simple as the common household tap shown in Figure 8.7 has nonfunctional requirements that make the difference between success and failure:

- *Look and Feel:* The product shall appear easy to operate.
- *Usability:* The product shall be able to be used by someone with wet hands.
- *Performance:* The full flow of water shall be achievable with two turns of the handle.
- *Operational:* The product shall continue to operate correctly with water up to temperatures of 70°C.
- *Maintainability:* The product shall allow any routine maintenance (such as changing a washer) to be completed in less than 4 minutes by a skilled operator.
- *Security:* The product shall not be able to be operated by a small child.
- Cultural and Political: The handle shall turn in the direction dictated by local custom.
- *Legal:* The product shall conform to the Queensland Plumbers and Drainers Board code of installation.

At this stage you have written a *description* and usually a rationale that captures the intention of the nonfunctional requirements. Some of them may seem a little vague, and some of them may appear to be well intentioned and little more. Please keep in mind that you have not finished with these requirements, because you have yet to write the fit criteria. When you do so, you will write a measurement to quantify the meaning of each requirement. We look at this task in the next chapter.

Fit Criteria 9

in which we show how measuring a requirement makes it unambiguous, understandable, and, importantly, testable

Fit, as we use the term here, means a solution completely satisfies the requirement. That is, the solution does exactly what the requirement says it must do or has the property the requirement says it must have, no more and no less. But to test whether the solution fits the requirement, the requirement itself must be measurable. As a simple example, if the requirement calls for a length of rope "of a suitable size," it is obviously impossible to test any delivered solution. By contrast, if the requirement says the rope shall be "2 centimeters in diameter and 2 meters long," then it becomes a simple matter to test whether the delivered solution fits the requirement.

Of course, attaching a measurement to a length of rope is easy. Attaching a measurement to some requirements is much more difficult, but still possible, and absolutely necessary.

The measurement of the requirement is the *fit criterion.* It quantifies the behavior, the performance, or some other quality of the requirement.

So far in this book we have mainly dealt with the *description* of the requirement. The description states the stakeholder's intention for the requirement, and is the normal thing stakeholders say when they are giving you requirements. But to know precisely what they intend, you must quantify the description. Once you measure the requirement—that is, express it using numbers—there is very little room for misunderstanding.

Agility Guide

A pleasing aspect (amongst many) of Kent Beck's eXtreme Programming technique is the insistence on writing test cases before writing the code. The test case defines some yardstick the implemented code has to match, and

> *I often say that when you can measure what you are speaking about, and express it in numbers, you know something about it; but when you cannot measure it, when you cannot express it in numbers, your knowledge is of a meager and unsatisfactory kind.*
>
> Source: Lord Kelvin

READING

Beck, Kent, and Cynthia Andres. *Extreme Programming Explained: Embrace Change* (second edition). Addison-Wesley, 2004.

203

what the tester does to ensure this match. The fit criterion is slightly simpler: It is the yardstick. By adding a fit criterion to the requirement, you are, in essence, writing its test case.

Do rabbit projects need fit criteria? Absolutely, if they are to develop the right code. Rabbits do not necessarily write fit criteria as such—after all, they may not even be writing the requirements—but *understanding* fit criteria means their code solves the real problem. We suggested in Chapter 8 that rabbits use a blog to discover the nonfunctional requirements. For each of the nonfunctional requirements yielded by the blog, we now suggest deriving the appropriate fit criterion, confirming it with the stakeholder, and writing the test case using that fit criterion.

Horse projects need to have a precise understanding of the meaning of requirements. It has been our experience that when the project has multiple stakeholders—this is the norm for horse projects—different stakeholders have different meanings for requirements. Adding a fit criterion to each requirement means it is virtually impossible for misunderstandings to occur. We recommend that horse projects write fit criteria for their requirements.

Elephant projects must use fit criteria. These projects are forced to produce a written specification to be handed on to some other party, either another part of the organization or an outsourcer. Having a specification containing only unambiguous, testable requirements is crucial to elephant projects if the other party is to deliver the correct product.

Why Does *Fit* Need a *Criterion?*

When you have a requirement for the product to carry out some function or to have some property, the testing activity must demonstrate the product does, indeed, perform that function or possess the desired property. To carry out such tests, the requirement must have a benchmark such that the testers can compare the delivered product with the original requirement. The benchmark is the fit criterion—a quantification of the product that demonstrates the standard the product must reach.

You should also consider the builders of the product. It stands to reason that once they know the criterion for the product's acceptance, they will build to that standard. If they are told their product will be used underwater, and the acceptance criterion is that the product must operate for as long as 24 hours at a depth of 15 meters, then they are unlikely to build the product out of anything except waterproof materials (see Figure 9.1).

Possibly the hardest part of testing a requirement against an agreed-upon measurement is defining the appropriate measurement for the requirement. If your stakeholder asks you for a product that is "nice," then you must find some way of measuring its niceness. This measurement must, of course, be agreed upon with your stakeholder. You really have no idea what he means

> *The idea is for each requirement to have a quality measure that makes it possible to divide all solutions to the requirement into two classes: those for which we agree that they fit the requirement and those for which we agree that they do not fit the requirement.*
>
> Source: Christopher Alexander, *Notes on the Synthesis of Form*

Figure 9.1

If they know the performance criterion the product must meet before it is accepted, the builders will naturally build a product to meet that criterion.

by "nice." But once you and your stakeholder reach agreement on how to measure it, the builders can construct the right product, and the testers can demonstrate that it is the right product—it fits the requirement.

So how do you find a measurement for "nice"? Suppose that after some interrogation, your stakeholder tells you that as far as he is concerned, "a nice product is liked by the staff members intended to use it." A little more probing reveals that "liked by the staff members" means they take to the product instinctively, and don't hesitate before using it.

This explanation gives us something to measure: the duration of hesitation before using the product, the time elapsed before complete adoption of it, or the user satisfaction level after a period of usage (the last criterion can be measured by staff survey, for example). Of course, you have to reach agreement with your client that your proposed measurement does, in fact, measure the sought-after quality. However, once you do reach an agreement, you have a satisfactory fit criterion for a "nice product." If your stakeholder had a different meaning for "nice," then you would simply derive a different fit criterion.

Keep in mind that any requirement can be measured. All you have to do is find a suitable scale.

Scale of Measurement

The scale of measurement is the unit you use to test conformance of the product. For example, if the requirement is for a certain speed of operation, then the scale is time—microseconds, minutes, months—to complete a given action or set of tasks. For a usability requirement, you can measure the time needed to learn a product, or the time taken before achieving a particular level of competence, or perhaps even the error rate of the work done using the product.

There is a scale of measurement for everything . . . almost.

Scales of measurement exist for all sorts of qualities. Color can be measured by specifying its component colors as a percentage of cyan, magenta, yellow, and black. Loudness and softness of sound are measured in terms of decibels. An amount of light is measured in units of lumens. Typefaces can be measured by noting type names and point sizes. In fact, there is a scale of measurement for almost everything. So far, the only thing that your authors have not been able to put a scale of measurement to is love—we cannot find a way of measuring how much you love someone.

Rationale

The rationale is the reason, or justification, for a requirement. We have found that attaching a rationale to the requirement makes it far easier to understand the real need. Quite often, stakeholders tell you a solution rather than their real requirement. Or they tell you a requirement that is so vague as to be (for the moment) unusable. In the example given previously, the client asked for a "nice" product. The justification, or rationale given, was the users would readily adopt the product.

Suppose the rationale had been different. Say, instead of ready adoption, the client gave you a rationale that indicated a "nice" product is so easy to use that its users make fewer errors than they do with the current product. The corresponding requirement has a different meaning, and the resulting fit criterion is completely different.

The rationale is not only a guide to help you find the fit criterion, but also a means to help you know when you have several different requirements masquerading as one. One stakeholder says "nice" means the product is pleasant to use, another says "nice" means the product is exciting, and yet another says a "nice" product encourages users to make return visits to it. In this case you have three different requirements, each with its own fit criterion that measures the desired property.

You have to pass along a way to measure the requirement's real meaning.

When asking stakeholders for their rationale for a requirement, you might appear to be like the child constantly asking a parent, "Why?" So be it. That is the role of the requirements analyst: to ask why and keep on asking why until you understand the meaning of the requirement. But you haven't finished yet, because you still have to pass along a way to measure the requirement's real meaning. That is why you derive the fit criterion.

To find an appropriate fit criterion, start by analyzing the description and rationale you have established for the requirement.

> *Description: The product shall make it easy for a buyer to find his chosen music.*

This requirement is fairly subjective and slightly ambiguous. The rationale provides more information on what is needed:

> *Rationale: Music buyers are used to convenience and will not tolerate slow or awkward searches for their chosen tracks.*

Now you know the requirement is about speed—which is fairly easy to quantify—and awkwardness—which is about complexity and perceived ease. For the speed component, a time limit for a search is an appropriate measurement. Suppose your market research people tell you ten seconds is the limit of the target audience's tolerance. To be better than the competition, you are shooting for six seconds.

For the awkwardness component of the fit criterion, your ergonomics people and your market research personnel both say that buyers must be able to find a piece of music in no more than three actions (an action here means a click, a gesture, a menu selection, or any other conscious action on the user's part).

Your measurement for these things would be this fit criterion:

> *Fit Criterion: The average music buyer shall be able to locate any piece of music within six seconds, using no more than three actions.*

Some fit criteria may, at first, be unattainable because of business or real-life constraints. Or your client may not be willing to spend the amount required for the implementation to meet the criterion. Thus sometimes you might negotiate an adjustment to the fit criterion to allow for the product's operating environment, intended usage, and client's budget. Think of these adjustments as *business tolerances*. As we are certain that some of the intended users of the product will be below-average performers, we would adjust the fit criterion to read as follows:

> *Fit Criterion: Ninety percent of music buyers shall be able to locate any piece of music within six seconds, using no more than three actions.*

Fit Criteria for Nonfunctional Requirements

A nonfunctional requirement is a quality that the product must have, such as usability, look and feel, performance, and so on. The fit criterion is a measure of that quality.

Some of the nonfunctional requirements may at first seem difficult to quantify. Ultimately, however, it is possible to measure all of them. If you cannot quantify and measure a requirement, it is not really a requirement. It might be several requirements written as one, or it might be incomplete, ill considered, irrational, haphazard, or just plain not a requirement. Either you can quantify it or you delete it.

Let's look at some examples.

> *Description: The product shall be user-friendly.*

This requirement at first seems vague, ambiguous, and not at all amenable to measurement. However, you can find a way to measure it. Start with the client: Can he tell you more precisely what he means by "user-friendly"? This is where the rationale comes in. For example, is the product meant to be easy to learn, easy to use, attractive and inviting, or some other meaning of "user-friendly"?

Suppose your client clarifies his intention toward "user-friendly" by saying, "I want my users to be able to learn how to use the product quickly." This rationale suggests a scale of measurement—the time taken to master given tasks. You can measure it by identifying a set of standard tasks and measuring the learning time needed before being able to complete them successfully. Alternatively, you can specify an amount of training time allowed before being able to use the product to a certain standard. Another measurement of how successful a user is at knowing the product could be the number of calls to a help desk or references to online help.

A suggested fit criterion for this "user-friendly" requirement is this:

> *Fit Criterion: New users shall be able to add a road, change a road, and delete a road within 30 minutes of their first attempt at using the product.*

Note that this fit criterion measures this particular meaning of "user-friendly." It does not necessarily apply to all instances of the client asking for a "user-friendly" product.

Earlier in this chapter you saw an example of a requirement that specified a "nice" product; the client said that "nice" meant the staff liked it. You can measure "like": If the staff likes the product, they will use it. You can measure how quickly they start using it, how much they use it, or how soon word gets

Figure 9.2

You can measure your users' liking for the product by surveying their work practices before and after the product is introduced, by measuring how long it takes them to start using the product once it is available, or by surveying them after a period of use to ascertain their liking for the product.

around that the product is good and users encourage one another to use it. All of these criteria quantify the client's desire that the staff like the product and use it (see Figure 9.2).

You could write a fit criterion like this:

> *Fit Criterion: Within three months of introducing the product, 60 percent of the users shall be using it to carry out the agreed-upon work. From those users, the product shall receive a 75 percent or more approval rating.*

Note how you clarify the requirement when you add the fit criterion. By negotiating a measurement, you transform the requirement from a vague and somewhat ambiguous intention into a fully formed, testable requirement. You will find that it is usually not possible to get the complete, measurable requirement in the first instance. It is unlikely that your stakeholders will express themselves in such precise terms. We suggest you go with the flow. Don't slow down your requirements-gathering processes to make the requirement measurable, but rather get the stakeholders' intention—you write this as the *description*—and the *rationale*. Then analyze your understanding, write your own best interpretation of the fit criterion, and improve it by asking your stakeholder whether it is an accurate measurement of the requirement.

Product Failure?

The fit criterion might be determined by asking your stakeholder, "What would you consider a failure to meet this requirement?" Suppose you have this requirement:

> Description: The product must produce the road de-icing schedule in an acceptable time.

Clearly, the scale of measurement here is time. Your client can tell you how much time he thinks would constitute a failure. For example, if the engineer has to wait for more than 15 seconds (or whatever) for the schedule, the client may consider the product unacceptable. Thus you have the following fit criterion, with suitable business tolerances applied:

> Fit Criterion: The road de-icing schedule shall be available to the engineer within 15 seconds from when he makes his request for 90 percent of the times that it is produced. It shall never take longer than 20 seconds.

There will be times, however, when you discover there is no agreement on a quality measure, and hence there can be no fit criterion. In these circumstances, it is possible that the original requirement is actually several requirements—each requirement has its own measurement—or the requirement is so vague, and its intention so unrealistic, that it is not possible to know whether it has been satisfied. For example, no fit criterion is possible for this requirement: "I want a product my grandmother would have liked had she been alive today."

Subjective Tests

Some requirements have to be tested using subjective tests. For example, if a cultural requirement for a product to be used in the public domain is "not offensive to any group," then the fit criterion must be along these lines:

> Fit Criterion: The product shall not be offensive to 85 percent of a test panel representing the makeup of the people likely to come in contact with the product. No more than 10 percent of the interest groups represented in the panel shall feel offended.

Although fit criteria are measures of the product's performance, it is usually cost-effective to test prototypes built specifically for the purpose.

The business tolerance here allows for the fact that you cannot count on 100 percent of humans passing any test. In this case the business tolerances shield the product from the fringe-lunatic extreme views, while at the same time allowing "offensive" to be measured.

It is likely you would use a prototype or simulation, and not the delivered product itself, for this kind of testing. Although fit criteria are measures of the product's performance, it is usually cost-effective to test prototypes built specifically for the purpose.

Numbers used in fit criteria are not arbitrary. Suppose you have a fit criterion of "reduce the time to perform [some task] by 25 percent of the current time." This means that the current time must be known and documented, not just guessed at. The reason for the target of a 25 percent reduction must be well understood, and agreed to by the client. Ideally, the reasoning behind wanting 25 percent—and not 20 percent or 30 percent—is backed by empirical data taken from a study of the business.

Look and Feel Requirements

Look and feel requirements specify the spirit, mood, or style of the product's appearance and behavior.

Many companies require their products to be in company colors. The rationale for this requirement is either adherence to branding standards or a desire to enhance customer recognition. These two are slightly different, however.

Let's look at branding standards first. The product either conforms to the standards or it doesn't. Your organization has a person, or department, who are responsible for the branding standards. Thus the fit criterion should specify the target standard and state who or what is to certify the product's compliance.

> *Fit Criterion: The product shall be certified as complying with this year's corporate branding standards by the head of marketing.*

Where the rationale is customer recognition, we suggest a fit criterion along these lines:

> *Fit Criterion: Sixty percent of the target audience will recognize the product as belonging to the corporation within five seconds of encountering it for the first time.*

Look and feel requirements may start out as "touchy-feely" statements of intent. However, by questioning, by repeatedly asking for a rationale, and by looking for measurable aspects, you will always find suitable fit criteria for them. Even something as vague as "cool" can be measured. How? By asking why it has to be cool, thereby finding the stakeholder's rationale for the requirement. Suppose the client says the product has to be "cool" to appeal to the target market of high school students. A fit criterion in this situation could be a rate of acceptance by a representative panel of high school students. Or perhaps it is the product selected by 75 percent of the panel when shown five sample prototypes. Or perhaps, when shown a simulation of the product, 85 percent of the representative high school panel say they would buy it.

Look and feel requirements may start out as "touchy-feely" statements of intent, but you will always find suitable fit criteria for them.

Usability and Humanity Requirements

Usability and humanity requirements specify the product's convenience and fitness for use by its intended users. Products are usually required to be easy to use, easy to learn, able to be used by certain types of users, and so on. To write the fit criterion for each of these requirements, you must find a measurement scale that quantifies the objective of the requirement.

Let's look at some examples.

> Description: The product shall be intuitive.

To measure "intuitive," you must consider the people to whom the product must be intuitive. In the IceBreaker example, you are told the users/actors are the road engineers; they have an engineering degree and meteorological experience.

> Rationale: The engineers must find it easy and intuitive; otherwise, they will not use it.

Now that you know this rationale, "intuitive" takes on a different meaning.

> Fit Criterion: A road engineer shall be able to produce a correct de-icing forecast within ten minutes of encountering the product for the first time without reference to any out-of-product help.

Sometimes "intuitive" really means "easy to learn." In this case, you ask how much time can be spent in training, and the resulting fit criterion might look like this:

> Fit Criterion: Nine out of ten road engineers shall be able to successfully complete [list of selected tasks] after one day's training.

Look for the real meaning of the requirement, and confirm it by having your stakeholders agree that your proposed fit criterion is the correct measurement of the meaning.

Fit criteria for usability requirements might also quantify the time allowed for given tasks, the error rates allowed (quantifying ease of use), the satisfaction rating awarded by the users, ratings given by usability laboratories, and so on. Look for the real meaning of the requirement, and confirm it by having your stakeholders agree that your proposed fit criterion is the correct measurement of the meaning

It might be appropriate for your usability requirements to have a fit criterion based on readability. Several readability scoring systems are availability. For example, the Flesch Reading Ease Score assigns a rating based on several factors in the text. The highest score is 100, and a suggested score is in the 60–70 range. The Flesch–Kincaid Grade Level Score rates text against the U.S. grade school levels of comprehension. For example, a score of 8.0 means that an eighth grader can understand the material. Suggested scores for a standard document are in the 7.0–8.0 range.

Accessibility requirements specify how easy it should be for people with common disabilities to access the product. This could result in a fit criterion like this:

> *The product shall be certified to be in compliance with the Americans with Disabilities Act.*

It may also be necessary to specify the relevant parts of the act and perhaps the body responsible for certifying compliance.

Performance Requirements

Performance requirements deal with the speed, accuracy, capacity, availability, reliability, scalability, and similar characteristics of the product. Most of the time, the nature of the performance requirements will suggest a measurement scale. Let us look at some examples.

Suppose you have this requirement:

> *Description: The response shall be fast enough to avoid interrupting the user's flow of thought.*

The word "fast" indicates you should measure time. Here is a suggested fit criterion:

> *Fit Criterion: The response time shall be no more than 1.5 seconds for 95 percent of responses, and no more than 4 seconds for the remainder.*

Similarly, the fit criterion for an availability requirement might be written as follows:

> *Fit Criterion: In the first three months of operation, the product shall be available for 98 percent of the time between 8 A.M. and 8 P.M.*

A fit criterion may be shown as a range. This is particularly appropriate for performance requirements. For example:

> *Fit Criterion: The product shall allow for 3,000 downloads per hour, although 5,000 per hour is preferred.*

The point of using a range is to deter the developers from constructing a product that could be overly expensive, and to make the best design trade-offs to fit the budget and design constraints.

As most performance requirements are themselves quantified, it should be fairly straightforward to write appropriate fit criteria. If the requirement is given to you in correctly quantified terms, then the fit criterion and the requirement are the same: Write one or the other.

If the requirement is given to you in correctly quantified terms, then the fit criterion and the requirement are the same.

Operational Requirements

Operational requirements specify the environment in which the product will operate. In some cases the product has to be used in adverse or unusual conditions. Recall our example from the IceBreaker product:

> *Description: The product shall be used in and around trucks at night, and during rainstorms, snow, and freezing conditions.*

The fit criterion for an operational requirement is a quantification of the successful usage in the required environment. For the preceding (somewhat unusual) operational requirement, the fit criterion quantifies the enabling of the operator to achieve specified tasks and the ability of the product to withstand the conditions. For example:

> *Fit Criterion: The operator shall successfully complete [list of tasks] within [time allowed] in a simulation of a five-year storm (this is an accepted quantification of meteorological conditions) and the product shall function correctly after 24 hours exposure.*

Operational conditions may also specify that the product must coexist with partner, or collaborating, systems. The fit criterion in this case will cite the specification of the partner system or the way to communicate with the partner:

> *Fit Criterion: The interfaces to the Rosa Weather Station shall be certified as complying with the National Transportation Communication ITS Protocol (NTC/IP).*

This criterion is testable—by engineers from NTC—and points the product's builders toward a known and accepted standard.

Maintainability Requirements

Maintainability requirements specify the expectations about the maintenance of the product. Usually the fit criteria for these requirements quantify the amount of time allowed to make certain changes. This is not to say that all maintenance changes can be anticipated, but where changes are expected, then it is possible to quantify the time allowed to adopt those changes.

> *Fit Criterion: New users shall be added to the system with no more than five minutes' interruption of normal service to existing users.*

If you are creating a software product, and there is a requirement to port it to another computer, this is specified in the maintainability section. The fit criterion quantifies the amount of time, or effort, to satisfactorily port the software.

Security Requirements

Security requirements cover the security of the product's operation. The most obvious requirement in this category specifies who is allowed access to what parts of the product, and under what circumstances. The fit criterion could be something like this:

> *Description: Only engineers using category A logins shall be able to make any additions, updates, or deletions to any weather station data.*
>
> *Fit Criterion: Of 1,000 additions, updates, or deletions to any weather station data, none shall be from other than category A engineer logins.*

File integrity is part of security. The most common source of damage to computer files is authorized users accidentally corrupting the data. Thus at least one requirement should refer to file integrity. Its fit criterion would be something like this:

> *Fit Criterion: After any operation, the product's weather station data shall be identical to the temperature transmissions as recorded by the transmitting weather station.*

This fit criterion says that the product's data must agree with the authority for that data. As most data is transmitted to the product from the outside—in this case, from a weather station—the transmitter must be the authority. Thus, if the product's data conforms to the authority's data, it is considered to be correct.

Cultural and Political Requirements

Cultural and political requirements, by their nature, are subjective and slightly more difficult to quantify. The fit criterion is usually based on who will certify the product's acceptability. The following examples of fit criteria should reveal their originating requirements:

> *Fit Criterion: The Shatnez Laboratory of Brooklyn shall certify that the product complies with the shatnez rules.[1]*
>
> *Fit Criterion: The ethics committee shall attest that the product displays no religious or political symbols, or words or symbols that could be construed as religious or political.*
>
> *Fit Criterion: The marketing department shall certify that all components are American made.*

Cultural requirements come about because different countries and different people have different customs, experiences, and outlooks. When you are specifying fit criteria for cultural requirements, remember that words used in some countries are unknown in others that speak the same language. Make sure that you are not making assumptions about how the fit criteria will be interpreted by defining your terms in section 5 of your requirements specification.

Legal Requirements

Legal requirements specify the conformance with laws. Here is a fit criterion that will apply to most legal requirements: Your client wins a court case brought by somebody who uses the product. However, fit criteria must be able to be tested in a cost-effective manner, and court cases are far too expensive to be indulged in lightly. Thus the majority of fit criteria will be along the following lines:

> *Fit Criterion: The legal department/company lawyers shall certify that the product complies with the [appropriate laws].*

Legal requirements are also written to ensure that the product complies with cited standards. Most standards are written by organizations that either have people who certify compliance—"standards lawyers"—or issue guidelines as to how you can certify compliance for yourself. In either case, fit criteria can be written to specify how compliance with the standard is to be verified.

Fit Criteria for Functional Requirements

A functional requirement is something that the product must do—an action it must take. The fit criterion specifies how you will know that the product has successfully carried out that action. For functional requirements, there are no scales of measurement: The action is either completed or not completed. Completion depends on satisfying an authority that the product has correctly performed the action. The authority in this case is either the source of the data or the adjacent system that initiated the action.

Functional requirements can be written for different kinds of action. For example, if the action is to record something, then the fit criterion is that the recorded data complies with the data as known to the authority. For example:

> Description: The product shall record the weather station readings.
>
> Rationale: The readings are necessary for preparing the de-icing schedule.
>
> Fit Criterion: The recorded weather station readings shall be identical to the readings as recorded by the transmitting weather station.

The authority in this case is the weather station: It initiated the action, and it is the source of the data. You can say the requirement is for the product to faithfully store the data (allow for the product to make necessary manipulations to the data) as sent from the weather station. If this is done correctly, then the product's data conforms to that transmitted by the station.

The fit criterion does not indicate *how* this conformance is to be tested. Instead, it is simply a statement the tester uses to ensure compliance.

If the functional requirement is to make some calculation, then the fit criterion says the result of the calculation must be consistent with the authority's view of the data. For example, if the requirement is that "the product shall record . . . ," then the fit criterion reads "the retrieved data shall agree with . . ." and cites the authority for the data. Usually this authority is the original source of the data. Where the requirement is "the product shall check . . . ," the fit criterion is "the checked data conforms with . . ." and again cites the authority for the data. "The product shall calculate . . ." results in a fit criterion of "the result conforms to . . ." and gives the algorithm (or source of the algorithm) for the result.

For the fit criteria to be complete, the specification must contain a definition of the terms used in the fit criteria.

The general rule for functional requirements is that the fit criterion ensures that the function has been successfully carried out. That brings us to test cases.

Test Cases

You might find it feasible to write test cases for your functional requirements.

You might find it feasible at this stage to think about writing test cases for your functional requirements. This approach is in line with the eXtreme Programming view, which advocates writing the test before writing the code. The basic idea is to force the programmer to concentrate on learning the success criterion for any part of the functionality.

Many requirements analysts feel uncomfortable delving into writing test cases. However, the testers for your organization will be—we are sure of this—delighted either to help you or to write the test cases for you. Testing is most effective early in the development cycle. Involving the testers in the requirements activity is always beneficial, because testers are the best people to tell you if your functional requirements are correctly (and testably) stated.

READING

Myers, Glenford, Corey Sandler et al. *The Art of Software Testing* (second edition). John Wiley & Sons, 2004.

Use Cases and Fit Criteria

You can apply a fit criterion to a use case.

A use case, whether it is a product use case or a business use case, is a set of actions triggered by a business event. You can think of a use case as a collection of requirements—both functional and nonfunctional—working toward a common end. Each requirement has its own fit criterion, which measures the requirement. If we can measure individual requirements, we can also measure the collection. In other words, we can apply a fit criterion to a use case.

To avoid confusion about this use case criterion, we call it the *outcome*. That is, this criterion is the intended outcome of the (business or product) use case if all works as intended. As we are talking about a collection of requirements, each with a fit criterion, you may prefer to think of the outcome as a summary (or even summation) of all the individual fit criteria.

The outcome does not replace the individual requirements' fit criteria. It does, however, help you communicate about the intention of the use case.

We suggest you make use of outcomes very early in your requirements gathering. During the blastoff (or as soon as you identify the business events), try to elicit from your stakeholders the intended outcome for each of their business events. You are asking, "When this business event happens, what does the business need to achieve?" The answer to this question is, with a little massaging on your part, the outcome or fit criterion for the business use case. As your business use cases evolve into product use cases, the same or very similar criteria can be applied. You will find, as we have, that an early outcome criterion eliminates a lot of misunderstandings about what each business use case is intended to accomplish.

As you capture individual requirements, and their fit criteria, keep in mind that each of them has to contribute in some way to the purpose of the product. If you have an outcome criterion attached to each use case, it is easier to ensure that all the requirements you are capturing contribute to the use case as a whole.

Fit Criterion for Project Purpose

We have already discussed writing the fit criterion for the project's purpose. Of course, we didn't call it a fit criterion back in Chapter 3 (we called it a measurement), but that is what it is. Let's look quickly at this idea again: The project's purpose is a statement of the reason for making the investment in the project or a definition of the problem it is intended to solve. If you plan to go to the trouble and expense of developing a product, then it makes sense to have an objective benchmark to measure the delivered product against.

The measurement of the purpose is exactly the same as a fit criterion for an individual requirement. The only difference is that the fit criterion measures a single requirement, whereas the purpose's measurement measures the entire project.

Refer to Chapter 3, Project Blastoff, for information on writing a measurable product purpose.

Fit Criteria for Solution Constraints

Section 4 of the Volere Requirements Specification Template contains constraints. We treat them as a special type of requirement that needs to be specified just like any other type of requirement. For example, in section 4a, you will find the solution constraints. These constraints place restrictions on the way that the problem must be solved; you could also say they mandate a solution to the problem. For example:

> Description: The software part of the product must run on Linux.

This requirement reflects management's desire to continue to use, or to start to use, Linux. It may or may not have a sound technological basis, but that is beside the point. You are being told that any solution you deliver has to comply with this constraint.

We can test compliance—either you comply with the requirement or you don't—as long as whatever it is that you have to comply with is itself measurable. For example, you can test whether you have complied with a law, but you can't test whether you have complied with a constraint that states "You shall be happy." In the case of the Linux constraint, you could write the following criterion:

> *Fit Criterion: All functionality of the software shall operate correctly when run using Red Hat Enterprise Linux version 4.*

Similarly, all other constraint requirements—for example, implementation environment, partner applications, commercial off-the-shelf software, open source software, workplace environment, time budget, and financial budget—should have fit criteria.

Summary

The fit criterion is an unambiguous goal that the product has to meet.

A fit criterion is not a test, nor is it the design for a test. Rather, a fit criterion is an unambiguous goal that the product has to meet. It is used as input to building a test case where the tester ensures that each of the product's requirements complies with its fit criterion.

Quantifying or measuring the requirement gives you a better opportunity to interact with your stakeholders. By agreeing on a measurement, you confirm that you have understood the requirement correctly, and that both you and your stakeholders have an identical understanding of it. You will also find quantifying it ensures that the requirement is both wanted and necessary.

Adding a fit criterion to a requirement encourages testers to participate in the requirements process. Testers should be involved early in the development cycle—we cannot stress this point enough. Testers can help you to specify the fit criteria. This is not to say that the testers should write the fit criteria. However, testers are the best source of knowledge about whether something can be tested, and whether the fit criterion contains the appropriate quantification. In other words, the testers act as consultants for the fit criteria.

The fit criterion is the requirement.

The fit criterion *is* the requirement. The description you write is the stakeholder's way of stating the requirement. If your stakeholders are like most of us, they speak using everyday language. Everyday language is, unfortunately, often ambiguous and sometimes not precise enough. You need a supplement to the requirement—a fit criterion that is stated in unambiguous, precise terms and, most importantly, uses numbers or a measurement to convey its meaning.

You derive a fit criterion by examining the requirement's description and rationale, and determining what quantification best expresses the user's intention for the requirement.

Fit criteria are also a vehicle for reaching a consensus among multiple stakeholders. Your attempts to clarify and measure will almost always result in hidden meanings becoming visible, hidden requirements bubbling to the surface, and, most importantly, the stakeholders agreeing on what is needed.

Fit criteria are usually derived after the requirement description is written. You derive a fit criterion by examining the requirement's description and rationale, and determining what quantification best expresses the user's intention for the requirement. You may sometimes find that this close examination results in changes to the requirement, but these changes are for the better and should be considered quite normal. Their occurrence simply means the requirement was not properly understood in the first instance. With patience and persistence, and with the wise use of measurements, you can ensure that each of your requirements is unambiguous, testable, and real.

Writing the Requirements

 in which we turn the
requirements into written form

Writing the requirements refers to the task of putting together a description of the product from the business point of view. Typically, this description is called a specification, and we use the term here to mean whatever description you are compiling, whether it is written or not. It is appropriate to think of this activity as *building* a specification: You assemble a specification, one requirement at a time, rather than writing it all at once.

Writing the requirements is not really a separate activity, but is done mainly during the trawling and prototyping activities as you discover the requirements. However, it makes sense in the context of this book to devote a chapter to discussing how a requirement is written. This is that chapter. See Figure 10.1.

Agility Guide

We imagine at this point in the book hard-core agilists are forcefully saying, "What happened to 'Working software over comprehensive documentation'? Why are you asking me to write the requirements when I can build working software?" Despite the title of this chapter, we are not asking you to actually write the requirements. We merely want you to formalize them to a point where all concerned stakeholders can agree that you have the correct requirement.

The important point to keep in mind here is the difference between a requirement and a solution. Working software is great, providing it solves the right business problem. The intention of formalizing the requirement is to ensure all interested stakeholders agree on the requirement, and to allow

> *No matter how brilliantly ideas formed in his mind, or crystallized in his clockworks, his verbal descriptions failed to shine with the same light. His last published work, which outlines the whole history of his unsavory dealings with the Board of Longitude, brings his style of endless circumlocution to its peak. The first sentence runs on, virtually unpunctuated for twenty-five pages.*
>
> Source: Dava Sobel, *Longitude*

Figure 10.1

You discover the intention of the requirements when you are trawling and prototyping. We refer to these as *potential requirements*. The writing activity transforms the resulting ideas and half-formed thoughts into precise and testable requirements. We call these *formalized potential requirements*. The Quality Gateway tests the requirement before adding it to the requirements specification.

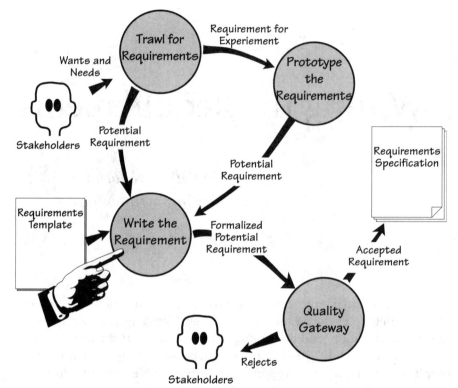

the designer and the software builder to construct the right implementation on the first attempt. We know of no more efficient way of arriving at working software.

Rabbit projects should not write a specification, but should consider some of the attributes of the requirement. Things such as rationale, fit criterion, and customer value can be added to your blog or wiki. This expansion can be done at any time once the requirement has been proposed. Think of this chapter as not so much writing a specification, but rather as enhancing your blog. The intention is not to make requirements gathering more bureaucratic, but to make software development more effective.

Horse projects should start with the requirements knowledge model (shown in Figure 10.2 later in this chapter). Make sure you know where and how these components are recorded. It is not necessary to have them all in one specification, but it is necessary to have them somewhere. Horses should consider the amount of specification they need. We describe here a complete and rigorous specification, but please assess your needs before producing each part of the specification.

Elephant projects will build a complete specification and should use some kind of automated tool to contain it. Many such tools are available, and the prime consideration is to allow the team of requirements analysts to access the specification simultaneously. Because of their size and fragmentation, elephant projects need to be ultra-concerned with having enough formality to ensure their requirements are traceable from the product to the work, and from the work to the product.

Turning Potential Requirements into Written Requirements

During the trawling and prototyping activities, the requirements you find are not always precise. They are ideas or intentions for requirements, and sometimes extremely vague and half-formed. By contrast, the requirements specification you intend to produce is the basis for the contract to build a product. As a consequence, it must contain clear, complete, and testable instructions about what has to be built. The task we tackle in this chapter is turning the half-formed ideas into precise statements of requirement.

This translation is not always straightforward, and we have found it useful to have some help. To do so, we make use of a specification template and a requirements shell. The template is a ready-made guide to writing a specification, and the shell is the container for an individual—we shall call it an "atomic"—requirement. Let's look first at the *knowledge* you are accumulating when producing a specification.

Knowledge Versus Specification

Before plunging into how to write requirements and assemble them to make a specification, it is worth spending a few moments to consider the knowledge or information you accumulate as you progress through the requirements process. By understanding this knowledge, you make better decisions on how the requirements specification is written, published, and distributed.

Let us start with the requirements knowledge model (Figure 10.2). Think of this model as a conceptual filing system, containing your requirements information. You can also think of it as an abstract way of looking at the contents of the template. Each rectangle in Figure 10.2 represents a class of requirements information. The way in which you store this information is not important, nor should you be too concerned about its format. The *information* is the crucial aspect of this conceptual model. Think facts, not documents or databases.

We are suggesting for convenience that most of this information can be contained within a specification. To that end, the numbers on the classes provide a cross-reference to the specification template.

Figure 10.2

The requirements knowledge model represents the information gathered during the requirements process. For convenience we use a UML class diagram to model this information. Each of the classes (shown as rectangles) is a repository of information about the subject (name of the class). The information can be in any form. The associations (lines) between the classes are relationships needed to make use of the information. The numbers attached to the classes correspond to the section numbers in the Volere Requirements Specification Template.

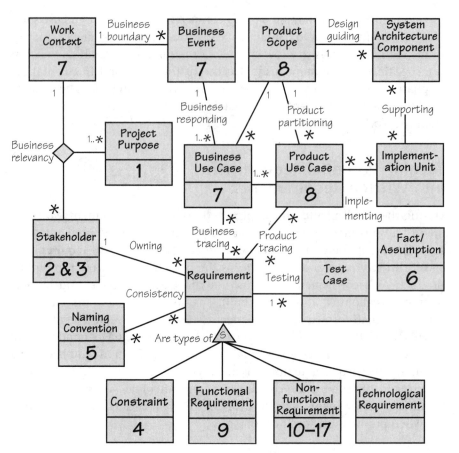

The lines represent necessary associations between the classes. For example, the classes Work Context, Project Purpose, and Stakeholder have an association between them because this association has a meaning to your project. Recall from Chapter 3 the trinity of scope, stakeholders, and goals. These three had dependencies on one another, so it is appropriate to model each dependency as an association we call Business relevancy.

Think of the knowledge model as an abstract representation of the requirements information you accumulate, manage, and trace. When your team has a shared understanding of their knowledge model, you are in a position to decide how you will format and store this knowledge. You decide what combination of automated and manual procedure you will use to record and keep track of the content. Typically projects use a combination of spreadsheets, word processors, requirements management tools, modeling tools, and manual procedures to manage the information represented by the knowledge model.

You should also consider the information contained by the knowledge model, and decide which parts of which classes are to be published in which documents. For example, Figure 10.2 includes an association called Product Tracing between the classes called Product Use Case and Requirement. An asterisk appears at both ends of the line, which means each product use case is made up of a number of requirements, and each requirement is potentially used by a number of product use cases. If you are keeping track of your requirements knowledge according to the model, you have a number of options for publishing it. You could select a specific product use case and publish it together with its associated requirements. Alternatively, you could select a particular requirement and produce a summary of all the product use cases that contain the requirement. When you have a well-organized knowledge model you can choose which parts of it should appear in which documents, and provide stakeholders with the information they need.

READING
For more details on building your own tailored requirements knowledge model, see Robertson, Suzanne, and James Robertson. *Requirements-Led Project Management: Discovering David's Slingshot.* Addison-Wesley, 2005.

The Volere Requirements Specification Template

Thousands of good requirements specifications have already been written. Your task of writing another one becomes easier if you make constructive use of some of the existing good specifications.

The Volere Requirements Specification Template was made by "standing on the shoulders of giants." Your authors borrowed useful components from specifications of many successfully built products, and packaged the best of them into a reusable template that can form the foundation of your requirements specifications.

The Volere template is a compartmentalized container for requirements. We examined requirements documents and categorized their requirements into types that prove useful for the purpose of recognition and elicitation. Each of the types is allocated to a section of the template. The template's table of contents lists these types:

Bernard of Chartres used to say that we are like dwarfs on the shoulders of giants, so that we can see more than they, and things at a greater distance, not by virtue of any sharpness of sight on our part, or any physical distinction, but because we are carried high and raised up by their giant size.

Source: John of Salisbury

The Volere Requirements Specification Template is found in Appendix B. This chapter will refer frequently to the template.

Project Drivers

1 The Purpose of the Project
2 The Client, the Customer, and Other Stakeholders
3 Users of the Product

Project Constraints

4 Mandated Constraints
5 Naming Conventions and Definitions
6 Relevant Facts and Assumptions

Functional Requirements

Nonfunctional Requirements

Project Issues

The template is set out in five main divisions. First come the *project drivers*. These factors cause the project to be undertaken in the first place. Drivers are such things as the purpose of the project—why you are involved in gathering the requirements for a product, and who wants or needs that product.

Next are *project constraints*. These issues have a strong influence on the requirements and the outcome for the product. The constraints are written into the specification at blastoff time, although you may have some mechanism in place for determining them earlier.

Think of these first two sections as setting the scene for the requirements that are to follow.

The next two divisions deal with the *requirements for the product*. Both the functional requirements and the nonfunctional requirements are explained here. Each requirement is described to a level of detail such that the product's constructors know precisely what to build to satisfy the business need and what benchmark is relevant for testing each capability of the delivered product.

The final division of the template deals with *project issues*. These are not requirements for the product, but rather issues that must be faced if the product is to become a reality. This part of the template also contains a "waiting room"— a place to store requirements not intended for the initial release of the product.

1 The Purpose of the Project

The first section of the template deals with the fundamental reason your client asked you to build a new product. That is, it describes the business problem the client faces and explains how the product is intended solve the problem.

1a The User Business or Background of the Project Effort

This description focuses on the work the user does, examining why it is not currently functioning as well as desired. There must be some problem or some significant opportunity to improve; otherwise, you would not be asked to develop a new product. The description may be quite brief:

> *The road authority is unhappy with the number of road accidents caused by ice.*

Alternatively, it may more fully describe the operational problem, usually giving the most weight to the most serious problems and the problems that your intended product best addresses.

> *Roads freeze in winter, and icy conditions cause road accidents that kill people. We need to be able to predict when a road is likely to freeze so our depot can schedule a de-icing truck in time to prevent the road from freezing. We expect a new product will provide more accurate predictions of icy conditions by using thermal maps of the district, road temperatures from weather stations installed in the roads, and the weather forecasts. This will lead to more timely de-icing treatment than at present, which will reduce road accidents. We also want to eliminate indiscriminate treatment of roads, which wastes de-icing compounds and causes environmental damage.*

Give references to any material that supports your statement. Any problem that is serious enough to warrant new product development is serious enough to be well documented.

> *Thornes, J. E. Cost-Effective Snow and Ice Control for the Nineties. Third International Symposium on Snow and Ice Control Technology, Minneapolis, Minnesota, Vol. 1, Paper 24, 1992.*

Perhaps there are no serious problems, just a significant business opportunity your client wishes to exploit. In this case, describe the opportunity.

> *Ice formation on roads is a serious problem in many countries, particularly in the northern hemisphere. There is currently no accurate way of predicting ice formation, and road treatment is unscientific at best and haphazard at worst. There is a significant market available if we produce an accurate ice forecasting and treatment-scheduling product. Our marketing department has identified 25 countries that would immediately buy such a product.*

Alternatively, the project may seek to explore or investigate possibilities. In this case the project deliverable, instead of a new product, would be a document proving that the requirements for a product can (or cannot) be satisfied.

> *Ice forecasting and truck scheduling have traditionally been done by separate entities. We suspect that treatment scheduling can be done far more effectively if it is combined with forecasting. Both activities would likely benefit by sharing data and optimization strategies. We wish to investigate whether there is a product development opportunity for our organization.*

1b Goals of the Project

This part of the specification describes what we want the product to do and what advantage it will bring to the overall goals of the work. Do not be too wordy in this section—a brief explanation of the product's goals is usually more valuable than a long, rambling treatise. A short, sharp goal will be clearer to the stakeholders and improve the chances of reaching a consensus for the goal.

> *To reduce road accidents by accurately forecasting and scheduling the de-icing of roads.*

If a goal is worthwhile, then it must provide some advantage or benefit. You can also think of it as adding value to the work. Rob Thomsett, a prominent management consultant, says that there are three categories of benefit:

- Value in the marketplace
- Reduced cost of operations
- Increased value or service to customers

Reducing road accidents can be counted as increasing a service to customers.

The advantage must be measurable. If you cannot measure it, it is not a worthwhile goal. How could you ever tell if your product has achieved the advantage it was intended to produce?

For example, suppose you have the following goal:

> *To produce a distributed quality-focused devolved groupware coordination and phased dynamic alliance monitoring solution.*

No possible advantage is stated here, and certainly nothing that can be measured. Instead of having a goal such as the above gibberish, we suggest that you look for a quantifiable benefit.

In Chapter 9, we referred to the measurement attached to a requirement as a fit criterion. The measurement of the goal is, in essence, the same thing. In Chapter 3, Project Blastoff , you saw how to arrive at a clear goal by using the PAM (Purpose, Advantage, Measurement) technique.

We came up with the following goals for the Icebreaker project:

Chapter 9 explains fit criteria in detail.

For more on how to write goals, refer to Chapter 3, Project Blastoff.

> *Purpose: To accurately forecast road freezing times and dispatch de-icing trucks.*
>
> *Advantage: To reduce road accidents by forecasting icy road conditions.*
> *Measurement: Accidents attributed to ice shall be no more than 15 percent of the total number of accidents during winter.*

> *Purpose: To save money on winter road maintenance costs.*
>
> *Advantage: Reduced de-icing and road maintenance costs.*
>
> *Measurement: The cost of de-icing shall be reduced by 25 percent of the current cost of road treatment, and damage to roads from ice shall be reduced by 50 percent.*
>
> *Supporting Materials: Thornes, J. E. Cost-Effective Snow and Ice Control for the Nineties. Third International Symposium on Snow and Ice Control Technology, Minneapolis, Minnesota, Vol. 1, Paper 24, 1992.*

These measurements are testable and provide guidance to help the project team focus their attention on those requirements that make the greatest contributions to meeting the goals. Although other goals may exist for this product, be careful not to include every individual requirement as a goal. A goal is an overriding requirement: It applies to the product as a whole. Thus

> *To save money on winter road maintenance costs.*

is a goal, whereas

> *The product shall record air-temperature readings, humidity readings, precipitation readings, and road-temperature readings received from weather stations.*

is a functional requirement that contributes to the goal.

You determine the goals at blastoff time. You must ensure that these goals are reasonable, attainable, simply stated, and worthwhile, and that they carry a measurement so you can test the delivered product to ensure that it satisfies the goal. If the goal does not have these properties, then history suggests the project is unlikely to deliver anything useful.

The goal is used throughout the requirements-gathering activity. Each requirement you gather must contribute, even if indirectly, to that goal. Requirements that do not contribute are not relevant and should be discarded.

2 The Client, the Customer, and Other Stakeholders

This section describes the stakeholders—the people who have an interest in the product. It is worth your while to spend enough time to accurately determine and describe these people, as the penalty for not knowing who they are can be very high.

Each of the stakeholders has some need the product has to fulfill. That is to say, the stakeholders are the sources of requirements. If you do not discover all of them, you are unlikely to discover all of the requirements.

This section of the specification identifies the stakeholders to the project team. Wherever possible, give the name and contact details for the stakeholder.

2a The Client

The client is the person who pays for product development. For products developed for in-house consumption, the client is sometimes known as the *sponsor* and may be the manager of the user department. For products

Chapter 3, Project Blastoff, provides a full explanation of each of the different types of stakeholders. Also refer to Appendix D, Project Sociology Analysis Templates, for guides to help you discover the stakeholders.

intended for external sale, your client may be the marketing department or product (sometimes program) management.

The person with the budget is normally regarded as the client, and it is he you have to satisfy with your product. Taking the time to understand who this person is will help you to know what kind of product you have to build. Name the client with an entry like this:

> The client for the product is Mack Andrews, the chief executive of Saltworks Systems.

2b The Customer

The customer is the person who buys your product. What kind of person is he? What attributes can you give to the customer, and what do you have to build to entice him to buy your product?

Describe the customer, and everything that you know about him.

> The customer for the product is the Northumberland County Highways Department, represented by director Jane Shaftoe.

If you are using personas as your customers, include a complete description of them in this section. A persona description is rarely too verbose.

2c Other Stakeholders

The other stakeholders are people who have some interest in the product or some knowledge needed for the development of the product. They do not necessarily have a financial interest—although the description does not preclude it—but do have an interest in the outcome for the product. It is important to identify and involve all relevant stakeholders—failure to do so may mean either that you miss vital requirements or that you end up with people actively working against your product.

The stakeholders are identified at blastoff time. They are listed in this section of the requirements specification to formalize their involvement and to give the requirements gatherers a list of people to interview. Wherever possible, give names and contact details for your stakeholders. You should also show any prioritization of stakeholders in this section.

3 Users of the Product

Users are the people who interact directly with your product. They are, of course, another type of stakeholder. Because of their major significance in the requirements-gathering effort, however, we have chosen to give them a section of their own in the template. In this section, you identify all the people who might conceivably make use of the product. The users become clear when you identify the product boundary during trawling. In this part of the specification, you describe them and their characteristics.

> *The engineers located at the truck depot are the main user group. The engineers have a detailed knowledge of road types, road locations, and road networks. They are all experienced in using personal computers for a wide variety of applications, including word processing and computer-aided design. All have a degree in engineering, and all of them speak English. Sonia Henning is the Road Engineering Supervisor.*
>
> *The Highways Department clerks are located at the Highways Department head office in Newcastle. Dick Button is the Clerical Supervisor. The clerks do not necessarily have any knowledge of the subject matter of roads and weather forecasts. Some of the clerks have used personal computers; however, do not assume familiarity with technology. Most have GCSE O levels, they are aged between 18 and 60, and all can read and speak English.*
>
> *The clerks work for local government organizations. Refer to the employment rules for specification of the types of disabilities that must be catered for.*

The product is to help the users do their work; you could also think of it as improving their work. You also write usability requirements to suit the characteristics of the users.

The functional requirements come from studying the users' work, so it is important to correctly identify the people actually doing the work at the moment. Similarly, the better the description of the users you write, the easier it is to determine the usability requirements. Make a point of including any unusual characteristics of the users—whether they might be angry, in a hurry, have only one arm free (for example, a waiter), and so on. This section of specification is where you detail your knowledge of the users. You take advantage of this work throughout the specification process to help you to define requirements relevant to these particular users.

You can find a discussion of user characteristics in Chapter 3, Project Blastoff, and more guidance in Appendix D, Project Sociology Analysis Templates.

4 Mandated Constraints

Constraints are global—they are factors that apply to the entire product. The product must be built within the stated constraints. Sometimes we know about the constraints, or they are mandated before the project gets under way. They are probably determined by management and are worth considering carefully—they restrict what you can do and so shape the product.

Constraints are requirements. That is, they are like the other requirements you gather during your trawling. The difference is that constraints are mandated, usually at the outset of the project.

4a Solution Constraints

Solution constraints are design decisions that mandate how the final product must look or what technology it must use or comply with. For example:

> *The product shall be able to be downloaded to 3G mobile phones.*

Here we see that management or marketing has decided the product will be successful if it is designed to comply with this constraint. Similarly, the client organization may have a standard stating that all new products are to use a specified programming language, or run on certain computers, or fit in with preexisting products.

Many projects chose at the outset to make use of available software products, such as shrink-wrap or open source products. The solution constraint is that the product under development must make use of the off-the-shelf (OTS) products and correctly interact with them.

While we discourage you from including any design details in your requirements specification—design and requirements are not the same thing—there will always be some mandates about the design dictated by the client or the organization. It would be unrealistic and unacceptable to ignore them.

However, despite this caveat and some obvious advantages of using certain designs, we warn you to examine the motive behind all design constraints. Is it given as a constraint because using the mandated technology offers a realistic advantage? Is there a real business need for this kind of solution? Or could it be that you are being given a perceived solution to the problem in lieu of a genuine statement of the true business need?

4b Implementation Environment of the Current System

Sometimes the constraint reflects management's desire not to buy a new load of hardware.

> *The product shall run on the existing network of personal computers.*

This constraint restricts any computerized solution to the existing technology. Thus the requirements may not specify a product that is so elaborate as to need different computing capabilities to implement it.

This section is also used to describe the current environment, or at least that part of it used by the new product.

4c Partner or Collaborative Applications

Almost all software projects have to construct a product that must interact with several other software products both inside and outside the owning organization. This section sets out for your developers what those other products are and explains why they are considered partners to the current product.

> *The product shall interface with the Rosa DM31 weather stations.*
> *The product shall interface with the Thermal Mapping Database.*
> *The product shall interface with the Road Engineering Computer System.*

Constraints might also be written when the solution intends to use OTS software as part, or all, of the new product. These types of restrictions are covered in section 4d of the specification. Just as these sections describe the technological environment, section 4e describes the anticipated workplace environment. This gives a picture of the workplace and any features, including the users who could have an effect on the design of the product.

4d Off-the-Shelf Software

This section is where you specify any brought-in software. Because of the abundant supply and myriad capabilities of OTS software available to almost all projects, it usually makes sense to use some of these products. This section identifies which brought-in products you intend to use. You might also use this section to specify the interfaces and special functionality necessitated by the OTS product; however, we find it is less confusing to include that functionality along with your other functional requirements.

4e Anticipated Workplace Environment

This section describes the workplace. Include it only if the workplace could have an effect on the requirements for the product.

4f Schedule Constraints

This section specifies the time allowed to build the product. When the requirements team knows the deadline, it helps team members restrict their requirements gathering to what it is possible to build in the allowed time.

4g Budget Constraints

This section shows the allowable resources—money or effort or people—for the project. It is intended to restrict the wildest ambitions and to prevent the team from gathering requirements for an Airbus 380 when the budget can buy only a Cessna.

> *The budget for building the product is $500,000.*

5 Naming Conventions and Definitions

It has been our experience that all projects have their own unique vocabulary. Failure to use this project-specific nomenclature correctly inevitably leads to misunderstandings, hours of lost time, miscommunication between team members, and ultimately poor-quality specifications.

5a Definitions of All Terms, Including Acronyms, Used in the Project

In section 5a of the requirements specification, start a glossary to define the important terms to be used by the stakeholders. This glossary should be enlarged and refined as the analysis proceeds, but for the moment, it should introduce the terms that the project uses and the meanings of those terms to your project.

> *Weather Station:* A weather station is capable of monitoring air temperature, humidity, precipitation, and road temperature. Four road-surface sensors can be attached to one weather station. Each sensor must be within 1 km of the weather station.
>
> *Thermal Map:* A region or other geographical area is surveyed to determine the temperature differences at various parts of the area. The resulting thermal map means the temperature at any part of the area can be determined by knowing the temperature at a reference point.

The names you use in the requirements specification should be the regular business names—that is, the names that the business stakeholders use in their everyday work. However, be prepared to suggest better names if the existing ones are misleading or include references to obsolete technology.

Good names are easily distinguishable and self-documenting. They should invoke the right meaning, thereby saving hours of explanation. Create your dictionary by writing each term and its definition. Include all abbreviations and acronyms that are used by your users.

We suggest you add *all* acronyms and abbreviations. We often encounter situations where team members use acronyms, but admit they do not know the meanings of those acronyms. This section gives you a place to register your acronyms.

This section is intended to serve as a reference for all the people who work on the project. It is also used in the Quality Gateway to ensure that all terms used to write the requirements conform to the terms defined here.

5b Data Dictionary for Any Included Models

The glossary described earlier is the basis for the analysis data dictionary. As the analysis data dictionary evolves, many of the definitions from the glossary are expanded in the dictionary by adding their data composition. We find it particularly useful to start the data dictionary here, as any models you include in your specification—we cannot overstate the value of having a context model as part of it—lack rigor without the attached data dictionary.

Use whatever dictionary notation you normally use. The notation is unimportant; the existence of the dictionary and the way you use it *are* important.

6 Relevant Facts and Assumptions

6a Facts

Relevant facts are external factors that have an effect on the product but are not covered by other sections. They are not necessarily translated into requirements but could be. Relevant facts alert the developers to conditions and factors that have a bearing on the requirements. For example, it may be that the IceBreaker product's specification would contain relevant facts:

> *Salt (NaCl) de-ices down to −6°C. Calcium chloride (CaCl) de-ices down to −15°C.*
>
> *One ton of de-icing material treats three miles of single-lane roadway.*

These facts must be taken into account when scheduling trucks to treat freezing roads. Note that they are not requirements as such, but have a strong effect on the outcome of the product.

Relevant facts are usually discovered when you are trawling for requirements, and particularly when you are discussing the business rules with your users. The background information given by the relevant facts section is required reading for new people on the project.

6b Assumptions

The assumptions you write in this section are those being made by the project team. The intention is to alert management to factors that might affect the product. The assumptions usually focus on the intended operational environment of the product, but may relate to anything that could, if the assumption does not come true, have a detrimental effect on the success of the product.

> *Roads that have been treated will not need treating for at least two hours.*
>
> *Road treatment stops at county boundaries.*

By stating these assumptions, the analyst says to the stakeholders, "Look at these. I am proceeding on the basis that these assumptions are true. The product that I specify assumes that they are true. If the product is not to stop road treatment at county boundaries, then please let me know right now."

Sometimes other products may be undergoing development at the same time as your product, and their delivery failure will affect your product. Similarly, you may be making assumptions about the performance or capacity of some as-yet-untested product. If that product does not perform as you assume it does, your product will be adversely affected.

> *Road Engineering's Apian system will be available for integration testing before November.*
>
> *The treatment trucks being built will be capable of operating at speeds up to 40 mph. They will have a material capacity of two tons.*

You may make assumptions about interfaces between the product under development and existing products. For example, the IceBreaker product must interact with the weather stations. These stations are being developed by an outside organization. Obviously, if there are variations in the way that they transmit their information, then the IceBreaker product will not work as planned.

> *The Bureau's forecasts will be transmitted according to its specification 1003-7 issued by its engineering department.*

Also, you may write assumptions about the availability and capability of bought-in components, the operational environment of the product, the capabilities of the development language, or anything else that will be used by the product.

It is anticipated—in fact, it is necessary—that all assumptions will have been resolved by the time the product is released.

7 The Scope of the Work

The first scope to be established is the scope of the work. It determines the boundaries of the business area to be studied and outlines how it fits into its environment. Once you understand the work and its constraints, you can establish the scope of the product. Keep in mind that the product has to fit seamlessly into the work, so it is appropriate to look first at the work.

We suggest using a context model to describe the scope of the work and its surrounding adjacent systems. We described this model and explained how to build it in Chapter 3, Project Blastoff, and again referred to it in Chapter 4, Event-Driven Use Cases.

Establishing the correct work scope is crucial to the success of the product. It is worth investing all the care, and time, necessary to ensure that the context is sufficient for you to understand the parts of the customer's business that could potentially benefit from the product. Without this, your chances of producing a satisfactory product are lessened.

The first two subsections, 7a and 7b, describe the work. We have looked at that topic in Chapter 3, so let us move on.

Context models are discussed in Chapter 3, Project Blastoff, and Chapter 4, Event-Driven Use Cases.

7c Work Partitioning

Once you have established the scope of the work, it soon becomes apparent that the work is much larger than one person can comfortably understand. There is a need to partition the work into smaller, more manageable, and more convenient pieces. *Business events,* as we described them in Chapter 4, Event-Driven Use Cases, are the most convenient way to partition the work.

Business events are things that happen in the outside world—the outside world is represented by the adjacent systems on your context model—that cause the work to respond in some way. Business events also happen when it is time for the work to carry out some prearranged obligation, such as producing reports, broadcasting news, or some other functionality needed to send information to the outside world.

Our projects maintain an event list showing for each business event:

For more on business event partitioning, see Chapter 4, Event-Driven Use Cases.

- Event number
- Event name
- Input or triggering data flow
- Output data flows
- One-sentence summary of the event response/business use case

If you have built any models of the response to the business event (that is, the business use case), then you put them in this section of the specification, tagged with the appropriate event number. The models can take a variety of forms: sequence diagrams, activity diagrams, data flow diagrams, and business task models, to name a few possibilities. Another option for key events is to build a business use case scenario. Chapter 6 provides details of how to do this.

The details of business use case scenarios are found in Chapter 6, Scenarios and Requirements.

8 The Scope of the Product

8a Product Boundary

We have made much mention of the difference between the scope of the work and the scope of the product. We won't belabor the point by repeating it here.

You have several options for showing the product's scope. We suggest a model is markedly better than a text description at demonstrating your scoping intentions to your stakeholders. The UML use case diagram, while far from perfect, is a popular model to show product scope.

Alternatively, you can use another context model similar to the work context. This time the central bubble is the product, and the adjacent systems are the actors.

The kind of model you use here is less important than using a model and having a clear demonstration of the functionality contained in your product.

8b Product Use Case List

The use case diagram is a graphical way of summarizing the product use cases that are relevant to the product. If you have a large number of product use cases (we find 15–20 is around the limit), then a list of product use cases is more manageable than the use case diagram.

8c Individual Product Use Cases

This section is where you keep details about the individual product use cases on your list. You can include a scenario for each product use case on your list or you might prefer to draw a sequence diagram. Also, here is where you keep any prototypes of the product use cases.

The Shell

The first eight sections of the requirements specification, which cover the drivers, constraints, and scope of the project, use a mixture of models and free text. However, the atomic functional and nonfunctional requirements should be written more formally using an agreed structure.

When you write atomic requirements, it is not sufficient to write free-form natural-language statements, as they lack the necessary rigor and are ambiguous. We have found that a number of components are necessary to make a complete requirement, and have implemented these components in what we call a *shell*.

Snow Cards

Before we discuss the components of the shell, we want to introduce the *snow card*. It is simply a card—white, of course—that contains the shell components. We borrowed the idea of a card from William Pena, an architect. Members of Pena's architectural firm use cards to record requirements and issues relating to buildings they are designing. The team members tape cards containing unresolved issues to the conference room walls, and then use this visual display to get a quick impression of the progress of the building.

We have found a similar use for these cards when gathering requirements. Figure 10.3 shows an example of a snow card. This low-tech approach to requirements gathering is convenient when trawling for requirements, but at some stage we transfer the requirement to an automated tool.

In our requirements seminars, we place small stacks of snow cards on the students' tables. The students use them to record requirements during the workshops. What always surprises us is that, even though the snow card is a low-tech device, the students take away all the unused ones at the end of the

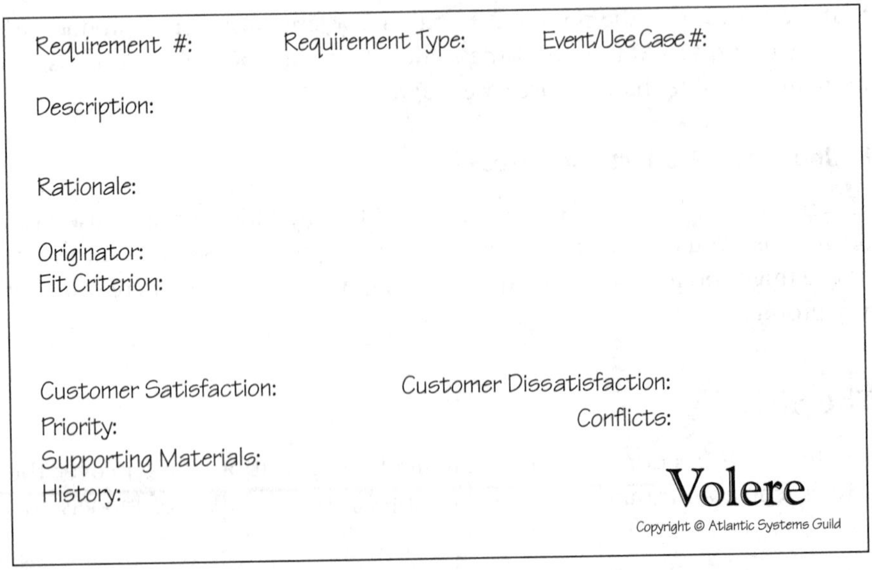

Figure 10.3

The Volere Shell in its snow card form. Each 8 inch × 5 inch card is used to record an atomic requirement. The requirements analyst completes each of the items as it is discovered, thereby building a complete, rigorous requirement.

Requirement #:   Requirement Type: Event/Use Case #:

Description:

Rationale:

Originator:
Fit Criterion:

Customer Satisfaction: Customer Dissatisfaction:
Priority: Conflicts:
Supporting Materials:
History:

Volere
Copyright © Atlantic Systems Guild

seminar. Later we get e-mails telling us how much they like using snow cards for the early part of the requirements-gathering process.

When working on our own projects, we use cards when we are interviewing stakeholders, and record requirements as we hear them. Initially the requirement is not fully formed, so we might simply capture the description and the originator. As time moves on and we have a better understanding of the requirements, we progressively add new components to the cards.

One advantage of loose cards is that they can be distributed among analysts. We have several clients who make use of cards in the early stages of requirements gathering. They find it convenient to pin them to walls, to hand them to analysts for further clarification, to mail them to users (we were intrigued to receive a snow card with our address and postage stamp on the back), and generally to be able to handle a requirement individually.

We were intrigued to receive a snow card with our address and postage stamp on the back.

Automated Requirements Tools

The low-tech approach is certainly feasible in the early stage of requirements gathering. However, if a number of analysts are working on your project, you will find an automated tool pays dividends as the work progresses and the number of requirements grows. The tool does not have to be elaborate. In fact, many of our clients find that a word processor or spreadsheet is satisfactory.

Free tools are also applicable: Blogs spring to mind here. It is easy enough to set up a blog or wiki on your in-house system, or to make use of one of the services available over the Internet. While it is not exactly a blog, your authors use Writely (*www.writely.com*) as an online collaborative tool. We are currently writing another book involving three authors and this approach works well for us. Other tools are also available, each with its own attractions and each with its own cost. Take your pick.

Look about. You are bound to find something that suits your requirements for recording requirements.

READING
Requirements tools change constantly. We maintain a list of available tools at *www.volere.co.uk/tools.htm.*

The Atomic Requirement

Now let us look at how an individual, complete, formalized requirement is constructed.

As we treat each of the items that make up the requirement, consider how you discover it and how well it applies to your organization. For this activity, we assume you are using the Volere Shell, or that you are using some mechanism to ensure that you capture the relevant parts of each requirement.

Start by identifying the requirement. Each requirement has three pieces of identification: its number, its type, and the event(s) and/or use case(s) that spawned the requirement.

Requirement Number

Each requirement must be uniquely identified. The reason is straightforward: Requirements must be traceable throughout the development of the product, so it is convenient and logical to give each requirement a unique number. We use "number" meaning any unique identifier, although it can be any kind of identifier you wish. To keep this assignment from becoming an onerous clerical task, we suggest you use a simple sequential number. It is not important how you uniquely identify the requirement as long as you identify it.

Requirement Type

The type comes from the Volere Requirements Specification Template. The template includes 27 sections, each of which contains a different type of requirement. We use the template section number as the type: The purpose of the product is requirement type 1, constraints are type 4, functional requirements are type 9, look and feel are type 10, usability requirements are type 11, and so on.

Attaching the type to the requirement is useful in several ways:

- You can sort the requirements by type. By comparing all requirements of one type, you can more readily discover requirements that conflict with one another.

- It is easier to write an appropriate fit criterion when the type of requirement is established.

- When you group all of the known requirements of one type, it becomes readily apparent if some of them are missing or duplicated.

- The ability to group requirements by type also helps with stakeholder involvement. For example, you can easily identify all of the security requirements and make them available for review by a security expert.

Event/Use Case Number

The context of the work is broken into smaller pieces using the business events as the partitioning tool. The work makes a response to each business event; this response constitutes a business use case. You decide which part of the business use case is to be handled by the product; we call this part a product use case. When you identify each product use case, you also identify the user or users who will interact with that part of the product; we call them actors.

Give each business event a number for convenient referencing. Similarly, each product use case is numbered. For traceability and change-control purposes, it is useful to keep track of all requirements generated by a business event. Each of your product use cases corresponds to a business event, so it is possible to use the same number to indicate the business event and the

| Requirement #: **75** | Requirement Type: **9** | Event/Use Case #: **6** |

Figure 10.4

The requirement
number, requirement
type, business event
number, and product
use case number.

product use case. If, however, you choose to cluster your requirements into sub-use cases, then you need a separate numbering system. Whatever your preference, you must tag each requirement so that you can identify which parts of the business it relates to (business events) and which parts of the product it relates to (product use cases). Figure 10.4 illustrates how requirements are identified.

Being able to collect together all the requirements for a product use case helps you find missing requirements and confirm the functionality with its users.

Description

The description is the intent of the requirement. It is an English (or whatever natural language you use) statement in the stakeholder's words as to what the stakeholder thinks he needs. Do not be too concerned about whether the description contains ambiguities (but neither should you be sloppy with your language), as the fit criterion eliminates any failings in the language. The objective when you first write the description is to capture the stakeholder's wishes. So for the moment just be as clear as you (and your user) can.

Rationale

The rationale is the reason behind the requirement's existence. It explains why the requirement is important and how it contributes to the product's purpose. Adding a rationale to a requirement helps you to clarify and understand it, and by so doing, you come to understand the requirement.

Originator

The originator is the person who raised the requirement in the first instance, or the person to whom it can be attributed. You should attach the originator's name to your requirements so you have a referral point if questions about the requirement arise or if the Quality Gateway rejects the requirement. The person who raises the requirement must have the knowledge and authority appropriate for the type of requirement.

Fit Criterion

A fit criterion is a quantified goal the solution has to meet—in other words, it is an acceptance criterion. While the description of the requirement is written in the language of the users, the fit criterion is written in a precise, quantified manner so that solutions can be tested against the requirement.

The fit criteria set the standard to which the builder constructs the product. While they do not say how the implementation will be tested, they do provide the benchmark to test against to determine whether the implementation meets the requirements.

Fit criteria are so important that we have devoted an entire chapter to them; visit Chapter 9 for more details.

Chapter 9 covers fit criteria.

Customer Satisfaction and Customer Dissatisfaction

The satisfaction ranking is a measure of how happy the client will be if you successfully deliver an implementation of the requirement. The scale ranges from 1 to 5, where 1 means that the client is unconcerned about the outcome and 5 means that the client will be extremely happy if you successfully deliver a product that meets the requirement.

The dissatisfaction rating is also on a scale of 1 to 5. This time the rating measures the amount of unhappiness the client will feel if you do not successfully deliver this requirement. A 1 means that the client will be unconcerned if the product appears without this requirement; a 5 means that your client will be extremely angry if you do not successfully deliver this requirement.

For example, this is a fairly normal and unremarkable requirement:

> *The product shall record changes to the road network.*

Naturally, your client expects the product to be able to record the road network so that it can tell the engineers which roads must be treated. The client is unlikely to get excited over this requirement, so the satisfaction rating may be anything from 3 to 5. However, if the product cannot record changes to roads, you would expect the client to be rather angry, and thus would give a dissatisfaction rating of 5. The high dissatisfaction score gives significance to this requirement.

Now consider this requirement:

> *The product shall issue an alert if a weather station fails to transmit readings.*

This feature of the product would be both useful and nice to have. Your client may give it a satisfaction rating of 5. However, the requirement is not crucial to the correct operation of the product: The engineers would eventually notice if readings failed to turn up from one of the weather stations. In this case the client may well rate the dissatisfaction as 2 or 3. In other words, if the product never does this, the engineers will not be too unhappy.

The satisfaction/dissatisfaction ratings are used to place a value on each of the requirements. The effect of asking your client to rate the satisfaction and the dissatisfaction is to make him consider the requirement more seriously. It also gives him an opportunity to let you know how he feels about each of the requirements. Later, you can weigh these ratings against the cost of each requirement.

The ratings are set either by your client or by a panel made up of the significant stakeholders. If the product is intended for sale to external customers, then these ratings should be assigned by a panel representing the potential customers.

An example of a complex case we have come across is one where mobile telephones were being developed for sale in different countries. The marketing people had identified that their customers' priorities differed from country to country. Thus the value ratings had to be separately assessed for each target country.

Priority

The priority of a requirement is the decision on the importance of the requirement's implementation relative to the whole project. The customer value ratings help to identify how the stakeholders feel about the requirements. The priority rating governs which requirements will receive priority when it comes to inclusion in the next release of the product. Priority is often the result of a decision reached by a group of stakeholders and sometimes reflects a compromise.

You can apply the idea of customer value and priority at the product use case level. As soon as you have identified your product use cases, ask your stakeholders to give a customer satisfaction rating and a customer dissatisfaction rating to each use case. If you know enough about the constraints, then you might also be able to do a rough prioritization for each use case by asking whether it should appear in the first or subsequent releases of the product.

For more on prioritization techniques, refer to Chapter 14, Reviewing the Specification.

Conflicts

Conflicts between requirements mean there is some contradiction between them, or one requirement makes another requirement less feasible. For example, a requirement for the product may be to calculate the shortest route to the destination. Another requirement might say the product is to calculate the quickest route to the destination. A conflict between these two requirements would arise if they were both considered to be the preferred route, and if traffic or other conditions meant that the shortest route was not always the quickest route.

Similarly, you may discover a conflict between two or more requirements when you design the product and begin to look at solutions. Perhaps the solution to one requirement means the solution to the other requirement is impossible, or at least severely restricted.

Conflicting requirements are a normal part of development. Don't be too concerned if conflicts between requirements appear. As long as you are able to capture the fact that the conflict exists, then you can work toward solving it.

Supporting Materials

Do not attempt to put everything in the specification. There will always be other material that is important to the requirements, and it may be simply cross-referenced by this item.

> *Supporting Materials: Thornes, J. E. Cost-Effective Snow and Ice Control for the Nineties. Third International Symposium on Snow and Ice Control Technology, Minneapolis, Minnesota, Vol. 1, Paper 24, 1992.*

We suggest you restrict entries under this heading to those references that have a direct bearing on the requirement.

History

This section is the place to record the date the requirement was first raised, dates of changes, dates of deletions, date of passing through the Quality Gateway, and so on. Add the names of people responsible for these actions if you think it will help later.

Writing the Specification

The Volere Requirements Specification Template and Volere Shell are convenient devices to use when writing a specification. The template is a guide to the topics to be covered by the specification, and the shell is a guide to what to write for each atomic requirement.

You should keep the business event list handy to allow for easy tagging of requirements to the business use case and/or product use case where the requirement originated. All requirements must have an identifier, so you must have some way of registering requirement numbers or otherwise guaranteeing that each requirement carries a unique identifier. Figure 10.5 illustrates this further.

Now let us consider the remaining requirement types from the template and discuss the appropriate entries for each of the sections.

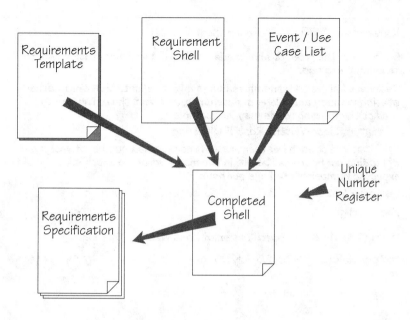

Figure 10.5

The specification is not so much written as assembled. The template provides a guide to the types of requirements, explaining how to describe each one. The components for each functional requirement and nonfunctional requirement are compiled using the shell as a guide. You can think of the requirements specification as an assembly of completed shells.

9 Functional Requirements

Think of the functional requirements as things the product must do or actions it must take. These requirements are the fundamental activities of the product. For example, a functional requirement may be something like this:

> *The product shall record the new weather stations.*

This requirement states an action that, if carried out, contributes to the goal of the product. If the goal is to predict when the roads will freeze, then it is necessary to collect data from weather stations, and thus it is necessary to know the existence and location of the weather stations. When new ones are added to the network, the product must be able to record their details.

Similarly, the following requirement also contributes to the product's purpose:

> *The product shall issue an alert if a weather station fails to transmit readings.*

This requirement is necessary if the product is to know about failures of the stations and the possibility of the product having incomplete data. However, these example functional requirements are not complete. You may also

Figure 10.6

A complete functional
requirement written on a
snow card.

Requirement #: **75**   Requirement Type: **9**   Event/Use Case #: **6**

Description: **The product shall issue an alert if a weather station fails to transmit readings.**

Rationale: **Failure to transmit readings might indicate that the weather station is faulty and needs maintenance, and that the data used to predict the freezing roads may be incomplete.**

Originator: **Roger Walters, Road Engineering**

Fit Criterion: **For each weather station the recorded number of each type of reading per hour shall be within the manufacturer's specified range of the expected number of readings per hour.**

Customer Satisfaction: **3**   Customer Dissatisfaction: **5**

Priority: **High**   Conflicts: **None**

Supporting Materials: **Specification of Rosa Weather Station**

History: **Raised by GBS, 28 July 05**

Volere
Copyright © Atlantic Systems Guild

think that they are too casual and possibly ambiguous. To complete each requirement, you must take the following steps:

● Give it an identification number.

● Designate the product use case and the business event this piece of functionality is derived from.

● If the rationale is not self-evident, include it.

● Designate the originator.

● Add a fit criterion.

● Describe any conflicts, if they are known.

● Include any supporting materials you consider useful.

Figure 10.6 illustrates the complete functional requirement. Let's look more closely at the description.

Description

The description details an action that the product must take—in other words, what the product must do. Take this example:

The product shall record air-temperature readings, humidity readings, precipitation readings, and road-temperature readings received from weather stations.

Note the level of detail. The requirement is written in plain English, provided it is not obviously ambiguous or open-ended. The description must be understandable and verifiable by technical and nontechnical stakeholders. It is not yet complete—each of the requirements is given a fit criterion that tightens the definition by making it testable.

Usually the requirement can be stated in one sentence. If you find yourself taking more than one sentence to describe it, then you may, in fact, be describing several requirements. If you use two verbs in the sentence, it might be that you are describing two requirements. It is good practice to write each requirement as a single sentence with a single verb. It will cause you fewer problems when you write the fit criterion and the time arrives to test the requirement.

It is good practice to write each requirement as a single sentence.

The functional requirements are usually derived from the steps of the use case scenario. For example, the use case step

> *Product determines which roads are likely to freeze and when they are likely to freeze.*

yields these requirements:

> *The product shall determine the current temperature of the road adjacent to the weather station.*
>
> *The product shall extrapolate temperatures for each meter of road using the thermal map.*
>
> *The product shall predict the temperature for each road-meter for each ten-minute interval using the weather forecast.*
>
> *The product shall record roads where ice will form within the given time parameter.*

See Chapter 6, Scenarios and Requirements, for a full description of how to write scenarios.

Again, note the level of detail. It should be enough for your client (or the user or the domain experts) to verify that the product will work correctly.

Nonfunctional Requirements

Nonfunctional requirements are the properties that the product must have. In this section you describe what the spirit of the product's appearance is, how easy it must be to use, how secure it must be, what laws apply to the product, and anything else that must be built into the product, but is not a part of its fundamental functionality.

Figure 10.7

A nonfunctional requirement.

Requirement #: **110**   Requirement Type: **11**   Event/Use Case #: **6**

Description: **The product shall be easy for the road engineers to use.**

Rationale: **It should not be necessary for the engineers to attend training classes to be able to use the product.**

Originator: **Sonia Henning, Road Engineering Supervisor**

Fit Criterion: **A road engineer shall be able to use the product to successfully carry out the cited use cases within 1 hour of first encountering the product.**

Customer Satisfaction: **3**   Customer Dissatisfaction: **5**

Priority: **Next release**   Conflicts: **None**

Supporting Materials:

History: **Raised by AG. 25 Aug 05.**

Volere
Copyright © Atlantic Systems Guild

See Chapter 9, Fit Criteria, for details on how to quantify nonfunctional requirements.

Nonfunctional requirements are written like other requirements. That is, they have all the usual components—they are identified, they have a type, they have a description, they have a fit criterion, and so on. Thus you write them just as you would a functional requirement (see Figure 10.7).

Project Issues

Chapter 8, Nonfunctional Requirements, describes these types of requirements and discusses how to write them.

Project issues are not requirements, but rather project concerns that are brought to light by the requirements activity. We sometimes include them in a requirements specification for fear they will become lost if we do not do so. However, if your organization already has procedures in place or suitable documents or files in which to record this information, then please do not add these issues to your requirements specification.

18 Open Issues

This section of the specification deals with issues that have arisen from the requirements activity, but have not been resolved yet. When you are probing around the user's business, questions often come to the surface, and they cannot for the moment be answered. Similarly, as you are gathering the requirements for a future product, it may well be that your stakeholders are unsure of how the work should be done in the future.

> *The feasibility study to determine whether to use the Regional Weather Center's online database is not yet complete. This issue affects how we should handle the weather data.*

Changes happen all the time, and some of them are certain to affect your product. The Open Issues section of the requirements specification may also contain notes on changes that have been proposed, but whose final outcome is not yet established.

> *Planned changes to working hours for drivers may affect the way that trucks are scheduled and the length of the routes that drivers are permitted to travel. The changes are still in the proposal stage; details will be available by the end of the year.*

19 Off-the-Shelf Solutions

This section looks at available solutions and summarizes their applicability to the requirements. This discussion is not intended to be a full feasibility study of the alternatives, but it should tell your client that you have considered some alternatives and determined how closely they match the requirements for the product.

Note the intention of this section. It does not say that there are some wonderful solutions just waiting to be taken down from the shelf, and never mind if they don't fit the requirements all that well. Instead, this section points out solutions that may be applicable and warrant further study.

If there are no suitable OTS products, then this section alerts the client that he may have to shoulder the cost of building something.

We suggest that this section include three headings:

- Is there a ready-made product open source or commercial off-the-shelf software that could be bought?
- Can ready-made components be used for this product?
- Is there something that we could copy?

For each of these headings, set out the alternatives that you think are suitable. If your findings are preliminary, then say so. It is useful to add approximate costs, availability, time to implement, and other factors that may have a bearing on the decision.

The point of this section is to consider alternative ways the product can be implemented, not to try and force-fit the requirements into a marginal product.

An all-too-common problem from a project perspective is preparing the change but not preparing for the change.

Source: Mike Russell

20 New Problems

Changes to the existing order often bring with them adverse effects. This section gives you the opportunity to examine and highlight any problems that the installation of the new product will create.

For example, there may be changes to the way that work is done, changes to interfaces with existing products, or changes to jobs that people currently do.

While it is not necessary to describe every facet of every change, you should use this section as an opportunity to alert your client to problems that he might possibly face.

21 Tasks

What steps have to be taken to deliver the product? This section highlights the effort required to build the product, the steps needed to buy a solution, the amount of effort to modify and install a ready-made solution, and so on.

Whatever route you plan to follow to install the new product in the user's business area should be known, and described, at the requirements stage.

Although your organization may have a standard approach to constructing or buying products, the requirements of the product usually necessitate at least some variations on this process. Management uses this section to assess the feasibility of the product, given the effort and cost required to produce it.

22 Migration to the New Product

When you install a new product, some things always have to be done before it can work successfully. For example, databases often have to be converted. There is usually new data to be collected, procedures to be converted, and many other steps to be taken to ensure the successful transition to the new product.

Often there are periods where the organization will run both the old product and the new product in parallel until the new one has proven that it is functioning correctly.

This section of the specification is where you identify the tasks necessary for the period of transition to the new product. This section is input to the project planning process.

READING

DeMarco, Tom, and Timothy Lister. *Waltzing with Bears: Managing Risk on Software Projects*. Dorset House, 2003.

23 Risks

All projects involve risk. By this, we mean the risk that something will go wrong. Risk is not necessarily a bad thing, as no progress is made without taking some chances. However, there is a difference between unmanaged risk—

say, shooting dice at a craps table—and managed risk, where the probabilities are well understood and the contingencies planned. Risk is a bad thing only if you ignore the risks and they become problems. Risk management involves assessing which risks are most likely to apply to the project, deciding on a course of action if they become problems, and monitoring projects to give early warnings of risks becoming problems.

This section of the specification contains a list of the most likely and the most serious risks for your project. For each risk, include the probability of it becoming a problem and any contingency plans.

It is also useful input to project management if you include the impact on the schedule, or the cost, if the risk does become a problem.

As an alternative, you may prefer to identify the single largest risk—the showstopper. If this risk becomes a problem, then the project will definitely fail. Identifying a single risk in this way focuses attention on the single most critical area. Project efforts are then concentrated on not letting this risk become a problem.

This section of the book is not intended to be a thorough treatise on risk management. Nor is this section of the requirements specification meant to be a substitute for proper risk management. The intention here is to assign risks to requirements and show clearly that requirements are not free—they carry a cost that can be expressed as an amount of money or time, and as a risk. Later, you can use this information if you need to make choices about which requirements should be given a higher priority.

READING

Boehm, Barry. *Software Risk Management*. IEEE Computer Society Press, 1989.

McManus, John. *Risk Management in Software Development Projects*. Butterworth-Heinemann, 2003.

24 Costs

The other cost of requirements is the amount of money or effort that you have to spend turning them into a product. Once the requirements specification is complete, use one of the estimating methods to assess the cost, and then express this cost as a monetary amount, or effort or time to build the product.

There is no best method to use when estimating. The important thing is to create your estimates using metrics directly related to the requirements. If you have specified the requirements in the way we have described, you will have the following metrics:

- Number of business events
- Number of product use cases
- Number of requirements
- Number of constraints
- Number of function points

READING

Garmus, David, and David Herron. *Function Point Analysis: Measurement Practices for Successful Software Projects.* Addison-Wesley, 2001.

Appendix C, Function Point Counting: A Simplified Introduction, describes function point counting as it can be used by requirements analysts.

You can use these metrics as the basis for estimating the time, effort, and cost of building the product. First you need to determine what each of these metrics means within the environment in which you are building the product. For example, do you know how long it will take you to do all the work necessary to implement a product use case? If you do not, then you can take one of the use cases and benchmark it.

We favor counting function points as a means to estimate the size of the problem. This approach is a commonly accepted sizing method, and so much is known about it that it is possible to make easy comparisons with other products and with other installations' productivity.

At this stage, your client needs to know what the product is likely to cost. You usually express this as a total cost to complete the product, but you may also find it advantageous to point out the costs of individual requirements.

Whatever you do, do not leave the costs in the lap of hysterical optimism. Make sure that this section includes realistic numbers and coherent estimates and questions based on those numbers.

25 User Documentation and Training

This section specifies the user documentation that will be produced as part of the product-building effort. This is not the documentation itself, but a description of what must be produced.

The reason for including this description is to establish your client's expectations, and to give your usability people and your users the chance to assess whether the proposed documentation will be sufficient.

26 Waiting Room

The waiting room holds requirements that cannot, for one reason or another, be part of the initial release of the product. If you are competent at gathering requirements, your users may often be inspired to think of more requirements than you can fit within the constraints of the project. While you may not want to include all of these requirements in the initial version of the product, neither do you want to lose them.

When you decide to put a requirement into the waiting room, you do not need to write it in detail. It might simply be one sentence summarizing an idea that someone has had. Just write until the idea is trapped well enough for you to be able to assess it later.

The waiting room has a calming effect on everyone because it shows their ideas are being taken seriously. Your users and client know the requirements are not forgotten, merely parked until it is time to review them and make decisions about whether they will be incorporated in the product.

27 Ideas for Solutions

Ideas for solutions are obviously not requirements, but it is impossible when gathering requirements not to become interested in how they might be implemented. Rather than discarding the ideas or—even worse—writing them as if they are requirements, a practical idea is to simply set aside a section of your specification for these ideas. Record each one faithfully in this area, and then hand them over, along with the requirements, to your designer.

In exceptional circumstances, you might consider writing your ideas for solutions against individual requirements. Take care when doing so, as it is all too easy to become engulfed in cool solutions and forget for the moment you are supposed to be gathering requirements.

We said at the beginning of the "Project Issues" section earlier in this chapter that all of these components do not necessarily belong in a requirements specification. The ideas for solutions are an ideal subject for a blog. This is, after all, the place for ideas, and blogs are a great place for creativity and building on one another's ideas.

Summary

Writing the requirements specification is not a separate activity, but one that is done in conjunction with other parts of the requirements process. Requirements analysts write requirements, or parts of requirements, whenever they find them. Not all requirements are completed at the same time.

This does not mean that writing the specification is a random activity. Business events, business use cases, product use cases, the template, and the shell make it possible to measure the degree of completion, and more importantly the areas in need of completion, at any time.

A requirements knowledge model is an abstract view of your filing system for managing your requirements knowledge. The model provides the basis for keeping track of the effect of one piece of knowledge on another.

Writing a good requirements specification is important. A well-written specification pays for itself many times over—the construction is more precise, the maintenance costs are lower, and the finished product accurately reflects what the customer needs and wants.

The Quality Gateway

in which we prevent unworthy requirements becoming part of the specification

The Quality Gateway is just that—a gateway into the requirements specification. That is, each requirement must be tested by the gateway before it may be included in the specification with the other correct requirements.

Consider the life of a requirement before it arrives at the Quality Gateway. The requirement could have originated anywhere or with anyone. You have been using a variety of trawling techniques to discover the requirements. Each requirement is captured—regardless of its completeness or coherency—whenever and however it appears. You catch requirements when they come out of people's mouths, when you observe them, when you read them. Your concern when trawling is to capture all of the requirements and not to miss anything. Your results can take a variety of forms (interview notes, sample documents, blogs, videos, scenario models, and rough sketches in your notebook, among others) and states of completion. All of this seeming randomness makes them difficult to review. At this stage of development, let us call these *potential requirements*.

The writing process we spoke about in Chapter 10 applies the template and the shell to the potential requirements and puts them into a consistent form. Once they are in that form, you can call them *formalized potential requirements*. This transformation should be thought of as a natural progression from the half-formed idea to a precise, unambiguous requirement. But you have one more thing to do before you can call it a completed requirement: You must test it.

When the formalized potential requirement arrives at the Quality Gateway, it should be complete enough that it can undergo tests to determine whether it should be accepted into the specification or rejected. If it is rejected, then it is returned to its source for clarification, revision, or discarding. See Figure 11.1.

> *Quality is never an accident. It is always the result of intelligent effort.*
>
> Source: John Ruskin

259

Figure 11.1

The Quality Gateway is the activity where each requirement is tested to ensure its suitability. "Suitability" in this context means that the requirement provides downstream activities with a clear, complete, unambiguous description of what to build. To ensure a suitable requirements specification, all requirements must be tested by the Quality Gateway. For a detailed process model of the Quality Gateway, refer to Diagram 4 and its supporting material in Appendix A.

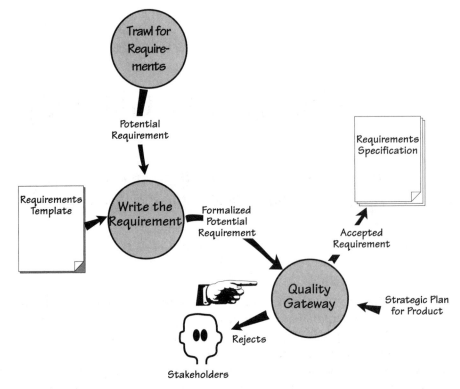

This chapter discusses the Quality Gateway as an activity within your requirements process. However, this activity is slightly different in that it is brought into play as each requirement is written: The requirement is tested and, if accepted, becomes part of the specification. You should also consider the *effect* of the Quality Gateway: When requirements analysts know the standards the gatekeepers use to test the requirements against, the analysts can use the same tests to improve their own requirements writing. Keeping the Quality Gateway tests in mind helps analysts raise questions earlier and improve the quality of the requirements that eventually pass through the formal Quality Gateway.

Agility Guide

This chapter discusses the Quality Gateway in its most formal incarnation. It is worth emphasizing that you can—in fact, you should—apply some or all of the Quality Gateway tests to a requirement at any stage of your requirements gathering. The way that you implement the Quality Gateway (who will do what, when they will do it, and how many times they will do it) depends on the degree of agility to which you aspire.

Rabbit projects rarely make use of written requirements. This lack of documentation makes it slightly harder to determine whether the requirement is the correct one. Nevertheless, before attempting to implement a requirement, the developer must ensure it is within scope, is testable, is not gold plating, and meets several other criteria that we will cover in this chapter. The Quality Gateway is applicable to rabbit projects, but probably not in the formal way we present the subject here. Rabbit team members should read this chapter and apply its principles as a checklist for reviewing their stories.

Horse projects probably use written requirements and an iterative development cycle. This practice results in a short time elapsing between the gathering of requirements and the release of a partial working version of the product. But putting the product in the user's hands quickly should not be viewed as a way of avoiding testing the requirements. Even for the fastest of cycles, it is still far more efficient and effective to spend a small amount of time testing the requirements before attempting any implementation. Horse projects should use an informal Quality Gateway. More on how to do this later.

Elephant projects produce a specification. The sheer size of elephant projects means that even small errors in requirements have the potential to balloon into major problems if not caught early. The size of the final specification precludes effective testing of the entire document—people stop seriously reading at about page 15 and start skimming. The idea of testing individual requirements or cohesive groups of requirements as they are generated is attractive in that it has every chance of success. Each requirement is tested. If it passes these tests (you must determine the tests appropriate for your type of project or product), it becomes part of the specification. As a result, the specification contains *only* tested, correct requirements.

Requirements Quality

At this stage, let us take a moment to consider the effect of requirements quality. After all, we are suggesting here that you make an effort to ensure the correctness of your requirements. Thus it is appropriate we lay out the reasons for undertaking this endeavor.

We are about to talk about a specification. Keep in mind that it need not take the traditional form of a written, sometimes long, usually boring document with sign-offs, versions, release dates, and so many other things appended. We recognize the need for this kind of document in some situations, and the lack of a need for it in others. So, for the purposes of this chapter, please read the word "specification" to mean the collection of one or more requirements held in whatever manner you use, including the requirements held inside your head.

The requirements specification is used by several downstream activities and eventually used to build the product, whatever it may be. As a result, if

For the purposes of this chapter, please read the word "specification" to mean the collection of one or more requirements held in whatever manner you use, including the requirements held inside your head.

the specification is wrong, the product will also be wrong. The Quality Gateway testing is meant to ensure, as far as possible, the correctness of the requirements.

Between 50 and 60 percent of errors in software development originate in the requirements and design activity. About 5 percent of these errors originate in the programming part of the development. This suggests, in the strongest possible way, the benefits that can be realized by putting a little effort into getting the requirements right. Errors are expensive and, if allowed to continue to the downstream activities beyond the requirements process, become more and more expensive.

The cost of repairing an error increases each time the development effort reaches a new phase. A requirements error that might cost $1 to correct during the requirements activity might cost up to $100 during implementation, and even ten times more if the error is not detected and corrected until the product is in the field.

READING

Jones, Capers. *Estimating Software* Costs. McGraw Hill, 1998.

The precise numbers from different researchers vary, but all of them point to a large increase in the cost of repair in downstream activities. And this cost increases regardless of which type of life cycle you use—waterfall, incremental, eXtreme Programming, whatever. All downstream activities have dependencies on the requirements. An undiscovered error in requirements means a disproportionate effort to correct it later. Capers Jones has calculated that the rework needed to remove requirements errors typically accounts for as much as 50 percent of software development costs.

The earlier an error is discovered, the cheaper it is to correct.

You may dispute some of the research, and you can dispute some of the numbers within reason, but the underlying fact remains true regardless of any other variable in the development cycle: The earlier an error is discovered, the cheaper it is to correct.

The numbers suggest—no, let's be honest here, they scream—that you should spend the time testing and correcting your requirements *during the requirements activity* instead of allowing incorrect requirements to percolate through to a downstream activity. Many development projects do not start testing until software is being implemented. This is far too late—most of the errors originated several activities before implementation—and far too expensive. At this point the cost of repair for the majority of errors can now be as much as 100 times more than it need be.

Simply put, testing the requirements is the cheapest and fastest way to develop your product.

Using the Quality Gateway

In medieval times, castles and fortified towns had gateways designed specifically to keep invaders and unwanted travelers out. The gateways usually sported a portcullis and were heavily defended by gatekeepers, people

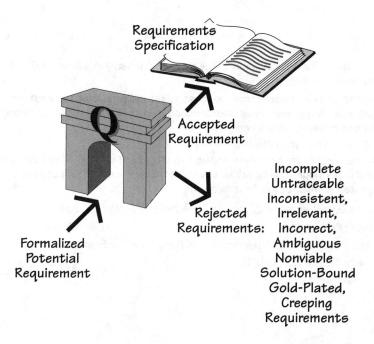

Requirements
Specification

Accepted
Requirement

Incomplete
Untraceable
Inconsistent,
Rejected   Irrelevant,
Requirements: Incorrect,
Ambiguous
Nonviable
Solution-Bound
Gold-Plated,
Creeping
Requirements

Formalized
Potential
Requirement

Figure 11.2

The Quality Gateway
tests each requirement
for correctness and
suitability. Accepted
requirements are added
to the specification.
Rejected requirements
are returned to their
originator.

charged with the protection of the inner sanctum. The Quality Gateway we describe here has the same role—to defend the specification against unwelcome requirements.

To pass through the Quality Gateway and be included in the requirements specification (remember the specification does not have to be a formal, written document), a requirement must pass a number of tests. These tests ensure that the requirements are complete and accurate, and do not cause problems by being unsuitable for the design and implementation stages later in the project. See Figure 11.2.

In the next part of this chapter, we discuss each of the requirements tests. As we do, keep in mind that it takes longer to describe the tests than it does to perform them.

Testing Completeness

In Chapter 10, Writing the Requirements, we discussed using the requirements shell as a way of making it easy to gather the components necessary to make a complete requirement. That chapter contains a discussion of each of these components.

Think of the requirements shell as a compartmentalized container for an individual atomic requirement, with each compartment being a component of the requirement. Earlier we suggested using the shell to help write the

Figure 11.3

An example of a complete requirement using the Volere Shell. All of the components are present, and the analyst has marked the requirement as having no known conflicts with other requirements. This requirement should pass the completeness tests.

Requirement #: **75**   Requirement Type: **9**   Event/Use Case #: **6**

Description: **The product shall issue an alert if a weather station fails to transmit readings.**

Rationale: **Failure to transmit readings might indicate that the weather station is faulty and needs maintenance, and that the data used to predict freezing roads may be incomplete.**

Originator: **George Shaw, Engineering**

Fit Criterion: **For each weather station the recorded number of each type of reading per hour shall be within the manufacturer's specified range of the expected number of readings per hour.**

Customer Satisfaction: **3**   Customer Dissatisfaction: **5**

Priority: **Release 1**   Conflicts: **None**

Supporting Materials: **Specification of Rosa Weather Station**

History: **Raised 28 July 05**

$Volere$

Copyright © Atlantic Systems Guild

requirement; now we use it to help you test the completeness of a requirement. (See Figure 11.3.) Note that we also refer to the shell as a "snow card." We use cards printed with these components for training purposes and low-tech requirements gathering.

Are There Any Missing Components?

The first test for completeness is to compare the requirement with the components of the shell. While it is not always necessary to have every component for every requirement, if some components are missing, there should be a reason for their absence.

Chapter 10 discusses the process of writing the requirements in detail.

The components of the shell come from successful requirements projects. Over the years, we have found these items to be valuable and to contribute to the clarity and reasoning of a requirement. They are measurements, or explanations, or pointers to other information, or requirements that will be used at several stages of the project. Thus it is advisable to include as many as are appropriate for the requirement.

The Volere Shell is packaged as part of the Requirements Specification Template in Appendix B.

Sometimes, however, not all of the shell components are necessary. For example, sometimes the description makes it obvious why the requirement is important. In that case there would be no point in writing the rationale. Sometimes the description can be dropped, because a clear and readable fit criterion is provided. Sometimes there are no supporting materials.

Naturally, if one of the components is missing, then its omission should occur because it is not necessary rather than because it is too difficult or has been overlooked. If the component is missing because you are still investigating it (and perhaps waiting for an answer from someone), then include that information in the requirement to forestall unnecessary questions:

> *Supporting Material: 10/10/05 waiting for county engineer to supply details of supporting material.*

The completeness test says that each requirement must have all relevant components, or you should record the reason why they have not been, or cannot be, completed.

Meaningful to All Stakeholders?

Once you are satisfied about the components of the requirement, you should ensure each component adds to the meaning and common understanding of the requirement.

This means that the requirement is written as clearly as possible. While we admire conciseness, you must ensure the requirement is written so all the needed information is included.

Test each component of the requirement and, from the point of view of each stakeholder, ask, "Is it possible to misunderstand this?" For instance, Figure 11.3 includes the following information:

> *Supporting Material: Specification of Rosa Weather Station*

We ask, "Is it possible to confuse this? Is there more than one specification of the Rosa Weather Station? Is there any doubt about where to find this specification?" The answers to these questions help us to be more precise about exactly what we mean. The resultant entry reads:

> *Supporting Material: Specification of DM32 Rosa Weather Station, release 1.1 published Jan 22, 2004*

Everything should be made as simple as possible, but not one bit simpler.

Source: Albert Einstein

READING
For more on stakeholders' viewpoints, refer to Sommerville, Ian, and Pete Sawyer. *Requirements Engineering.* John Wiley, 1998.

Testing Traceability

Remember the old story of the World War I general who needed to get a message back to headquarters? He gave the message to his next in command: "Send reinforcements; we're going to advance." The message was passed between runners and shouted to other messengers until at last it reached headquarters. There an exhausted messenger blurted out, "Send three and fourpence; we're going to a dance." The same sort of thing happens when too many transitions separate the origin of a message and its final delivery point.

The path followed in the story is very much the same as that a requirement goes through in its many stages before it is finally delivered as a working product. Each stage is a transformation, fraught with the possibility that the requirement may become misunderstood, applied wrongly, or somehow scrambled in the translation by any of the people involved in the development of the product.

It is vital for future maintenance that you are able to connect the original requirement to the part of the delivered product that implements the requirement. In other words, the beginning of the development process must somehow be connected to the end of it. You need to ensure the specified requirement is actually the requirement that is implemented. Figure 11.4 illustrates the connections between requirements components and their implementation.

Figure 11.4

This partial requirements knowledge model shows the connections between the components of the requirements specification. The connections are necessary for tracing the components through their development. For example, the *Product Scope* is delineated by a number of *Product Use Cases* (the asterisk at an end of the connection means "many"), and each *Product Use Case* is a cluster of many *Requirements*. An atomic *Requirement* can be either a *Constraint,* a *Functional Requirement,* or a *Nonfunctional Requirement.* The *Work Context* is the subject of a number of *Business Events,* each of which responds with a *Business Use Case.* These can be implemented in the product as one or more *Product Use Cases.* (Chapter 4, Event-Driven Use Cases, discusses this relationship.) To maintain traceability, you need to know which requirements belong to which product use cases, which business events are implemented with which business and product use cases, and so on.

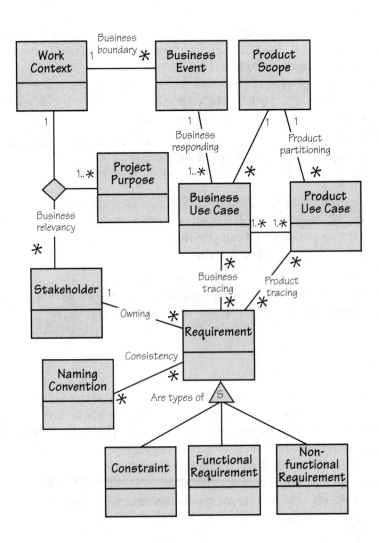

To make sure it is traceable, each of your requirements must have the following characteristics:

- A unique identifier
- An indicator of the type of requirement or constraint (we use the section number of the template in which the requirement appears)
- References to all of the business use cases or product use cases that contain the requirement
- References to the stakeholder who is the originator of the requirement
- Consistent use of terminology

If the requirements are traceable, then when changes happen, it is far easier to find the parts of the product affected by the change and to assess the impact of the change on the rest of the product. Keep in mind that the requirements can and will change at any stage during the product's life. Keeping your requirements traceable means that you can design the most effective way to accommodate the change.

You can find a more complete requirements knowledge model in Chapter 10, Writing the Requirements.

Is the requirement uniquely identifiable and cross-referenced to business use cases, product use cases, dependent requirements, and conflicting requirements?

Consistent Terminology

When a poet writes a poem, he intends that it should inspire rich and diverse visions in anyone who reads it. The requirements analyst has the opposite intention: He would like each requirement to be understood in precisely the same way by every person who reads it. Requirements specifications are not poetry—they are not even novels where a subjective interpretation is sought. The requirements specification must have only one interpretation if the developer is to build the right product. Otherwise, there is an obvious danger of building a product that satisfies the wrong interpretation of the requirement.

To specify a requirement so it is understood in only one way, you should define the terms you are using and the meanings of those terms within the specification. Section 5 of the Volere Requirements Specification Template is called Naming Conventions and Definitions. This section is a repository for the terms that are used for this particular project. The terms are given a definition that is agreed by the stakeholders. This section acts as a reference point for the words used to write the requirements.

The next act of consistency is to test that every requirement uses terms in a manner consistent with their specified meanings. It's not enough to define the terminology: We have to make sure that each term is used correctly. For example, in a requirements specification we once audited, we found the term "viewer" in many parts of the specification. Our audit identified six different meanings for the term, depending on the context of its use. This kind of terminology defect causes problems during design and/or implementation. If

Does the specification contain a definition of the meaning of every essential subject matter term within the specification?

Is every reference to a defined term consistent with its definition?

you are lucky, a developer realizes there is an inconsistency, but then has to reinvestigate the requirement. If you are not lucky, the designer inadvertently chooses the meaning that makes most sense to him at the time and implements that one. Any stakeholder who does not agree with that meaning will naturally consider the product to fail the requirement.

One last word about inconsistency: You should expect it, and you should look for it as part of the process of specifying requirements. When you discover inconsistencies, they point to a need for further investigation and perhaps negotiation.

Relevant to Purpose?

When trawling for requirements, you are certain to come across some absolutely charming, well-stated, complete requirements that are perfect in all respects, except they are irrelevant to the purpose of your product. This happens on most projects. Users become enthusiastic and start adding everything they can think of; developers add requirements because they want to make the product all-encompassing or just plain cooler. Unfortunately, this kind of irrelevancy quickly leads to requirements creep, with the probable result that the project runs significantly over time and over budget, and even then doesn't deliver the product it set out to build in the first place.

In Chapter 3, which covered the project blastoff, we discussed how to identify the purpose of the project and to write it down as quantified project goals. These goals serve as the arbiter of relevancy throughout the project.

To test a requirement for relevancy, compare its intention with the project goals. The test is fairly simple: Does this requirement contribute to the purpose of the project? Does this requirement help make the product, directly or indirectly, meet the project's purpose?

As an example, imagine that you are working on the IceBreaker project and you come across this requirement:

> *The product shall maintain a lookup table of the times of sunrise and sunset throughout the year.*

At first this requirement appears to be relevant. The product has to predict the formation of ice on roads, and ice usually forms at night. Thus this requirement appears to contribute to the project goal:

> *Project Goal: To accurately predict when ice will form on road surfaces and to efficiently schedule the appropriate de-icing treatment.*

Chapter 3, Project Blastoff, discusses how to define the purpose of the product.

Does this requirement contribute to the purpose of the project?

However, if we dig a little deeper, we discover that the temperature of the road surface actually determines whether ice will form, and road temperature is monitored and transmitted by weather stations. In other words, whether it is night or day does not override the actual temperature. Ice is perfectly capable of forming during the daylight hours. There is no reason for the product to have any knowledge of day or night.

Requirements can contribute indirectly to the product. Sometimes the requirement may call for the product to do something that has no immediate connection to the purpose; however, without this requirement, the product could not achieve its purpose. As an example, consider this requirement:

> Description: The product shall record the durations of truck activity.

See section 8 of the Volere Requirements Specification Template in Appendix B for a sample context model. Also refer to Chapter 3, Project Blastoff, for information on how to set the context.

At first glance, this requirement appears to have nothing to do with the goal of the product, which is to efficiently schedule trucks to treat roads with de-icing material. But look at the rationale for this requirement:

> Rationale: De-icing trucks may not be scheduled for more than 20 hours out of each 24-hour period.

Now the reason for the requirement is apparent. The Quality Gatekeeper can allow this requirement to pass, because it makes a contribution toward meeting the goals of the project.

Also consider that many of the nonfunctional requirements contribute indirectly to the project's goals.

Irrelevant requirements should be returned to their source with a short explanation. Be prepared to invest a little time in this communication, as an "irrelevant" requirement may indicate that a stakeholder has misunderstood the purpose or signal that a new business area is opening. In other words, you have to make a judgment as to whether the requirement is truly irrelevant or the original scope has become incorrect because of business changes.

The scope of the product also determines relevancy of the requirements. The scope results from making decisions about the product use cases. This effort should lead to section 8 of the requirements specification, which contains a product context diagram showing the flows of information between the product and the actors/adjacent systems. You can use these flows as a test for relevancy.

For example, suppose that you are given the following potential requirement. Does it fit within the scope we have defined for IceBreaker?

> The product shall record the overtime worked by the truck drivers.

Is every requirement relevant within the stated boundaries of this product?

Look at the product boundaries. A product context model shows the boundaries of the product by the flows of information that enter or leave the product. Compare the preceding requirement with the boundary flows. Do any of the flows have anything to do with recording truck drivers' working overtime? Are there flows that indicate the product is dealing with working hours? Is there anything on the context model that indicates overtime hours should be stored within the product?

In the IceBreaker example, nothing makes the overtime requirement relevant. There is no information flow that could possibly have any data content related to working hours. If you included this requirement, it would not connect to anything else in the product, and so would be redundant functionality.

When considering relevancy, pay particular attention to the following sections of your requirements specification:

- Users (section 3): Who are you building the product for, and is it a product suitable for these users?
- Requirements Constraints (section 4): Is the product relevant within the constraints? Have all the constraints been observed by the requirements?
- Relevant Facts (section 6): Have the requirements failed to account for any external factors?
- Assumptions (section 6): Are the requirements consistent with any assumptions you are making about the project?

Testing the Fit Criterion

See Chapter 9 for a full explanation of how to write fit criteria.

Requirements can be ambiguous. In fact, any English-language (or any other language) statement is probably ambiguous in some way, as well as being subjectively understood. This is obviously not the way that we should write requirements. As a consequence, in addition to the natural-language *description* of the requirement, we write a *fit criterion*. The fit criterion is a quantification of the requirement, which, as far as possible, uses numbers (numbers have no ambiguity) instead of words to express the requirement.

The fit criterion is a measurement of the requirement.

The fit criterion is a measurement of the requirement that enables the testers to determine, without recourse to subjective judgments, whether the delivered solution meets, or fits, the requirement.

> Description: The product shall appear easy to use.
>
> Rationale: The client needs the users to voluntarily and quickly adopt it.
>
> Fit Criterion: First-time users shall hesitate no more than ten seconds before starting to use the product. The number of people refusing to use the product shall be fewer than 15 percent.

It is crucial to accurate requirements specification that each requirement carries a fit criterion. The first question to ask is, "Does the requirement have a correctly defined fit criterion?" Any requirements that do not must be considered to be incomplete, as a large degree of uncertainty remains about the requirement. It is really this simple: If you can't measure it, you don't understand it. The next question for the fit criterion is, "Can it be used as input to designing acceptance tests?" You may need help from the testing people to answer this question. The fit criterion is not the design for the test, but indicates what needs to be tested so as to ensure the delivered solution complies with the original requirement. At this stage you should also consider whether there is a cost-effective (within the project's constraints) way of testing a solution to this requirement.

Does each requirement have a fit criterion that can be used to test whether a solution meets the requirement?

The fit criterion must also meet the purpose of the project. We have discussed how the requirement must conform to the project purpose, so it makes sense that the measurement of the requirement must likewise conform to this purpose.

While the fit criterion uses numbers to express the requirement, the numbers themselves must not be subjective, but must be based on evidence. For example:

> *Description: The product shall be easy to learn.*
>
> *Fit Criterion: A user shall be able to learn to process a claim within 30 minutes of starting to use the product for the first time.*

The question to ask about this fit criterion is, "Where did the 30 minutes come from?" Is it simply the whim of a stakeholder or the requirements analyst? Or is it based on evidence that a learning curve longer than 30 minutes means the users will become discouraged and give up? It is, of course, useful if the requirement writer has included a reference to the evidence in the Supporting Materials component of the requirement.

The fit criterion uses a scale of measurement. For example, if the requirement states the product is to be fast, then the scale of measurement for the fit criterion is probably time. Check whether the scale of measurement is appropriate for the requirement, and whether acceptance tests run using that scale will, in fact, show whether the product meets the requirement.

The fit criterion measurement may include some business tolerances. For example, if the fit criterion specifies that a number of people have to perform certain tasks within certain time limits, then the business tolerance allows a small percentage of the test panel to fail. This tolerance exists because you cannot expect 100 percent of humans to be able to do everything. Similarly, products that handle material or deal with imperfect outside world artifacts might be allowed a certain margin of error, or business tolerance. Consider whether the business tolerance is based on appropriate evidence.

Viable within Constraints?

Constraints are described in section 4 of the Volere Requirements Specification Template in Appendix B.

Viable requirements are those that are workable within the project—they conform to the constraints set down for the project and the product. Constraints cover such things as the amount of time available to build the product, the anticipated workplace environment, the users of the product, constraints on the design of the product, and so on.

Each requirement is tested for viability within the constraints. This means you must consider each of the constraints, and ask whether the requirement contradicts it in any way.

For example, the users of the product can be considered a constraint. Whatever product you are specifying must be consistent with those users. The product must be easy for the user to operate, but sophisticated enough to provide the needed functionality. As an example, the following requirement for the IceBreaker product is not viable:

> *Truck drivers shall receive weather forecasts and schedule their own de-icing.*

Truck drivers do not have the necessary information at hand to predict the time a road will freeze. They do not know which roads have been treated and which are in a dangerous condition. Coordinating a number of trucks treating multiple roads stretching over the whole of a county is a matter for centralized control.

You might also consider whether the organization is mature enough to cope with a requirement.

Do you have the technological skills to build the requirement?

Do you have the technological skills to build the requirement? It is an easy matter to write a requirement, but it is sometimes a different, more difficult thing to construct a working solution for it. During the requirements activity there is little point in specifying a product that is beyond your development capabilities. This test is a matter of assessing—unfortunately there can be no measurement here—whether the requirement is unachievable given the technical capabilities of the construction team.

Do you have the time and the money to build the requirement?

Do you have the time and the money to build the requirement? This test means estimating the cost of meeting the requirement, and assessing it as a share of the total budget. (The budgets should be listed as a constraint in section 4 of the requirements specification.) If the cost of constructing a requirement exceeds its budget, then the customer value attached to the requirement indicates how you should proceed: High-value requirements are negotiated, while low-value requirements are discarded.

Is the requirement acceptable to all stakeholders?

Is the requirement acceptable to all stakeholders? This is simple self-defense. If a requirement is unpopular with some of the stakeholders, then history tells us that it is futile to include it in the product. Stakeholders have been known to sabotage the development of products because they disagree with part of the product. Users have been known to ignore and not use products because not all of the functionality was as they thought it should be.

Do any other constraints make the requirement nonviable? Do any of the partner applications or the expected work environment contradict the requirement? Do any solution constraints—constraints on the way that a solution must be designed—make the requirement difficult or impossible to achieve?

Requirement or Solution?

The description of a requirement is often stated in terms of a solution. We all unconsciously talk about requirements in terms of how we think they should be solved. We talk about solutions rather than requirements because of our personal experience of the world. This results in a statement that focuses on one possible solution—not necessarily the most appropriate one—and hides the real requirement.

The more abstract the requirement, the less likely it is to be a solution.

Examine the requirement. Does it contain any element of technology? Is it written in a way that describes a type of procedure?

The more abstract the statement, the less likely it is to be a solution. For example, if you write

> *The product shall be easy to use.*

then it is a requirement. By contrast, if you write

> *The product shall use Java script for the interface.*

then it is a solution. Note the use of a technology, "Java script," in the requirement.

Sometimes we unconsciously state solutions. For example, this is a solution:

> *The product shall have a clock on the menu bar.*

Both "clock" and "menu bar" are parts of a solution. We suggest that the real requirement is

> *The product shall make the user aware of the current time.*

When you write the requirement in an abstract manner, other solutions become possible. There are ways other than a clock to make people aware of the time—the astrolabe is one. There are ways other than Java script to make products easy to use.

There will be requirements or constraints that sound like solutions. For example, if your product is shrink-wrapped software, and your client thinks that having a browser-like interface is a selling point, then that becomes a requirement. You would write "a browser-like interface" as one of the solution constraints in section 4 of the specification.

Examine your requirements. Investigate any that are solutions and ask whether they are what the client really wants. Could you rewrite them as requirements without the technological content?

Also, ask, "Why?" For example, suppose that you have the following requirement in your Quality Gateway:

> *Users shall use passwords to access the system.*

Why is this a requirement? "Because we don't want unauthorized people to access confidential information." Now you are discovering the real requirement:

> *The product shall allow only authorized users to access confidential information.*

There are lots of ways to assure confidential access to information— passwords are just one of them. However, if passwords have been specified because the new product must conform to the organization's use of passwords, then the requirement is really a design constraint and is perfectly acceptable.

Of course, from time to time people will come up with great ideas for solutions. Keep them in section 19, Off-the-Shelf Solutions, or section 27, Ideas for Solutions, of the requirements specification. You should always trap great ideas when you think of them. But don't be tempted to distort the product's requirements to fit the great solution idea. It may be great, but it may also be the solution to a different problem.

For more on writing requirements rather than solutions, look at Chapter 7, Functional Requirements, and Chapter 8, Nonfunctional Requirements.

The customer satisfaction/ dissatisfaction ratings indicate the value that the customer places on a requirement.

Customer Value

The customer satisfaction and customer dissatisfaction ratings attached to a requirement indicate the value the customer places on a requirement. The satisfaction rating measures how happy the customer will be if you successfully deliver an implementation of the requirement, and the dissatisfaction rating measures how unhappy the customer will be if you do not successfully deliver this requirement. See Chapter 10, Writing the Requirements, for a discussion of customer satisfaction and customer dissatisfaction.

We have found that this two-step approach helps people to think more objectively about a requirement rather than mechanically giving it a number on a scale from one to ten or, even worse, a high, medium, or low value.

You may decide to substitute Quality Function Deployment (QFD) for this exercise. QFD was developed by the Japanese car industry to ensure that all requirements are expressed "in the voice of the customer." QFD includes a matrix for identifying the customer importance rating. The difference between the customer importance rating and the customer value is that, rather than having one importance rating, customer value has two ways of rating each requirement.

The real test for the Quality Gateway is whether the requirement carries an appropriate rating of the value that the customer places on the requirement.

Your customer, or a panel made up of the significant stakeholders, sets the ratings with your help. Later, these ratings are weighed against the cost of the requirement and, if necessary, used to help make choices between requirements and assign implementation priorities. Although this activity may seem to be something of an arduous exercise, knowing precisely what value to attach to a requirement is very worthwhile.

If you have a large number of requirements that have a satisfaction/dissatisfaction rating of 5/5, then it indicates that the values have not been thoughtfully rated. As this process is the best opportunity your customer has of letting you know what is important and what is not, we suggest you reject the ratings and ask they be done again. Perhaps for the next rating exercise you should set a limit—say, 75 percent—of the number of requirements that may have a "5/5" rating. Make sure that your customer understands your reason for doing so is to understand what is most important to his business; then if you need to make trade-offs, you can choose the most relevant ones. Another reason for attaching customer values to the requirement is to determine what is, and what is not, gold plating.

> See Chapter 14, Reviewing the Specification, for a discussion of how to use the customer value ratings to prioritize requirements.

> **READING**
> For a good summary of QFD, see Macaulay, Linda A. *Requirements Engineering.* Springer, 1996.

> **READING**
> For more on customer satisfaction and dissatisfaction ratings, refer to Pardee, William J. *To Satisfy and Delight Your Customer.* New York, 1996.

Gold Plating

The term "gold plating" comes from the domain of bathroom taps. Some people like to have gold-plated taps. Of course, the water does not flow out of gold-plated taps any better than it does from chrome-plated ones. The difference is that the gold-plated tap costs more and might, to some eyes, look a little better. This term has been taken up by the software industry to mean unnecessary features and requirements that wind up contributing more to the cost of a product than they do to its functionality or usefulness.

Does it matter if this requirement is not included?

Let's look at an example. Suppose a requirement for the IceBreaker product states that it shall play a piece of classical music when an engineer logs on. Our knowledge of the IceBreaker product leads us to suspect that this is a gold-plated requirement. It does not appear to contribute to the overall goals of the product. But maybe the truck depot supervisor thinks that the product would be more pleasing to the engineers if it plays music to them.

This requirement is gold plating. It is there because it might be "nice to have." No one would mind if the requirement were omitted from the product. So the first test of gold plating is, "Does it matter if the requirement is not included?" If no one can truly justify its inclusion, then it may be considered gold plating.

A low dissatisfaction rating indicates a requirement that is probably gold plating.

The second, and perhaps more reliable, test is to look at the customer satisfaction/dissatisfaction ratings attached to the requirement. A low dissatisfaction rating indicates a requirement that is probably gold plating. After all, when the customer says that it does not matter if this requirement is not included, then he is signaling a requirement whose contribution to the product is not vital.

We hasten to add that we do not advocate excluding all gold-plated requirements from your product. It is often a good idea to add that little something extra, that extra little bit of chocolate. Sometimes a little gold plating makes a difference to the acceptance of the product. Sometimes we take great pleasure in unnecessary but delightful features. Look at your iPod the next time you charge it. The screen indicates it is charging by displaying a graphic of a battery being filled. Note the speed: The filling speed decreases as the battery nears its full charge. Your screen saver, the sounds attached to alerts, changing screen colors and wallpaper, pictorial and customizable icons: The list of gold-plated items that please us goes on and on.

The point is that you should know whether a requirement is gold plating. If you decide to include a gold-plated requirement, it should be a conscious choice. If you discover that you cannot implement all of the requirements within the project constraints, then gold-plated requirements are prime candidates for exclusion.

Requirements Creep

Requirements creep refers to new requirements entering the specification after the requirements are considered complete. Any requirements appearing after this point are considered to be requirements creep.

Requirements creep has been tagged with a bad name, usually because of the disruption to the schedules and the bloated costs of product delivery. Without wanting to defend requirements creep, we do think it prudent to look at some of the causes of creep and to discuss how we can approach this problem.

First, most creep comes about because the requirements were never gathered properly in the first place. If the requirements are incomplete, then as the product develops, more and more omissions must of necessity be discovered. The users, aware that product delivery is now imminent, ask for more and more "new" functions. But are they really new? We suggest they are requirements that really were part of the product all along. They were just not, until now, part of the requirements specification.

Similarly, if the users and the clients are not given the opportunity to participate fully in the requirements process, then the specification will undoubtedly be incomplete. Almost certainly the requirements will creep as delivery approaches and the users begin asking for functionality they know they need.

We have also observed creep that came about because the original budget (for political reasons) was set unrealistically low. When the incredibly noticeable creep set in, it was not so much a matter of the requirements creeping, but of the product bringing itself up to its correct functionality.

Requirements also change. Quite often they change for the very good reason that the business has changed, or new technological advances have made change desirable. These kinds of changes are often seen as requirements creep. In truth, if changes that cause new requirements happen after the official "end" of the requirements process—and they could not have been anticipated—then this type of requirements creep could not have been avoided.

Whatever the reason, whether good or bad, you must be able to identify the reason for the creep. Moreover, you must be able to respond appropriately.

A little earlier in this chapter we spoke about the relevancy of requirements, and noted how the requirement must be both relevant to the product purpose and within the scope of the work. If requirements are creeping outside the scope or are not relevant to the product purpose, then we suggest you have serious cause for concern. Is the scope correct? Are the goals for the product correct and realistic? We cannot hope to diagnose your exact problem in this book, but we suggest you look long and hard at the root cause of your requirements creep.

The best way to minimize requirements creep is to engage in a good requirements process, with the active and enthusiastic participation of the stakeholders. That, and to start with a reasonably sized project. Anything less and you must expect some creep to happen to your requirements. When it does, identify the cause and use that knowledge to fine-tune your requirements process.

We have not spoken about the effect of requirements creep on your budget. Let's look at that issue along with another problem, requirements leakage.

Most creep comes about because the requirements were never gathered properly in the first place.

If changes that cause new requirements happen after the official "end" of the requirements process—and they could not have been anticipated—then this is unavoidable requirements creep.

Requirements Leakage

Requirements leakage refers to those requirements that somehow "leak" into the specification. Think of this as the way water can leak into a rowboat as you cross a lake. A little water may not harm you, but too much of it and your chances of getting safely to the other side are seriously diminished. You can also think about requirements leakage as unrecognized and uncontrolled requirement creep. Nobody knows where the requirements leaked from or who is responsible for them. Nobody wants to own them. And yet, leaking requirements have an effect on the budget. Either they are rejected or the project plan is adjusted to reflect the current reality.

Capers Jones reports for the average project, about 35 percent of the requirements appear after the requirements process is deemed to have ended. That is, about one third of all the requirements have crept or leaked into the specification.

The effect of this insidious growth in the requirements is shown in Figure 11.5. The graph depicts the cost of delivering functionality. You should create a graph like this one to make everyone realize that functionality is not free. Look at what happens when the size of the product creeps up by 35 percent. The effort needed expands by a little more than that. And yet, this is the part of the product that somebody expected to get for free. When the requirements grow beyond what was originally anticipated, the budget

READING

Jones, Capers. *Software Quality: Analysis and Guidelines for Success.* International Thomson, 2000.

Figure 11.5

When you know the rate of productivity at your organization, it is a fairly simple exercise to convert the size of the product into the amount of effort or cost. When the size of the product increases (creeps), the amount of effort needed must also increase. It is this increase, which is due to uncontrolled requirements creep or leakage, that causes many projects to fall behind schedule or fail completely.

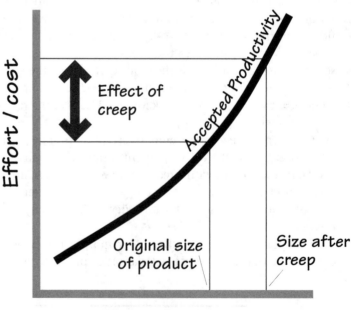

must grow proportionally. But how often do you hear, "Just one more little thing—it won't affect the budget"? It does affect the budget. Each requirement has a cost attached. So what to do about it?

The Quality Gateway must ensure all requirements carry the name of the originator. Knowing who asked for it gives you the starting point from which to assess the need for the requirement. Next the Quality Gateway ensures each requirement carries valid customer satisfaction/dissatisfaction ratings. These ratings tell you the value your client/customer places on the requirement. If it is high, then creeping requirements might be tolerated (with an adjustment to the budget). The rationale attached to the requirement must also make sense. We have often found that leaking requirements do not make sense or are outside the scope. If you have the measurements we advocate attaching to your requirements, then you can confront the originator of the rogue requirement and justifiably reject its inclusion in the specification.

To stay in control means you have to, at all times, be aware of how much functionality you are delivering. This statement implies you measure the functionality of the product. Capers Jones advocates basing the development on a contracted number of function points at an anticipated cost per function point. Suppose we start with an average delivery rate of 16 function points per person-month.[1] So, for a 1,000-function-point product to be delivered, the cost is 62.5 person-months. If the functionality to be delivered creeps by 25 percent, that's 250 function points; to accommodate this growth, another 16 or so person-months has to be added to the budget. While this type of ongoing calculation does allow requirements to creep, it ensures that the creep is recognized, budgeted, and paid for.

As a footnote to this point, we have observed that some government departments are starting to contract out their software at a rate per function point. The size of the product can be anything the government wants it to be, but the contracted cost per function point of delivery remains the same. This idea may work for you, too.

FOOTNOTE 1:
Please note this number is an average, and different technologies and application areas have an effect on it. So do your own in-house development skills.

Implementing the Quality Gateway

We have described the Quality Gateway as a process for testing requirements. Now you have to decide how you will implement it in the context of your own organization.

The first decision focuses on who is involved in the Quality Gateway. Is it one person? If so, who? Should it be a small group? If so, will it be made up of testers or requirements analysts? Does the group include the project leader? Is the client represented? The answers to these questions are as varied as the organizations that have implemented Quality Gateways.

We suggest you start your Quality Gateway with two people—perhaps the lead requirements analyst and a tester. Keep in mind this gateway is meant

We suggest you start your Quality Gateway with two people—perhaps the lead requirements analyst and a tester. The gateway is meant to be a fast, easy test of requirements, not a laborious process involving half of the development team.

to be a fast, easy test of requirements, not a laborious process involving half of the development team. We have clients who implement their Quality Gateway electronically. The requirements analysts e-mail all requirements to the gatekeepers, who then add the accepted ones to the specification. They report this strategy is both convenient and effective.

Clients who use requirements tools typically assign an attribute to the requirement that indicates whether it has been tested and approved by the gatekeepers. The gatekeepers are, naturally enough, the only people to have write permission for this attribute.

Culture is an ingrained part of organizational life. You must respect it when you implement a Quality Gateway.

An important facet of any organization is its culture. This culture is every bit as strong as the culture you find when visiting different countries, when talking to people from different ethnic backgrounds, or when observing groups of people who are outside your normal way of life. Culture is an ingrained part of organizational life, and you must respect it when you implement new procedures.

The degree of formality also brings up many questions: How formal does the Quality Gateway need to be? Should you issue inspection reports? Should you hold prearranged Quality Gateway inspection meetings? And so on.

Most of the time we advise clients to keep their Quality Gateway procedures as informal as will allow for the satisfactory checking of their requirements. Some organizations deal with complex, technical subject matter; their Quality Gateways are of necessity formal and rigorous. Some clients deal with more accessible subject matter, where all the participants in the requirements-gathering process are well versed in the business; their Quality Gateways are so informal that they happen almost without anybody noticing.

The use of automated tools can help to reduce the amount of human intervention in the Quality Gateway process.

The use of automated tools can help to reduce the amount of human intervention in the Quality Gateway process. Some requirements-gathering tools can do the preliminary mechanical checking—ensuring that all the components are present, use the correct terminology, are correctly identified, and so on.

Existing procedures may also play a part in your Quality Gateway. If people already have the job of inspecting work, then they are likely to be involved in your Gateway. If inspection procedures exist, then they should be adapted for requirements rather than trying to implement a whole new process.

Alternative Quality Gateways

We have discussed the Quality Gateway as a process whereby appointed gatekeepers test all requirements before the requirements become part of the requirements specification. We have said that this endeavor should be a permanent, but informal process. Of course, there are other ways of testing the quality of your requirements.

Requirements analysts can test each other's requirements, for example. This informal "buddy pairing" approach works well when the analysts are able to approach their work in an ego-free manner. The partners check each other's output and trap errors early in the process. This strategy works best when a pair of analysts has learned to be objective about each other's work.

In "buddy pairing," requirements analysts test each other's requirements.

Sometimes the process is far more formal and rigorous. One elephant project we worked on implemented the Quality Gateway as a four-stage process. First, each individual developer has a checklist and uses it to informally review and improve requirements throughout the development process.

The second stage is a peer review, in which another member of the team formally reviews each written requirement. We found it very effective for the peer reviewer to be someone from the test team. Rather than review the entire specification, these reviews concentrate on all the requirements related to a particular use case. The results of the review are recorded for the requirement as part of its history.

The third stage is a team review that includes customers and users. Problem requirements that have not passed the Quality Gateway tests are presented by one person, and are discussed and possibly resolved by the team members.

The fourth, and final, stage is a management review that is mostly concerned with looking at a summary of the Quality Gateway successes and failures. The results of this review are used to manage and fine-tune the requirements project.

See Chapter 2, The Requirements Process, and Chapter 15, Whither Requirements?, for more on tailoring your process.

Whatever your situation, you should think of the Quality Gateway both as a way of testing the requirements before they become part of the specification, and as a way of improving the quality of your requirements process.

Summary

The Quality Gateway applies a number of tests to formalized potential requirements. The gateway tests individual requirements to assess whether they meet the following criteria:

- Completeness
- Traceability
- Consistency
- Relevancy
- Correctness
- Ambiguity
- Viability
- Being solution-bound

● Gold plating

● Creep

The requirements are tested during the requirements activity. That is, by preventing incorrect requirements from becoming part of the specification, the Quality Gateway prevents incorrect requirements from becoming part of the product. Eliminating errors early is the fastest and cheapest way of developing products.

Testing the requirements has a beneficial effect on the writers of those requirements. When an analyst knows his requirements will be subjected to certain tests, then naturally he writes them so they will pass the tests. This, in turn, leads to better requirements practices as well as more effective use of analytical time when less errors are generated.

The way you implement the Quality Gateway should reflect the particular needs and characteristics of your organization. In any event, be sure to implement your Quality Gateway so that all requirements, with no exceptions, must pass through it before they can become part of the specification.

Prototyping the Requirements

12

in which we use simulations to help find requirements

One of your authors, Suzanne, recently bought a phone to replace one that had decided to stop working. Time was pressing—she was trying to catch a train to a client meeting—and as the brand of phone was known to her, the device never came out of the box before she produced a credit card, took delivery, and rushed to catch the 08:15 to Reading. Once settled into her seat on the train, she lifted the phone out of its box. The phone had all of the attributes advertised on the outside of the box, looked impressively smart, and functioned perfectly except for one thing: Several of the buttons were too small to use. Suzanne has average-sized hands and is quite dexterous, but the phone refused to be turned on or answered except by stabbing the buttons with surgical precision and a sharp instrument. On her return from the client the phone shop was still open and she was able to exchange the phone for an adult-hand-friendly model, but the question lingered: Why didn't this fairly straightforward requirement come to light prior to manufacture? Didn't anyone with adult hands try dialing using a prototype?

Think about all those requirements your client requested after delivery of previous products—the subtle little ones that seemed so obvious after the event. Why weren't they discovered earlier? The answer usually is that the potential users could not envision those requirements. Or, to be brutally honest, they were not given the right opportunity to envision the requirements. Prototypes help people to "see" their requirements when a text specification might not.

We want to emphasize one point at the outset: We are talking here about using prototypes as a way of eliciting requirements from the stakeholders. We are not talking about using prototypes as a design tool, even though your designers may use them later for such purposes. The cool interfaces, the eye

> " By acting out their real work in the prototype, customers can make their unarticulated knowledge explicit. Fleshing out the prototype with the customers' own data and work situations gives them the touchstones they need to put them in the experience of doing the work. "
>
> Source: Hugh Beyer and Karen Holtzblatt, *Contextual Design*

> " Prototypes can reduce creeping requirements by somewhere between 10 percent and 25 percent. "
>
> Source: Capers Jones

283

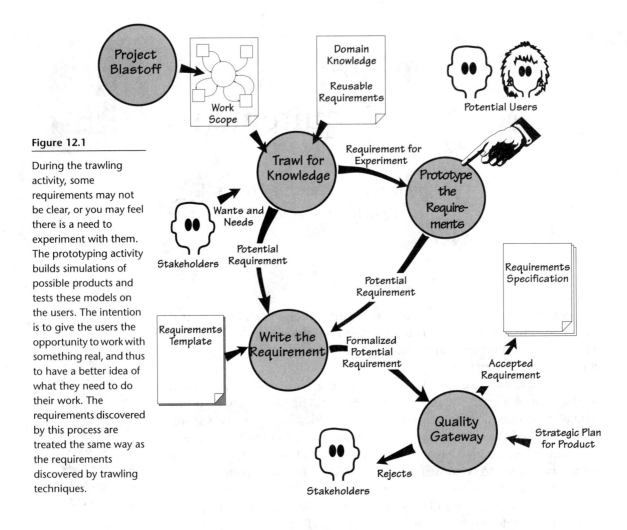

Figure 12.1

During the trawling activity, some requirements may not be clear, or you may feel there is a need to experiment with them. The prototyping activity builds simulations of possible products and tests these models on the users. The intention is to give the users the opportunity to work with something real, and thus to have a better idea of what they need to do their work. The requirements discovered by this process are treated the same way as the requirements discovered by trawling techniques.

candy, the good-looking windows and panes are not the issue. Requirements prototypes are used to help your stakeholders understand and communicate the product's requirements. And, of course, they allow you to experiment and invent. Requirements prototypes should be seen as a trawling technique. You are gathering requirements, but in this case you are using prototypes to help elicit the stakeholders' needs. See Figure 12.1.

Sometimes when you are using a product—be it a hairdryer, a personal organizer, or a word processor—you may discover additional requirements:

● "I wish that this hairdryer had completely variable speeds, rather than just two."

● "I would like the organizer to dial the phone for me."

● "I want to 'save as' to the client's ftp site."

Requirements often do not emerge until someone actually uses the product. But by then it is too late—the product already exists. The objective of requirements gathering is to find the requirements *before* the product is built.

Prototyping is an adjunct to the other requirements-gathering techniques we discussed in Chapter 5, Trawling for Requirements. It is particularly useful in the following situations:

- The product has not existed before, and it is difficult to visualize.
- The stakeholders for the product have no experience with either the kind of product or the proposed technology.
- The stakeholders have been doing their work for some time and are stuck in the way that they do it.
- The stakeholders are having trouble articulating their requirements.
- The requirements analysts are having trouble understanding what is required.
- The feasibility of a requirement is in doubt.

Agility Guide

This chapter discusses prototypes as a way of discovering the requirements. So far in this book, we have made it plain enough that, regardless of your aspirations for agility, learning and understanding the requirements make the difference between building the right product and the wrong one. We also hope we have clarified the difference between requirements and the solution to those requirements.

With that in mind, we advocate building prototypes—usually a paper or whiteboard prototype—and testing them to see if they would satisfy the users' work. Of course, the users' agreement is not the end of it. Requirements analysis is a much broader church than "Do you like this one?" The analyst has to ensure the particular piece of work fits with the overall architecture of the work. Security, maintenance, and other nonfunctional requirements must be considered. In short, the prototypes are merely the beginning—albeit a very useful beginning—and not the end of the requirements gathering.

Rabbit projects almost always use prototypes. However, we want to make a distinction between developing a prototype with the intention that once the stakeholder agrees, the prototype becomes the working version, and developing a throwaway requirements prototype. Prototypes as we discuss them here are considered expendable. They are an aid to understanding the users' work, without which you cannot deliver the optimal product.

Horse projects have a larger number of stakeholders than rabbit projects, and use prototypes slightly differently. Although horse projects use requirements prototypes to gather requirements, they need a mechanism with which to test the prototypes against different stakeholders in different locations. These projects also write a specification, and we suggest you rely more on stakeholders' agreement with the prototypes rather than asking them to read through the entire requirements specification.

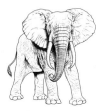

Despite the formality of elephant projects, prototyping also has a role here. Prototypes should be used when stakeholders, or groups of stakeholders, are having problems explaining what they need. In these situations, prototypes act to clarify the stakeholders' intentions. The formal requirements are still written once the prototype has served this purpose.

We should mention some numbers given to us by software statistician Capers Jones. For smaller applications of about 1,000 function points, Jones discovered that, on average, the prototypes built by the project team contained about 10 percent of the final delivered functionality. For large applications (typical of elephant projects) of 100,000 function points, prototypes covered only about 2 percent of the total functionality. This research points out a problem unique to elephant projects: They are bigger and they have more complex functionality. As a consequence, they should take more advantage of prototyping to discover that functionality.

Prototypes and Reality

When gathering requirements, you are asking your stakeholders to imagine what they need their future product to do. The results you uncover are limited by the stakeholders' imaginations and experiences, and by their ability to describe something that for the moment does not exist.

The prototype makes the product real enough to prompt stakeholders to bring up requirements that might otherwise be missed.

In contrast, a prototype gives the stakeholder something real, or at least something that has the appearance of reality. The prototype makes the product real enough for stakeholders to bring up requirements that might otherwise be missed. Our colleague Steve McMenamin refers to prototypes as "requirements bait": When stakeholders see the functionality displayed by a prototype, it inspires them to raise other requirements. In this way, by demonstrating possibilities through prototypes and giving stakeholders a seemingly real experience, you capture the additional requirements—sometimes there are quite a lot of these—that might otherwise have waited until the product was in use to come to the surface. See Figure 12.2.

Prototypes are also used to play out the consequences of requirements. You inevitably come across those strange requirements that have a single advocate who swears he would be lost without it. Who knows whether his requirement is a great idea that will make the product better or merely a complex way of doing something that doesn't need to be done? The prototype does. Building a prototype of hard-to-fathom requirements makes them visible. It gives everyone the opportunity to understand them, discuss them, possibly simplify them, and then decide whether their merits warrant their inclusion in the final product.

Figure 12.2

A requirements prototype is used to display the functionality of a potential product. The prototype's purpose is to prompt stakeholders to tell you whether you have understood the needed functionality and, as a result of "using" the prototype, to give you additional requirements suggested by it.

As noted earlier, the prototypes discussed here are throwaway prototypes; they are not intended to evolve into the finished product. Of course, they might, but that is incidental to the requirements gathering. Requirements prototypes are intended to help elicit requirements. They are created to get feedback from the stakeholders and to generate new requirements.

A prototype is a simulation. It attempts to appear as if it is a product that the stakeholders could use to do their work. But not the work that they have been doing in the past—instead, the prototype models the work that you envisage they might do in the future if given the help of the product that you are demonstrating. You show your stakeholders a prototype of a product—possibly several alternative prototypes—and ask if they could do their job using a product something like the prototype. If the answer is yes, then you capture the requirements demonstrated by that version of the prototype. If the answer is no, then you change the prototypes and test again.

The stakeholders who must decide whether your prototype is a reasonable demonstration of the proposed work face a somewhat difficult situation. They bring to the prototyping exercise some work-related baggage. They have been doing their job for some time (you probably wouldn't be asking them to test your prototypes if they hadn't), and their perception of their work may be very different from yours. This difference in perspectives requires tact on your part to discover which aspects of reality are uppermost in the minds of the people you are dealing with. Which metaphors do they use for their work, and how do they envision themselves while they are

Which aspects of reality are uppermost in the minds of the people you are dealing with? Which metaphors do they use for their work, and how do they envision themselves while they are doing their work?

doing their work? On top of this, you are asking them how they feel about doing different work—the work that you are proposing for the future. Adopting the new product could mean jettisoning artifacts and ways of working that they feel quite comfortable with. It is no easy task for the stakeholders to turn away from their experience and their comfort, and to accept a new, as-yet-untried way of doing their work.

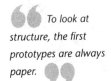

Build a prototype that relates to the physical anchors in the user's world.

The lesson is clear: We must always try to use prototyping techniques that conform, in some way, to the artifacts and experiences that are most familiar to the stakeholders. This means adjusting your prototyping approach for each work situation.

Let's look at some of the possibilities available for requirements prototypes. We can then talk about how they might be gainfully employed. We'll start with the simplest option: the low-fidelity prototype.

Low-Fidelity Prototypes

> *To look at structure, the first prototypes are always paper.*
>
> Source: Hugh Beyer and Karen Holtzblatt, *Contextual Design*

Low-fidelity prototypes help stakeholders concentrate on the subject matter by using familiar media. Such things as pencil and paper, whiteboards, flip charts, Post-it notes, index cards, and cardboard boxes can be employed to build effective low-fidelity prototypes (Figure 12.3). In fact, these prototypes may take advantage of anything that is part of the stakeholders' everyday life and do not require an additional investment.

The low-fidelity prototype is not meant to look all that much like the finished product. This is both good and bad. The good part is that no one will confuse the prototype with an actual product. It is obviously built with a minimal investment in time, and most importantly it gives no indication that it is anything other than an easy-to-change mock-up. The low-fidelity prototype encourages iteration, and it more or less indicates that you are not expecting to get the right answer on your first attempt. The bad part is that such a prototype sometimes requires more effort on the part of the stakeholder who is testing it to imagine that the whiteboard sketch is potentially his new product. However, the ability to make changes easily and the speed

Figure 12.3

Effective prototyping tools do not have to be complex or expensive.

with which you can sketch out a prototype usually help you to bring things to life to help stakeholders take more advantage of their imaginations.

We find that prototyping is more convenient, and ultimately more accurate, if the prototype involves a single business use case or a single product use case. As the prototype involves some simulated product, we will assume you are prototyping a product use case. We introduced business and product use cases back in Chapter 4. Recall that a business use case is an amount of work, triggered by an external business event occurring or by a predetermined time being reached, that takes place in a single, continuous time frame. It also has a known, measurable, testable outcome. A product use case is the part of the business use case to be done by the product. Because of the single, continuous time frame, it provides you with an appropriate amount of work as the subject of your prototype.

Let's look at prototyping by examining an example use case. The "Monitor untreated roads" use case, as shown in Figure 12.4, is suitable for our purposes. This use case is triggered periodically when it is time to monitor the road treatment: The engineer checks whether all the roads that are scheduled to be treated with de-icing material have been covered by one of the trucks. Thus we have to find all the requirements for this part of the product.

Your aim in building this low-fidelity prototype is to unearth the existing requirements that must be carried into the new product, along with the new, undreamed-of requirements. Let's assume the engineers are currently working with a system that supplies them with a list of roads, and use that as a starting point.

You can quickly sketch a low-fidelity prototype of the current situation, and then begin to explore improvements to it. The prototype focuses on what the product could do, for the moment ignoring any implementation details.

The point of sketching a low-fidelity prototype is to be quick. Demonstrate each requirements suggestion with another sketch or several alternative sketches. You might intentionally serve up several prototypes of the same use

Prototyping is more convenient, and ultimately more accurate, if done one use case at a time.

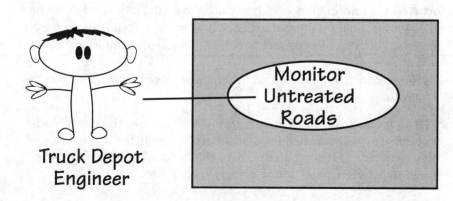

Truck Depot Engineer

Figure 12.4

The truck depot engineers are responsible for ensuring that all roads in danger of freezing are treated with de-icing material. Use case number 11, "Monitor untreated roads," represents this part of the work.

case, asking for the stakeholders' preferences and possibly more suggestions for alternatives. Once your stakeholders see you are simulating potential ways of solving their problem and realize their input is not only welcome but also necessary, they will almost certainly help you by suggesting their own enhancements and requirements. Experience has taught us a valuable lesson: Once you get people involved by making the problem visible, they tend to become very creative and imaginative—and sometimes your problem evolves into one of keeping pace with their imagination.

Get started by sketching what the stakeholders[1] might be doing when using the product for the use case. Ask the stakeholders what part the product will play in their work, and note their ideas. In the "Monitor untreated roads" use case, stakeholders would most likely want the product to provide following information:

- Roads scheduled for de-icing
- Roads that have been de-iced
- Relative positions of roads

Now ask the stakeholders what they would do with this information. At this point you are not trying to design a solution to this immediate problem, but rather want to explore ideas for what a potential product *might* do and what the work *might* be with that product:

- "What is the best way of presenting the needed information?"
- "Is the requested information the right information for the work being done?"
- "Could the product do more or less of the work?"

Assume for the moment there are no technological limitations. Also, keep in mind you are not designing the product, but are capturing all the things it might possibly do to help the stakeholders do their work.

Sketch pictures to elicit ideas from the stakeholders. If they are having trouble getting started, then inject some ideas of your own. Ask them to imagine that they are doing the job of monitoring untreated roads. What other pieces of information would they need to do the job? Would they have to look for information somewhere else? Is all of the information in the current version of the prototype necessary to do the job of monitoring untreated roads?

As the prototyping proceeds and the engineers see your sketches, you hear the following:

"That's great. Now wouldn't it be great if we could see the major roads that have not been treated for three hours? But only the major roads— the secondary ones don't matter so much. Our current system can't distinguish between major and secondary roads."

FOOTNOTE 1:
We say "stakeholders" rather than "users," because there are probably people other than users who are interested stakeholders for any use case.

Paper is eminently practical and meets the primary need: It makes it possible to express the structure of the system and makes it hard to overfocus on user interface detail.

Source: Hugh Beyer and Karen Holtzblatt, *Contextual Design*

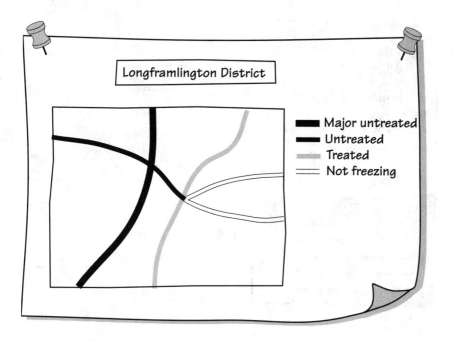

Longframlington District

■ Major untreated
■ Untreated
▬ Treated
═ Not freezing

Figure 12.5

By drawing this low-fidelity prototype on a flip chart or whiteboard, with the help of the truck depot engineers, you identify their requirements. They want the product to highlight the major roads within a district that have not been treated and are in a dangerous condition.

How long does it take you to add that requirement to your sketch? About ten seconds? How long would it have taken to modify the installed product if the engineers had asked for this requirement after delivery? Enough said.

By working with the engineers you generate a prototype that is possibly quite different from what they have at the moment. That is the point of the prototype—to change the work, and to discover new and better ways of doing the work. By encouraging the engineers to tell you more and more about the job, you uncover requirements that otherwise would not come to light. See Figure 12.5.

When you sketch a low-fidelity prototype, you demonstrate your ideas to the stakeholders and encourage them to iterate by changing and improving your ideas. Recall that a part of the requirements process is inventing a better way to do the work. (See Figure 12.6.) The prototype is an invention vehicle for you and your stakeholders to experiment with and to see how the proposed product could contribute to the new work.

Low-fidelity prototypes give the best value when you use them early in the development cycle. The stakeholders can give you more feedback earlier in the process when they are less fixated on the design or appearance of the product and are more interested in the overall structure and broad-brush functionality. At this stage, the users' ideas for the product should be fluid, and quick and easy experimentation will yield the best product.

The low-fidelity prototype is not a work of art, but rather an idea-generating device.

Figure 12.6

The low-fidelity prototype is informal and fast. No one will mistake it for the finished product. Because it is easy to change, stakeholders are willing to iterate, experiment, and investigate alternative ideas.

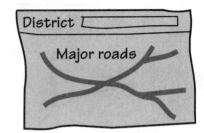

High-Fidelity Prototypes

High-fidelity prototypes are built using software tools and have the appearance of working software products. They appear to do whatever the use case does, and they display most of the characteristics of working software products. Development of such a prototype gives stakeholders the opportunity to "use" a realistic-looking product and decide whether the product displays the correct requirements.

Because the prototype behaves as the stakeholders would expect the final product to behave, it gives them the chance to explore the *potential* of the product, ideally leading them to suggest improvements and new requirements. But herein lies a problem: Because the prototype looks so much like a working product, the stakeholders may be tempted to concentrate on its appearance and possibly forego making functional improvements. To do so would defeat the purpose of requirements prototyping.

Putting aside the slight risk of stakeholders misunderstanding their role in the prototyping activity, the high-fidelity prototype has a lot to offer. It is interactive, which encourages the user to explore. The icons and data displayed on the screen are representative of the data and icons used to do the actual work. The stakeholders should feel at home with the prototype: They can open windows, update data, and be told whether they have made an error. In other words, the prototype simulates the real work.

The requirements analyst creates lifelike work situations, then asks the stakeholders to operate the prototype as if they were doing real work. By observing the stakeholders' reactions and noting their comments, the analyst finds even more of the product's requirements.

Prototyping has a beneficial effect on the discovery of requirements that otherwise might be missed. The high-fidelity prototype, because it is more detailed than the low-fidelity version, gives the stakeholders greater opportunities to explore all the possibilities for the use case. For example, stakeholders may explore the exception and alternative paths: "What happens if no more trucks are available, but some of the trucks have been scheduled to treat secondary roads?" "Can I bypass the parameter stage or set up a default set of parameters?"

An extensive set of high-fidelity prototyping tools is available to the requirements analyst. In many cases, the tool indicates how you should go about collecting your requirements. Tools can be of the interface builder types, which incorporate functionality to easily build screens and simulate functionality. Many of these tools are backed by a database, thereby enabling you to construct small to medium-size working applications.

Slightly more formal in their application are programming languages such as Visual Basic, REALbasic, and Perl. They can also be used to quickly construct lifelike prototypes. In some cases prototypes built in these languages go on to become the working product, but that is not the initial intention of the requirements prototype.

Content management systems such as Mambo and Drupal allow prototyping of Web-based products. These tools are more than just prototyping tools—the final result may be the full-strength version of the product. Care must be taken to ensure the requirements for the other aspects of the product—security, maintainability, and so on—keep pace with the front end as it is being prototyped.

We will not attempt to list all products that could be used for high-fidelity prototypes. Any such list would be out of date before you picked up this book. We suggest searching the Web and, in particular, the open source community (sourceforge.net) as the best resource for software suitable for requirements prototyping.

The high-fidelity prototype is effective for discovering usability requirements. As the user attempts to work with it, the analyst observes which parts of the prototype are pleasing and easy to use, and which usability features need improvement (see Figure 12.7). The user's actions thus provide input to the usability requirements.

In addition to analyzing the feedback you get from stakeholders, consider the designer's contribution. Any good designer will likely have something to say and ideas to contribute to the prototype. Designers, being the people they are, are usually happier working with real and visual objects than with abstract concepts. They typically see the prototype as a natural artifact that they can try out and improve. By showing your prototypes to your designers, you almost certainly will benefit from their ideas.

> *Prototypes are requirements bait.*
>
> Source: Steve McMenamin

Figure 12.7

The high-fidelity prototype is a faithful demonstration version of the proposed product. This example shows a screen shot from Mambo (used with permission), an open source content management system. Users are invited to log on the demonstration site and alter the prototype as they wish, thereby demonstrating the ease of using such products for prototyping.

Also consider the value of a high-fidelity prototype when you are developing a product for the mass market. In this situation, the prototype serves as a vehicle for soliciting feedback from customer representative groups. Your potential customers will voice their preferences and explain whether your product is something they are willing to buy. At the same time, the high-fidelity prototype is useful for making realistic comparisons with competing products. Your product must match, and preferably beat, anything available elsewhere.

Storyboards

Storyboards are a prototyping technique borrowed from the film and cartoon industries. When a cartoonist is planning a cartoon, he sketches a number of linked pictures. These pictures identify the story line and guide the cartoonist in how many detailed pictures he needs to draw. A similar path is followed with movies: The script is sketched out on a storyboard, with a panel for each scene showing the actors, close-up or long shot, mood of the scene, and dialog for that scene. The director and the storyboard artist work on each panel, prototyping the movie, until the director is satisfied the story is being effectively told. Then they shoot the movie as it is laid out in the storyboard.

Brad and Janet take the family away for the weekend.

HomeSafe senses the car leaving, locks the doors, and turns on the burglar alarm. It also activates the random lights program. HomeClimate turns down the heating.

Before they return, Janet phones HomePlate to check the food supplies at home. She asks HomePlate to thaw a frozen chicken.

From the driveway, Brad phones HomeSafe to open the garage door and unset the burglar alarm.
HomeMusic plays their favorite homecoming music.
HomePlate starts cooking the chicken.

Building a storyboard means thinking of the proposed functionality as a story and breaking it into a series of steps, or discrete actions (Figure 12.8). Draw each action as a panel of the story. Many storyboards show the user at a screen in each panel, but, if possible, you should try to show the remainder of the work being done. Do not under any circumstances worry about your artistic ability. Stick figures with cartoon bubbles to indicate dialog are perfectly adequate. Don't be embarrassed to show your storyboard to your stakeholders. They probably are no better at drawing than you are. You are not trying to create great art, just produce a communicable representation of some work being done.

Sometimes one picture is enough to illustrate all the actions and outcomes for a use case (see Figure 12.9). For more complex use cases, or for playing out of several use cases or aspects of the whole product, you need a sequence of pictures.

We find storyboards to be a good starting point when exploring a business situation involving interactions between real people. Somehow, people identify with the sketched figures (no matter how badly drawn) and provide a lot of input on what can happen during the course of the product use case.

Figure 12.8

A storyboard demonstrates to the potential users how a product—in this case, different parts of a product—could work. Each panel represents an identifiable part of the story. The requirements analyst uses this kind of prototype to play through the product, experimenting with it and learning the requirements.

Figure 12.9

Some storyboards abandon the panel format and show most of the product in one layout. This example comes from an air traffic control project your authors are involved with. The storyboard uses Post-it notes and cards to show the different functionality of the proposed product. The tape and string are work flow connections between the functions. (Photo courtesy of Neil Maiden.)

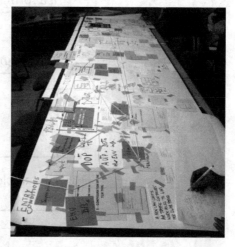

Object Life History

This prototyping technique goes by many names. The object life history is a state model (also known as a state transition diagram) that shows which states the objects for a class (sometimes called entities) may take, and illustrates the transitions between those states. Whatever you call it, the idea is to take a key business object—one whose subject matter is the concern of a number of use cases—and use a state model to show the things that might happen to that object during its lifetime. When you have completed the life history of the object, consider whether there are sufficient functional requirements to cover all the happenings.

Figure 12.10 shows a state model for a road, one of the more important business objects in the IceBreaker system. A state is a steady condition for the object, and each rectangle in the model identifies a different state that this object will be in at one time or another. For example, the road object is normally in the condition of being *safe for use*. It continues in that steady condition until something happens to change the state. In this case, the safe state is interrupted by a prediction that, due to ice formation, the road is about to become *unsafe for traffic*.

Once that interruption happens, the road is in a different state. It will remain in the unsafe state until something else happens to change it. The diagram indicates that there are three possibilities: (1) the road can be *treated*, in which case it moves back to being safe; (2) the surface temperature can rise enough so the ice melts; or (3) enough ice can form to make the road truly

READING

Maiden, Neil, and Suzanne Robertson. *Integrating Creativity into Requirements Processes: Experiences with an Air Traffic Management System.* International Conference on Software Engineering, May 2005.

Figure 12.10

This state model or object life history for the business object *Road* identifies the states in which a road can exist and the events that cause a transition from one state to another.

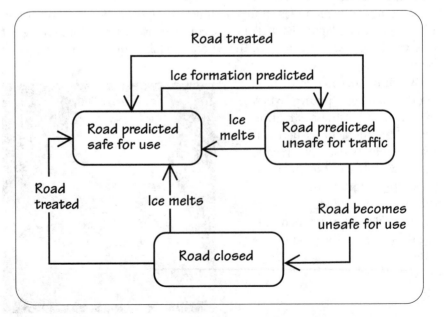

dangerous, in which case it is *closed* to traffic. Treating it or waiting for the ice to melt is the way to make this road safe to use again.

What's the point of this model? The story. In this example it is the story of a road and the things that might happen to it within the scope of the work that we are studying. Here is part of this story:

"When the A1(M) road was predicted to be unsafe for use last January, we could not treat it before it became unsafe for use and we had to close the road."

You can see this part of the story reflected in the state model in Figure 12.10.

The story is told not so much by the states, as by the transitions between states. These transitions are caused by the business events that affect the work. Using Figure 12.10 as an example, "Ice formation predicted" is a transition brought about by business event 8, "Time to detect icy roads." (Chapter 4 has a complete list of business events for IceBreaker.) "Road treated" is the result of business event 9, "Truck treats a road." If you examine the state model, you should be able to correlate all of the transitions with the business events.

The story is told not so much by the states, as by the transitions between states.

When we built the first version of this model, we found that we had the requirements for all the events shown in the object life history model, except one. Our original model said that a closed road becomes safe for use when it is treated. When we showed this model to a user, he pointed out that the road would also become safe when the ice melts. We had missed this transition out of the "Road closed" state.

Thus the model told us that there are more requirements. In fact, it identified a new business event, "Time to monitor closed roads," to see whether the roads have become safe without treatment. The new business event should added to the context model, and the business use case explored and its requirements written.

We suggest you build object life histories for the key business objects. Your intention is to discover more about the work and to unearth any additional business events that must be taken into account.

The Prototyping Loop

Although you can employ a variety of techniques for prototyping, the same strategy applies to using any of them. This strategy consists of three prototyping activities: design and build, test, and analyze (Figure 12.11). Let's look at them in more depth.

Figure 12.11

Prototyping begins with a "Requirement for experiment." This could be a single requirement, a product use case, or some hypothesis to be proved or disproved. The user tests the prototype, and the results are analyzed. Note the output of the *Analyze* process: "Potential requirements." The requirements learned from the test are recorded. Any needed modifications to the prototype are used to redesign and rebuild it. The process continues until the *Analyze* process ceases to reveal further requirements.

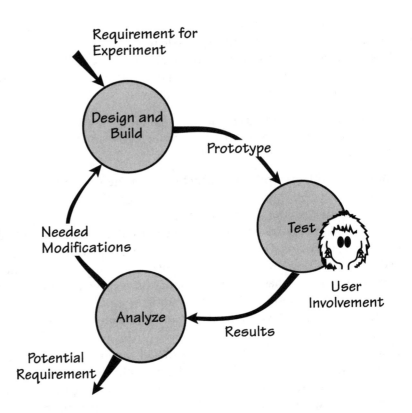

Design and Build

Design is the activity of deciding what you are trying to model with your prototype and what you are trying to achieve. The subject of the prototype may be a single requirement or (more likely) a product use case. Similarly, the prototype might be built to prove some idea, to disprove some idea, or for any other reason. For the sake of simplicity, we will assume you are prototyping a product use case. Now, what is the use case meant to achieve, and what are its functional outcomes? Once you have decided the functional outcome of the prototype, then that part of its design becomes clearer.

The other question is harder: What are you trying to achieve with this prototype? Are you looking for the functional requirements or nonfunctional ones such as usability, operational, or security requirements? Are you exploring a use case that is largely unknown, or are you building a prototype to confirm the requirements for a fairly well-understood piece of work? Are you trying to prove a proposed requirements is not workable? For any of these questions, consider how you will know when you have achieved your purpose. To put it another way, how will you measure the success of the prototype?

Also consider these issues:

- Identify the operational environment in which the product will eventually be used to do work. For example, it could be an office, a factory, a school, a laboratory, a family household, or a public building. (You might already have defined the environment in section 13, Operational Requirements, of your requirements specification.)

- Identify the stakeholders whose input you need to get information for this prototype. (You might already have defined these people in sections 2 and 3 of your requirements specification.)

- Decide how you will make clear to each person why you need his input and what advantage he will get from being involved in the prototyping effort.

- Plan how you will run each prototyping session. Will you work with the stakeholders, or will you leave the prototype with them and return when they have had a chance to assess it?

The answers to these questions provide you with the input needed to slant the design of the prototype to fit the particular situation. Designing is mapping the world of the user into the prototype. What artifacts does the user want represented in the prototype? What are the user's metaphors for this use case, and how does he see the product's contribution to the work that he is doing?

Designing is mapping the world of the user into the prototype.

We have already discussed building prototypes, so we will not linger on that part of the process. Suffice it to say that given today's high-fidelity prototyping tools and the wide variety of low-fidelity methods, the actual construction of the prototype is a relatively straightforward affair. This means you might be able to build your prototypes with your stakeholders present, and it should leave you more time to spend testing the prototype together.

Testing in the User Environment

In testing, the users and other stakeholders use the prototype as a simulation of their work while you objectively record their feedback.

The exact way you run the tests depends on the kind of prototype you are using and your objectives in using prototypes in the first place. Stakeholders can be left alone for some time to experiment with high-fidelity prototypes; later you can meet to discuss the results. You usually have to demonstrate the low-fidelity prototypes to the stakeholders, so the testing is more casual and the feedback is more interactive.

We recommend that you include your usability experts in this kind of testing. It has been our experience that usability people are often not invited to become involved until the product has very nearly reached the production stage. It is assumed that only a few fine-tuning corrections to the usability

Include usability experts in your prototyping cycle.

aspects will be necessary to complete the product. However, this is far too late to consider this critical issue. Usability must be built into the product from the beginning, not bolted on at the last moment. We have included usability (section 11 in the template) for a very good reason: Usability is a nonfunctional requirement. That is, it is an integral part of the product and not an optional accessory that can be sprayed on like a last-minute paint job.

The objective of prototyping is to get feedback. Let's look at how we analyze this feedback.

Analyzing the Results

Your aim in analyzing the prototyping results is to identify potential requirements and to determine whether it is worth modifying the prototype and running more tests in the user environment.

There are two things you are looking for with your analysis. First, you want to see whether the stakeholders uncovered any new potential requirements. Second, you want to determine whether it is worth modifying the prototype and running more tests.

In Figure 12.11, note that one of the outputs of the analysis activity is a flow of requirements. When you examine the results of the prototype test, you are looking for requirements. Either the test confirms the requirements you thought were correct and built into the prototype, or the stakeholders discovered new requirements by using the prototype.

It is important you capture these requirements. The prototype is not sufficient by itself, because it is only a *simulation* of the specification. You still need to extract the real requirements; otherwise, you are left with prototyping code that may not convey the underlying requirements to the developer.

A prototype is not the same thing as a requirements specification; it is a simulation of the specification. You still need to extract the real requirements.

Sometimes your prototyping results may indicate that it would be worth modifying your prototype and conducting further tests with it. For example, the road engineers told us that they would like the IceBreaker product to identify roads in danger of closing; then they could make rescheduling decisions based on the seriousness of the closure.

The seriousness factor was something new, and its inclusion affected a number of other requirements. We decided that a good way of learning more about the potential new requirements was to modify the prototype and ask the engineers to test it again and provide more feedback.

Review the results of your prototyping. Are you still discovering new requirements? The number of potential requirements your analysis reveals is significant. Consider whether you have found enough requirements to make it worthwhile to continue modifying and testing that prototype. Or were there too many? If you have a truly large number of requirements, does it indicate that you may not know enough about the work situation? Would other methods be more appropriate to learn how the work should be done?

Is your prototyping effort still contributing to your stated reason for building the prototype? If the answer is yes, then you might decide to put more effort into modifying and testing the prototype. If your measurements indicate that you are learning less, then the prototype has probably served its purpose.

You are likely to go around the prototyping loop several times, each time getting a different result. Revisit your objectives and results each time.

When you build a requirements prototype, think of it as a technique for helping you learn about the requirements so the eventual product is based on real, well-defined user needs.

Summary

Requirements prototypes are simulation models designed to help you learn more about the stakeholders' requirements. The aim of a prototype is to make it easier for people to imagine what it might be like to use the real product to do work. Ideally, working with this model will stimulate them into remembering requirements they have forgotten, or thinking of ideas that might not otherwise occur to them until they begin using the real product.

Low-fidelity prototypes offer a quick way to put together a mockup of a product using familiar technology such as pencil and paper, whiteboards, flip charts, and so on. These prototypes encourage stakeholders to focus on what the product does, rather than how it will appear. They help to discover missing functionality and to test the scope of the product.

High-fidelity prototypes use software tools and give a strong appearance of reality. Their advantage is obvious: It takes little imagination to see the prototype as a working system. We suggest that you adopt prototypes of both kinds as a regular part of your requirements process.

Reusing Requirements

*in which we look for requirements
that have already been written
and explore ways to reuse them*

In our everyday lives we all consciously (or, more commonly, unconsciously) reuse knowledge. If we are experienced drivers, then we do not consciously think about how to drive. We can make a cup of tea without rediscovering how many spoons of tealeaves we should use. We write a letter without looking up where to put the recipient's address, and how to start and end the letter. In these and many more everyday situations, we reuse knowledge. It is knowledge that we have gained by studying and practicing what we have already discovered for ourselves, or more often what others have already defined. It does not occur to us to start all over and reinvent how to make a pot of tea. Instead, we reuse the knowledge that already exists and enhance it to suit our particular situation.

> *Engineers? You want to be engineers? Then remember that engineers don't invent things when they can find something that can be reused.*
>
> Source: Tomoo Matsubara

When specifying the requirements for a new product, you can often save a lot of effort if you start by asking, "Have these requirements or similar ones already been specified?"

What Is Reusing Requirements?

Although they might have many of their own special features, the products you build are not completely unique. Someone, somewhere, has already built a product containing some requirements that are germane to your current work. When you take advantage of work that has already been done, your efficiency as a requirements gatherer increases significantly. Early in your requirements projects look for reusable requirements that have already been written, and incorporate these "free" requirements into your own project. See Figure 13.1.

Figure 13.1

Reusing requirements entails making use of requirements written for other projects. They can come from a number of sources: a reuse library of specifications, other requirements specifications that are similar or in the same domain, or informally from other people's experience.

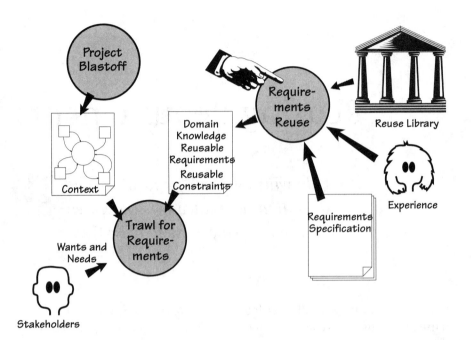

Successful reuse starts with having an organizational culture that consciously encourages reuse rather than reinvention.

Refer to Chapter 3 for more on how to run a project blastoff meeting.

But these requirements are not exactly free: You have to do something for them. Successful reuse starts with having an organizational culture that consciously encourages reuse rather than reinvention. If you have this attitude, then you are in a position to include requirements reuse in your requirements process.

Naturally, to determine whether you have any relevant reusable requirements, you need to know something about the work that you are investigating. When you run a project blastoff meeting, pay particular attention to the first seven sections of the requirements specification:

1 *The Purpose of the Project:* Are there other projects in the organization that are compatible or that cover substantially the same domains or work areas?

2 *The Client, the Customer, and Other Stakeholders:* Can you reuse an existing list of stakeholders, a stakeholder map, or a stakeholder analysis spreadsheet?

3 *Users of the Product:* Do other products involve the same users and thus have similar usability requirements? Also refer here to stakeholder maps and spreadsheets.

4 *Mandated Constraints:* Have your constraints already been specified for another project?

5 *Naming Conventions and Definitions:* You can almost certainly make use of parts of someone else's glossary, rather than having to invent all of your own glossary.

6 *Relevant Facts and Assumptions:* Pay attention to relevant facts from recent projects. Do other projects' assumptions apply to your project?

7 *The Scope of the Work:* Your project has a very good chance of being an adjacent system to other projects that are under way in your organization. Make use of the interfaces that have been established by other work context models.

When you are looking for potentially reusable requirements, don't be too quick to say your project is different from everything that has gone before it. Yes, the subject matter is different, but if you look past the names, how much of the underlying functionality is substantially the same? How many requirements specifications have already been written that contain material that you can use unaltered, or at least adapted, in your own specification? See Figure 13.2.

For more on stakeholder maps and stakeholder analysis, see Appendix D, Project Sociology Analysis Templates.

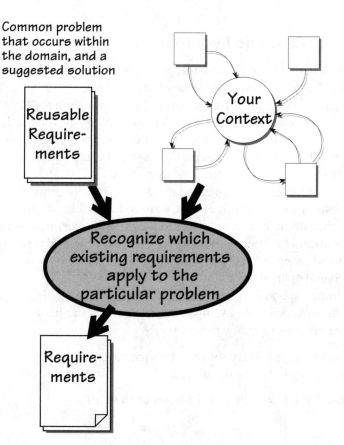

Common problem that occurs within the domain, and a suggested solution

Reusable Require-ments

Your Context

Recognize which existing requirements apply to the particular problem

Require-ments

Figure 13.2

At project blastoff time the subject matter of the context, together with its adjacent systems and boundary data flows, should indicate the potential for reusing requirements from previous projects.

The blastoff deliverables provide a focus for identifying reusable knowledge that might not otherwise be found.

One of the benefits of using a disciplined process for writing requirements specifications is that you naturally produce requirements that are more easily reusable by future projects.

We have found that significant amounts of specifications can be assembled from existing components rather than having to be invented from the ground up.

The stakeholders who participate in the blastoff meeting are wonderful sources of reusable components. Ask them about other documents that contain knowledge relevant to the work of the project. Consider whether someone else has already investigated subject matter domains that overlap with your project. Closely examine the blastoff deliverables. They provide a focus for identifying reusable knowledge that might not otherwise be found.

When you are trawling for requirements, continue to look for reusable requirements by asking the people you interview about them: "Have you answered these questions, or questions like them, before? Do you know of documents that might already contain the answers to these questions?" This fairly informal approach means that you encounter potentially reusable requirements in many different forms. Some are precisely stated and hence directly reusable; others merely provide clues or pointers to sources of knowledge. One of the benefits of using a disciplined process for writing requirements specifications is that you naturally produce requirements that are more easily reusable by future projects.

Sources of Reusable Requirements

When you want to learn to cook the perfect fried egg, one of the best ways to get started is to learn from someone whose fried eggs you admire. They tell you the egg should be less than five days old, and the butter—slightly salted is best—should be heated until it is golden but not brown. You break the egg, gently slide it into the bubbling butter, and then spoon the golden liquid over it until the white turns opaque. You serve the egg with a sprinkling of fresh coriander and offer the diner Tabasco sauce.

Informal experience-related reuse of requirements: We do this when we ask questions of our colleagues. We want to learn from one person's experience so that we do not have to start our own endeavors from scratch.

This is informal experience-related reuse of requirements; we do this when we ask questions of our colleagues. We want to learn from one person's experience so that we do not have to start our own endeavors from scratch. We might not always find out everything we want to know, and we might make changes to what we are told, but we use the information discovered to build on other people's knowledge.

More formal reusable requirements for the domain of fried-egg cookery come from cookbooks. For example, Jenny Baker, in her book *Simple French Cuisine*, instructs us to follow these steps:

"Heat sufficient oil . . . fry the tomatoes with a garlic clove . . . break the eggs on top and cook gently until set."

In *Italian Food*, Elizabeth David advises us to do this:

"Melt some butter . . . put in a slice of mozzarella . . . break two eggs into each dish . . . cover the pan while the eggs are cooking."

You can think of a cookbook as a requirements specification—it's just written for a different context of study than the one you are currently working on. Even though the preceding examples have some differences, both have aspects that could be reused as a starting point for writing a new recipe for fried eggs. This means once you know the context of your work, you can look for requirements specifications that deal with all or part of that context and use them as the source of potentially reusable requirements.

The examples we have used here come from a domain of cooking fried eggs. Within that domain, each writer has written her specification from a specific viewpoint. Elizabeth David focuses on cooking eggs the Italian way, whereas Jenny Baker writes about eggs in France. The two writers give you specific instructions for producing the desired result in a particular situation—in other words, their recipes work just like a normal requirements specification.

Now let's stand back a little and look at an abstraction. In *How to Cook: Book One*, Delia Smith investigates the subject of egg cooking with a view toward learning as much as she can about the subject of eggs. She has made an abstraction of knowledge that is relevant regardless of whether you want to cook Italian, French, or Trinidadian egg dishes. Smith writes about how to tell whether an egg is fresh, how long to cook an egg, when to use oil, when to use butter, and so on. In terms of requirements engineering, we could say that she has built a domain model on the subject of eggs.

A *domain* is a subject matter area. A *domain model* is a generic model of knowledge that applies to any product built for use in that domain. Consider the knowledge that Smith passes on about eggs. It is usable for almost any recipe (specification) that involves eggs. We see more about domain analysis later in this chapter.

You can reuse requirements or knowledge from any of the sources that we have discussed: colleagues' experiences, existing requirements specifications, and domain models. The only thing necessary is that you can recognize the reusable potential of anything you come across. Recognition itself requires that you perform abstractions, so as to see past the technology and procedures that are part of existing requirements. Abstraction also involves seeing past subject matters to find recyclable components. We have more on abstraction later in this chapter; for now, let's look at making use of the idea of patterns.

Once you know the context of your work, you can look for requirements specifications that deal with all or part of that context and use them as the source of potentially reusable requirements.

READING

Three cookery writers who have made knowledge about cooking accessible and reusable are Elizabeth David, Jenny Baker, and Delia Smith. Any of the books by these writers can help you improve your cooking skills and enjoyment of food.

David, Elizabeth. *Italian Food*. Penguin Books, 1998.

Baker, Jenny. *Simple French Cuisine*. Faber & Faber, 1992.

Smith, Delia. *How to Cook: Book One*. BBC Worldwide, 1998.

Requirements Patterns

A pattern is a guide. It gives you a form to follow when you are trying to replicate, or make a close approximation of, some piece of work. For example, the stonecutters working on classical buildings used wooden patterns to help them to carve the column capitals to a uniform shape. The tailor uses patterns to cut the cloth so that each jacket is the same basic form, with minor adjustments made to compensate for an individual client's body shape.

But what about patterns in a requirements sense? Patterns imply a collection of requirements that make up some logical grouping of functions. For example, we can think of a requirements pattern for selling a book in a shop: Determine the price; compute the tax, if any; collect the money; wrap the book; thank the customer. If this is a successful pattern, then it pays you to use the pattern for any future bookselling activities, rather than reinvent how to sell a book.

Refer to Chapter 4, Event-Driven Use Cases, for more on the connection between business events and use cases.

Typically we use requirements patterns that capture the processing policy for a business use case. If we use the business use case as a unit of work, then each pattern is bounded by its own input, output, and stored data. As a consequence, we can treat it as a stand-alone mini-system.

Requirements patterns improve the accuracy and completeness of requirements specifications. You reduce the time needed to produce a specification because you reuse a functional grouping of requirements knowledge that has already been specified by other projects. To do so, look for patterns that may have some application in your project. Keep in mind that the pattern is usually an abstraction and you may have to do a little work to adapt it to your own needs. However, the time saved in completing the specification and the insights gained by using other people's patterns are significant.

Christopher Alexander's Patterns

READING

Alexander, Christopher, et al. *A Pattern Language: Towns, Buildings, Construction.* Oxford University Press, 1977.

The most significant collection of patterns—and one that inspired the pattern movement in software design—was published in *A Pattern Language*, written by a group of architects headed by Christopher Alexander. The book identifies and describes patterns that contribute to functionality and convenience for everyday human life within buildings, living spaces, and communities. The book presents these patterns to architects and builders for use as guides for new building projects.

The Waist High Shelf (illustrated in Figure 13.3) is the name of one of the patterns defined by Alexander and his colleagues. In this case they looked at many people, such as the authors and readers of this book, and observed what happens when we enter and leave our houses. Suppose it is time to leave for work, and you are in a hurry. You need your keys, your sunglasses, your building pass, and the book you have to return to a colleague. If these things are difficult to find, you become irritated, probably forget something, and have a bad start to the day. The Waist High Shelf pattern is based on the observation that we need somewhere to put our keys and whatever other bits and pieces we have when we arrive, so that we can easily find them again when we leave.

The pattern specifies there should be a horizontal surface at waist height (a convenient height to reach), located just inside the front door (you do not

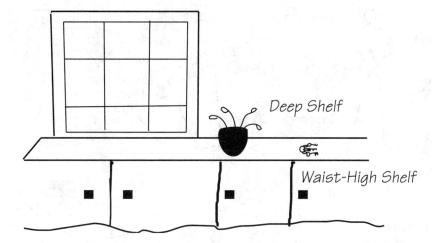

Figure 13.3

Alexander defined the Waist High Shelf pattern because, as he observed, "In every house and workplace there is a daily 'traffic' of the objects which are handled most. Unless such things are immediately at hand, the flow of life is awkward, full of mistakes: things are forgotten, misplaced."

have to carry objects farther than necessary), and big enough for you to deposit items that are commonly transported in and out of the house. In your authors' house, the Waist High Shelf pattern implemented itself without us realizing it. We noticed that we naturally put our keys on one of the steps of the staircase that is on your right as you come through our front door. We also noticed that, without being told, our visitors also leave their keys on the "waist high step."

Note the role of the pattern. It is a guide, not a rigid set of instructions or an implementation. It can be reused—there is no need to experiment and reinvent the pattern. It is a collection of knowledge or experience that can be adapted or used as is.

Now let us look at patterns as they apply to requirements.

A Business Event Pattern

Let's start by looking at an example of a requirements pattern. We can then discuss how the pattern was built and how it can be used by future projects. This pattern is based on the response to a business event:

> *Pattern Name: Customer Wants to Buy a Product*
>
> *Context: A pattern for receiving product orders from customers, supplying or back-ordering the product, and invoicing for the product.*
>
> *Forces: An organization has demands from its customers to supply goods or services. Failure to meet his demand might result in the customer seeking another supplier. Sometimes the product is unavailable at the time that the order is received.*

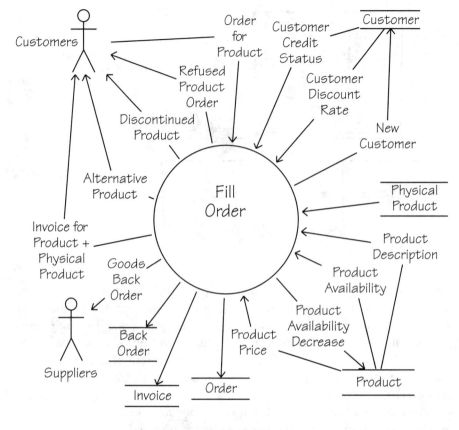

Figure 13.4

This context model defines the boundaries of the pattern *Customer Wants to Buy a Product*. The arrows identify flows of data and material. All flows coming into the process *Fill Order* are used by that piece of work to carry out the business rules that produce the flows coming out of *Fill Order*. Some flows come from or go to adjacent systems such as *Suppliers* or *Customers*. Other flows come from or go to stores of information such as *Product* or *Back Order*, as indicated by a pair of parallel lines. Of course, this diagram is merely a summary showing the boundaries; the individual requirements are inside the process *Fill Order*.

Solution: The following context model, event response model, and class diagram define the pieces of the pattern. Each actor, process, data flow and data store, business object, and association is defined in detail in attached text using the same names as are used in these models.

Context of Event Response

The context model in Figure 13.4 is a summary of the subject matter covered by the Customer Wants to Buy a Product pattern. You use the diagram to determine whether the details of the pattern might be relevant to the work you are doing. The flows of data (or material) around the boundary of the context indicate the kind of work being done by this pattern. If the majority of these flows are compatible with the inputs and outputs of your event, then the pattern is probably usable in your project.

Once you have decided that the pattern is suitable for your use, it's time to move on to the details. These can be expressed in a number of different ways. The technique that you use depends on the volume and depth of your knowledge about the pattern. For example:

- A step-by-step text description or scenario of what happens after a Customer sends an Order for Product
- A formal definition of all the individual requirements related to the Fill Order process
- A detailed model that breaks the pattern into subpatterns and their dependencies before specifying the individual requirements

Processing for Event Response

Figure 13.5 illustrates how a large pattern can be partitioned into a number of subpatterns. From this diagram, we can identify other potentially reusable clusters of requirements. For instance, the diagram has revealed a subpattern called Calculate Charge along with its interactions with other subpatterns.

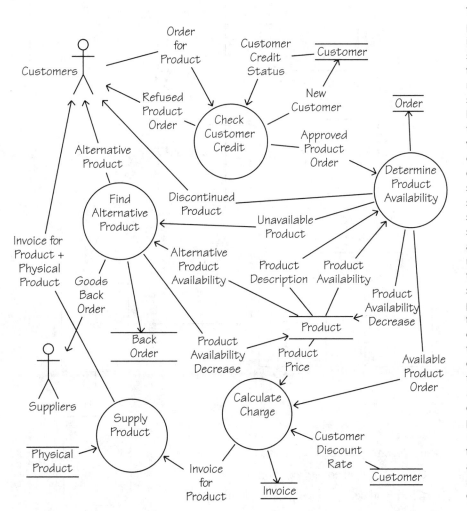

Figure 13.5

This diagram breaks the process *Fill Order* (shown in Figure 13.4) into five subprocesses (groups of functionally related requirements) and shows the dependencies between them. Each of the subprocesses (shown with a circle) is connected by named data flows to other subprocesses, data stores, or adjacent systems. Each subprocess also contains a number of requirements. Rather than forcing an arbitrary sequence on the processes, this model focuses on the dependencies between the processes. For example, we can see that the process *Determine Product Availability* has a dependency on the process *Check Customer Credit*. Why? Because the former needs to know about the *Approved Product Order* before it can do its work.

We can use this subpattern independently whenever we want to specify the requirements for calculating any type of charge. The interactions indicate which other patterns might also be relevant to us when we are interested in the pattern for calculating a charge. Other ways of depicting this pattern are to use a UML activity diagram, a sequence diagram, or a scenario.

Data for Event Response

The class diagram in Figure 13.6 shows us the objects that participate in the pattern Customer Wants to Buy a Product along with the associations between them. We can cluster the attributes and operations unique to each

Figure 13.6

This class diagram shows the objects and associations between them that are part of the pattern *Customer Wants to Buy a Product.* Consider the business rules communicated by this diagram. A *Customer* may make zero or many *Orders,* each of which is invoiced. The *Order* is for a collection of *Order Lines.* An *Order Line* is for a *Product,* which might be a *Service Product* or a *Goods Product.* Only *Goods Products* can have a *Back Order.* Now consider how many situations in which these business rules, data, and processes might be reused.

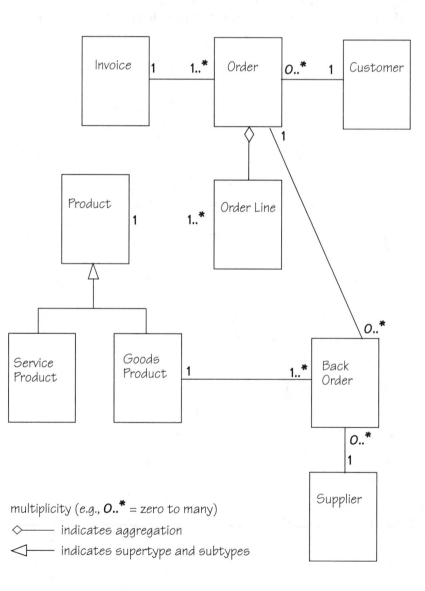

multiplicity (e.g., *0..** = zero to many)

◇———— indicates aggregation

◁———— indicates supertype and subtypes

object. For instance, the object Product has a number of unique attributes, such as its name and price; similarly, it has some unique operations such as calculate discounted price and find stock level. Because we have this cluster of knowledge about the object called Product, whenever we need to specify requirements for a product we can potentially reuse some or all of this knowledge.

Once again, you have many options regarding which models you use to model data. We have used a class model here, but you could just as effectively use an entity–relationship model or any other sort of data model that identifies classes and their associations.

Forming Patterns by Abstracting

The requirements pattern we have been discussing is the result of analyzing many business events—quite often from very different organizations—that deal with the subject of a customer wanting to buy a product. We derived the pattern by making an abstraction that captures all of the common processing policy for this type of business event. Thus the pattern contains the business policy that applies when almost any customer wants to buy almost any kind of product. If your project includes a business event centered on a customer wanting to buy something, then this pattern is a realistic starting point.

The same rubric applies with other events and other domains. Form your patterns by eliminating the idiosyncrasies that exist in many businesses and looking for the general case. Look past the specific to see the general. Look away from the technology the organization currently uses to see the business policy that is being processed. Think of the work, not in its current incarnation, but as a model for work that can be done in the future.

Of course, you can have many patterns, covering many business events and domains. To file them so that they are accessible, we organize these patterns in a consistent way according to the following template (which is really a pattern itself):

Pattern Name: A descriptive name to make it easy to communicate the pattern to other people.

Forces: The reasons for the pattern's existence.

Context: The boundaries within which the pattern is relevant.

Solution: A description of the pattern using a mixture of words, graphics, and references to other documents.

Related Patterns: Other patterns that might apply in conjunction with this one; other patterns that might help to understand this one.

Patterns for Specific Domains

Suppose that you are working on a system for a library. One of the business events within your context is almost certain to be Library User Wants to Extend Book Loan. Figure 13.7 shows a model of the system's response to this event. When a Library User submits a Loan Extension Request, the product responds with either Refused Loan Extension or Loan Extension Approval.

Your work on the project in the library domain has led to the specification of detailed requirements for a particular product. As a by-product of doing this work, you have identified some useful requirements patterns, clusters of business-event-related requirements that are potentially reusable on other projects in the library domain.

READING

For many examples of reusable domain models, refer to Hay, David. *Data Model Patterns: Conventions of Thought.* Dorset House, 1995.

When you specify requirements using a consistent discipline, you make them more accessible to other people and hence reusable. If you, or someone else, began another project for the library, a good starting point would be the specifications that you have already written. They are usually a prodigious source of recyclable requirements within this domain.

Now imagine that you are working on a system in a very different domain, that of satellite broadcasting. One business event within this context is Satellite Broadcaster Wants to Renew License. When the satellite broadcaster submits a Broadcast License Request, the product responds with either Rejected License or New License. Figure 13.8 summarizes the system's response to the event.

Figure 13.7

A summary of the library system's response to the event *Library User Wants to Extend Book Loan.*

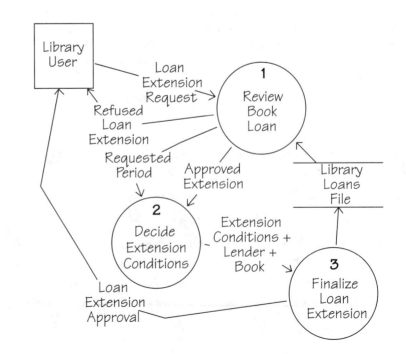

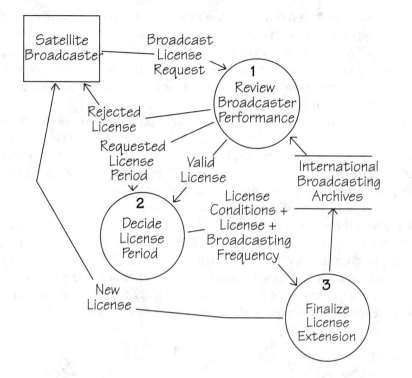

Figure 13.8

A model of the satellite broadcasting product's response to the event *Satellite Broadcaster Wants to Renew License.*

When you work on the requirements for the satellite broadcasting project, you also discover requirements patterns that are potentially reusable on products within this domain.

Now let's look a little farther afield. We have talked about the idea of identifying and reusing requirements patterns within a specific subject matter domain. But how can we use patterns outside the originating domain?

Patterns Across Domains

At first glance, the event responses to Library User Wants to Extend Loan and Satellite Broadcaster Wants to Renew License appear to be very different. Indeed, they are different in that they come from very different domains. Nevertheless, let's revisit the two event responses, this time looking for similarities. If we find shared characteristics, we have a chance of deriving a more abstract pattern that could be applied to many other domains.

Both books and broadcasting licenses are Things to Be Renewed. The business decides whether to renew an item in response to requests from a Renewer. The business rules for renewing books or licenses share some similarities. For instance, the business checks whether the Renewer is eligible to renew the thing; it decides the conditions of renewal; it records the decision and informs the Renewer. By looking at several different responses, we can make an abstraction: We have some processing policy that is common to all renewable items. We also discover that some attributes of a Thing to Be Renewed are the same regardless of whether we are talking about a book or a broadcasting license. For example, each Thing to Be Renewed has a unique identifier, a standard renewal period, and a renewal fee.

Figure 13.9 shows the result when we make an abstraction of the processing policy from the two business use cases. Here we are using abstraction to identify common characteristics. This means we look past what we see on the surface, and find useful similarities or classifications. It also means we ignore some characteristics in our quest to find common ones.

Ignore the physical artifacts and subject matters. For example, in Figure 13.9 ignore the artifacts of library books and broadcasting licenses. Instead, concentrate on the underlying actions of the two systems, with a view toward finding similarities that you can use to your advantage. If, for example, a part of a route allocation system has functional similarities to a container storage system (one of the authors actually found these similarities), then the work done for one system could be recycled for the other.

Figure 13.9

This business use case model is the result of finding the similarities between a business use case in the library domain and a business use case in the satellite broadcasting domain.

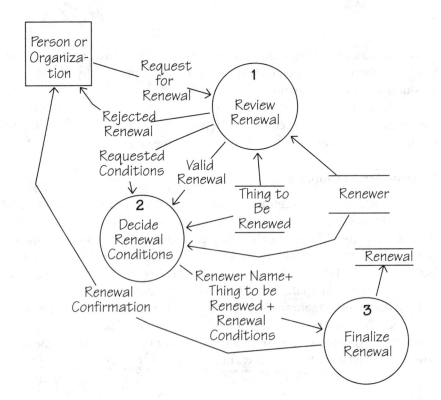

The skill of identifying and using patterns is tied to several other abilities:

- The ability to see work at different levels of abstraction
- The ability to categorize, or classify, in different ways
- The ability to see that telescopes and glass spheres filled with water are both magnifying devices
- The ability to spot similarities between apparently different things
- The ability to disregard physical artifacts
- The ability to see things in the abstract

READING

Gamma, Erich, et al. *Design Patterns: Elements of Reusable Object-Oriented Software.* Addison-Wesley, 1995. Gamma's book is a leading work on object-oriented design patterns.

Domain Analysis

Domain analysis is the activity of investigating, capturing, and specifying generic knowledge about a subject matter area. You could think of domain analysis as non-project systems analysis: The goal is to learn about the business policy, data, and functionality—not to build something. The knowledge gained about the domain is used, and ideally reused, by any project that builds a product to be used within that domain.

Domain analysis works in the same way that regular systems analysis does. That is, you work with domain experts to extract their hitherto unarticulated knowledge, and you record it in a manner that allows other analysts to reuse the knowledge. This suggests that regular analysis models—event-response models, activity diagrams, sequence diagrams, class diagrams, state models, data dictionaries, and so on—are the most useful, as these kinds of models have the greatest currency in the analysis world.

READING

Prieto-Diaz, Ruben, and Guillermo Arango. *Domain Analysis and Software Systems Modeling.* IEEE Computer Society Press, 1991.

Once the domain knowledge has been captured and recorded, then it becomes available to anyone who builds a product for that domain. The domain knowledge applies to any product for that domain. The point is not to rediscover knowledge that has always existed, but to reuse the models of knowledge.

The point is not to rediscover knowledge, but to reuse models of knowledge.

Of course, there is always the problem of precisely what constitutes a domain. Simply saying "banking," "insurance," or "microsurgery" is not enough. The definition of a domain lies in its interfaces with other domains. It is what enters and leaves that defines the domain, not the domain name. Look back at the context model in Figure 13.4. The flows that enter and leave define the scope of this domain, not its name of Customer Wants to Buy a Product. However, once you have established the boundaries of the domain, it becomes fairly easy to identify useful business events, data, and functions.

Domain analysis is a long-term project. That is, the knowledge gained is reusable, but this benefit will be realized only if you get the opportunity to reuse the knowledge. An investment in domain analysis is like any other investment: You must have a good idea that the investment will be paid back.

In the case of domain analysis, your investment is rewarded if several projects in that domain use the domain knowledge. Also, keep in mind that there is no limit to the number of times that domain knowledge can be reused.

Trends in Reuse

When you build a model of some aspect of a system, you immediately make those aspects visible; as soon as you make them visible, they become potentially reusable. Research and experience have provided many models for defining various aspects of requirements. For example, at the beginning of a project you can make a system visible by drawing a context diagram to model the intended context of the work. You can partition the subject matter into business events, use cases, and classes, each of which you can model. The choice of which models you use is not important; what is important is that you and your colleagues all work with the same models so that you have a communication medium for making your work visible and hence potentially reusable.

Reuse and Objects

Using the principles of object orientation, we partition and implement system knowledge so that everything relating to one class of subject matter is packaged together.

For instance, the IceBreaker system includes a class called Truck. This class contains all the attributes of a truck, such as its tonnage, registration number, and model description. It also contains all the operations that are unique to a truck, such as Maintain Truck and Show Truck Capacity. The definition of the class called Truck is probably reusable, as a starting point, in any system that deals with trucks or similar vehicles.

The use of objects has encouraged greater formality and consistency in the way people define and talk about system knowledge. This consistency has helped to raise consciousness about the possibilities of reuse. If we express our knowledge in a more consistent way, then it is more widely communicable and there is every chance that we can use it more than once. Another reason that object orientation contributes to reuse is that it has led to convergence toward a common notation. The Unified Modeling Language (UML) is becoming a standard notation for building object-oriented models.

Reuse Is Now a Job?

Back in 1993, the Second International Workshop on Software Reusability was held in Lucca, Italy. Most of the papers presented at the conference focused on the subjects of reusing code, design, or architecture. In other words, the thinking was that only the hard artifacts—code, objects, and so

READING

For a thorough discussion of the wide implications of reuse, refer to Jacobson, Ivar, Martin Griss, and Patrik Jonsson. *Software Reuse: Architecture Process and Organization for Business Success*. Addison-Wesley, 1997.

READING

For an overview of the Unified Modeling Language, refer to Fowler, Martin. *UML Distilled: A Brief Guide to the Standard Object Modeling Language*. Addison-Wesley, 2003.

on—could be reused. Very few papers at the conference looked at the idea of reuse earlier in the development cycle—namely, the requirements themselves.

Things have changed a lot since then. The practice of reuse is moving upstream, so that today we are seeing reuse of the more abstract artifacts. Requirements are commonly recycled; patterns are exchanged on the Internet. Working conferences on patterns are held regularly and result in the sharing of knowledge and publication of new patterns. This change in emphasis brings with it greater rewards. For instance, if a requirement has already been implemented, then it has a design and some code or objects associated with it. If you reuse this requirement, providing your implementation environment is similar, you probably get the design and the code and objects for free. By reusing knowledge gleaned from earlier stages in the development cycle, you get the advantage of the downstream products. But reusing material taken from later in the cycle does not bring the same advantages as mining the upstream products.

When we saw this advertisement in April 1998, it was very unusual:

> "We invite applications to investigate Software Reengineering Patterns as an approach to the problem of reengineering legacy systems. This project, funded under the EPSRC Managed Programme "Systems Engineering for Business Process Change," is jointly run by the Computer Science Department and the Management School of the University. Candidates should have excellent communication skills, and either a PhD in a related area or relevant industrial or commercial experience."

Today it is no longer uncommon to see job advertisements that ask for people who have pattern-related skills. This trend indicates that we are starting to think of the discovery and management of reusable patterns as a real job. If we are prepared to invest in knowledge as a tangible asset, then we can reap the benefits of requirements reuse.

If you reuse a requirement, you probably get the design and the code and objects for free. By reusing knowledge gleaned from earlier stages in the development cycle, you get the advantage of the downstream products.

READING

For more on thinking behind the reuse of analysis models, refer to Robertson, Suzanne, and Kenneth Strunch. *Reusing the Products of Analysis.* Second International Workshop on Software Reusability, Position Paper. Lucca, Italy, March 24–26, 1993.

Summary

We can and do informally reuse requirements knowledge by talking to our colleagues and reusing our own experience. Requirements modeling techniques produce deliverables such as work context models, use case models, scenarios, and atomic requirements specifications, among many others. All of these deliverables serve to make requirements visible.

The visibility of requirements makes them potentially reusable to a much wider audience. The interest in patterns and domain analysis is spurring our industry to become more aware of the advantages and possibilities of reusing requirements.

Reviewing the Specification

*in which we decide whether our
specification is correct and complete,
and set the priorities of the requirements*

At some stage in your requirements process, you will want to release your specification. It does not have to be complete at this stage: it could be a partial version for the next iteration; a version of the specification you want to publish for marketing reasons; or any other version. But before releasing the specification, you need to review it.

We use the term "specification" here to mean whatever collection of requirements you have. It does not have to be a paper specification. It does not even have to be formal; it could be a blog, wiki, or something similar. It might hold only the requirements for the next release. Whether it is complete remains to be seen. Whether it conveys the correct information also remains to be seen. This review ensures the specification is fit for its intended purpose before you hand it over to anyone else.

Figure 14.1 illustrates how the Quality Gateway and the specification review work together. The Quality Gateway tests an individual requirement, ensuring it is correctly stated, unambiguous, within scope, testable, traceable, and not gold plating. When a requirement successfully passes through the Quality Gateway, you can have confidence in the correctness and viability of that requirement.

Chapter 11 discusses the Quality Gateway in depth.

But what about the specification as a whole? You know it is made up of correct requirements, but collectively do they tell the whole story? Before passing the specification along, you must review it with following points in mind:

- Determine whether any requirements are missing.

- Prioritize so the builders understand the importance and the urgency of the requirements.

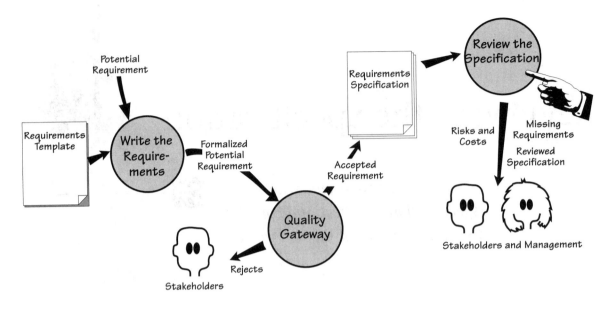

Figure 14.1

You have arrived at the point in the process where you want to consider the specification as a whole. The Quality Gateway has tested and accepted individual requirements, which were then allowed into the specification. Now it is time to assess the requirements as a complete specification.

● Check for conflicts between requirements that could prevent one or the other from being satisfied.

Additionally, your project management should perform two tasks:

● Estimate the cost of construction.

● Evaluate the risks faced by the project.

This review of the requirements specification can be carried out at any time; ideally, it should be an ongoing activity. You might, for example, review the specification as a check on the progress of the requirements activity. The quality (or lack thereof) of the specification tells you more about progress than its volume does. You might also review a partial specification. That is, given that you are working with an iterative cycle and want to review the requirements for a small number of selected product use cases, you might wish to proceed with building them while the analysts continue gathering the remainder of the requirements.

Agility Guide

Rabbit projects rarely write a complete specification. The review process discussed in this chapter is useful not for reviewing a specification, but rather for checking completeness in such projects. Rabbits should look at the sections of this chapter covering non-events and the CRUD check. The section on prioritization, while created with written requirements in mind, is also relevant for rabbit projects.

Horse projects have some kind of specification. It does not have to be as formal as an elephant specification, but knowing it is complete and relevant is desirable. Horses may not build all of the models we describe here, but that's okay: The review process still works without all of them being present. Horse projects should definitely formally prioritize their requirements.

Elephant projects always have a complete specification. The likelihood of complete or partial outsourcing is high, and this review ensures that the specification handed to the outsourcer will result in the correct product being built. Models are a key part of the review process for these types of projects. Elephants will certainly have modelers as part of the team. That fact makes this chapter particularly relevant to elephants.

Reviewing the Specification

The review process follows an iterative cycle until all problems have been resolved. That is, when errors are discovered, their corrections are reviewed and, if necessary, the specification looked at again to ensure none of the corrections introduced new problems. This iteration continues until you stop finding errors. We recommend you keep a record of discarded requirements to prevent their accidental reintroduction and to monitor which kinds of requirements are being rejected. This kind of documentation might prevent the reappearance of the unwanted requirements in future projects. The types of errors you discover in this review suggest what you need to do to improve your requirements process.

This review gives you an ideal opportunity to reassess your earlier decision on whether to go ahead with the project. A seriously flawed specification or indications that the costs and the risks outweigh the benefits are almost always indications that you need to consider project euthanasia.

A seriously flawed specification or indications that the costs and the risks outweigh the benefits are almost always indications that you need to consider project euthanasia.

Inspections

The specification review should be undertaken as an inspection. For those readers unfamiliar with the term, *inspections* (*Fagan inspections,* to attribute them correctly) are a formalized process of ensuring the quality of documents. Much has been written about Fagan inspections, and we do not propose to add to that body of literature here. A brief outline of the process is sufficient.

The inspection process kicks off with a planning activity in which the materials and the inspectors are determined. A moderator usually handles this task. The inspectors are given an overview of the document under consideration, and they have about three days to study the material. The inspection meeting proper—limited to two hours—studies the document using checklists. These checklists, which are lists of potential errors, are updated

READING

The original paper (one of the most cited papers in software history) is Fagan, Michael. Design and Code Inspections to Reduce Errors in Program Development. *IBM Systems Journal*, vol. 15, no. 3 (1976), pp. 258–287. Fagan inspections have been incorporated into several books.

READING

Gilb, Tom, and Dorothy Graham. *Software Inspection*. Addison-Wesley, 1993.

Wiegers, Karl. *Peer Reviews in Software: A Practical Guide*. Addison-Wesley, 2001.

The Volere Requirements Specification Template is found in Appendix B.

Scenarios are discussed in Chapter 6.

when new errors are discovered. The author reworks the document, and the moderator ensures all defects have been removed. If necessary, the moderator arranges a follow-up inspection.

Fagan inspections teach us that a certain amount of formality in our processes can, indeed, be beneficial in accuracy and efficiency. Much statistical evidence shows that inspections reduce the cost of development, and that projects employing inspections are more likely to meet their deadlines.

You can easily adopt some of the Fagan rules. For instance, try these tactics:

● Assign a moderator to take responsibility for arranging the inspection and distributing the materials.

● Give inspectors three days to read the document and prepare for the inspection.

● Limit inspections to two hours and no more than two inspections a day.

● Have between three and eight inspectors.

All of these guidelines make sense in the context of inspecting a requirements specification.

Find Missing Requirements

The first check in the review determines whether all of the requirements types appropriate to your product are present in the specification. Use the Volere Requirements Specification Template and its requirements types as a guide in determining whether your specification contains the requirements of the types called for by the nature of the product. The goal of the project, together with any strategic plan for the product, usually indicate the appropriate types of requirements. For example, if you are developing a financial product but you have no security requirements, something is definitely missing. Similarly, a Web product that lacks either usability or look and feel requirements is certainly in trouble.

The functional requirements should be sufficient to complete the work of each use case. To check this, play through each of the product use cases as if you were the product. If you do everything the requirements call for, do you arrive at the outcome for the use case? Are your users (you should have them with you when you perform this role-play) satisfied the product will do what they need for their work?

Look for exceptions to the normal things the product must do. Have you generated enough exception and alternative scenarios to cover these eventualities, and do your functional requirements reflect this? Revisit your scenarios and, for each step, determine whether exceptions can occur there or whether an exception can prevent that step from being reached.

Check each product use case against the nonfunctional requirement types. Does it have the nonfunctional requirements that it needs and that are appropriate for this kind of use case? Use the requirements template as a checklist. Go through the nonfunctional requirements types, read their descriptions, and ensure that the correct nonfunctional requirements have been included.

Have All Business Use Cases Been Discovered?

The strategy described in this book shows you how to partition the work according to the business events that affect it. For each business event, you then determine the work's response—the business use case—and decide how much of that response will be carried out by the product—the product use case. You gather the requirements one product use case at a time. This strategy is effective, providing you discover all of the business events. Missing business events must, inevitably, result in missing requirements.

But how do you know whether you have discovered all the business events? The procedure for making this determination uses the outputs of your requirements process and system modeling. In other words, you do not have to produce more stuff, just make more use of what you have.

You do not have to produce more stuff to do the review, just make more use of what you have.

Figure 14.2 illustrates the procedure for confirming the completeness of your list of business events. Follow along the model of this procedure as we describe its activities.

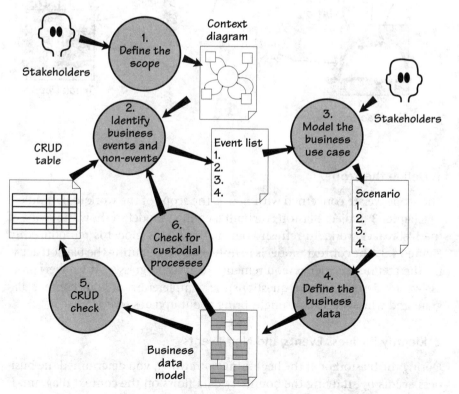

Figure 14.2

The procedure for determining all business events have been found. The process is iterative, going through all activities until the *Identify business events and non-events* activity fails to discover any new ones. At this stage of the requirements process, you should have done most of these things.

Figure 14.3

The context diagram of the work shows the data entering and leaving the scope of the work. These data transfers are referred to as boundary data flows. We use these flows to determine the business events.

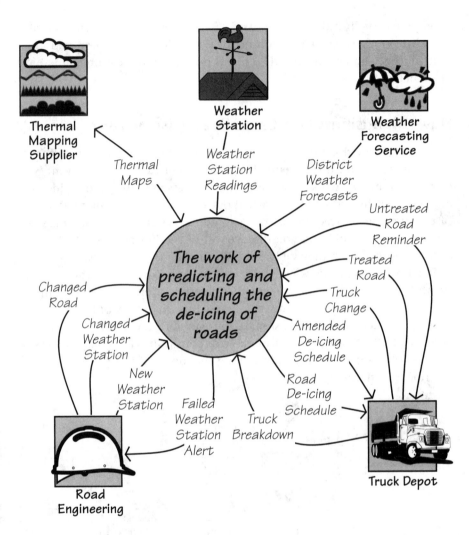

1. Define the Scope

The scope we are concerned with here is the scope of the work to be studied. In Chapter 3, Project Blastoff, we built a context model to show the scope of the IceBreaker work. To refresh your memory, this model is reproduced in Figure 14.3. The context model is mainly completed during the blastoff activity, then refined further as requirements analysis progresses. The review process we are describing here questions the completeness of your context diagram and where necessary, might bring about updates to it.

2. Identify Business Events and Non-Events

During the blastoff or at the beginning of trawling, you determined the business events by studying the boundary data flows on the context diagram. If an external business event happens, the adjacent system sends a data flow to the work to elicit a response from it. Thus each incoming boundary data flow indicates the potential for an external business event. The outgoing flows are either the output of the response to an external business event (the work responds by processing the incoming flow and produces the outgoing flow) or the result of a time-triggered event (such as reporting, sending out letters or alerts, and so on). In other words, each flow on the context model is somehow connected to a business event.

Chapter 4, Event-Driven Use Cases, contains complete coverage of how to determine business events from the context model.

The output of this activity is a list of business events, like that shown in Table 14.1 for the IceBreaker work.

EVENT NAME	INPUT	OUTPUT
1. Weather Station transmits reading	Weather Station Readings	—
2. Weather Bureau forecasts weather	District Weather Forecasts	—
3. Road Engineering advises changed roads	Changed Road	—
4. Road Engineering installs new Weather Station	New Weather Station	—
5. Road Engineering changes Weather Station	Changed Weather Station	—
6. Time to test Weather Stations	—	Failed Weather Station Alert
7. Truck Depot changes a truck	Truck Change	—
8. Time to detect icy roads	—	Road De-icing Schedule
9. Truck treats a road	Treated Road	—
10. Truck Depot reports problem with truck	Truck Breakdown	Amended De-icing Schedule
11. Time to monitor road de-icing	—	Untreated Road Reminder

Table 14.1

The Business Event List for the IceBreaker Work: These business events cause the work to respond. The inputs and outputs are the boundary data flows connected to the event. When you have listed all of the boundary flows from the context model, you have determined all of the possible business events . . . for the moment.

Non-Events. Once you have linked each of the boundary data flows to a business event, it is time to look for the non-events. The term "non-events" is a play on words. Non-events are events that happen if another event does not happen. For example, two non-events appear in Table 14.1. Event 9 is called "Truck treats a road." But what happens if the truck does *not* treat the road? This is a "non-event." It shows up as event 11, "Time to monitor road de-icing"—the work checks whether the roads have been treated as directed and, if they have not, issues a reminder.

In many businesses there is a business event called "Customer pays invoice"—a common enough event. But what happens if the customer does not pay the invoice? The corresponding "non-event" is "Time to send reminder notice to nonpayers."

Go through your own list of business events and ask, "What happens if this event does not happen?" Not all business events have a non-event, but checking the list for their existence may help you to discover some of the missing events.

Add any new events discovered through this exercise to the list of business events, and update the context model with the appropriate flows. Continue searching the list of existing events for more non-events, but don't be overly concerned if you don't find one for every event. Sometimes the answer to the question, "What happens if this event does not happen?" is "Nothing."

3. Model the Business Use Case

READING

Robertson, James, and Suzanne Robertson. *Complete Systems Analysis: The Workbook, the Textbook, the Answers.* Dorset House, 1998. This book is a thorough treatment of business use case modeling.

This step is not part of the requirements review, but something you have already done. As part of the requirements investigation, you will have built models or scenarios to help you and your stakeholders understand the desired response to the business event. Given that scenarios are the most commonly used models, we show a scenario in the schematic of the review process in Figure 14.2. However, the precise type of model you use is less important than the fact that you build models at all. A satisfactory model helps you understand and communicate the functionality and data for the business use case.

4. Define the Business Data

The next part of the review process is a step you might have already done: building a model of the stored data needed by the work that you are studying. You can use a class diagram, an entity relationship model, a relational model, or whichever data-modeling notation you prefer. As long as it shows classes, entities, or tables, and the associations or relationships between them, it will suffice. This data model is progressively confirmed and updated as a result of your requirements investigation.

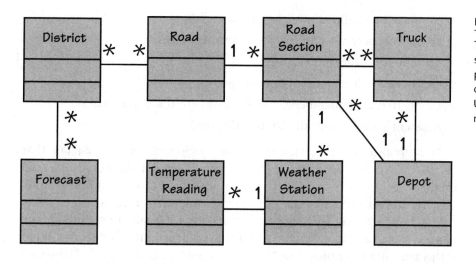

Figure 14.4

This model shows the stored data used to predict and schedule the de-icing of roads. It uses UML class model notation.

If building this kind of model is beyond your normal skill set, ask one of the database people to do it for you. They will have to build such a model at some stage; they may as well do it now, when it can serve more purposes than just aiding the logical database design. However, you must insist the database person builds a model of the *business data*, and does not start designing a database. They are two different things.

Figure 14.4 shows a sample model of the data used by the IceBreaker work.

An alternative way of describing the business's stored data is to simply list the classes of data used by the business. Data classes (also called "entities") are the subject matter of stored data. In other words, they are the things that we store data about. You can think of a class as a collection of data elements (their correct name is "attributes") for something that is important to the business. The "something" can be real, such as a customer or a product you sell; or it can be abstract, such as an account, a contract, or an invoice. The important thing to note is that the class does not have an alphanumeric value. For example, an account has no alphanumeric value. The account number has such a value, but the account number is an *attribute* of the account class, not the account itself. Thus classes are things that have identifiers attached to them: Books have an ISBN to identify them; credit cards have a card number.

Do not agonize too long over identifying the data classes. You should do as well as you can without spending the rest of the month on it. Some heuristics are generally helpful in identifying classes by defining their properties:

- Things, concrete or abstract, used by the business
- Things that are identified—accounts, sales opportunities, customers
- Subjects of data, not the data itself

- Nouns with a defined business purpose
- Products or services—mortgages, service agreements
- Branches of organizations, locations, or constructions
- Roles—case officer, employee, manager
- Events that are remembered—agreements, contracts, purchases
- Adjacent systems from the context diagram

You can also find the classes from your context model—the diagram that shows the data flowing into and out of work. In general, the stored data used by the work comes in via data flows and leaves via other data flows. Think about it this way: If there is data inside the work, there must be some flow of data to bring it there. That means you can dissect the data flows found in the context model and look at their attributes. Ask questions about them: "What is this attribute describing?" or "What is the subject of this data?" These subjects are your classes. Analyze all flows, both inward and outward, in the context model. You are looking for "things" that conform to the properties of classes listed earlier. When you have analyzed all of the flows, you have most likely identified all of the business data classes.

Now we get to the fun part.

5. CRUD Check

Each class of data (check these on your class model) must be Created and Referenced. Some are also Updated and/or Deleted. You build a CRUD table, such as the one shown in Table 14.2, to determine whether every class has all the appropriate actions performed on it.

Table 14.2

The CRUD Table: Each cell shows the identifier of the business event that creates, references, updates, or deletes the entity.

CLASS	CREATE	REFERENCE	UPDATE	DELETE
Depot	—	7	—	—
District	—	2, 8, 10	—	—
Forecast	2	8, 10	—	—
Road	3	4, 8, 9, 10	3	—
Road Section	3	4, 8, 10, 11	3, 9	—
Temperature Reading	1	6, 8, 10	—	—
Truck	7	8, 9, 11	7, 10	—
Weather Station	4	1, 6	5	—

If a class is referenced without first being created, it means the creation event is missing. If a class is created without being referenced, then either an event is missing or there is superfluous data. Some classes (but not all) are updated and/or deleted; of course, for this to happen they must have been created.

Holes in the CRUD table raise questions about missing business events. For example, the classes Depot and District show no creating business event. Thus the context is incomplete: It does not have the incoming flows to create these classes of stored data. When you find this situation, you must revisit your stakeholders to find out more about these missing business events. When you determine what they are, add them to the event list, update the CRUD table, and continue the process.

The "Delete" column of the CRUD table shows classes that are deleted for business policy reasons only. This is not the same as archiving or cleaning up the database. For example, if a Depot were to be taken out of service, then it is essentially deleted. However, a Forecast is never deleted—there is no essential business policy reason for doing so.

6. Check for Custodial Processes

The work's processes can be fundamental or custodial. *Fundamental processes* are connected to the reason for the product's existence—for example, analyzing the roads, recording the weather forecasts, scheduling the trucks to treat the roads. *Custodial processes* exist to maintain—keep custody of—the stored data. These processes make changes to the data solely to keep it up-to-date. These changes are not part of the fundamental processing.

For example, a fundamental process for a credit card company is to record any purchases you make using its card. This is, of course, a business event that happens when you hand over the card in the store. But from time to time, you might move to a new home. When you advise the credit card company of this change of address, it uses a custodial process to update its stored data. A similar business event would occur if you changed your name or changed the card's PIN.

To do this, go through the class model and the CRUD table, checking whether you have enough custodial processes to maintain all of the work's stored data. Check that where a class has changeable attributes, there is a custodial business event to change them.

Repeat Until Done

Stages 1 through 6 of the business event discovery process are iterative. That is, you continue to go through the process—identifying business events; modeling the business use cases; adding to the class model; checking that the classes are created, referenced, updated, and deleted—until activity 2, "Identify business events and non-events," fails to reveal any new events. At that stage, you can be confident that there are no more business events relevant to your work.

You might also investigate the automated tools at your disposal, as some of this procedure can be automated. It is not that hard to do, but if you can get some automated help, why not?

Customer Value

Each requirement should carry a customer satisfaction and customer dissatisfaction rating. (See Figure 14.5.) The satisfaction rating measures how happy your client (or a panel of stakeholders) will be if you successfully deliver the requirement; the dissatisfaction rating measures how unhappy the client will be if you fail to deliver the requirement.

The satisfaction and dissatisfaction ratings are the best mechanism your client has to let you know which requirements are the most valuable.

The satisfaction and dissatisfaction ratings indicate the value of the requirement to your client. They are normally appended to each requirement, although you may elect to attach the ratings to each product use case as a measure of the client's value for the successful delivery of that part of the work.

The client normally determines the satisfaction and dissatisfaction ratings. If the client is paying for the development of the product, then it stands to reason that he should be the one to put a value on the requirements. Some organizations prefer to have a small group of the principal stakeholders assign the ratings.

The satisfaction and dissatisfaction ratings are the best mechanism your client has to let you know which requirements are the most valuable. Use these ratings to communicate with your client or the other stakeholders and to encourage them to tell you the value they place on each requirement. If your client or your stakeholders have trouble assigning ratings to the requirements, then you must do it yourself and check their reactions. Naturally, the

Figure 14.5

The satisfaction and dissatisfaction scales measure your client's concern about whether requirements are included in the final product. A high score on the satisfaction scale indicates that the client is happy that the requirement will be successfully delivered; a high score on the dissatisfaction scales indicates that the client is very unhappy that the requirement is not to be included in the product.

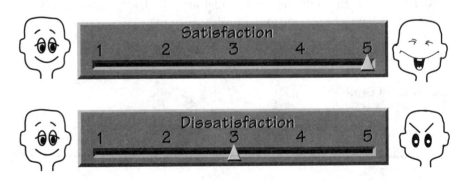

value you place on a requirement may be very different to that of your client. Ultimately, the stakeholders must bear the responsibility of the wrong requirements being implemented if they do not participate in this exercise.

Consider the value of a requirement after it has been rated. For example, if a requirement scores 5 for satisfaction and 5 for dissatisfaction, then your client really wants that requirement. However, if a requirement scores 2 and 2, then the client doesn't care if this requirement does not make it to the final product. Requirements with low values should be either dropped from the specification or put into the Waiting Room (section 26 of the specification template) until the next release of the product.

READING

For more on customer value ratings, refer to Pardee, William J. *To Satisfy and Delight Your Customer.* Dorset House, 1996.

Prioritizing the Requirements

One problem with requirements is that there are always too many of them. Prioritizing gives you a way to choose which ones to implement in which versions of the product. Decisions about prioritization are complex because they involve different factors and these factors are often in conflict with each other. Also, because the various stakeholders probably have different goals, it may prove difficult to reach agreement about priorities.

To prioritize requirements, you can group them together into logical (to you) groups. These groups are then prioritized as a unit, on the assumption that all the composing requirements have the same priority as the group as a whole. A group might be a use case, a component, a feature, or any other grouping of requirements that it makes sense to prioritize as a unit instead of treating them individually.

You can group requirements together and prioritize them as a unit.

To make it easier to read, for the next few pages, we use the term "requirements" to mean "groups of requirements," "features," "product use cases," or any other grouping you care to use.

Prioritization Factors

The following factors commonly affect prioritization decisions:

● The cost of implementation
● Value to customer or client
● Time to needed to implement the product
● Ease of technological implementation
● Ease of business or organization implementation
● Benefit to the business
● Obligation to obey the law

Not all of these factors are relevant to every project, and the relative importance of each factor differs for each project. Within a project, the relative importance of the factors is not the same for all of the stakeholders. Given this combinatorial complexity, you need some kind of agreed-upon prioritization procedure to provide a way of making choices. Part of that procedure is to determine when you will make prioritization decisions.

When to Prioritize

How soon should you make choices? As soon as you understand what you have to choose from. The more visible you make your knowledge, the more chances you have to make and help others make informed choices.

If your requirements have a well-organized structure, you can prioritize them early in your project. The process described in this book includes a project blastoff. You use this meeting to assess your level of knowledge about the contents of the first eight sections of the requirements specification template. Build a work context model and partition it using business events. At that point, because you have some identifiable pieces, you can do a rough prioritization and assign a priority rating to each business use case—something like "high," "medium," and "low" will work fine for the moment. You can use the results of this prioritization to decide which parts of the business to investigate first. In addition, you can use this first prioritization to guide your version planning.

When you start to write atomic requirements, you should progressively consider whether to prioritize them. If any requirements obviously have low value, then tag them as such. Use the customer satisfaction and customer dissatisfaction ratings, discussed in the previous section, to help other people make choices.

Your stakeholders often assume the term "requirements" means these capabilities will definitely be implemented. "Requirements" are really desires or wishes that we need to understand well enough to decide whether to implement them.

Part of the reason for progressive prioritization is expectation management. Your stakeholders often assume the term "requirements" means these capabilities will definitely be implemented. "Requirements" are really desires or wishes that we need to understand well enough to decide whether to implement them. For example, we might have a requirement that is really high priority but, due to a mixture of constraints, we cannot meet its fit criterion 100 percent. However, we do have a solution that will fit the fit criterion 85 percent.

If you have been progressively prioritizing throughout the project, people are able to accept such compromises without feeling cheated. Prioritization prepares stakeholders for the fact you cannot implement all the requirements.

You can use any of a number of procedures to prioritize your requirements. We have already talked about customer satisfaction and dissatisfaction as a way of understanding the values people put on requirements. These ratings can provide input for deciding on and assigning priority ratings to the requirements.

Requirement Priority Grading

You can grade your requirement priority however it suits your way of working. A common way of grading requirements is "high," "medium," and "low." But you can use any other grading that suits you. For example, some people grade requirements by release or version number: R1, R2, R3, and so on. The idea is that the R1 requirements are the highest priority and are intended to appear in the first release, the R2 requirements appear in the second release, and so on. But suppose that after you have tagged the requirements by release, you discover you have too many requirements in the R1 category. At that point you need to prioritize the R1 requirements into high, medium, and low categories.

The idea of sorting the requirements into prioritization categories is often referred to as *triage*. This term (from the French verb *trier*, meaning "to sort") comes from the field of medicine. It was first adopted during the Napoleonic wars when field hospitals were not capable of treating all soldiers who had been wounded. The doctors used triage to place the patients into one of three categories:

● Those who would live without treatment
● Those who would not survive
● Those who would survive if they were treated

READING

Davis, Al. *Just Enough Requirements*. Dorset House, 2005.

Simmons, Erik. Requirements Triage: What Can We Learn from a Medical Approach. *IEEE Software*, May 2004, p. 86.

Due to scarce medical resources, the doctors treated the third group only. The idea of triage can be used in project work using the categories:

● Those requirements needed for the next release
● Those requirements definitely not needed for the next release
● Those requirements you would like if possible

If the first and last categories leave you with more requirements than will fit into your budget, you need to prioritize further.

Prioritization Spreadsheet

A prioritization spreadsheet (Figure 14.6) enables you to prioritize the overflow requirements. Ideally, and especially if you have done a good job on progressive prioritization, these requirements will fit into the medium-priority (would like if possible) category. In other words, you have been able to fit all the high-priority requirements into your budget. If this is not the case, then prioritize the high-priority requirements and either drop the medium- and low-priority requirements or tag them for future releases.

Earlier in this chapter, we identified seven prioritization factors (or you may use any other prioritization factors relevant to your project). On our spreadsheet (see Figure 14.6), we have limited the number of factors to four.

READING

The downloadable Volere Prioritization Spreadsheet (*www.volere.co.uk*) offers a way to prioritize requirements. The spreadsheet contains some examples you can replace with your own data.

	A	B	C	D	E	F	G	H	I	J	K	L
1	**Volere Prioritization Spreadsheet**											
2	Copyright © The Atlantic Systems Guild 2006											
3												
4	Requirement/Product Use Case/Feature	Number	Factor - score out of 10	%Weight applied	Factor - score out of 10	%Weight applied	Factor - score out of 10	%Weight applied	Factor - score out of 10	%Weight applied		Total Weight
5			Value to Customer	40	Value to Business	20	Minimize Implementation Cost	10	Ease of Implementation	30	Priority Rating	100
6	Requirement 1	1	2	0.8	7	1.4	3	0.3	8	2.4	4.9	
7	Requirement 2	2	8	3.2	8	1.6	5	0.5	7	2.1	7.4	
8	Requirement 3	3	7	2.8	3	0.6	7	0.7	4	1.2	5.3	
9	Requirement 4	4	6	2.4	8	1.6	3	0.3	5	1.5	5.8	
10	Requirement 5	5	5	2	5	1	1	0.1	3	0.9	4	
11	Requirement 6	6	9	4	6	1.2	6	0.6	5	1.5	6.9	
12	Requirement 7	7	4	2	3	0.6	6	0.6	7	2.1	4.9	
13	Requirement											
14	Requirement											
15	Requirement											
16	Requirement											
17	Requirement											
18	Requirement											
19	Requirement											
20	Requirement											

Figure 14.6

This prioritization spreadsheet is downloadable from *www.volere.co.uk*.

Trying to manage more than four prioritization factors makes it difficult, if not impossible, to agree a weighting system.

The "% Weight Applied" column shows the percentage importance assigned to each factor. You arrive at this percentage weight by stakeholder discussion and voting. The percentage weights for all factors must total 100 percent.

In column 1, list the requirements you want to prioritize. These might be atomic requirements or clusters of requirements represented by product use cases, features, or business use cases.

Give each requirement/factor combination a score out of 10. This score reflects the positive contribution to the factor made by this requirement. For example, for requirement 1, we assigned a score of 2 for the first factor because we believe that it does not make a very positive contribution to the "Value to Customer" attribute. The same requirement scores a 7 on the "Value to Business" attribute, because it does make a positive contribution to our business. The score for minimizing the cost of implementation is 3; we think this requirement is relatively expensive to implement. It scored an 8 in terms of its ease of implementation, reflecting the relative simplicity of implementing this requirement.

For each score, the spreadsheet calculates a weighted score by applying the percent weight for that factor. The priority rating for the requirement is calculated as the total of the weighted scores for the requirement.

You may use a variety of voting systems to arrive at the weights for the factors and the scores for each requirement. Of course, the spreadsheet is merely a vehicle for enabling a group of stakeholders to arrive at a consensus when prioritizing the requirements. By making complex situations more visible, you make it possible for people to communicate their interests, to appreciate other individuals' opinions, and to negotiate.

Conflicting Requirements

Two requirements are conflicting if you cannot implement them both—the solution to one requirement prohibits implementing the other. For example, if one requirement asks for the product to "be available to all" and another says it shall be "fully secure," then both requirements cannot be implemented as specified.

As a first pass at finding conflicting requirements, sort the requirements into their types. Then examine all entries that you have for each type, looking for pairs of requirements whose fit criteria are in conflict with each other. See Figure 14.7.

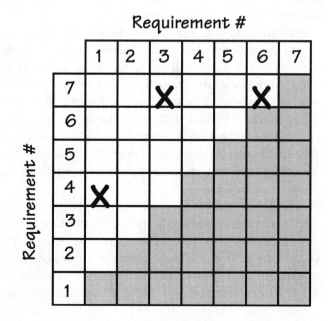

Requirement #

Figure 14.7

This matrix identifies conflicting requirements. For example, requirements 3 and 7 are in conflict with each other. If we implement a solution to requirement 3, it will have a negative effect on our ability to implement a solution to requirement 7, and vice versa.

Of course, a requirement might potentially conflict with any other requirement in the specification. To help you discover these problems, here are some clues to the situations where we most often find requirements in conflict:

● Requirements that use the same data (search by matching terms used)

● Requirements of the same type (search by matching requirement type)

● Requirements that use the same scales of measurement (search by matching requirements whose fit criteria use the same scales of measurement)

A spreadsheet is a useful tool when you are performing this check. For nonfunctional requirements, consider the requirements that are of the same type. For example, a usability requirement should not, say, have a fit criterion specifying that "users shall be able to carry out all the use cases without any training" if the users in question are research scientists dealing with masses of variable data. Although the product should be as easy to use as possible, we would nevertheless anticipate several months of training will be necessary before the scientists can use it correctly. Thus the fit criterion on the usability requirement is in conflict with the specification of the users.

Another helpful technique for identifying and assessing dependencies between requirements is Quality Function Deployment (QFD), which was popularized in Japan in the 1960s. Its intention is to enable customers, marketing, development, production, design, and managerial staff to work together effectively from the time that a project is started. The heart of the technique is communication of the voice of the customer (or the requirements) throughout the development of the product. QFD uses a tool called the House of Quality (so called because it has the shape of a house), which is a matrix for identifying functional and organizational interdependencies throughout a product's development life.

For functional requirements, look for conflicts in outcomes. As an example, suppose one requirement for the IceBreaker project calls for de-icing trucks to be routed by the shortest distance, and another specifies the trucks must be given the quickest route. These two requirements do not necessarily mean the same thing, and they may result in different outcomes.

Conflicts may arise because different users have asked for different requirements, or users have asked for requirements that are in conflict with the client's idea of the requirements. This type of overlap, which is normal for most requirements-gathering efforts, indicates you need to establish some sort of conflict resolution mechanism.

You, as the requirements analyst, have the most to gain by settling conflicts as rapidly as possible, so we suggest that you play a lead role in resolving them. When you have isolated the conflicting requirements, approach each of the users separately (this is one reason why you record the source of each requirement). Go over the requirement with the user and ensure that both of you have the same understanding of it. Reassess the satisfaction and dissatis-

READING

Hauser, John R., and Don Clausing. The House of Quality. *Harvard Business Review,* May–June 1988.

❝ *The foundation of the house of quality is the belief that products should be designed to reflect customers' desires and tastes—so marketing people, design engineers, and manufacturing staff must work closely together from the time a product is first conceived.* ❞

Source: John Hauser and Don Clausing

faction ratings: If one user gives low marks to the requirement, then he may not care if you drop it in favor of the other requirement. Do this with both users and do not, for the moment, bring them together.

When you talk to each user, explore his reasoning. What does the user really want as an outcome, and will it be compromised if the other requirement takes precedence? Most of the time we have been able to resolve conflicts this way. Note that we use the term "conflict" here, not "dispute." There is no dispute. There are no positions taken, no noses put out of joint by the other guy winning. The users may not even know who the conflicting party is.

If you, as a mediator, are unable to reach a satisfactory resolution, then we suggest that you determine the cost of implementing the opposing requirements, assess their relative risks, and, armed with numbers, call the participants together and see if you can reach some compromise. Except in cases of extreme office politics, stakeholders are usually willing to compromise if they are in a position to do so gracefully without loss of face.

Ambiguous Specifications

The specification should, as far as is practical, be free of ambiguity. You should not have used any pronouns and should be wary of unqualified adjectives and adverbs—all of these introduce ambiguity. Do not use the word "should" when writing your requirements; it infers that the requirement is optional. But even if you follow these guidelines, some problems may remain.

The fit criteria are devices to quantify each of the requirements, and thus make them unambiguous. We describe fit criteria in Chapter 9, explaining how they make each requirement both measurable and testable. If you have correctly applied fit criteria, then the requirements in your specification will be unambiguous.

This leaves the descriptions of the requirements. Obviously, the less ambiguity they contain, the better, but a poor description cannot do too much damage if you have a properly quantified fit criterion. However, if you are concerned about this issue, then we suggest that you select 50 requirements randomly. Take one of them and ask a panel of stakeholders to give their interpretation of the requirement. If everyone agrees on the meaning of the requirement, then set it aside. If the meaning of the requirement is disputed, then select five more requirements. Repeat this review until either it becomes clear that the specification is acceptable or the collection of selected requirements to test has grown so large (each ambiguity brings in five new ones) that the problem is obvious to all.

If the problem is bad, then consider rewriting the specification using a qualified technical writer.

The terms used in the requirements must be those defined in the Naming Conventions and Definitions section of the specification. If every word has an agreed-upon definition and you have used the terms consistently, then the meanings throughout the specification must be consistent and unambiguous.

Risk Analysis

Risk analysis is not directly connected with requirements; rather, it is a project issue. However, at this stage of the requirements process you have a complete specification of a product that you intend to build. You have invested a certain amount of time deriving this specification, , and you are about to invest even more time in building the product. Now seems like a good time to pause for a moment and consider the risks involved in proceeding.

You, as the requirements analyst, do not have to handle the risk analysis by yourself. If your organization is of a reasonable size, there should be someone on staff who is trained in risk assessment.

Risk analysis identifies the risks the project faces along with the probability of a risk manifesting itself as a problem. In some cases, the impact caused by the risk becoming an actual problem is so severe it forces you to take preventive action. In other cases, the impact is extreme to the point it is a "showstopper"—the entire project must be abandoned. In the case of severe impact, it is necessary to determine how you can mitigate that risk.

In other cases—they have to be assessed on a project-by-project basis— the likelihood and the impact are slight enough that it is preferable to wait and see if the risk does, in fact, become a problem. Some risk remains, however, so it pays to have a contingency plan for the possibility of the risk turning into a problem.

Quite a lot of help is available for identifying risks. Several books have been published that provide checklists of risks. In his book, Capers Jones gives the percentage of projects that have suffered from each of the risks he identifies. This data can be used to help you assess the probability of the risk affecting your project.

As mentioned earlier, this book is not intended to be a treatise on risk, but we do urge you to realistically consider the risks your project is running. If you believe some of the risks might have a significant impact, then you would likely benefit from calling in some risk assessment help. In the meantime, you can identify many of the risks just by looking through the early part of the requirements specification.

READING

DeMarco, Tom, and Tim Lister. *Waltzing with Bears: Managing Risk on Software Projects.* Dorset House, 2003. This book contains strategies for recognizing and monitoring risks.

Jones, Capers. *Assessment and Control of Software Risks.* Prentice Hall, 1994.

Project Drivers

1. **The Purpose of the Project.** Is the purpose of the product reasonable? Is it something your organization can achieve? Or are you setting out to do something you have never done before, with only hysterical optimism telling you that you can deliver the objective successfully?

2. The Client, the Customer, and Other Stakeholders. Is the client a willing collaborator? Or is he uninterested in the project? Is the customer represented accurately? Are all stakeholders involved and enthusiastic about the project and the product? Hostile or unidentified stakeholders can have a very negative effect on your project. What are the chances that everyone will make the necessary contributions? What risks do you run by not having the cooperation you need?

3. Users of the Product. Are the users properly represented? While user representative panels are useful, experience has shown that they are frequently wrong in their assessment of what the real users want and need. Are the users (or their representatives) capable of telling you the correct requirements? Many project leaders often cite the quality of user contributions to requirements as their most serious and frequently encountered risk.

Many system development efforts result in substantial changes to the users' work and the way that users work. Have you considered the risk that the users will not be able to adapt to the new arrangements? Remember that humans do not like being changed, and your new product is bringing changes to your users' work. Are the users capable of operating the new product? Consider these risks carefully, as the risk of the users not being prepared to change may turn out to be a substantial problem.

Project Constraints

4. Mandated Constraints. Are the constraints reasonable, or do they indicate design solutions with which your organization has no experience? Is the budget reasonable given the effort needed to build the product? Unrealistic schedules and budgets are among the most common risks cited by projects.

6. Relevant Facts and Assumptions. Are the assumptions reasonable? Should you make contingency plans for the eventuality that one or more of the assumptions turns out not to be true? It pays to keep in mind that assumptions are really risks.

Functional Requirements

7. The Scope of the Work. Is the scope of the work correct? Do you run the risk of not including enough work to produce a satisfactory product? If the scope is not large enough, then the resulting product will not do enough for the user. A failure to define the work scope correctly always results in early requests for modifications and enhancements to the product.

8. The Scope of the Product. Does the scope of the work include all the needed functionality, or just the "easy stuff"? Is it feasible within the budget and time available? Having the wrong product scope risks having many change requests after delivery.

Other commonly cited risks include creeping user requirements and incomplete requirements specifications. Risk analysis does not make all of these risks disappear, but it does mean that you and management become aware of problems that might arise and can make appropriate plans for monitoring and addressing them.

Measure the Required Effort

Measuring the amount of effort needed is not usually the responsibility of the requirements analyst. We mention this topic here because now that the requirements are known, you have an ideal opportunity to measure the size of the product. Common sense suggests that you do not proceed past this point without knowing this size, and thus the effort needed to build the product.

To this end, we have included a short introduction to function point counting in Appendix C. The appendix is not intended to teach you everything there is to know about function point counting, but rather to show how this technique works and suggest it as an effective way to estimate size.

The work you have done in gathering the requirements provides input to the measuring process. For example, the context model is a rich source of things to measure. A data model (if you have one) also provides input to measurement. You can even simply count the number of requirements you have written. All of these are measurements, and all are vastly preferable to guesswork and blind acceptance of imposed deadlines. One of the most commonly encountered risks is the risk of making poor estimates of the time needed to complete the project. This risk almost always eventually manifests itself as an actual problem, where the solution is usually to take shortcuts, skimp on quality, and end up delivering a poor product even later than originally planned. Such a risk can be avoided by allocating the short time needed to measure the size of the product and, thereby, the required effort to build it.

Summary

The purpose of the specification review is to assess the correctness, completeness, and quality of the requirements specification. The review also gives you an opportunity to measure the value, cost, and risk attached to building the product, and to assess whether it is worthwhile to continue development of the product.

Consider the model shown in Figure 14.8. It provides a composite measure of the overall worth of the product, or the worth of a product use case. Suppose that you have devised a suitable scale for each axis. The low end of the scale is at the intersection of the axes, and the high end is at the extremities.

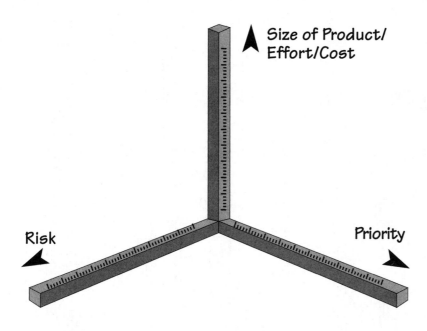

Figure 14.8

Each axis represents one of the factors that determines whether the product is worthwhile. The size/cost axis can be assessed using function points or some other size measurement; it represents the cost of construction. The priority axis represents the value placed by the stakeholders on the product. The risk axis represents the severity of risks determined by the risk analysis activity.

Rank the risk, the size of the product or the effort/cost to build it, and the priority along the corresponding scale. What does the profile look like? If you have high scores for effort and risk, but a low score for priority, you should consider abandoning the product: The benefit from having it is outweighed by the risk and effort required to build it.

You can use the same model to compare the desirability of individual requirements, clusters of requirements, or product use cases. This type of analysis is helpful when your requirements cannot be met within the constraints (usually time and budget) and you are trying to decide which ones should have priority.

The products you would like to build are those that score highly on customer value and low on the other scales. You will not often see this nirvana-like state, but take note of whether the profile of your product indicates that it is one to build or one to avoid.

Whither Requirements?

in which we consider some other
issues for the requirements

Sometimes, the way we talk about the requirements process makes it sound as if this process has a clean start and finish: We begin on day 1 with a blank sheet and knowledgeable stakeholders, and once we have specified the requirements for a product, our job is over. We would certainly like that to be the case. In reality, requirements, like anything else, need to be managed—and not just while the requirements are being gathered, but for as long as the product exists.

In this chapter, we look at some of the management issues attached to requirements. Although this is not a complete treatise on managing a requirements effort, we will explore some major issues:

READING
Robertson, Suzanne, and James Robertson. *Requirements-Led Project Management: Discovering David's Slingshot.* Addison-Wesley, 2005.

- Adapting the requirements process to suit the project
- Tools for recording and manipulating your requirements
- Publishing the requirements for communicating to different people and organizations for different purposes
- Tracing the requirements through the development of the product
- Dealing with change
- A retrospective to improve your process

All of these issues have an impact on how you manage your requirements.

Adapting the Process

As we mentioned earlier in this book, the Volere Requirements Process is a distillation of experience from many different projects that built different products in different countries under different circumstances. The process provides a source from which you can select the parts that apply to your particular project. We have found the most effective way to adapt the process is to focus on the deliverables. This adaptation reflects what quality and quantity of each deliverable you need, what form the deliverable should take, who should produce it, and how it should be reviewed.

The complete Volere Requirements Process model is in Appendix A.

Look at the process model in Appendix A, and specifically at the generic deliverables produced by the process. In particular, examine the interfaces between the processes on Diagram 0 of the process model. For instance, between the processes called Project Blastoff and Trawl for Knowledge is an interface representing a deliverable called Work Context. When you adapt the generic process, you decide how this deliverable (and all other deliverables) are produced by your project. Sometimes this deliverable is produced by a number of people, possibly working in a number of locations. In that case your process must define who will do what and how you will keep track of the pieces and fit them together.

Your aim is to discover where and how you would most benefit from changes to your way of specifying requirements. If you have a current process for producing requirements specifications, then sketch out a rough model of your current process to help get your thoughts in order. Review this model, marking any areas where you know you would like to make improvements.

If you have a current process for producing requirements specifications, then sketch out a rough model of your current process to help get your thoughts in order. Mark any areas where you would like to make improvements to this model.

To begin, concentrate on the deliverables on Diagram 0 of the generic process model; these deliverables, which are at a summary level, provide a way of talking about the big picture. When you are considering the overall requirements process, you identify those parts of the process where you think it will benefit you to explore the deliverables described in the detailed lower levels of the model.

For each deliverable, consider how each one would best be produced within your project environment using your resources:

● What is the deliverable called within your environment? Refer to the definitions of the terms used in the generic process model and identify the form of the equivalent deliverable in your organization.

● Does your current name for the deliverable facilitate communication, or would changing it help clarify any misunderstandings? For example, many projects have a deliverable called "high-level requirements," but no two people seem to have the same idea as to what "high-level" means. This loose terminology results in an enormous amount of wasted time.

● What is the deliverable used for within your environment? If the deliverable does not have an agreed-upon purpose within your project, and if that purpose does not have a quantifiable benefit, then omit it from your process.

● Does the deliverable have to be a physical artifact? Can it be trusted to be remembered without recording it?

- Who produces the deliverable? Specify which parts of the deliverable are produced by whom. Also, when several people are involved, define the interfaces between their work.

- When is the deliverable produced? Map your project phases to the generic process.

- Where is the deliverable produced? A generic deliverable is often the result of fragments that are produced in a number of geographical locations. Define the interfaces between the different locations and specify how they will work.

- Who needs to review the deliverable? Look for existing cultural check-points within your organization. Do you have recognized stages or phases in your projects when peers, users, or managers review your specification?

- Now turn your attention to the generic processes that produce the deliverables. How do they fit into your project? You might already have done a great deal of this thinking by examining the deliverables; this examination is simply a double check of your earlier work.

- To summarize the answers to the preceding questions, create a rough sketch of the process model and relevant detail levels for your project. Use this sketch to help plan who does what and how they communicate with each other.

- When you discover deliverables that are already effectively produced by your current process, retain those parts of your process and use the generic process to improve or replace the parts where you discover problems.

- Question any existing procedures. Is there a good business reason for each activity that touches this deliverable?

An important issue when designing a process to fit your project is to consider your needs for the publication of the requirements specification. Some of these needs might become clear to you when you are reviewing the activities in your process. However, we find it is a good way to discover misunderstandings is to ask, "When and why do we publish the requirements specification?" We shall look at this issue later in this chapter. First, however, let's consider how you might store your deliverables.

What About Requirements Tools?

Many products are on the market, and as many are available for free, that can help with your requirements. Tools can apply automation to the clerical tasks of tracing requirements, linking test results to requirements, change management, semantic analysis, and so on. While these tools are undoubtedly useful, they should be treated as tools—and nothing more. That is, they should serve as aids to your own efforts, and not as replacements for them. Despite

READING

For information about currently available tools, your authors maintain a listing at *www.volere.co.uk/ tools.htm*. Ian Alexander maintains a list at *easyweb.easynet.co.uk/ ~iany/other/other_sites.htm*. The INCOSE list is at *www.paper-review.com/tools/ rms/read.php*.

the claims of some vendors, there is no requirements tool that can actually interview a user or determine what your client really needs.

We will not go over the features available on the various tools. By the time you read this book, these features will have changed, some of the vendors will have gone out of business, and new ones will have appeared. If you want to know what is available, then we direct you to the Internet, where you can find the most up-to-date information. We maintain a list on our Volere site, and other helpful sources are cited in the margin.

Instead of looking at the features of these tools, we want to look the other way—at your *requirements* for the tools.

Mapping Tools to Purpose

If there is an overriding message in this book, it is this: Understand the requirements before building the product. This point also applies when you are buying a requirements product. Before you, or your manager, succumb to the elaborate claims of the tool salesman, consider what you want your tool to do—your requirements for a requirements tool. If your requirement is to manage the requirements deliverables, then consider those deliverables when making a purchase decision.

Figure 15.1 is a class model of the key requirements deliverables, described in the template, along with the inter-deliverable associations needed to manage the requirements.

Let's look at this model. Each component of the requirements specification is represented by a class. The classes are tagged with the corresponding section numbers from the Volere Requirements Specification Template. The associations between the classes indicate a need to understand the links between those classes. For example, the classes Work Context and Business Event have an association, which indicates a need to keep track of the links between the two. The 1 and the asterisk (*) indicate that each Work Context has potentially many Business Events associated with it. Thus, if we have a work context, then we need to know how many business events affect it, and we need to link those business events back to the work context.

Now we have a requirement for a requirements tool: We would like the tool to keep track of this association and alert us to any problems. We would also like the tool to record the details of the Work Context and each Business Event as well as the associated business use case defined in section 8 of the template. For example, the template tells us that, to define a Work Context, we need to record things like the adjacent systems and the details of the interfaces between those adjacent systems and the work we are investigating. This information is usually recorded as a context diagram, but it could be documented in other ways. Similarly, we need to record the details of the associated business event and business use case. Normally we create several

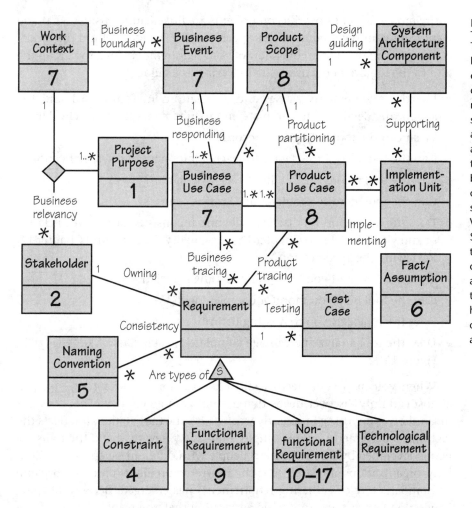

Figure 15.1

The requirements knowledge model. This class diagram shows the components of the requirements specification (rectangles) and the necessary associations between them (lines). The boldfaced numbers correspond to the section numbers of the Volere Requirements Specification Template that describe the components. The asterisks and numbers on the associations indicate how many components can participate in the association.

scenarios—the normal case and the exceptions and alternatives—to account for the details of a business use case.

To make requirements easier to think about, we categorize them into the subtypes of Constraints, Functional, Nonfunctional, and Technological requirements. We need to record and retrieve each of these subcategories. We also need to know which Technological requirements were added to which Product Use Case.

When we look at the association between a Requirement and a Product Use Case in Figure 15.1, we see that a Product Use Case has many Requirements attached to it. This is normal, as you would need to assemble all of the product use case's requirements for a functional review. But the model also shows a Requirement having associations with many (indicated by the asterisk) Product Use Cases. In other words, sometimes the same requirement is included in several different product use cases. Rather than describe the entire model, look at how the components are linked and consider what you want from your own requirements specification. The idea behind the model is that you can use it as an overview of your requirements for a tool. Map the tool to the requirements using the following as a guide:

- Use the requirements classes and associations in Figure 15.1 and the supporting details in the template and requirements shell as a checklist.
- What can the tool help you to record?
- Can the tool record the details for each component of the specification?
- Can the tool record the details of each association?
- Can the tool identify problems and inconsistencies?
- Does the tool report on discrepancies and inconsistencies between classes of knowledge? (Refer to Chapter 11, The Quality Gateway, and Chapter 14, Reviewing the Specification.)
- Does the tool alert you to possible missing associations?
- Can the tool help you monitor completeness?
- Does the tool alert you to missing definitions of terms?
- Does the tool analyze percentage complete of each class of knowledge in Figure 15.1?

When you map your needs against the capabilities of a tool, you will almost certainly discover needs that are not completely met. This does not mean there is anything inherently wrong with the tool. Rather, it reflects the fact that requirements engineering is a relatively new field and the tools are being developed by many different people with different perspectives. Similarly, organizations are developing their own requirements processes because no standard way of gathering requirements has emerged. Because of these issues, don't expect any tool to do everything that you want.

To meet all of your needs, you must design your own requirements environment. Define how all parts, automated and manual, interface with each other. In other words, you need your tools to support, as seamlessly as possible, all the activities that you carry out within your requirements process.

Publishing the Requirements

When should you publish your specification? What should it contain? What form should it take? The Volere Requirements Specification Template is a container for organizing your requirements knowledge and one form for the arrangement of a published specification. Of course, there are other ways to arrange the requirements knowledge, and you will save time if you choose the one that best suits your situation.

Harking back to our previous discussion, a well-designed requirements management tool makes it easier for you to publish the specification in different forms. But no matter which combination of tools you employ to maintain your specification, the important thing is that you understand the benefit for each class of requirements knowledge and each association that you maintain. If you maintain these associations, then you can publish the specification in whatever form best suits your purpose. In this section, we describe some publication versions that are typically useful in particular kinds of situations. We have annotated each part with the relevant sections of the requirements template.

Contractual Document

You have to publish a specification for an outsourcer who is responsible for building the product. This specification is the basis for your agreement with the outsourcer.

- Product constraints (sections 1–4).
- Definition of terms used in the specification (section 5).
- Relevant facts and assumptions (section 6).
- List of business events and work context diagram (section 7).
- Product boundary diagram (section 8).
- Class diagram or data model (section 9) conforming to the terms specified in section 5.
- Product use case list including a fit criterion for each use case (section 8).
- Individual functional and nonfunctional requirements clustered by product use case (parts of sections 9–17).
- Estimate of size in function points or another recognized unit of measurement (section 24).

See Appendix C, Function Point Counting: A Simplified Introduction, for information on how to use function points to estimate the size of of your product.

Management Summary

Sometimes you need to publish a version of the specification that provides a management checkpoint. The amount of detail you include depends on the reason for the management checkpoint, but here is a list of the contents typically found in such a document:

- Product constraints (sections 1–4).
- Relevant facts and assumptions (section 6).
- Definition of terms used in the specification (section 5).
- Work context diagram (section 7).
- Business event list (section 7).

● Product boundary diagram (section 8).

● Product use case list including a fit criterion for each use case (section 8).

● Estimate of size—a count of what you know, at this stage, about each of the classes of requirements, such as the number of business events, number of use cases, number of functional requirements, number of non-functional requirements, or number of terms. Depending on how far you have progressed, you might be able to include the estimated number of function points (section 24).

Marketing Summary

When your marketing department is working in parallel to make publicity plans, then you need to publish a version of the specification that focuses on what the product does for the customer.

● Product constraints (sections 1–4).

● Definition of terms used in the specification (section 5).

● Work context diagram (section 7).

● Business event list (section 7).

● Product boundary diagram (section 8).

● Product use case list including a fit criterion for each use case (section 8).

● If marketing is concentrating on a particular group of use cases, then include the detailed functional and nonfunctional requirements for those use cases (parts of sections 9–17).

User Review

When you publish the specification for users, you should focus on those parts of the specification that affect the users' work. The most common purpose for publishing this version of the specification is to verify the specified product is the one users are expecting. Another reason is to provide technical writers with the basis for the user manual.

● Work context diagram (section 7).

● Definition of terms used in the specification (section 5).

● Product boundary diagram (section 8).

● Product use case list including a fit criterion for each use case (section 8).

● Individual functional and nonfunctional requirements clustered by product use case. Limit these requirements to the use cases that are directly concerned with these users' work (parts of sections 9–17).

Reviewing the Specification

When reviewing a specification, you need all sections of that specification. If you are reviewing individual product use cases, then group all of their requirements together. Quite a few requirements may be part of multiple product use cases. Although this grouping requires a little shuffling of the requirements, you should review each product use case to ensure the completeness of its functionality and to confirm it has the appropriate nonfunctional requirements. If you are reviewing one particular type of requirement, then arrange the requirements by type.

Requirements Traceability

A requirement is traceable if you can identify all parts of the product that exist because of the requirement and, for any part of the product, you can identify the requirement or requirements that caused it. Similarly, no part of the product should lack a set of related requirements. Requirements must be traceable to maintain consistency between the product and the world using the product.

If you want to change some aspect of the product, you must identify which requirements are affected by the change. You need to trace the effect of the change not just within the product, but also within the business affected by the product. Similarly, if there are new or changed requirements in the business, you need to trace which other business requirements and which parts of the implemented product are affected. No matter which part of the world changes, you need to be able to trace the requirements both backward and forward.

When you are specifying requirements, give each requirement a unique identifier, use terminology consistently to specify the requirement, and identify which business use cases and which product use cases are associated with that requirement. So far, so good. When you design a solution to meet the requirements, you must know which parts of each requirement are satisfied by each piece of technology. The problem is that when implemented, the requirements are translated into whichever form is appropriate for the technology; because they are implemented using more than one piece of technology, they may become fragmented.

Let's use an example from the IceBreaker product to demonstrate how we trace requirements.

Tracing a Business Event

Earlier in this book, we discussed dealing with largeness and complexity by partitioning the context of the work using business events (see Chapter 4). Whenever you apply some kind of partitioning, you create a need for traceability. In this case the traceability needs to connect the business event to the work context.

One of the business events in the IceBreaker system is

> *Business Event 10: Truck depot reports problem with truck.*
>
> *Truck Breakdown (input flow from Truck Depot)*
>
> *Amended De-icing Schedule (output flow from Truck Depot)*

In this business event, the truck depot tells the engineers that one of the trucks has broken down. The engineers now need to reschedule the work of the broken-down truck. The engineers review the schedules of the trucks, find an available truck, reschedule the de-icing work, and inform the truck depot.

Part of the requirements process calls for us to study the work related to this business event—the business use case—and determine how much of the work is done by the product and how much by the user. We looked at this issue in Chapter 4, when we discussed event-driven use cases and ways to determine the product scope. The part of the business use case done by the product is the product use case.

When we determined how much of the work should be done by the Ice-Breaker product, we came up with the following product use case:

> *Product Use Case 10: Amend De-icing Schedule whose user is the Truck Depot Engineer.*

Traceability need: to trace a product use case to the business use case, and vice versa.

Here we have created another traceability need because we fragmented the business use case by partitioning it into work to be done by the product and work to be done by the business. We need to be able to trace the product use case to the business use case, and vice versa. To do so, we can assign a unique identifier to each business use case and to each product use case, and then create a connection between them. Bear in mind that more than one product use case might be associated with a particular business use case. Also, the same product use case might be related to more than one business use case.

The requirements specification for the product contains detailed specifications (functional and nonfunctional) for all requirements related to the product use case. For example:

> *Requirement 81: The product shall record when a truck has gone out of service.*

This requirement might turn out to be related to more than one product use case, which leads us to another traceability need: We must be able to trace all product use cases that are affected by a requirement, and vice versa. To do so, we decide to tag each requirement with the identifier of all relevant product use cases.

When you design the product, you decide which implementation technology will be used for each requirement. Several types of technology might be used to implement the product use cases within the product. In addition, several types of technology might be used to implement the parts of the business use case that are outside the boundaries of the product.

Figure 15.2 identifies the technological raw material we can use to implement the response to business event 10, "Truck depot reports problem with truck." Some of this solution technology (e.g., the Weather Station, Truck Driver, Engineer, Road Section, and Truck) might have been specified as a requirements constraint in section 4 of the specification. In other words, whatever solution is chosen must use this technology. Other parts of the technology (e.g., the Autoscheduling Software, Computer, Database, and Satellite) have been selected by the designer taking into account the constraints such as the budget.

Traceability need: to trace all product use cases that are affected by a requirement, and vice versa.

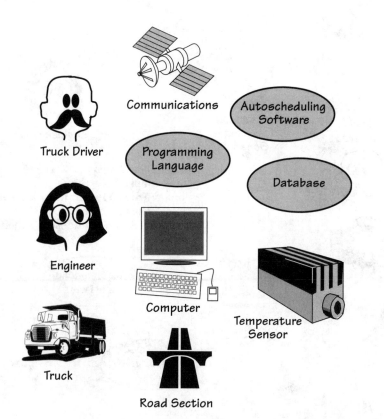

Figure 15.2

Looking at the technology available to us, including anything we can buy, we find these items are useful for implementing the business use case.

When the designer decides which parts of the business use case will be carried out by which pieces of technology, he allocates all parts of the business use case to achieve the best-fit implementation. The complete design defines how all parts of the business use case are implemented.

The requirements for the response to the event "Truck depot reports problem with truck" are allocated to a variety of technologies (Figure 15.3). When a truck breaks down, the truck driver communicates this fact to the engineers using the radio transmitter in his truck. Then, to activate the product use case, the engineer uses a scheduling dialog on the computer to reschedule the work of the broken-down truck. The requirements within the product use case are implemented using software written for the computer, the purchased autoscheduling software, and the database system. The engineer communicates the amended de-icing schedule to the appropriate trucks via radio.

We need to keep track of which requirements—or parts of requirements—are implemented by which pieces of technology. This traceability enables us to verify that the requirements specified are the ones implemented. To do so, we might decide to maintain up-to-date allocated business use case models that are cross-referenced to individual requirements and product use cases.

Traceability need: to keep track of which requirements, or parts of requirements, are implemented by which pieces of technology.

Figure 15.3

The event response for "Truck depot reports problem with truck" is allocated to a variety of technology.

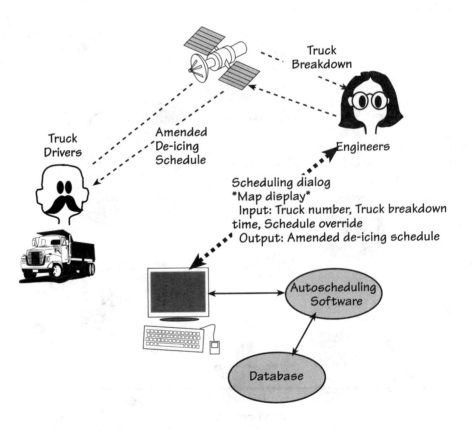

Dealing with Change

When we launch a product into the world and people start to use it for their work, experience tells us that the requirements will inevitably change (Figure 15.4). Users will probably think of something that they would like to change about the product that might make it easier for them to do their work. These changes will likely continue throughout the life of the product.

The world changes: New technologies appear, new business opportunities emerge, new ways to do things are found. In fact, it is usually some change that kicks off a product development effort. Something has changed so much that the old product, whatever it was, cannot cope, and so a new product is built. Thereafter, the new product is changed and changed until it, too, becomes old. At that point, some large change causes the old product to be replaced by a yet newer one.

The product changes because the demands placed on it change. Consider the house in Figure 15.4, and consider your own house. Is your house exactly how it was when you first moved into it? Houses change over time, because your needs change. You start a family, granny moves in with you, you want a new carpet or a new kitchen, and so on. All of these desires represent changes to requirements, and all cause (as soon as you can afford it) changes to the product. The house, like any other product, evolves over time.

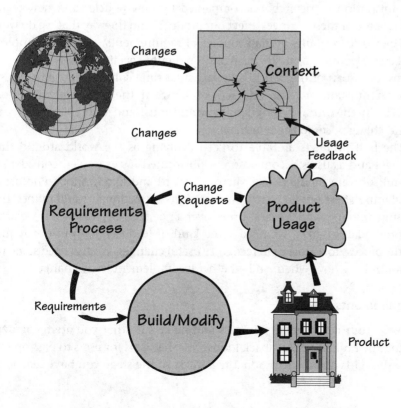

Figure 15.4

When a product is used, it is likely to generate changes. Throughout the lifetime of the product the world will change, which will in turn cause other changes to the product.

There are both good and bad changes. Good changes come when the product has been in use for a long time, and the user wants to extend its capabilities to accommodate some new requirements. Keep in mind that these requirements have emerged from the user's experience with using the product; they could not possibly have been foreseen by the original requirements analysts. This is good because the life of the product is being extended, and the product itself is proving to be fundamentally sound.

Bad changes come when the user asks for changes that should have been foreseen or that result because the original scope of the requirements gathering was not large enough.

If you start with a large enough scope—and we repeat our warnings about the scope being much more than the anticipated automated product—then the product is far more likely to be suitable over the long term. It is more likely to be a closer match to the user's work, and it is more likely to fit seamlessly into the work environment.

Changes in the World

There are many other changes we cannot anticipate—new happenings in the world, things that did not exist when we specified the requirements for our product. For example, democratic governments change from time to time (no doubt we are all thankful for these periodic overhauls), and each incoming administration is inevitably accompanied by new policies and new regulations. Some of these changes affect our products and the way that we do work.

The world contains myriad sources of requirements: people, technology, processes, politics, and so on. A requirements specification is based on a snapshot of part of that world at a particular time. Of course, the world is in a constant state of flux. Interactions between the various requirements sources in the world are dynamic, continuous, and unpredictable; as the world changes, so do the requirements.

The best products are able to keep evolving as the world around them changes and as users become more sophisticated. As examples, consider successful software products like Microsoft Word and Excel, Adobe Photoshop, and Linux. These products have increased their functionality and refined their nonfunctional qualities many times over since their beginnings. If we are to accommodate change, we need some kind of feedback loop in our requirements process to enable us to recognize useful changes. We also need some way of controlling how, when, and whether we implement these changes.

READING

The subject of how to recognize, model, and examine feedback in systems is discussed in Senge, Peter. *The Fifth Discipline*. Doubleday, 1990.

Requirements Feedback

Look at your requirements process and make sure that you are recognizing change by building in feedback loops—mechanisms for users to pass on their new thoughts about the product regardless of the stage you have reached in the development process. We have seen some organizations in which people are made to feel guilty if they change their minds about anything, especially if their earlier decisions have been written down. We do not advocate random and uncontrolled change; instead, we encourage people to tell the truth so that you can make rational decisions about how to react to that change. If you do not allow for feedback, then your systems become obsolete—fast. Encourage feedback by asking people to review requirements: "What could possibly happen to change this requirement, and is there anything I can do to make that change less painful?"

Your mechanisms for encouraging requirements feedback must continue throughout the life of the product. The requirements change over time; we know this for certain. So why not treat requirements as if they were any other kind of product and maintain them? You probably have a maintenance agreement for your personal computer or your dishwasher. Why not draw up the same kind of maintenance agreement with the product users (Figure 15.5)? Visit the users to perform regular maintenance checks. Use trawling techniques such as observation, interviewing, and apprenticing with the user on a regular, ongoing basis. The same methods that uncovered the requirements in the first place can help you unearth new requirements and keep the product healthy.

Good feedback mechanisms help you recognize change. Having recognized new circumstances, you have to decide what to do about them. Thus you need a change control procedure to define each change and monitor its status. In his survey on factors that contribute to successful requirements

> Factors that contribute to successful requirements specification:
> ● Formal requirements-gathering process
> ● Use of requirements change control
> ● Augmentation of written requirements with prototypes
> ● Use of requirements quality control
> ● Use of function points based on requirements
> ● Use of reusable requirements

Source: Jones, Capers. *Survey on Requirements.* Software Productivity Research, 1997.

Figure 15.5

A requirements maintenance agreement involves regular maintenance checks with the product's users. Use trawling techniques to discover new and changing requirements as early as possible.

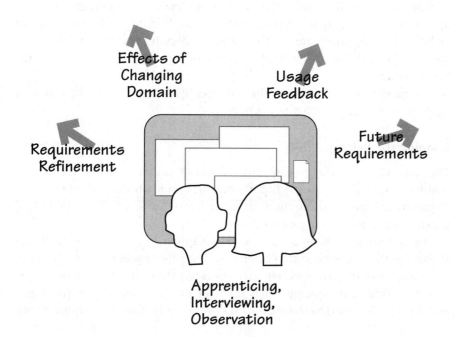

Effects of Changing Domain

Usage Feedback

Requirements Refinement

Future Requirements

Apprenticing, Interviewing, Observation

specification, Capers Jones reports on the use of requirements change control. As we mentioned in our discussion of traceability, without change control the real product becomes something different from the product you are managing, so that the project is out of control.

Requirements Retrospective

READING

Keith, Normen. *Project Retrospectives: A Handbook for Team Reviews.* Dorset House, 2001.

When you finish your requirements specification, you usually face pressure to get on with the rest of the project. But before you leave your requirements process, stop and give yourself a chance to learn from what you have done. A retrospective is a tool for gathering the wealth of experience that might otherwise be lost—an expensive loss when a day or two's effort retains it for all time. The result of the retrospective is a written summary explaining what you learned from your project and how you think other people might gain from your experience.

What to Look For

Focus on reviewing the effectiveness of the way you gathered and specified your requirements. Look at each part of the process you followed, and identify which parts worked well and which parts did not.

Find the major mistakes, but don't assign blame. The retrospective cannot be used as a witch-hunt. If project members suspect that management will punish them for making mistakes, then they will naturally cover up those mistakes. You can really be effective only in an organization free from fear.

Find the major successes, but don't dole out rewards. This practice encourages people to highlight anything they did in the hope of being rewarded rather than prompting them to look at the project dispassionately. The retrospective process has to be kept completely separate from the personnel reward system.

The main question to ask in the retrospective is this: "If you had to do it again, how would you do it and why?"

Running the Retrospective

The Volere Requirements Process model in Appendix A contains a detailed procedure for running retrospectives and writing reports. Refer to Process 6, "Do Requirements Retrospective."

The way you run the retrospective depends on how many people are involved. Your aim is to get input from everyone who contributed to the requirements specification; there are a number of ways to do this. Figure 15.6 illustrates a retrospective process.

The best advice that we can give you is to appoint a facilitator. A facilitator is someone who has no vested interest in the project and no self-interest in the outcome of the retrospective. His task is to gather the project experience.

The facilitator encourages each member of the project team (manager, technical staff, client) to share his own observations about the requirements.

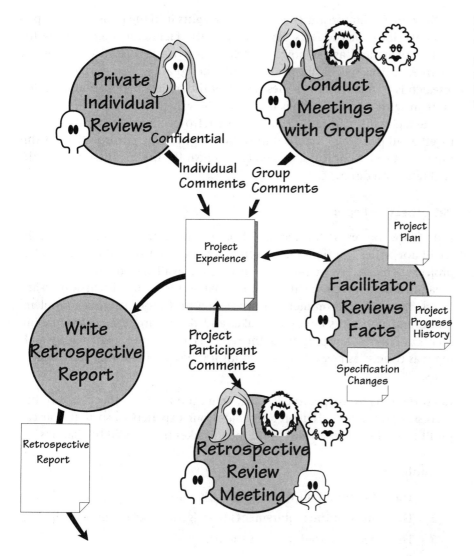

Figure 15.6

Your retrospective should seek input from everyone who was involved in producing the specification.

These individual comments are usually gathered via interviews, but can be collected anonymously. Responses by individual project members are not publicized, as confidentiality encourages people to speak more freely.

Separate meetings are arranged by the retrospective facilitator, with homogenous groups of people involved in requirements—project management, project technical staff, and stakeholders. Each group considers the specification process from its own perspective and gives the facilitator issues to add to the list. The facilitator brings up points from his private contact with team members for clarification and concurrence. Each group is offered the chance to add or change the issues.

Now the facilitator, armed with some insights into the project and its participants, looks at the facts. For example, the facilitator might review the project plans and assess how the deliverables tracked to it, or count the changes to the specification after initial acceptance. The purpose of this research is to quantify the issues raised by the project members and to gain more insights into why things happened the way they did.

The facilitator can hold a full project retrospective meeting that brings together all personnel involved in earlier stages of the retrospective. At this time managers, technical staff, and clients hear the findings described by the facilitator and discuss each.

Retrospective Report

If no follow-on research is required from the full retrospective meeting, the facilitator writes the final retrospective report, often with the assistance of project members. The report, which is made available to everyone in the organization to review, includes contact names for further discussion on any issues. It outlines recommended procedures and tools, describes problems found and possible solutions to take, and details any project disappointments or failures. The purpose of the report is to pass on experience, by making it as concise as possible. It also helps if it has an interesting table of contents:

Requirements Retrospective Report. Our requirements specification had successes and failures. This report shares our experiences so that you can profit from the successes and avoid the mistakes that caused the failures.

Contents

1 The most important things that we learned
2 The history of the requirements (abridged, use diagrams to help)
3 The objectives—did we meet them?
4 The process we used—did it work?
5 Communication—within the team
6 Communication—with the world
7 Did we miss any stakeholders?
8 The tools we used and what we learned
9 How we tested the requirements
10 Management—how did we do it?
11 Project reviews—what we learned
12 Design issues
13 Our greatest successes

Your Notebook

Many years ago your authors developed the habit of carrying a personal notebook and using it to record observations, ideas, meeting notes, plans—anything we feel like writing about or drawing a picture of. We use our notebooks for both personal and work-related subjects arranged in sequential order of writing. We have found that the habitual use of a personal notebook has some interesting effects.

In particular, we tend to write things down more often. The notebook is intended purely for our own use, so we are not inhibited by thinking, "I haven't got time to write this really well." As long as we can read it, that is all that matters.

We are not alone in using notebooks in this way. Richard Branson, the millionaire chairman of the Virgin Group, always carries a notebook. He produces it whenever he talks with employees or customers, and uses it to make notes on the conversations. The result is always a list of things to be done, improvements to be made, and problems to be fixed. Most chief executives talk to employees and customers, but the next day have largely forgotten what was said.

The benefit you will realize from using a notebook in a similar way is the amazing number of good ideas that you will come across when you review your notebook—ideas that you do not remember having are there for you to use. Your notebook becomes a tool for helping you learn and become more observant about the world. In short, it becomes your own personal retrospective report.

The End

This brings us to the end of our book. Throughout this text we have tried to show you the little things about requirements—the small quality issues—that make such a large difference to your work. Seemingly minor things, such as searching for a measurement for "an attractive product," using apprenticing to understand what the guy on the factory floor is trying to achieve, or sketching a low-fidelity prototype. can make a major difference—a difference that makes your work with requirements all the more effective and enjoyable.

Please use this book as we intended: not as a set of canonical rules that must be obeyed, but as a reliable companion to intelligent work. And as you work, take the time to observe (or, better still, measure) the difference that having good requirements makes to both your development efforts and your products. It is a difference worth pursuing.

Volere Requirements Process Model

in which we present, for your reference,
the complete Volere Requirements Process

The Volere requirements process is a product of The Atlantic Systems Guild. For information on other products and services contact:

The Atlantic Systems Guild Ltd.
11 St. Mary's Terrace
London W2 1SU
UK
suzanne@systemsguild.com
james@systemsguild.com
www.volere.co.uk
www.systemsguild.com

The Volere Requirements Process Model

This requirements process model is organized as a hierarchy of processes. To find more about the details of a process, look at the diagram or process notes with the same number. For example, the Requirements Process Model Summary (the first diagram) includes a process (number 1) called Project Blastoff. Diagram 1 will show you more details about this process. When you look at Diagram 1, you will see that it contains processes 1.1, 1.2, and 1.3. To find the details of each of these processes, look at the diagram or process note with the same number. At the end of the model, a dictionary specifies the terms used in the model.

This is a model of the *generic processes* necessary to elicit, specify, and review requirements. The model focuses on *content*. The *dependencies* between the processes are defined by the *interfaces*. This model does not imply any sequence, but rather is an *asynchronous* network. Any combination of processes can be active at any time.

Making This Work for You

Suppose that you want to make improvements to the way that you discover and communicate requirements. but you are not sure where to start. Clearly, you do not want to change everything. You need to identify where you would realize the greatest benefits. Here's how you can use the model to help you do that.

Start with the process model summary and concentrate not on the processes but on the flows of information. For each flow of information, ask these questions:

- Do we have this information defined in our project?
- Who are the stakeholders who originate this?
- Who takes responsibility for it?
- Are there other stakeholders who should be involved?
- How do we record it?
- Do we have anything missing (refer to the definition of the flow to help here)?
- Are there any negative impacts from the way that we are gathering or communicating this information?
- Is there any way we could minimize fragmentation of this information flow?
- Are there benefits in making a change?
- Does the change involve procedures, job specifications, or training?

When you discover flows that you think you would benefit from changing, then delve deeper into the generic process for hints on how to make appropriate and effective change to your own processes. Your improvement might be a combination of things like these:

- Add a new procedure
- Change an existing procedure
- Involve different stakeholders at different stages
- Communicate knowledge in a different form
- Replace or refine one of your existing documents
- Provide training and coaching
- Adopt different trawling techniques

- Partition the work more functionally
- Formally define and track a project goal

The list of possibilities is a long one, but all of them are contained in the process model.

The process model is a summary of all the things that you need to do—somehow or other, to some degree of detail—to discover and communicate requirements. The model is intended to provide a requirements process that you can use to improve your own environment. When you tailor the model, you synchronize it to your own environment by repartitioning it to add checkpoints (reviews, milestones) that are suitable for your environment and by identifying who will be responsible for carrying out each process. You also package the interfaces in the form that suits the way that you work.

Finding More Information

The chapters in this book contain additional information about all the subjects covered in the process model.

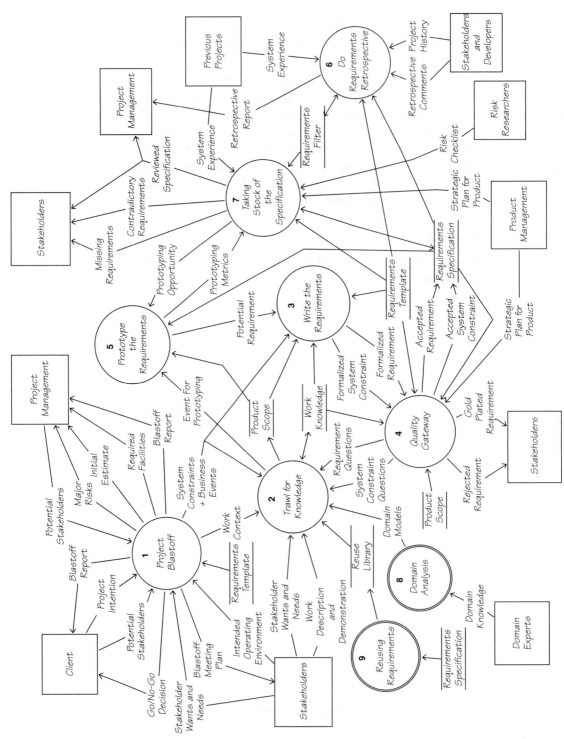

Diagram 0 Requirements Process Model Summary

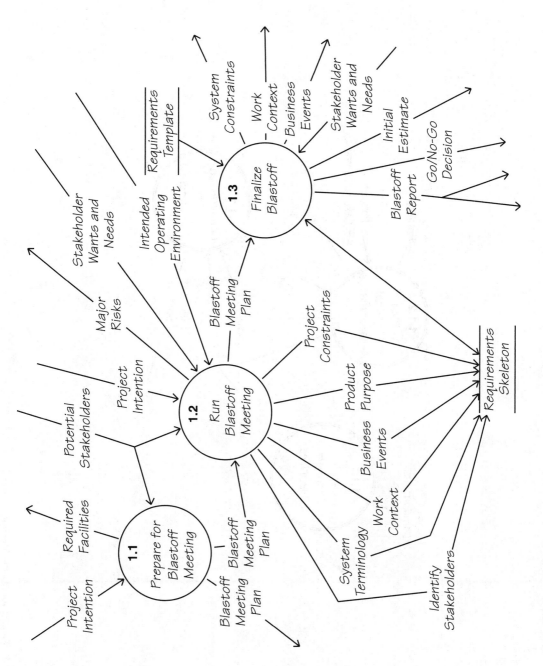

Diagram 1 Project Blastoff

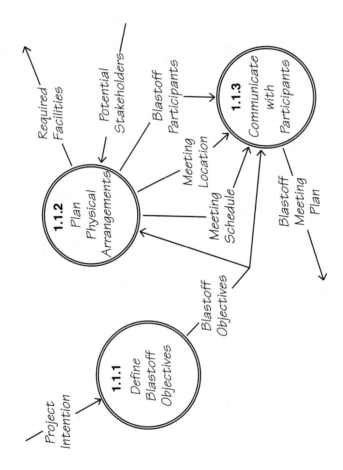

Diagram 1.1 Prepare for Blastoff Meeting

Define Blastoff Objectives (Process Notes 1.1.1)

Define the deliverables to be produced by the blastoff. Examine the Project Intention and decide whether the blastoff is to produce:

- Project Goals: This will always be produced.
- Work Context Model: There may be an existing model that will provide a starting point for this project; otherwise, the blastoff must produce a new context model.
- Identified Stakeholders: Always.
- Anticipated Developers: Examine the kind of product wanted by the customer. Use previous project experience to determine the skills needed for this product. The anticipated developers is a list of the people and skills that are most likely to work on this project.
- System Events: These, at some level, will always be delivered by the blastoff.
- Event/Use Case Models: These are produced in a blastoff to prove the feasibility of the project. When the project is large and there are no dominant transactions, then there is little point in producing use case models during the blastoff. When the project has a few critical transactions, then preliminary use case/event models will be very helpful to determine whether the product can be built.
- System Terminology: A preliminary terminology must be produced by the blastoff, unless there is a well-established standard terminology in use by the organization. For example, some industries have national or international standards for their terminology.
- Scenario Models: These fall into the same situation as events/use cases.

Plan Physical Arrangements (Process Notes 1.1.2)

The job of this process is to define the physical arrangements necessary to produce the blastoff objectives.

Determine the participants from the potential stakeholders in accordance with what is needed for the type of project. Include everyone who could possibly have a stake in the product. It is better to include possible stakeholders than exclude them. If the extra people do not have a real interest in the product, they will certainly find that they have better things to do and leave your stakeholder group.

Plan the facilities and accommodation carefully. Keep in mind that you will have a number of people at the meeting. If you wish to keep them there, then make sure that you have adequate facilities to make their time well spent.

Make sure you have defined these items:

- The location of the blastoff meeting
- Directions for how to get there
- Name and contact details of the facilitator
- Dates and times
- Time needed for the blastoff (number of days/hours)
- List of participants

Communicate with Participants (Process Notes 1.1.3)

Ensure that all the participants know the place and duration of the blastoff meeting. Send all participants an agenda, and ensure that they understand what is expected of them before they arrive. It is important that you impress on participants how they can contribute to the value to the product by participating in the blastoff, why they are doing it, and what the value of the product is to your organization. Send a list of participants with each invitation. Each participant must respond and commit to being there, and you must be certain that all participants come equipped to do the task.

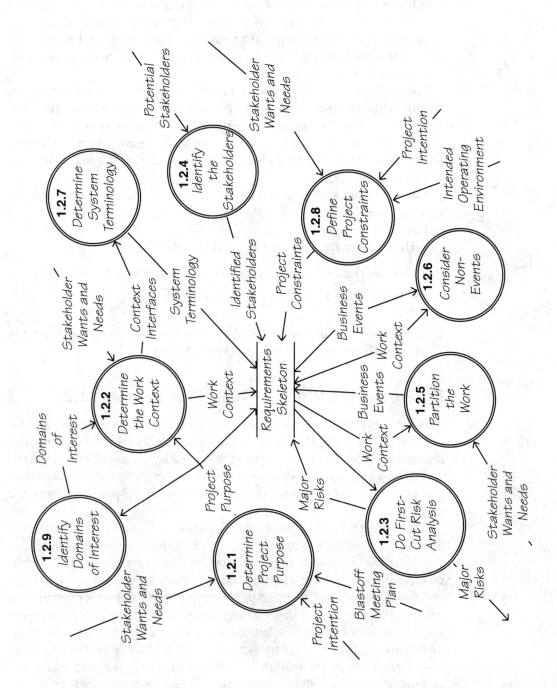

Diagram 1.2 Run Blastoff Meeting

Determine Project Purpose (Process Notes 1.2.1)

This task is to ask, "What do we want this system for?", but not to say how we will achieve it. The system purpose is a clear, unambiguous, measurable statement of precisely what product your client wants to get at the end of the project. It should consist of a short statement, one or two sentences at most, or a few bulleted points.

The real intention of this task is to ask, "Is this project feasible?" If you cannot state the objective so that all stakeholders agree with it, then the project cannot achieve anything worthwhile. Similarly, you must be able to state the purpose such that you will know when you have achieved it. If your words demonstrate the criteria to be used to measure the purpose, then they will be strong and clear.

Failure to make a suitable statement of the system purpose means that you should seriously consider abandoning or deferring the project until your stakeholders can agree.

Each system purpose statement should contain the following:

- A short description of the purpose (try to describe it in one sentence)
- The benefit to be gained from the purpose (ask why the client has the purpose)
- A measurement of the fit criterion that you will apply to determine whether the benefit, and thus the purpose, has been met

Determine the Work Context (Process Notes 1.2.2)

The context is the starting point for requirements. The context diagram isolates the part of the world that you will study to satisfy the project objectives. It shows the interfaces between your project and other people, organizations, and technology. It is the best place to reach the initial agreement on which part of the world is related to your project and what the product is expected to do.

The context is rarely as large as it should be—it should include the entire application domain. You must be careful not to have too small a context or a context that represents only the intended computer system. Users often describe the system they want in terms of what they think a computer can possibly do. Thus, by accepting this description of a computer system as a context, you miss out on other opportunities to automate or improve processes. Your context should include the business processes that are relevant to understanding the subject matter of your project. Some of the business processes carried out by the end users (provided they help you understand the application domain) will be within your detailed context of study.

Do First-Cut Risk Analysis (Process Notes 1.2.3)

This analysis assesses the major risks associated with building the desired product. It is necessary for the team to ask two questions:

● "What are the main risks we face if we build this product?"
● "What will happen if that risk becomes a problem?"

For example, suppose that the product is to be a new reservation system for a holiday tour operator. The following major risks might be associated with this kind of system:

● "What happens if we are not ready for the holiday season?"
● "The system is to be used by travel agents. What if we build a system that takes too long to learn to use?"
● "The system must interface with airline systems. What happens if the airline systems change before our system is built?"

It is necessary to be brutally honest when stating risks. Some risks may seem like criticisms of people at the blastoff meeting, so, if necessary, make it possible to contribute risks anonymously.

Risks are the worst-case scenarios that you can imagine. Here are some suggested risks to examine:

● Do we have an unrealistic schedule for delivering this product? (This is the most common risk of all.)
● What could happen if we don't have the product on time?
● Do we unrealistic expectations for this product?
● Do we have the people skills needed to build this product?
● What new skills are needed?
● Have we built this kind of product before?
● What kind of things have gone wrong on other projects at our installation?
● What kind of things have gone wrong with this kind of system, at your installation or elsewhere?
● What have we done badly in the past?
● What external influences are there on the project? For example, are there proposed changes to laws affecting this product? Will the company be reorganized before the product is delivered?
● What new technology is needed for this product?
● Are we dependent on products being delivered by external forces?
● Are we making unrealistic assumptions about any other products that this project needs?

- Do we have the correct management structure for this project?
- Are we in danger of "gold plating" the product?

Being honest about the risks at this stage will considerably improve your chances of successfully building your product.

Identify the Stakeholders (Process Notes 1.2.4)

Identify all the people who have a vested interest in the product being built: These are the stakeholders. Stakeholders participate in the requirements-gathering phase, as it is the stakeholders who determine the product they need built.

You are looking for people who will be affected by the product or participate in its development. While the stakeholder list must not be so large as to include everyone in the building, neither must it exclude people who have a real interest in the product. To do so will result in later repercussions that may well scuttle your project.

Stakeholders must be individually named. Do not accept "someone from the accounting office."

Here is a checklist of potential stakeholders:

- Client: The person responsible for paying for the development
- Customer: The person(s) or group(s) who will pay for the product
- User (potential at this stage): The person(s) or group(s) who will use the product to do work
- Sponsor Name: The person with organizational responsibility for the project
- Marketing Department
- Developer(s): Person(s) or group(s) responsible for developing the product
- Domain Expert(s): Sources of subject matter knowledge
- Technical Expert(s): Person(s) or group(s) who have expertise in the subjects relating to the product's nonfunctional requirements (e.g., machines, legal, operational environment; see the requirements template for an exhaustive list)
- Tester(s): Person(s) responsible for testing the quality of the requirements

For each stakeholder identify these items:

- Stakeholder name
- Stakeholder specialization (e.g., accounting, pricing, manufacturing)
- Estimated amount of time the stakeholder will need to contribute to the project (It's difficult to know this at blastoff time because it depends on

how much you know about the project. but it's worth considering whether you have an indication of the number of days/weeks and the frequency of the involvement.)

Refer to Chapter 3, Project Blastoff, for more guidance in doing a complete stakeholder analysis.

Refer to Appendix D, Project Sociology Analysis Templates, for tools to help you analyze the sociology of your project.

Partition the Context (Process Notes 1.2.5)

Partition the context into business events.

The term "events" is used here to mean the business events that have an effect on the system. You will need to study these events to have enough knowledge to decide the best scope for the product.

Start outside the system, and look for those happenings that result in a communication between an adjacent system and your work context. For example, when a customer places an order for some service from your system, it is a business event.

The system does not initiate the event, but has to respond to it. Thus, when any signal arrives from outside your context and your system must make some response, it is a business event.

Remember that these are business events, not the individual events that happen when the user clicks a button.

Consider Non-Events (Process Notes 1.2.6)

Non-events are what happens if an event doesn't happen. For example, suppose that you have a fundamental event, "Customer pays for goods." The non-event is what happens if the customer does not pay. Is there another event that happens, such as "Follow up on bad payers"?

Examine each business event and ask if it has one or more associated non-events. Add the new events to your list of business events.

Add the new data flows to your work context diagram.

Determine Business Terminology (Process Notes 1.2.7)

Establish recognized names for the data items and other objects used by the developers and the users.

Begin with the context diagram. Write a description of the data flows around the context. The intention is to converge on common terms to be used for each of the data items used by the system.

The result of this task is a list of agreed-upon terminology and definitions.

Define Project Constraints (Process Notes 1.2.8)

Define the mandated constraints on the way that the product must be produced.

Look for real constraints (as distinct from opinions about how the problem should be solved):

- Solution constraints: Mandated technology
- Deadlines: Any known deadlines
- Financial budget
- Current system constraints

Each constraint should be testable. In other words, how will you know whether you have met the constraint?

For each project constraint, ask, "Why it is a constraint?" This question will help you distinguish between real project constraints and solutions posturing as constraints.

Refer to the Volere Requirements Specification Template for more guidance in writing constraints.

Identify Domains of Interest (Process Notes 1.2.9)

The product purpose is the basis for determining which subject matter domains we need to study.

For each product purpose statement, ask, "Does this objective mention or imply subject matter areas that we need to study to build this product?" For example, suppose that one purpose is to provide rail transport for members of the general public. Then we can say that we need to study the domains of rail transport and the general public.

The next interesting question is, "How much of each of these domains is relevant to the product that we intend to build?" We address this question when we set the context of the problem.

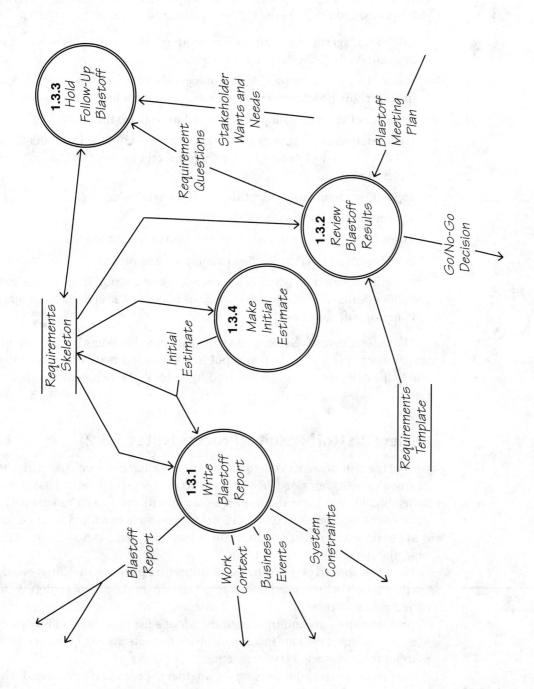

Diagram 1.3 Finalize Blastoff

Write Blastoff Report (Process Notes 1.3.1)

Write a report describing what was accomplished by the blastoff meeting. The report should include the following items:

- Context diagram with an explanation of the major decisions that determined the boundary of the system.
- Stakeholder list showing the stakeholders identified by the blastoff. Also include those people who were excluded as stakeholders, and say why.
- Developer list naming all people needed to work on this project.
- Preliminary event or use case list. Show those events/use cases identified so far. This list will not be complete, but serves as input to the first estimates of effort.
- Top ten requirements as identified by the stakeholders.
- System terminology as accepted at that point.
- Major risks. These are to be brought to management's attention.
- Initial estimate of effort needed to complete the project.
- Recommendation on whether to proceed. If the decision is not to proceed, include reasons for not proceeding plus changes (if any) that would make it appropriate to proceed.

The requirements skeleton is the first step toward building a requirements specification. Everything that you put in the requirements skeleton is used and built on by the processes involved in building the requirements specification.

Review Blastoff Results (Process Notes 1.3.2)

Look at the requirements skeleton and compare what has been collected with the requirements template. Determine whether there is enough of a skeleton to reasonably complete the requirements specification. The template is a guide to the requirements specification that you have to write. The intention is not to have a complete specification at this stage, but to know if, given the time, the specification can be built.

Were the objectives from the blastoff meeting plan met? In other words, are the blastoff deliverables enough to get started on the task of gathering the correct requirements?

Are there any outstanding questions? Make a list of all outstanding problems. If the deliverables are incomplete, then the outstanding questions serve as input to a follow-up blastoff meeting.

This process makes the decision on whether the project is to go ahead. The go/no go decision must be a conscious task. The question may be asked several times during the blastoff meeting.

Jim Highsmith and Lynne Nix, in "Feasibility Analysis—Mission Impossible" (*Software Development,* July 1966), produced the following checklist for identifying when you should *not* go ahead with a project:

1 Major political issues are unresolved by the blastoff.

2 Key stakeholders won't participate in the blastoff (and therefore probably the project).

3 Risks (probability of adverse consequences) are too high (technical, economic, organizational).

4 The cost–benefit ratio isn't favorable enough, especially when benefits are not measurable.

5 The internal staff's experience and training is insufficient for the project.

6 Requirements are unclear, or keep changing radically during the blastoff.

7 The risk–reward ratio is unfavorable. High risks usually need a high reward to be worthwhile.

8 Clients (in a multidisciplinary project) can't agree on exactly what the problems or objectives are.

9 No executive wants to be the project's sponsor.

10 Implementation planning seems superficial.

● There must be a measurable statement of the system objectives.

● The customers must be satisfied that the product is worthwhile.

● The developers must satisfied that they will be able to build the product.

● Both have to be satisfied with the estimates to build the product.

● The end users have to be satisfied that the product will be beneficial to them.

If things are do not look promising at this stage, it is far more economic to abandon the project now rather than in several years' time. Remember that the principal objective of the blastoff is to determine whether the project is feasible.

Hold Follow-Up Blastoff (Process Notes 1.3.3)

This mini-blastoff meeting is run in the same way as the previous meeting, but specifically addresses the outstanding requirements questions. Unless these questions can be answered, the risk is too great to proceed with the project.

Keep in mind that you are trying to achieve the blastoff objectives, not to know everything about the system.

Make Initial Estimate (Process Notes 1.3.4)

Make your first estimate of the effort required to build the product.

The estimate at this stage does not have to be highly precise, but must be realistic. It can be based on such simple metrics as the number of events that the system has to respond to or the number of use cases that will make up the system. The event/use case provides you with a manageable chunk that you can use as the basis for making an estimate. Estimate the average amount of effort for implementing one event and then use this figure to estimate the effort for all events within your context.

Depending on how much you know about the data, you may be able to make an initial function point count for the system. The type of count and the counting boundary (the context) have been defined, and an approximation of the data and transaction function types are also known.

An estimate can also be made on simple metrics such as the complexity of the data. Roughly speaking, this is the number of data entities that the system will use. It is necessary to know the average cost of installing a data entity for this kind of estimate. While it is not the most accurate of possible estimates, it provides a starting point.

Keep in mind that the applicability of the previous history of effort required per function point (or whatever) will be tempered if this is the first time that you have used the proposed development technology. Allow generous time for the learning curve.

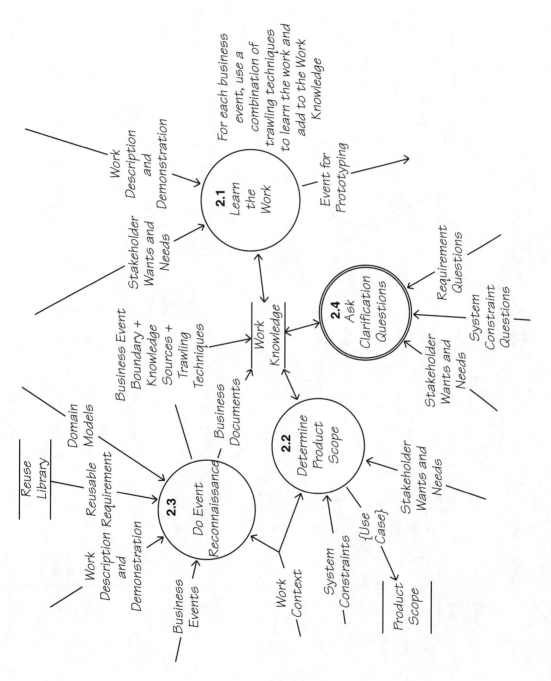

Diagram 2 Trawl for Knowledge

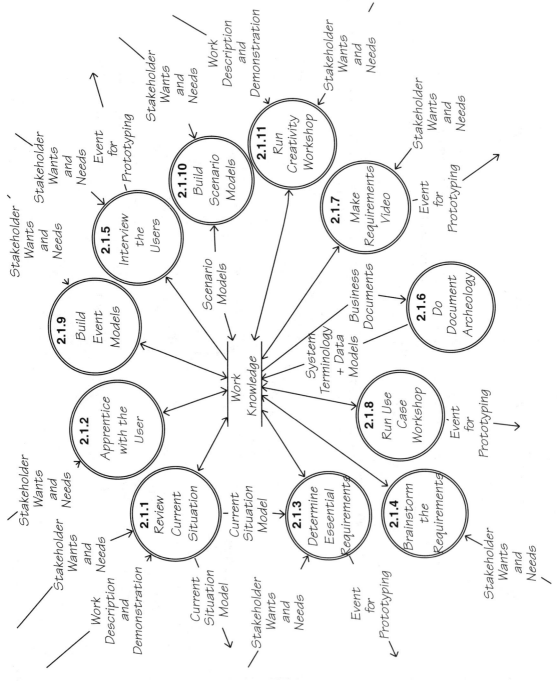

Diagram 2.1 Learn the Work

Review Current Situation (Process Notes 2.1.1)

When you review the current situation, keep in mind that you are not attempting to specify the system, but merely to establish the situation that the users currently face. It is highly likely that the users will describe their business in a way that includes the mechanisms they use to get the work done. These mechanisms are not requirements for the new system: You must look beyond them to see the underlying policy of the users' system.

Despite any bad reputation the current system may have, it is not totally worthless. It may have many functions that are making a positive contribution to the business. This means, of course, that some parts of the current system must be included in any future system. You may implement them differently with new technology, but their underlying business policy will remain almost unchanged. Thus the review of the current system ensures that you understand the situation before introducing any improvements.

The current situation model can be used as the input to business process reengineering.

Apprentice with the User (Process Notes 2.1.2)

This process is based on the idea of masters and apprentices. The developer becomes apprenticed to the user, sitting with the user to learn the job by observation and asking questions. It is unlikely that many users can explain what they do in enough detail for the developer to capture all the requirements. Users cannot be expected to have the required presentation and teaching skills to effectively present their work to others. However, people are very good at explaining what they are doing while they are doing it. If the user is doing his job in his normal workplace, he can provide a running commentary and provide details that might otherwise be lost. It is probably only while working that the user is able to precisely describe his task, tell you why he is doing things, and explain what exceptions can occur.

Apprenticeship removes the need to talk in generalizations. If we are away from our work, we tend to describe it in abstract terms and to describe generalized cases. The abstraction is useful in one sense, but it does not hold enough detail for it to work every time. (You can see this effect when a user shows you his work-around for special cases.) By sitting alongside the user, the apprentice receives a running commentary, and gets to see all the cases and the actions the user takes for each.

Finally, the apprentice learns the task, and demonstrates this by actually doing the job under the user eyes.

Use this approach:

- When the user is not good at abstraction
- When the user does not have time to talk to you
- When you do not know which questions to ask

Determine Essential Requirements (Process Notes 2.1.3)

The objective is to find the underlying essence of the system, and not accidentally reintroduce an existing technology or a requirement that exists because of an existing technology.

The developer is also looking for which skills people use and how they see themselves when they do the work. Which conceptualizations and metaphors do they use?

Create abstract requirements by seeing the application without its technology. For example, a bank in London had 20 different products. Each product was (on the surface) a different way of guaranteeing that exporters got paid for their goods in foreign countries. The products included letters of credit, guaranteed foreign bank loans, guaranteed funds, and so on. At first, the way the users handled each product seemed different. However, a common essence emerged as the developers studied the real work and looked past the current technology. The end result was that a single core implementation was created, then dressed differently for each product. In some cases, this different window dressing involved little more than changing a few titles on screens.

Brainstorm the Requirements (Process Notes 2.1.4)

Brainstorming is a method for generating ideas. The intention here is to produce as many requirements for the new product as possible. Do not be concerned about whether the ideas from the brainstorm session are all usable. The intention is simply to create as many ideas as possible. Subsequently, you will eliminate any that are too expensive, impractical, impossible, and so on.

Here are some simple rules for brainstorming:

- Participants in the brainstorming process should come from as wide a range of disciplines with as broad a range of experience as possible. This brings many more creative ideas to the session.

- Suspend, or at least defer, judgment, evaluation, and criticism. Simply record requirements as they are generated. The practice of not judging, evaluating, or criticizing is the fastest way to develop a creative and energized atmosphere for the brainstorm group.

- Produce *lots* of ideas. Come up with as many ideas as possible. Quantity will in time produce quality.

- Try to come up with as many ideas as you can that are unconventional, unique, crazy, wild, and so on. The wilder the idea, the more creative it probably is, and the more likely it is to turn into a really useful requirement.

- Piggyback a new idea on top of another.

● Write every idea down, without censoring. "Ideas disappear faster than water evaporates unless written down" (Alex Osborn, the founder of brainstorming).

● If you get stuck, "seed" the session with a word pulled randomly from a dictionary. This word serves as a starting point for word association in the process of generating ideas.

After the brainstorming session, the results can be evaluated, and the best requirements can be explored by more conventional methods.

Interview the Users (Process Notes 2.1.5)

Interviewing the users is the traditional approach to requirements gathering. However, when used on its own, it may not be the most effective strategy. We strongly suggest that interviews not be used as the sole method of gathering, but that they be used in conjunction with other techniques when they will be more effective.

The requirements engineer can draw up questionnaires in advance. While this gives some structure to the following interview, we have found that users have to be highly motivated to actually fill them in prior to meeting the engineer. We suggest that you send the user, or whomever you are interviewing, an agenda of the topics that you wish to cover. This gives the user a chance to have material at hand or to ask subject-matter experts to be present.

The user should not be completely passive during the interview. We strongly urge you to build models (e.g., event-response, use case, scenario) while you are talking with the user during the interview. This gives you and your user immediate feedback, and allows you to test the accuracy of what you are being told. We also prefer that the user participate in the modeling efforts. You must make allowances for their notational idiosyncrasies: You can correct them later.

You can also interview the user while watching the work being done. This has the advantage of you being able to direct your questions to the task at hand, and gives the user a better chance to describe the task. People are not good at describing their jobs, but are usually good at telling you what they are doing while they are doing it.

When people describe things to you, especially such conceptual and difficult things such as requirements, they usually have difficulty being precise. They will also describe things in abstract terms, and have difficulty defining precisely what they mean. The idea of laddering is that you can conceptually go up or down from what they are saying, depending on what you need to know. Going down the ladder means that you decompose what you are told to find the layer of fact below the statement, then decompose again to find the next lowest layer. You might also need to ladder up—that is, move the conversation to a higher level of abstraction.

For example, you may be asked for a system that responds quickly to customers' needs. To go down the ladder, you would ask for a meaning or measurement for "quickly." "While the customer is on the telephone" is a measurement, and the next lowest level will yield "You have to find the customer's record in one second." By going down the ladder of abstraction, you arrive at a deterministic answer.

Going up the ladder is also useful. It leads to outcomes and criteria: "The system has to respond quickly so customers do not become impatient."

Think about the level of the interview, and always try other levels. They are often very revealing.

Do Document Archaeology (Process Notes 2.1.6)

Document archaeology entails determining the underlying processes and requirements by inspecting the documents and files that the organization uses. It should not be used on its own as a requirements-gathering technique, but as a prelude to more intensive interviews and as the basis of modeling efforts.

In document archeology, you begin by collecting samples of all documents, reports, forms, files—in fact, anything that is used to record or send information. Regular telephone calls should not be excluded.

Inspect the document (for simplicity's sake, the term "document" here means all of the above) looking for nouns, or "things." These can be column headings, named boxes on forms, or simply the name of a piece of data on the document.

For each noun, ask these questions:

- What is the purpose of this thing?
- Who uses it, why, and what for?
- What are all the uses the system makes of this thing?
- If I have thing A, must I also have thing B, and must I not have thing C?
- Can this thing have a value? For example, is it a number or a code or quantity?
- If so, to what collection of things does it belong? (Data modeling enthusiasts will immediately recognize the need to find the class that owns the attribute.)
- What is that thing used for?
- Does the document contain a repeating group of things?
- If so, what is the collection of things called?
- Can I find a link between things?
- What process makes the connection between them?

- What are the rules attached to each thing? In other words, what piece of business policy covers the thing?
- What processes ensure that these rules are obeyed?
- Which documents give the users the most problems?

These questions will not in themselves reveal all the requirements for the system. They will, however, give you plenty of material and direction for further investigation. We also suggest that you use document archeology as part of your data modeling approach.

Make Requirements Video (Process Notes 2.1.7)

Video can be used to co-develop software. The users and developers participate in workshops and brainstorming sessions, and the proceedings are videoed. Interviews and on-site observations are also recorded. The videos are used to first record, and then confirm, the proceedings. In addition, videos can be shown to developers who do not get the opportunity to meet face-to-face with the users.

Video can be used as an adjunct to interviewing and observing the users in their own workplace. Users have their own way of accomplishing tasks, their own ways of categorizing the information that they use, and their own ways of solving problems that have worked well for them in their own situation. Thus, by using video to capture the users at work, you are capturing their ways of doing their jobs and their concerns, and not imposing your own expectations and preferences.

Video can also be used in a more structured way one business use case at a time. Select the business use case and ask the users to work through typical scenarios that they encounter with that activity. As they work, the users describe the special circumstances, the additional information they use, the exceptions, and so on. The shrugs, grimaces, gestures, and other body language that are normally lost when taking notes are faithfully recorded for later playback and dissection.

Run Use Case Workshop (Process Notes 2.1.8)

This workshop is conducted with the participation of the appropriate customer/user and the requirements team. The first segment of the workshop generates the scenarios; this effort needs input from the users/customers. The idea is to talk through a use case/event and to extract from the user the essential things that have to happen when this business event takes place. You are trying to define a series of user-recognizable steps that complete the work of this business use case. You ask the user to verify/improve/change the steps that you have written down. The resulting use case scenario is a very rough sketch of the requirements for the use case.

After the use case workshop, the requirements analysts go back to their offices and derive and specify the individual requirements from the knowledge in the use case scenarios.

Build Event Models (Process Notes 2.1.9)

You are looking at the functional part of the system. Break the whole system into its constituent business events. We will use the term "event" to signify this partitioning as a convenient way to look at each of the system's functions.

The objective of partitioning the system into events is to provide a way of breaking up the system in a consistent and communicable way. Event partitioning is nothing more than a special knife for carving a system into logical, minimally related pieces. However, despite its simplicity, it gives you several advantages:

- The events are minimally connected, so you can study isolated pieces without getting involved in all the details of the system.
- Events can be readily measured using function points or other measuring methods. Thus it is easier to make estimates that are based on real measurements.
- Management can use event partitioning to monitor progress.
- The main benefit to the requirements process is that events allow you to separate the actions of the system, and deal with the system's functionality in a way that is familiar to your users.

Finding Business Events

The work context is the best place to identify events. All of the data flows that connect the system to the outside world are somehow part of an event. Start by looking for the adjacent systems that communicate with the work context. Each discrete business data flow connected to them is a potential event. Some of these will be simple data flows that have to be stored by the system. Others will be complex interactions with the adjacent system that persist until the piece of business has been completed.

Some of the data that flows from the system does so as a result of a temporal event. Use these data flows to identify more of the events. Ultimately, you must be able to account for all of the data flows that bound the system. The flows will either trigger an event or result from one. Some events have both input and output flows.

Once you have listed all the events, consider the functionality of each. It may be necessary to model some of the events to more clearly see the requirements. However, at this stage you should try not to get bogged down in detailed modeling. It is suggested that scenario models may be the tools that give you enough of a description for each function to write its functional requirements.

Build Scenario Models (Process Notes 2.1.10)

Scenarios are stories built to illustrate the way that a user might operate an intended system. The scenario is built to illustrate the user's viewpoint of a business event and is used to clarify the implications of a requirement.

Scenarios can be built using a variety of media. The simplest scenario might be straight text, but is more likely to be pictures or diagrams. In fact, you should use any format and media that feels comfortable to the user.

Run Creativity Workshop (Process Notes 2.1.11)

When you ask stakeholders for their requirements, they may describe what is uppermost in their mind and what they think is possible. In a competitive world you also need to discover requirements that are not obvious—that is, requirements that are undreamed of but would make a difference to the success of the product. Inventing requirements is the process of exploring the work and asking what requirements you would have if you did not have the obvious (sometimes irrelevant) constraints.

Techniques for running creativity workshops include the following:

- Using ideas from brainstorming
- Asking people to imagine futuristic requirements that their grandchildren might have
- Consciously removing the constraints
- Building models and simulations

The best time to run creativity workshops is close to the beginning of the project—in other words, before people have become fixed in their ideas but after you have done a preliminary analysis of the work context, business events, goals, and stakeholders. At this point you can run a creativity workshop to encourage new and creative ideas.

For more on how to run creativity workshops, see Chapter 5, Trawling for Requirements.

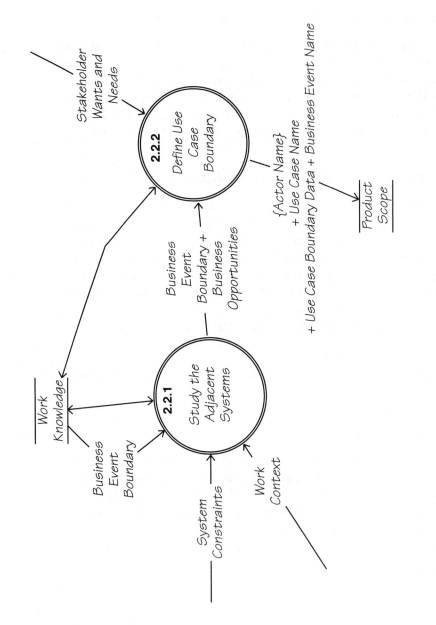

Diagram 2.2 Determine Product Context

Study the Adjacent Systems (Process Notes 2.2.1)

For each business event, if you have built an event response model as part of the process of learning the work, then use that model to help you study the adjacent system and the event processing. Otherwise, depending on your knowledge of the event and the complexity of the event, it might help you to sketch an event response model.

Look for business opportunities that show how the product can help to achieve the product purpose within the project constraints.

For each input data flow and output data flow between an adjacent system and a process, consider the system constraints and the work context and ask these questions:

● What work does the adjacent system do to produce or use the interface?
● Are we studying enough of the adjacent system to be able to identify business opportunities?
● Is there any work done by the adjacent system that could be done by the product?
● Could all or some of the work done by the process be done by the product?
● Are there any opportunities for helping people to be better at their jobs?
● What are the aspirations, desires, and concerns of the adjacent systems?

Define Use Case Boundary (Process Notes 2.2.2)

Determine the use case(s) for business events. For each business event:

● Consider the business opportunities.
● Review the work knowledge.

Decide the boundary between the product and the actor. For each use case (there might be more than one per business event):

● Define the actor names.
● Define the use case name.
● Define the use case boundary data.
● Record the product context by adding the use case to a use case diagram.
● Keep track of which business event name(s) is (are) related to this use case.

If you have more than 15 to 20 use cases, then a use case diagram will be too complex and you will need to draw a leveled use case diagram or create a use case list.

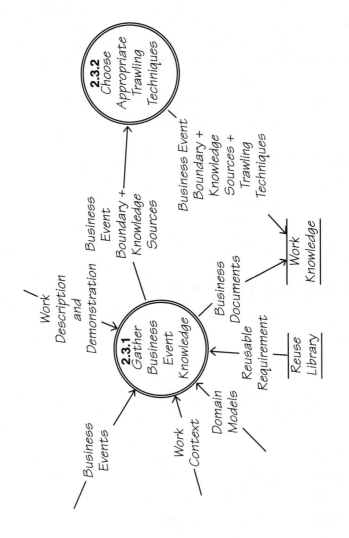

Diagram 2.3 Do Event Reconnaissance

Gather Business Event Knowledge (Process Notes 2.3.1)

This activity is concerned with taking stock of all the work knowledge that exists for each business event. Use the event boundaries as a guide for gathering all the work knowledge and the sources of that knowledge. The results of this activity are the starting point for learning the detailed work.

For each business event, look for any business documents that might contain knowledge about the work related to the event. Look for reports, forms, specifications, user manuals, organization charts, feasibility studies, product documentation, marketing blurbs—any document that might contain requirements buried in its depths.

List the names of sources of the work knowledge:

● People within the boundaries of the work context
● Adjacent systems
● People outside the boundaries of the work context
● The name of a group of people who might have knowledge of this event

Are there any domain models that contain knowledge about this event? Are there any reusable requirements that contain knowledge about this event?

Choose Appropriate Trawling Techniques (Process Notes 2.3.2)

To choose the most suitable trawling techniques for a business event, you need to consider the following issues:

● What are the potential sources of knowledge?
● What type of requirement are you searching for: policy architecture, stored data, person–machine interface, essential activity?
● Will you be able to speak directly to people?
● Is the knowledge conscious, unconscious, or undreamed of?

Here are some guidelines on the strengths of a number of trawling techniques:

1   Review the current situation.
    – Good for uncovering unconscious requirements
    – Helps when adding new requirements or doing maintenance changes to an existing system
    – Use as the basis of business process reengineering

2 Apprentice with the user.

 – Helps to uncover unconscious and conscious requirements

 – Useful when users are "too busy" to talk

3 Determine the essential requirements.

 – Helps to separate requirements from solutions

 – A good way to understand the real purpose of the system

 – Helps in uncovering unconscious requirements and provides insights that trigger undreamed-of requirements

4 Interview the users.

 – A good technique for discovering conscious requirements

5 Brainstorm.

 – Helps uncover undreamed-of requirements

 – Very useful when inventing new products with unknown/potential users

6 Conduct use case workshops.

 – Involves the users in explaining vague, complex, and difficult events

 – Good for uncovering conscious and unconscious requirements

7 Undertake document archaeology.

 – Used when your source of information is documents

8 Build event models.

 – If the business event boundaries are vague, then investigate them by doing some detailed systems analysis modeling.

9 Make requirements videos.

 – Useful when users' time is limited

 – Can be studied, analyzed, and used by a group after the video is made

 – Helps when the context is vague

See Chapter 5, Trawling for Requirements, for more guidance on trawling techniques.

Ask Clarification Questions (Process Notes 2.4)

Review the requirement questions and system constraint questions. Use the requirements template to help you.

Can you determine the requirement type?

Are there any measurement examples for this type of requirement? You could use these to help to formulate your questions:

Which stakeholders are most likely to be able to provide the answers to these questions? Use your stakeholder analysis to help with this task.

What is the best medium/way to ask the question? Do you need to ask it in person or is it possible to do it by telephone, e-mail, Web site, or prototype?

Your question should include everything that is already known about the requirement.

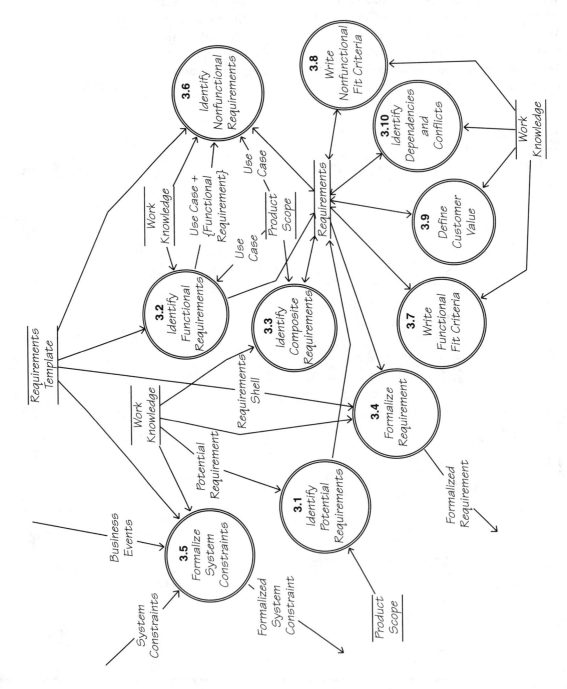

Diagram 3   Write the Requirements

Identify Potential Requirements (Process Notes 3.1)

Not all requirements are discovered as a result of setting a context and working toward a logical and connected partitioning. Instead, many individual requirements are discovered while trawling for knowledge.

This process analyzes the potential requirements discovered as a result of trawling. For each potential requirement:

● Write a description using the form "The product shall . . ." followed by the action that the product must take.

● Give the requirement a unique number.

● Review the product context and see if you can identify which use case(s) this requirement is connected to.

● Record the source (preferably names of people) of the requirement.

● Record the requirement rationale. Why is this requirement important to the business?

Refer to Chapters 7, 8, and 10 for more guidance in writing requirements.

Identify Functional Requirements (Process Notes 3.2)

When the use case is large and/or complex and/or unfamiliar, it is difficult to make the leap directly from the use case to the requirements. A scenario provides a steppingstone to the functional requirements in this situation.

From the point of view of the actor(s), write the scenario by listing the steps that the product must go through to do the work of the use case. For each scenario step, find the functional requirements by breaking the step into testable one-sentence statements. Ask what the product has to do to complete the work of this step. The following questions are helpful in this regard:

● What data must be received by the product?

● What data must be produced by the product?

● What data must be recorded by the product?

● What checks must be made by the product?

● What decisions must be made by the product?

● What calculations must be made by the product?

Each of the above questions might produce a number of functional requirements. For each requirement:

● Write a description using the form "The product shall . . ." followed by the action that the product must take.

● Give the requirement a unique number.

- Attach the use case number to the requirement.
- Record the source (preferably names of people) of the requirement.
- Record the requirement rationale. Why is this requirement important to the business?

Chapter 7 focuses on functional requirements.

Identify Composite Requirements (Process Notes 3.3)

A composite requirement (also known as a "high-level requirement") does not have its own testable fit criteria, but rather "summarizes" a number of other individually testable requirements. Composite requirements are useful as a way of talking about the combined effect of a number of individually testable requirements. Sometimes a composite requirement is a sign of vagueness or uncertainty.

It is useful to have a composite requirement for each use case. Then you can summarize the requirements at the use case level but you still have connections to each of the testable requirements that compose the particular use case.

When you define a composite requirement, be sure that you have a reason for doing so and that you are not simply taking refuge in generality.

Formalize Requirement (Process Notes 3.4)

Refer to the requirements shell that is packaged with the requirements template. For each requirement, use the shell as a guide and define each of the components defined on the shell.

For detailed advice and examples of each type of requirement, refer to the requirements template.

Formalize System Constraints (Process Notes 3.5)

Refer to the requirements shell that is packaged with the requirements template. For the product purpose and the project constraints, use the shell as a guide and define each of the components defined on the shell. For other types of system constraints (e.g., client, customer, user) refer to the requirements template.

For detailed advice and examples of each type of system constraint, refer to the requirements template.

Identify Nonfunctional Requirements (Process Notes 3.6)

You can use the functional requirements as a trigger to help you find the non-functional requirements by using the following approach:

I. For each use case
    A. For each functional requirement
        1. For each type of nonfunctional requirement listed in the requirements template
            a. Should there be one or more of these nonfunctional requirements to support this functional requirement?

You can also use a higher-level approach and look for nonfunctional requirements by comparing the use case with each of the types of nonfunctional requirements.

Write Functional Fit Criteria (Process Notes 3.7)

The objective of this process is to take a requirement and use the work knowledge to produce a requirement fit criteria for a functional requirement. The process looks for unambiguous criteria that make it possible to classify any solution to the requirement as either "fits the requirement" or "does not fit the requirement."

The template contains many examples of how to determine requirement measurements.

For each requirement, fit criteria for a functional requirement specify how you will know that the product has successfully completed the required action, provided that you have defined the terms (refer to section 5 of the requirements specification template) used in the description and purpose/rationale of the requirement. Then your fit criteria will take the following form:

- The specified retrieved data will agree with the specified data that was input.
- The specified checked data will agree with the specified checking rules.
- The result of the calculation will agree with the specified algorithm.
- The specified recorded data will agree with the specified retrieved data.

In other words, if your terminology is unambiguously defined, it is part of the definition of the fit criteria for functional requirements.

You might consider writing the test case as an alternative to the fit criterion for a functional requirement.

Write Nonfunctional Fit Criteria (Process Notes 3.8)

The objective of this process is to take a requirement and use the work knowledge to produce a requirement fit criteria for a nonfunctional requirement. The process looks for unambiguous criteria that make it possible to classify any solution to the requirement as either "fits the requirement" or "does not fit the requirement."

The template contains many examples of how to determine requirement measurements.

- Decide what type of requirement you are dealing with; the template will help with this task.

- Is it really a requirement? Requirements are often mistakenly stated as solutions. If this is the case, then you need to ask the stakeholders what the real requirement is, independent from how you might solve it.

- If the requirement is concerned with something that you can touch, see, smell, hear, or taste, then it is easier to find an objective measurement.

- If a noun is not concerned with something that you can touch, see, smell, hear, or taste, then you have a nominalization. A nominalization is created when a verb describing an ongoing process is turned into a noun.

- Suppose you come across this requirement: Maintenance must be reliable. "Maintenance" is a nominalization. You can clarify a nominalization by trying to place bounds on the meaning. Turn the nominalization back into a verb and ask this question: *Who* is nominalizing about *what*, and *how* are they doing it? In the preceding example, ask: *Who* is *maintaining what*, and *how* are they doing it? This technique will help you to identify the real meaning of the requirement; from there you will be able to define an appropriate fit criterion.

- Some requirements are vague nominalizations because no one really knows what they mean or want.

Define Customer Value (Process Notes 3.9)

Define the customer value by asking the customer to look at the requirement from two points of view:

- Customer Satisfaction: "How happy will you be (on a scale from 0 to 5) if I give you a solution that satisfies the fit criteria for the requirement?"

- Customer Dissatisfaction: "How unhappy will you be (on a scale from 0 to 5) if I do not give you a solution that satisfies the fit criteria for the requirement?"

Your aim is to understand the customer's real priorities and to guide the customer in communicating which issues are of greatest importance to him. The aim is to have some rational basis for making choices about which/when/whether to implement requirements.

Use the same procedure when you have several different groups of customers, each with a different set of priorities. Your aim is to discover and record the different priorities so that you can make reasoned choices and trade-offs.

Identify Dependencies and Conflicts (Process Notes 3.10)

Whenever you find a requirement that is in conflict with any other requirement, then you should record the conflict. A conflict happens when two or more requirements cannot all be implemented at the same time—that is, the implementation of one requirement prevents the others from being implemented.

The first step in resolving a conflict is to recognize that it exists and start thinking about it independently from the people whose opposing views might be thought to "cause" the conflict.

You might not discover all of the conflicts at this stage. Later, when you review the requirements specification, you will do a more formal search for conflicts.

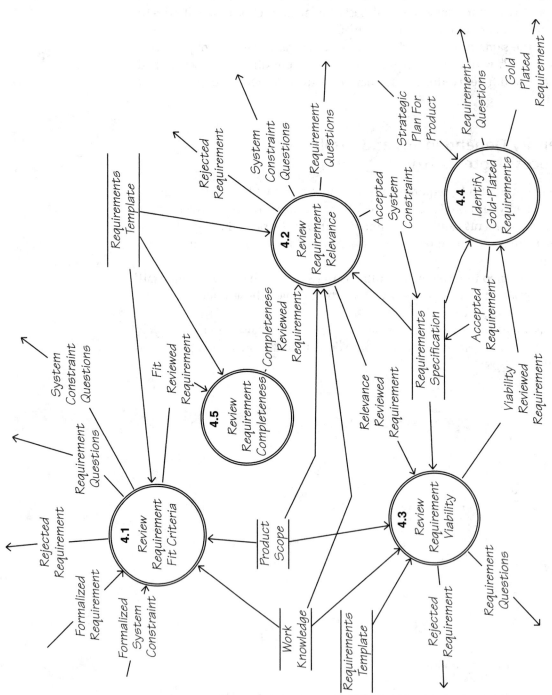

Diagram 4.0 Quality Gateway

Review Requirement Fit Criteria (Process Notes 4.1)

The purpose of the requirement fit criteria is to set communicable limits that the people involved in the project can understand well enough to test each solution. Ask your testers to help with this process.

Does the formalized requirement or formalized system constraint have a requirement fit criterion that provides an unambiguous way of testing any eventual solutions to determine whether they conform with that fit criterion?

Some requirements are easier to quantify than others. Functional requirements are the easiest of all, because they are bounded by a tight context and because we have had much more experience in quantifying them.

Suppose we have a requirement for a customer to send us orders. We can specify exactly which data describes a customer, how many customers we have, and what the projected growth/attrition rate is. Thus we could say that the requirement fit criteria for a customer are that any solution must record all of the defined data values for the defined number of customers and that it must be able to cope with the defined projected growth.

Now suppose the requirement states that when a customer sends us an order, we must respond fast. This performance requirement does not have an unambiguous requirement fit criterion. It would be impossible to test a solution and determine whether it conforms to this requirement, because different people might interpret "fast" differently. Thus we need to quantify how fast is "fast." This step forces many questions out into the open. Does "fast" have a different value in different circumstances? Does "fast" have the same value for all customers or all types of orders? The idea is to arrive at a value, a range of values, or a statement that can be used to test the fit of eventual solutions to that requirement.

The more abstract the concept, the more difficult it is to come up with a specific value for a requirement fit criteria. Provided you have a requirement relevant to the context, however, it is always possible to up with a quality measurement that conforms to our definition.

Suppose a requirement says that the system's automated interfaces must be "easy to use." Now we need a requirement fit criteria for "easy to use." Remember: We are looking for criteria so that we can test whether a solution satisfies the requirement. In this case it's impossible to find a number, but we can still ask the question, "How will we know whether a given solution fits this requirement?" Perhaps we can agree that a test panel of novice users must be able to get an answer to a query of grade 3 complexity within five minutes of first encountering the product.

Raise a question about any requirement or system constraint that does not have a testable fit criterion.

Review Requirement Relevance (Process Notes 4.2)

Is the requirement within the product context? If not, then raise a question because it might be an irrelevant requirement.

Is the requirement really a requirement, or is it a solution? Solutions masquerading as requirements are most common in the case of nonfunctional requirements or system constraints.

Look at the context of study and ask whether this requirement is a constraint that is imposed by the context. If the answer is yes, then you have a real requirement. If the answer is no, then you have a constraint that has been imposed because of someone's implementation bias or because someone has an incomplete understanding of the context.

Review Requirement Viability (Process Notes 4.3)

Given the current situation and the context of the project, is this requirement viable?

Is the organization mature enough to cope with a system that satisfies this requirement?

Do we have the technological skills to satisfy this requirement?

Would it be more realistic to scrub the requirement?

You are trying to raise questions early about requirements that are not viable within the conditions of this project.

Identify Gold-Plated Requirements (Process Notes 4.4)

Review each requirement to determine whether it is a real requirement or whether it is "gold plating." The key question is this: Does the requirement contribute to the strategic plan for the product? Go back to the purpose of the project (requirement type 1) and compare this requirement with the measurable purpose.

Sometimes, even though a requirement is gold-plated, you might choose to include it because it helps to overcome a personality or political problem. The important issue is to know that the requirement is gold-plated and to have a stated reason for including it.

Review Requirement Completeness (Process Notes 4.5)

Review the requirement against the requirements shell in the Volere Requirements Specification Template. If any of the components listed on the requirements shell are missing, then do the following:

● Highlight the missing components.

● Record the reason for the absence of the component.

● Question whether the requirement needs more trawling for knowledge.

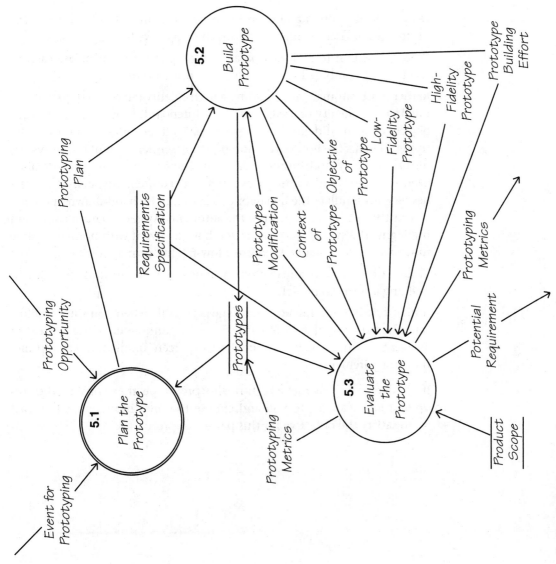

Diagram 5 Prototype the Requirements

Plan the Prototype (Process Notes 5.1)

This task decides what sort of prototype is best for a given prototyping opportunity.

Make a prototyping plan to satisfy this objective by considering the following:

● Do you need to build a new prototype from scratch? Could any existing prototypes be used or adapted to suit this objective?

● Would it be best to build a separate prototype for this event/use case, or should it be combined with one or more other events?

● Rather than automatically building a high-fidelity (automated) prototype, might a low-fidelity (pencil, paper, or whiteboard) prototype satisfy your objective? A low-fidelity prototype is particularly suitable when you are trying to focus the user's attention on the essential content of the system (business policy and business data). In these circumstances, a detailed event/use case model and an experienced requirements analyst are the best way to simulate the behavior of a system. The hand-drawn approach diverts the user's attention from the automated system characteristics and highlights the system purpose. If you have an event with nonmeasurable functional requirements, then use a low-fidelity prototype.

● Would it help you to consider one or more detailed business scenarios by building a scenario model?

● A high-fidelity (automated) prototype is suitable when you want to illustrate the behavior of an interface, when you cannot define the context of an event, or when you have more than 50 percent unmeasurable nonfunctional requirements.

If you decide to construct a high-fidelity prototype, then consider the prototyping tools available to you and choose the one that requires the least effort to satisfy the objective for this particular prototype.

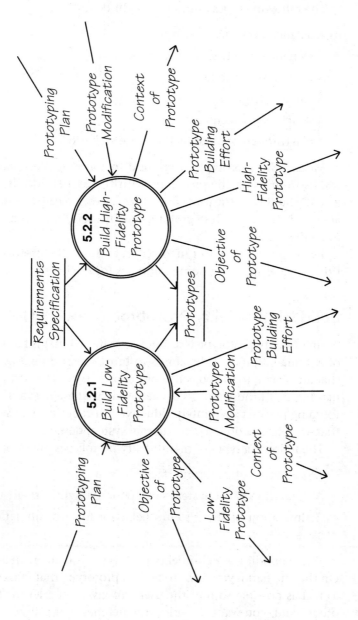

Diagram 5.2 Build Prototype

Build Low-Fidelity Prototype (Process Notes 5.2.1)

A low-fidelity prototype is a simulation model that is drawn by hand. Its aim is to bring alive those aspects of the system that are related to the objective of the prototype.

The following types of models might be suitable:

- A detailed event/use case model
- A scenario model for the event/use case
- An entity/state model
- A context diagram
- A sketch of a screen layout
- A playthrough of a product use case scenario

Modify the prototype to respond to the usage feedback. This feedback results from using the prototype with the user(s). Ideally, the prototype is actually built with the user's assistance, in which case this task is done in parallel with the task "Test prototype with users," and the usage feedback is immediate.

Keep track of the effort involved in building the prototype; this information provides input for doing estimates for the later phases of the project.

Build High-Fidelity Prototype (Process Notes 5.2.2)

A high-fidelity prototype is a simulation model that is built using some kind of automated product. Its aim is to bring alive those aspects of the system that are related to the objective of the prototype. The best prototyping products highlight those aspects of the system that are relevant to the user. A prototyping product is counterproductive if it requires the user to know things that are relevant only to the internal system design.

The following types of high-fidelity prototypes might be suitable:

- A simulation of a user interface
- A simulation of the system's behavior for a given event/use case
- A simulation of the system's behavior for a combination of events/use cases

When building a high-fidelity prototype, you are in an awkward position. On the one hand, you want to build a prototype that makes the system look as real as possible so that the user will give you relevant feedback. On the other hand, you want the user to remember that this simulation is not the real system and you can't deliver all the functionality just like that. You can reflect the unreality by the names you use. For instance, a customer name of

Alice in Wonderland serves as a continual reminder that there's a lot to do before the prototype becomes a real system.

Modify the prototype to satisfy the usage feedback. This feedback results from using the prototype with the user(s). Ideally, the prototype is actually built with the user's assistance, in which case the usage feedback is immediate. If the prototyping product has an interface that is understandable to the user, then the prototype can be built in conjunction with the user, and this task can be done in parallel with the task "Test prototype with users." Otherwise, it is better for the analyst to build the prototype and then test it with the user.

Keep track of the effort involved in building the prototype. This information provides input for doing estimates for the later phases of the project.

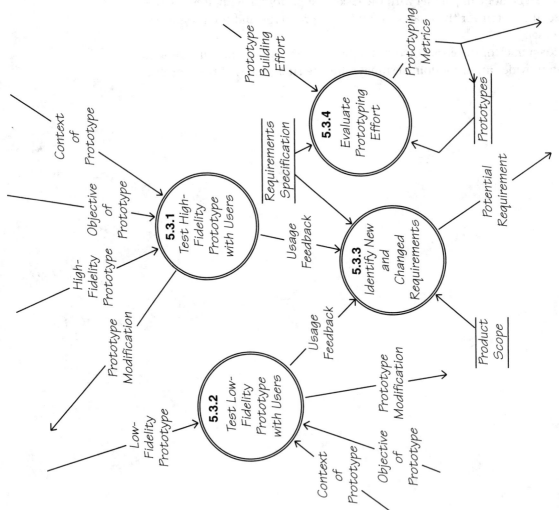

Diagram 5.3 Evaluate the Prototype

Test High-Fidelity Prototype with Users (Process Notes 5.3.1)

This task tests should ideally be done in parallel with the task of building the prototype. However, if the process of building the prototype involves procedures that are irrelevant to the user (due to the nature of the prototyping product), then it is better to build the prototype before showing it to the user.

The trouble with high-fidelity prototypes is that they are often so convincing that users are convinced that they are real, and think that you can build the whole system in half an hour. Remind the users that this model is a prototype. It's like a stage set—it appears to be real until you look behind the facade and discover that it is only simulated functionality.

Demonstrate the prototype to the users and ask questions like these:

- Does this model behave as you expected?
- Can you imagine yourself using a product that works like this to do useful work?
- Does anything about the prototype irritate you?

Review the objective of the prototype, and ask whether the prototype is leading you toward satisfying that objective. Depending on the objective of the prototype, you might decide to leave the prototype with the users for a period of time so that they can experiment with it and give you feedback at a later date. Identify any prototype modifications that are necessary to bring the prototype closer to satisfying this objective.

If you have satisfied the objective of the prototype, then the usage feedback will consist of user comments, new requirements, and requirements changes that emerge as a result of using the prototype.

Test Low-Fidelity Prototype with Users (Process Notes 5.3.2)

This task is ideally done in parallel with the task of building the prototype because the process of building a low-fidelity prototype makes the business problem clear to the user. Review the objective of the prototype, and ask whether the prototype is leading you toward satisfying this objective.

Ask questions like these:

- Is any information missing from the prototype?
- Are the business rules correct?
- Does the prototype cover the intended context of the prototype?

Identify any prototype modifications that are necessary to bring the prototype closer to satisfying the objective of the prototype. If you have satisfied the objective of the prototype, then the usage feedback will consist of user comments, new requirements, and requirements changes that emerge as a result of using the prototype.

Identify New and Changed Requirements (Process Notes 5.3.3)

This task reviews the usage feedback that is generated as a result of using the prototype. The aim is to discover new potential requirements by comparing the usage feedback with the requirements in the requirements specification and the strategic plan for the product.

● Does the specification already contain a requirement that satisfies this usage feedback?

● Can this usage feedback be expressed as a measurable requirement?

● Does this usage feedback contribute to the strategic plan for the product?

If the usage feedback passes these preliminary tests, then treat it as a potential requirement. Before it can be added to the requirements specification, it will have to pass through the Quality Gateway like all other potential requirements.

Evaluate Prototyping Effort (Process Notes 5.3.4)

This task evaluates the prototype-building effort and defines some prototyping metrics. These metrics are input to the task of estimating how long it will take to analyze and design similar-sized components in the real system.

● Calculate the number of function points contained in this prototype.

● What problems did you experience when building this prototype?

● What lessons did you learn?

The metrics will be used to help identify future prototyping opportunities and to help make estimates for future stages of the project.

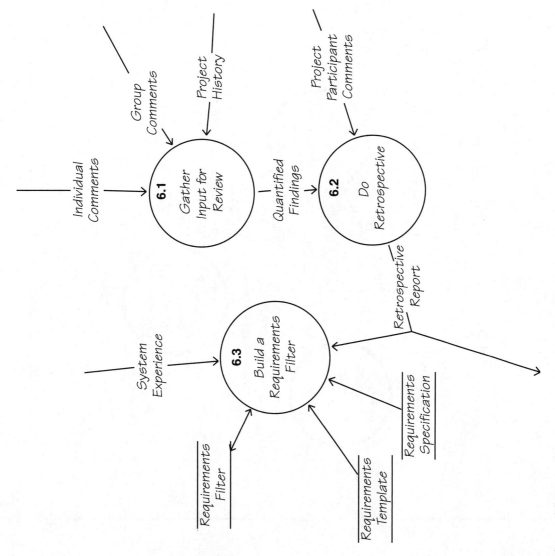

Diagram 6 Do Requirements Retrospective

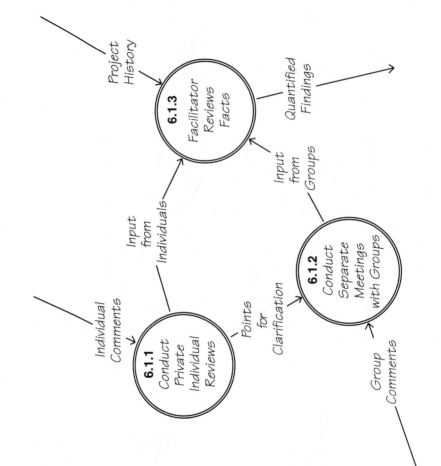

Diagram 6.1 Gather Input for Review

Conduct Private Individual Reviews (Process Notes 6.1.1)

The facilitator has private contact with each project member (developer, stakeholder, manager). The contact is often initiated by questionnaire. The individual responses submitted by project members are never publicized, and often the questionnaire is unsigned. Another way of gathering input from individuals is by asking them to talk into a tape recorder.

The purpose of this initial private contact is to provide the facilitator with a realistic guide to the issues of the project. Here are some sample questions:

- If you had to do it again, what would you do differently?
- What would you do the same way?
- What was your best experience?
- What was your worst experience?
- Which tools were most helpful?
- Which tools impeded progress?
- How do you rate the traceability of your requirements?
- Would you work with the same team again? Why?
- What single change would result in most improvement to product quality?
- How do you rate management support?
- What did you learn by doing this project?

Conduct Separate Meetings with Groups (Process Notes 6.1.2)

This series of meetings involves the retrospective facilitator (or a team of facilitators if the project had many personnel) and the project management, developers, users, and clients in homogenous groups. The purpose is to understand that particular group's experience of the project.

During these sessions the facilitator might bring up points for clarification that have arisen as a result of his private reviews. Each group is asked for its input to add to or change the issues.

Facilitator Reviews Facts (Process Notes 6.1.3)

The facilitator, or team of facilitators, reviews the facts gathered from individual and group input as well as the actual history of the project. The aim is to quantify the findings.

Compare the plan for producing the requirements specification with the actual progress:

- What are the differences?
- How many changes were made during the requirements specification process?
- Is the project suffering from requirements creep?

The facilitator also compares the project plans with the actual progress and reviews the changes to the specification.

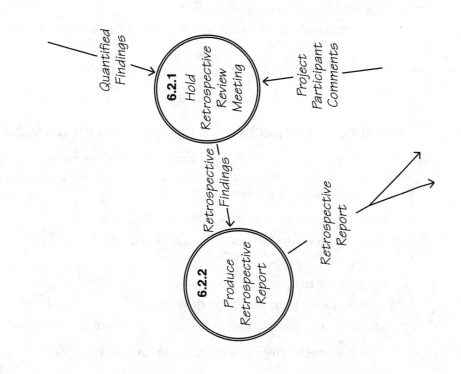

Diagram 6.2 Do Retrospective

Hold Retrospective Review Meeting (Process Notes 6.2.1)

The retrospective review meeting includes all people who have been involved in any of the earlier stages of the retrospective (individual reviews or group reviews). Managers, clients, technical staff, and all stakeholders meet to hear the findings described by the facilitator(s). The following guidelines are suggested for this review:

- Remind participants of the objective of the retrospective: to learn from experience by capturing and packaging the noteworthy experiences of the project so that other people can benefit from that knowledge.
- The facilitator presents each finding.
- The participants discuss each finding, and any new comments are noted by the facilitator.
- If there is disagreement on any points, then the facilitator notes both opinions.

Produce Retrospective Report (Process Notes 6.2.2)

Your aim is to have as many people as possible read the retrospective report with interest. Design this report so that it captures people's attention and is easy to find one's way around:

- Write the report in clear, straightforward language.
- Avoid words whose only purpose is to provide bulk.
- Be honest.
- Use pictures to help with explanations.
- Include quotes from project participants.
- Maintain anonymity unless individuals have requested otherwise.

Here is a sample table of contents for a retrospective report:

Retrospective Report on Requirements Specification

Our project had successes and failures. This report shares our experiences so that you can profit from the successes and avoid the mistakes that caused the failures.

Contents

1 The most important things we learned
2 The history of the project (abridged)
3 The project objectives: Did we meet them?

4   The process we used: Did it work?

5   Communication: within the team

6   Communication: with the world

7   The tools we used and what we learned

8   How we tested our requirements

9   Management issues

10   Project reviews

11   Requirements issues

12   Design issues

13   Some things we did right

14   Why our faces are red

15   Actions to take

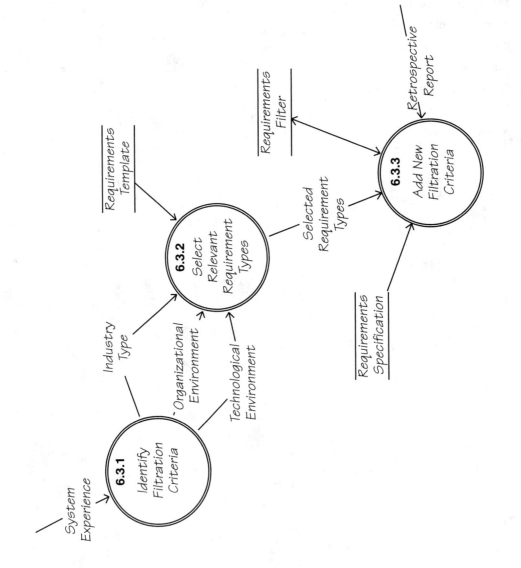

Diagram 6.3 Build a Requirements Filter

Identify Filtration Criteria (Process Notes 6.3.1)

A requirements filter provides an objective measurement of the quality/ degree of uncertainty/degree of completion (the content) of a requirements specification irrespective of the form in which it is produced. It offers a way of applying a fixed measurement to variable artifacts.

The filter is relevant in the following circumstances:

- When requirements specifications are produced by another organization
- When requirements specifications are produced in diverse forms
- When requirements specifications are produced by a variety of people who work in different ways

The filter is used as a tool for trapping missing requirements, irrelevant requirements, and inconsistent requirements.

The first step in building a filter is to identify the industry type for which it will be used. For example, a banking system would have different filtration criteria than an air defense system, simply because requirements that are very important in one industry might be totally irrelevant in another.

Next, define the organizational environment in terms of the roles of people involved in producing your requirements specifications.

Describe the typical technology that applies to your projects for this industry type.

Select Relevant Requirement Types (Process Notes 6.3.2)

For each requirement described in the requirements template, ask these questions:

- Does this requirement apply to the industry type or organizational environment or technological environment for which I am building a requirements filter? If so, then add the requirement to the requirements filter.
- Thinking about a requirement will often trigger ideas about other requirements that are not mentioned in the requirements template. Are any other requirements relevant to the requirements filter that you are building? If so, then add them to the requirements filter.

Add New Filtration Criteria (Process Notes 6.3.3)

This task is concerned with making your requirements filter more useful by adding new knowledge to it.

Every time you produce a requirements specification for this industry type, organizational environment, or technological environment, review the specification to see whether it includes any types of requirements that are not included in the filter. Add the new types of requirements to the requirements filter; they then become additional criteria for reviewing future requirements specifications.

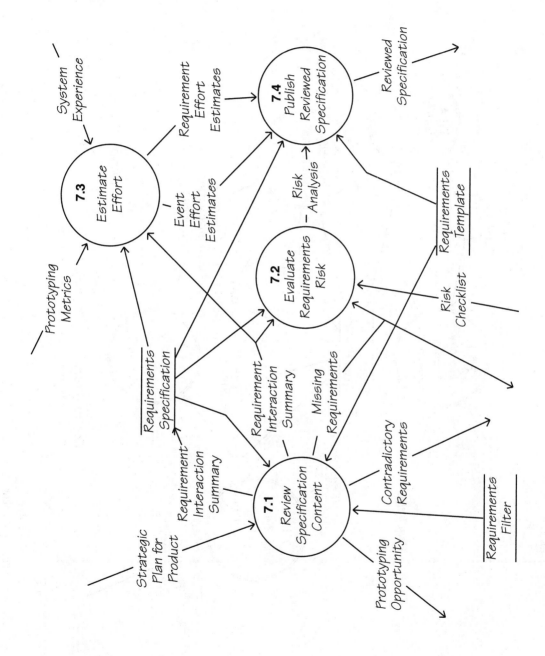

Diagram 7 Review Requirements Specification

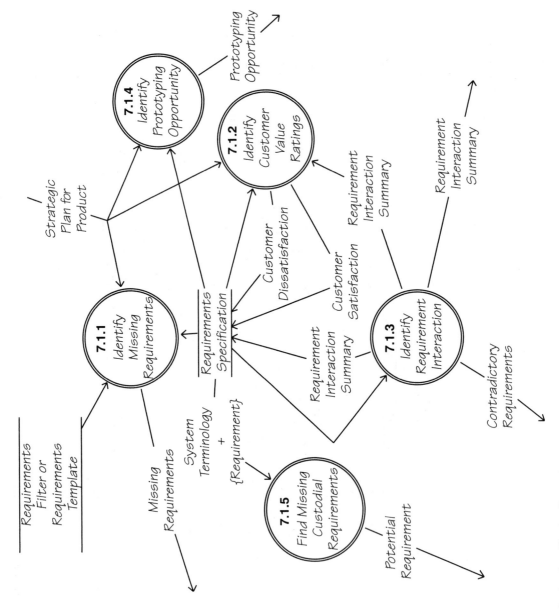

Diagram 7.1 Review Specification Content

Identify Missing Requirements (Process Notes 7.1.1)

If you have built a requirements filter, then use it to drive this task. Otherwise, use the requirements template.

Remember that each requirement should already have been individually reviewed. Your concern here is to cross-check the requirements to discover any missing ones.

For each requirement type in your filter/template, do the following to discover requirements that have been missed:

- Identify all requirements of this type defined in the requirements specification.
- If there are no requirements of this type, and if the strategic plan for the product indicates that there should be requirements of this type, then tell the requirements trawling step that this is a missing requirement.

Compare each event/use case in your specification with each type of nonfunctional requirement. Ask this question to help you identify missing requirements: Is this type of nonfunctional requirement relevant to this use case/event?

Identify Customer Value Ratings (Process Notes 7.1.2)

When evaluating design alternatives, it is helpful if you know which requirements are absolutely vital and which ones are there because someone thought they would be "nice to have."

Ask your stakeholders to grade each requirement for customer satisfaction on a scale from 1 to 5:

1 = Unperturbed if this requirement is satisfactorily implemented
5 = Very happy if this requirement is satisfactorily implemented

Ask your stakeholders to grade each requirement for customer dissatisfaction on a scale from 1 to 5:

1 = Unperturbed if this requirement is *not* satisfactorily implemented
5 = Extremely unhappy if this requirement is *not* satisfactorily implemented

The dependencies between requirements will help you assign the customer satisfaction and dissatisfaction ratings. For example, if you have a requirement with a satisfaction rating of 5 and that requirement is dependent on three other requirements, then the dependent requirements are also likely to have a satisfaction rating of 5.

The point of having a satisfaction rating and a dissatisfaction rating is that they guide the stakeholders to think of the requirements from two different perspectives. In addition, they help you uncover what stakeholders care about most deeply.

Identify Requirement Interaction (Process Notes 7.1.3)

Two requirements interact if a design solution to one of them makes it more difficult (or easier) to do anything about the other. Identifying requirement interaction at the specification stage provides input when you evaluate the requirements' risk and estimate the effort needed to satisfy the requirements.

Requirement interactions exist in the following situations:

- Two functions use some of the same policy.
- Two functions use some of the same data.
- Two functions have contradictory measurements.
- The solution to one requirement has an effect (either negative or positive) on the solution to another requirement.

Identify Prototyping Opportunity (Process Notes 7.1.4)

The task here is to identify which parts of the requirements would benefit most from the building of a prototype.

For each event or use case in the requirements specification, ask the following questions:

- Does the event/use case have a high customer reward (or penalty), or is it composed of a set of requirements that have a high customer reward (or penalty)?
- Is the event/use case central to the strategic plan for the product?
- Is the event/use case composed of more than 50 percent unmeasurable requirements?
- Can you specify the benefit of building a prototype for this event/use case?

For each event/use case, if the answers to these questions are all yes, then you have identified a prototyping opportunity.

The point of building prototypes during requirements specification is to find requirements that have been forgotten and to clarify requirements that are not clear. For this reasons, Steve McMenamin refers to prototypes as "requirements bait."

Find Missing Custodial Requirements
(Process Notes 7.1.5)

Custodial processing relates to the maintenance or housekeeping for the system's stored data. Most systems store data that must be able to be changed. For example, the addresses of customers change from time to time. The processing necessary to keep the address up-to-date has nothing to do with the fundamental activities of the system—this is the custodial processing.

For each item of stored data, determine whether it has any custodial requirements. Should the user be able to change, or perhaps delete, it? Can the custodial activity be part of a fundamental process, or must you establish a new event/use case?

Also, examine the context model for data flows from the outside that indicate data to be changed. Look for flows that directly change stored data, such as "Customer Address Change." As some of these may be missing from the context, look for flows that bring data into the system that may need to be changed. For example, perhaps a flow establishes a new customer. The data stored by this activity would have to be changed at some point in the future. If it is missing, add the changing data flow to the context, and make it a requirement to change the stored data.

Consider all of the external entities for the system. If it is a service provider (e.g., if it manufactures goods handled by the system or transports goods), then there may be a need to create, change, and delete the information held about this external entity.

Similarly, inspect all of the data items stored by the system. Determine whether they need to be maintained in any way.

Finally, determine whether the maintenance must be a separate requirement or whether it can be included in the same events/use cases as other fundamental requirements.

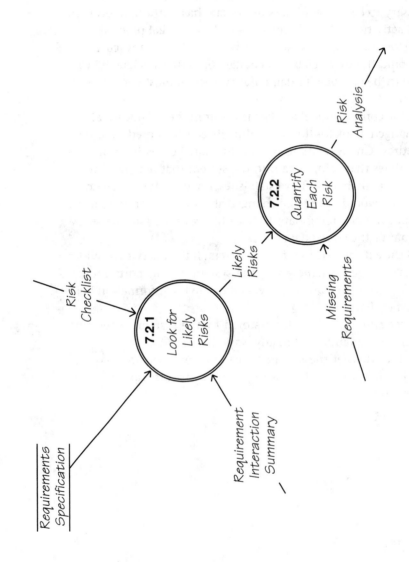

Diagram 7.2 Evaluate Requirements Risk

Look for Likely Risks (Process Notes 7.2.1)

This task looks for all the risks that could potentially affect your project. The completeness of the requirements specification is a powerful indicator of likely risks. There is nothing wrong with having risks, provided you look for them, define them, and monitor them. The real problems come when people deny the risks and then get a nasty surprise when a concealed risk turns into a problem.

Many risk checklists have been produced by researchers; some of these are suggested in the bibliography in this book. Use one of these checklists as your starting point and add new risks as you encounter them.

For each risk on the checklist, review your requirements specification to see whether there is any indication of this risk. For instance, one of the risks on your checklist might be inadequate customer involvement. Does anything in your requirements specification indicate that you have this risk? Suppose that in the section on user participation requirements, you see that specific user names and roles have not been specified. This omission indicates a likely risk. If you can't specify who will be involved, then it's likely that no one will be available when needed for the project.

For each requirement in your specification, if the requirement measurement is not specified, then it is an indication of a likely risk. Can you think of anything that might go wrong with analyzing, designing, and/or implementing a solution to this requirement? If your answer is yes, then you have discovered a likely risk.

If you discover a risk for a requirement, then dependent requirements will probably be affected by the same risk.

Quantify Each Risk (Process Notes 7.2.2)

This task does a detailed assessment of the likely risks. Quantify each one of these risks by specifying the following risk elements, as defined by Tim Lister and Tom DeMarco:

- Risk Number: To monitor and communicate the state of the risk.
- Risk Description: One sentence describing what problem might occur (e.g., we might need to involve users from an external organization).
- Risk Weight: Number of function points involved in this risk (e.g., 200 function points).
- Risk Probability: Percentage probability of this risk materializing (e.g., 30 percent based on what we know after specifying the requirements).
- Risk Cost: Estimated cost associated with this risk materializing (e.g., $100,000).

- Risk Schedule Impact: Estimated effect on the schedule (e.g., +3 months, +6 months).

- First Indication (e.g., none of the stakeholders within our organization is prepared to define the requirements for value-based investment).

Look at each missing requirement and ask this question: Is this type of requirement relevant within the system, and would I expect to have this requirement specified? For instance, in a safety-critical system you would expect to have a detailed specification of requirements that relate to damage to people and property, whereas in an inventory control system it would be reasonable for this type of requirement to be absent. If you determine that a relevant requirement is missing, then quantify it as a risk and add it to the risk analysis.

The resulting risk analysis contains an assessment of all the risks that you have identified as a result of reviewing your requirement specification.

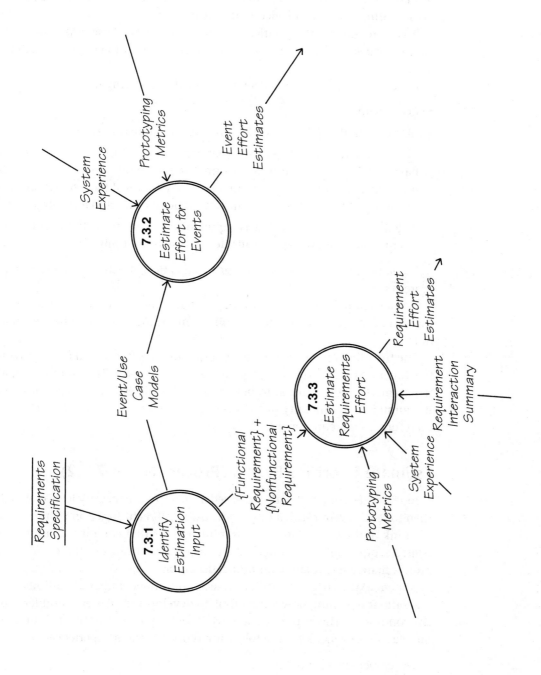

Diagram 7.3 Estimate Effort

Identify Estimation Input (Process Notes 7.3.1)

Each of your requirements that has passed through the Quality Gateway will contain a measurement. You can use your measurable requirements as input to estimating the effort needed to do the project.

If your requirements specification includes events or use cases, then you have manageable chunks that you can use as the input to your effort estimation.

For each event/use case you should have the following items:

● Event name.

● All functional requirements that are connected by this event.

● All nonfunctional requirements that are connected by this event. If you have not identified the nonfunctional requirements, then you can still make an estimate based on events. However, you will have to use an estimated weighting to assess the impact of the nonfunctional requirements.

● A definition of all data that is input to or output from the event. This might come from the world outside the system or it might be stored data.

If you have an event description or specification, it will make the estimate more accurate.

If your requirements specification does not include events or use cases, then you can use the individual requirements as input to your effort estimation.

Use the functional requirements to estimate the effort based on the essential functions and data within your context of study. The nonfunctional requirements provide input to help you weight the estimates depending on the number and difficulty of the nonfunctional requirements that relate to each functional requirement.

Estimate Effort for Events (Process Notes 7.3.2)

If you have described all of the required inputs to the necessary level of detail, then for each event estimate the effort using Albrecht function points.

Think of the events/use cases as mini-systems that combine a number of related requirements. Throughout the project, you can use the events as a project management and communication tool.

System experience from other projects run under similar conditions provides input regarding how long it took to develop a similar event under similar conditions. This input, if you have it, helps you to weight the estimates more accurately. Look for the following types of system experience:

● Developer experience

● Management experience

- Stakeholder experience
- Experience with the intended technology

If you have built any prototypes, then you can use the prototyping metrics as input when estimating the effort necessary for similar events within the system.

Event effort estimates = {event name + estimated function points}
+ total estimated function points for all events
+ estimate of what effort a function point means in this environment

According to Capers Jones, the U.S. industry average is $1,000 per implemented function point.

Estimate Requirements Effort (Process Notes 7.3.3)

You would use this approach if you have not identified event-related clusters of requirements. Estimate the effort using Albrecht function points. System experience from other projects run under similar conditions provides input regarding how long it took to develop a similar event under similar conditions. This input, if you have it, helps you to weight the estimates more accurately. Look for the following types of system experience:

- Developer experience
- Management experience
- Stakeholder experience
- Experience with the intended technology

If you have built any prototypes, then you can use the prototyping metrics as input when estimating the effort necessary for similar events within the system.

Requirement effort estimates = {requirement ID + estimated function points}
+ total estimated function points for all requirements
+ estimate of what effort a function point means in this environment

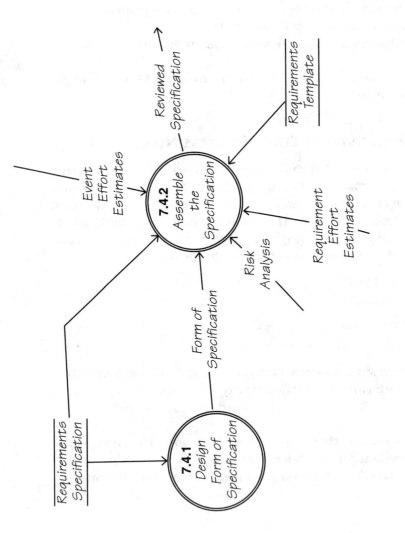

Diagram 7.4   Publish Reviewed Specification

Design Form of Specification (Process Notes 7.4.1)

This task designs the media that you will use to communicate the contents of the requirements specification. The most commonly used approach is to print the specification on paper. Today's technology provides some other alternatives:

- PDF document
- Web page
- A Lotus Notes document

The design of the specification form (typeface, colors, graphics, indexing) makes a great deal of difference to whether anyone will be able to, or will want to, read it. Consider the idea of using a graphic designer to advise you on the form of your specification.

Assemble the Specification (Process Notes 7.4.2)

When you assemble the specification. make sure that you make it easy for the reader to find his way around.

Use the requirements template as a guide for organizing the specification. Add an index.

Dictionary of Terms Used in the Requirements Process Model

Accepted Requirement
  [Functional Requirement |
  Nonfunctional Requirement |
  Project Constraint]
  A requirement that has passed through the Quality Gateway and will be included in the requirements specification.

Actor Name
  An actor is a human being (usually), a job, another computer system, or another organization—anything that interacts with the product. Every use case has at least one actor.

Assumptions
  Refer to section 6 of the Volere Requirements Specification Template for more details about assumptions.

Blastoff Meeting Plan
Advice to the stakeholders on the schedule, location, and objectives for the project blastoff meeting.

Blastoff Objectives
Deliverables to be produced by the blastoff are some combination of the following depending on the Project Intention:

- Project Goals
- Work Context Model
- Identified Stakeholders
- Anticipated Developers
- System Events
- Top 10 Requirements
- Event/Use Case Models
- System Terminology
- Scenario Models

Blastoff Participants
Name and contact details for each person who is invited to attend the project blastoff meeting.

Blastoff Report
Report describing what was accomplished by the blastoff meeting.

Business Documents
Reports, forms, specifications, user manuals—any document that might contain requirements buried in its depths.

Business Event
Business Event Name
+ (Event Input + Adjacent System Name)
+ {Event Output + Adjacent System Name}
The work context boundaries of a business event.

Business Event Boundary
Event Name
+ {Input Data Flow + Adjacent System Name}
+ {Output Data Flow + Adjacent System Name}
The boundary for studying a business event.

Business Events
{Business Event}
A list of the business events within the work context. This first-cut functional partitioning is the basis for future detailed analysis and design work. Refer to section 7 of the Volere Requirements Specification Template for more detailed information about business events.

Business Opportunities
Ideas for how the product can help to achieve the Product Purpose within the Project Constraints.

Client Name
The name of the person or organization who will pay for the development of the product.

Context Interfaces
Named interfaces between your system and the world outside your scope of study.

Contradictory Requirements
Contradictions between requirements, discovered during the requirements review.

Current Organization and Systems
Description of the people who work for the organization, their roles, their responsibilities, their interactions, and the technology that they use to do their work.

Current Situation Model
A model that describes aspects of an existing system. It usually focuses on the current partitioning of the problem and the interfaces between the pieces.

Customer Name
The name of the person(s) or organization(s) that will buy, or are expected to buy, the product.

Customer Value Ratings
Customer satisfaction on a scale from 1 to 5:
1 = Quite happy if this requirement is satisfactorily implemented
5 = Very happy if this requirement is satisfactorily implemented

Customer dissatisfaction on a scale from 1 to 5:
1 = Slightly perturbed if this requirement is not satisfactorily implemented
5 = Extremely grumpy if this requirement is not satisfactorily
    implemented

Domain Models
Models that capture the essence of a particular area of subject matter.

Event Effort Estimates
Estimated effort in implementing a solution to a use case/event.

Event for Prototyping
Produced when we suspect that building a prototype might lead to a better
understanding of the requirements for this event or the discovery of other
requirements.

Event/Use Case Model
Event Name + {Functional Requirement}
+ {Nonfunctional Requirement}
+ Event Input
+ Event Output
+ (Event Description)
A model that isolates the effect of one event/use case on the processes and
data within the context of a system.

Event/Use Case Models
{Event/Use Case Model}

Existing Documents
Reports, forms, specifications, user manuals—any document that might
contain requirements buried in its depths.

Fit Reviewed Requirement
Description of Requirement
+ Purpose of Requirement
+ Requirement Source
+ Requirement Type
+ Unique Identifier for a Requirement
+ Requirement Fit Criteria
+ Customer Satisfaction
+ Customer Dissatisfaction
+ Requirement Dependencies
+ Requirement History

Formalized Requirement
[Functional Requirement |
Nonfunctional Requirement]
A potential requirement that has been formally written according to the guidelines in the Volere Requirements Specification Template.

Formalized System Constraint
System Constraints
A system constraint that has been formally written according to the guidelines in the Volere Requirements Specification Template.

Functional Requirement
Requirement
Refer to section 9 of the Volere Requirements Specification Template for more details.

Go/No-Go Decision
Recommendation based on blastoff results regarding whether to proceed with the project plus the reason for that recommendation.

Gold-Plated Requirement
A requirement that is not essential to solving the stated business objectives.

Group Comments
Retrospective comments made by the group.

High-Fidelity Prototype
An automated prototype.

Identified Stakeholders
Client Name
+ {Customer Name}
+ Sponsor Name
+ {User Group}
+ {Developer}
+ {Domain Expert}
+ {Technical Expert}
People who have been identified to have an interest in the product and whose input is required during requirements gathering. Refer to sections 2 and 3 of the Volere Requirements Template for more detailed information on stakeholders.

Individual Comments
Retrospective comments made by an individual. There might be a need to keep these confidential.

Initial Estimate
First-cut estimate of the effort required to build the system.

Input from Groups
Input from groups collected by the facilitator.

Input from Individuals
Input from individuals collected by the facilitator.

Intended Operating Environment
Details of the environment in which the product will be installed.

Intended Operating Environment Description
A detailed description of the hardware, software, people, and environmental factors under which the product must operate.

Knowledge Sources
Any person, place, organization, or document that contains or might contain knowledge about the work within the work context.

Low-Fidelity Prototype
A non-automated prototype usually built using some combination of graphic models, screen layouts, and written examples.

Major Risks
A blitzed list of the major risks associated with building the product.

Meeting Location
Address of the place at which the project blastoff meeting will be held.

Meeting Schedule
Time(s) and date(s) for which the project blastoff meeting is scheduled.

Missing Requirements
Requirements types that should be included.

Nonfunctional Requirement
Requirement
Refer to sections 10–17 of the Volere Requirements Specification Template for more details about nonfunctional requirements.

Objective of Prototype

Why we are building the prototype; what we expect to gain; what are the questions to which we require answers.

Points for Clarification

Meetings with individuals sometimes raise questions that the facilitator needs to clarify when meeting with groups.

Retrospective Comments

Individual Comments
+ Project Participant Comments
+ Group Comments

Retrospective Report

A report whose purpose is to communicate noteworthy experiences of the project in a form that is usable by other people.

Potential Requirement

A need that has been discovered as a result of learning the work. It might turn out to be a requirement but we will not be sure until it has been formalized and has passed through the Quality Gateway.

Potential Stakeholders

A list of people considered to have an interest in the project.

Product Scope

Use Case
+ {Business Event Name}

Project Constraint

Refer to section 6 of the Volere Requirements Specification Template for more details.

Project Constraints

Constraints on the way that the product must be produced:

- Technology to be used (or not used)
- Budget
- Time
- Operating environment

Project History

Project Plans + Project Progress History + Specification Changes

Project Intention
Guidelines from the customer:

- Product desired from the project
- Anticipated budget
- Technological constraints
- Problem the product is intended to solve
- Anticipated scope
- Reasons for doing the project

Project Participant Comments
Comments made by participants at the retrospective meeting

Project Purpose
Business problem(s) that this product is intended to solve plus criteria for determining whether the objective(s) have been met. Refer to section 1 of the Volere Requirements Specification Template for more details about project purpose.

Prototype Building Effort
Time to Build Prototype
+ Context of Prototype
+ Form of Prototype

Prototypes
{[Low-Fidelity Prototype | High-Fidelity Prototype]
+ Prototyping Metrics}

Prototyping Metrics
Context of Prototype
+ Number of Function Points
+ Form of Prototype
+ Time to Build Prototype
+ Problems Experienced
+ Lessons Learned
Measurements of how long it took to build a particular prototype within a particular environment.

Prototyping Opportunity
Context of Prototype
+ Objective of Prototype
+ Interested Stakeholders
+ {Requirement}

Prototyping Plan
Context of Prototype
+ Objective of Prototype
+ Interested Stakeholders
+ [Low-Fidelity Prototype | High-Fidelity Prototype]
+ Existing Prototypes
+ Prototyping Tool

Quantified Findings
The result of the facilitator reviewing all comments from individuals and from groups.

Rejected Requirement
A requirement or constraint that has failed to pass through the Quality Gateway.

Relevance Reviewed Requirement
A requirement that has passed the Quality Gateway's relevance test.

Relevant Facts
Refer to section 5 of the Volere Requirements Specification Template for more details.

Required Facilities
All the physical arrangements necessary to satisfy the Blastoff Objectives, including:

- Accommodations
- Stationery
- Catering
- Equipment

Requirement
Requirement Number
+ Requirement Type
+ {Use Case Number}
+ Requirement Description
+ Requirement Rationale
+ Requirement Source
+ Fit Criteria
+ Customer Satisfaction
+ Customer Dissatisfaction
+ {Requirement Dependency}

+ {Requirement Conflict}
+ Supporting Materials
+ Requirement History

This identifies all components of a complete functional or nonfunctional requirement. The components are gradually added during the process of trawling for knowledge and writing the requirements.

Requirement Interaction Summary

Lists interactions between requirements. Two requirements interact if a design solution to one of them makes it more difficult (or easier) to do anything about the other. Identifying requirement interaction at the specification stage provides input when evaluating requirements risk and estimating effort.

Requirement Measurement

Description of Requirement
+ Purpose of Requirement
+ Requirement Type
+ Unique Identifier for a Requirement
+ Requirement Fit Criteria
+ Customer Satisfaction
+ Customer Dissatisfaction

Requirement Questions

Outstanding questions that prevent a project blastoff from being considered complete or that prevent a requirement or constraint from passing through the Quality Gateway. Contains everything that is currently known about the requirement or constraint.

Requirement Type

[Functional | Nonfunctional]

Requirements

{Requirement}

Requirements Filter

A tool for assessing the completeness of a requirements specification.

Requirements Skeleton

Product Purpose
+ Work Context
+ Identified Stakeholders
+ Business Events

+ System Terminology
+ Initial Estimate
+ Major Risks
+ Project Constraints
+ Intended Operating Environment Description
Used to keep track of the knowledge discovered during the blastoff.

Requirements Specification
    Product Purpose
    + Product Context
    + Identified Stakeholders
    + {Use Case}
    + System Terminology
    + {Functional Requirement}
    + {Nonfunctional Requirement}
    + {Project Constraint}
    + Assumptions
    + Relevant Facts
    + Project Issues
    + Requirement Interaction Summary

Requirements Template
    Template for a requirements specification. See the example Volere Requirements Specification Template.

Reusable Requirement
    A requirement that has been put into the Reuse Library because it is considered to be a candidate for reuse.

Reuse Library
    {Reusable Requirement}
    A collection of potentially reusable requirements.

Reviewed Specification
    Requirements Specification
    + Risk Analysis
    + Effort Estimates

Risk Analysis
    Detailed assessment of all risks identified by doing a risk analysis of the requirements specification.

Risk Checklist
Risk checklists produced by researchers such as Capers Jones and Barry Boehm.

Stakeholder Wants and Needs
Functional requirements, nonfunctional requirements, and constraints that the stakeholders want the system to have.

Strategic Plan for Product
Product management's input into the constraints that apply to the product. External influences might cause this plan to change during the course of the requirements specification.

System Constraints
Product Purpose
+ Identified Stakeholders
+ Business Events
+ System Terminology
+ Project Constraints
+ Relevant Facts
+ Assumptions

System Experience
Relevant experience of the stakeholders in building similar products, using similar technology, dealing with similar problems, and/or working in a similar environment.

System Terminology
Definitions of the terms that people use for data within the context of this project. Refer to section 4 of the Volere Requirements Specification Template for more details.

Trawling Techniques
A variety of techniques used by requirements engineers and business analysts for discovering requirements.

Usage Feedback
User comments, new requirements, and requirements changes as a result of using a prototype.

Use Case
Use Case Name
+ {Actor Name}
+ Use Case Boundary Data

User Group
    User Group Name
    + User Group Skills

Work Context
    A summary of the parts of the world that we intend to study to satisfy the
    system objectives. The model shows the adjacent systems (square boxes),
    our specific interest in each adjacent system (interfaces), and the intersec-
    tions of those adjacent systems (context process). Refer to section 8 of the
    Volere Requirements Specification Template for more detailed informa-
    tion about the work context.

Work Description and Demonstration
    Current Organization and Systems
    + Business Documents
    + Stakeholder Experience

Work Knowledge
    Work Context
    +Business Documents
    + Market Surveys
    + Job Descriptions
    + Company Reports
    + Current Organization and Systems
    + Stakeholder Experience
    + {Business Event Boundary + Knowledge Sources + Trawling Techniques}
    + {Potential Requirement}
    + Event Models
    + System Terminology
    + Data Models
    + Scenario Models
    Any artifact that contains knowledge about the subjects within the con-
    text of the work.

Volere Requirements Specification Template

a guide for writing a rigorous and complete requirements specification

Contents

Preamble

The first edition of the Volere Requirements Specification Template was released in 1995. Since then, organizations from all over the world (see experiences of Volere users at *www.volere.co.uk*) have saved time and money by using the template as the basis for discovering, organizing, and communicating their requirements.

Please be aware this template is copyright © The Atlantic Systems Guild Limited, and is intended to form the basis of your requirements specification. It may not be sold or used for commercial gain or other purposes without prior written permission. Please include the copyright notice in all uses.

Updates to this template are posted on our Web sites at *www.systemsguild.com* and *www.volere.co.uk*.

Volere

Volere is the result of many years of practice, consulting, and research in requirements engineering. We have packaged our experience in the form of a generic requirements process, requirements training, requirements consultancy, requirements audits, a variety of downloadable guides, and this requirements template. We also provide requirements specification writing services.

Public seminars on Volere are run on a regular basis in Europe, the United States, Australia, and New Zealand. For a schedule of courses, refer to www.systemsguild.com.

Requirements Types

For ease of use, we have found it convenient to think of requirements as belonging to a type.

Functional requirements are the fundamental or essential subject matter of the product. They describe what the product has to do or what processing actions it is to take.

Nonfunctional requirements are the properties that the functions must have, such as performance and usability. Do not be deterred by the unfortunate name (we use it because it is the most common way of referring to these types of requirements)—these requirements are as important as the functional requirements for the product's success.

Project constraints are restrictions on the product due to the budget or the time available to build the product.

Design constraints impose restrictions on how the product must be designed. For example, it might have to be implemented in the hand-held device being given to major customers, or it might have to use the existing servers and desktop computers, or any other hardware, software, or business practice.

Project drivers are the business-related forces. For example, the purpose of the project is a project driver, as are all of the stakeholders—each for different reasons.

Project issues define the conditions under which the project will be done. Our reason for including them as part of the requirements is to present a coherent picture of all factors that contribute to the success or failure of the project and to illustrate how managers can use requirements as input when managing a project.

Testing Requirements

Start testing requirements as soon as you start writing them.

You make a requirement testable by adding its *fit criterion*. This fit criterion measures the requirement, making it possible to determine whether a given solution fits the requirement. If a fit criterion cannot be found for a requirement, then the requirement is either ambiguous or poorly understood. All requirements can be measured, and all should carry a fit criterion.

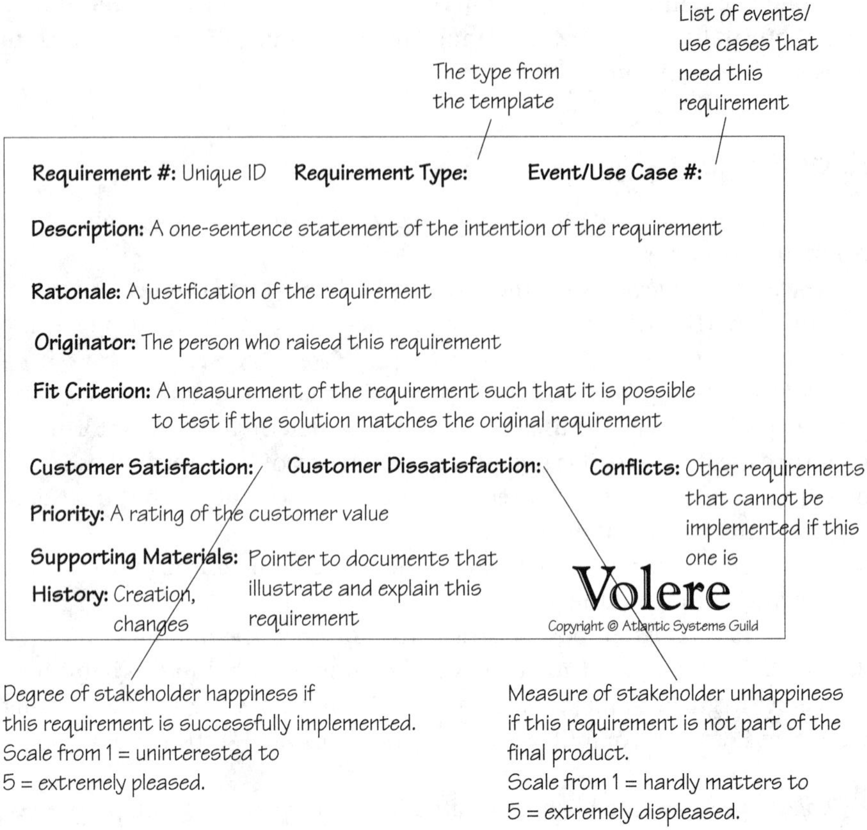

Figure B.1

The Volere Shell is a convenient way of ensuring you have all the components to make a complete requirement. This shell can, and should, be automated.

The type from the template

List of events/ use cases that need this requirement

Requirement #: Unique ID   **Requirement Type:**   **Event/Use Case #:**

Description: A one-sentence statement of the intention of the requirement

Ratonale: A justification of the requirement

Originator: The person who raised this requirement

Fit Criterion: A measurement of the requirement such that it is possible
to test if the solution matches the original requirement

Customer Satisfaction: **Customer Dissatisfaction:**   **Conflicts:** Other requirements
that cannot be
implemented if this
one is

Priority: A rating of the customer value

Supporting Materials: Pointer to documents that

History: Creation,   illustrate and explain this
changes   requirement

Volere

Copyright © Atlantic Systems Guild

Degree of stakeholder happiness if
this requirement is successfully implemented.
Scale from 1 = uninterested to
5 = extremely pleased.

Measure of stakeholder unhappiness
if this requirement is not part of the
final product.
Scale from 1 = hardly matters to
5 = extremely displeased.

Requirements Shell

The requirements shell is a guide to writing each atomic requirement (see Figure B.1). The components of the shell (also called a "snow card") are discussed fully in Chapter 10, Writing the Requirements.

1   The Purpose of the Project

1a   The User Business or Background of the Project Effort

Content

Content, Motivation, Examples, and Considerations
A short description of the business being done, its context, and the situation that triggered the development effort. It should also describe the work that the user intends to do with the delivered product.

Motivation

Without this statement, the project lacks justification and direction.

Considerations

You should consider whether the user problem is serious, and whether and why it needs to be solved.

1b   Goals of the Project

Content

This boils down to one sentence, or at most a few sentences, that say why we want this product. Here is where you state the real reason the product is being developed.

Motivation

There is a danger that this purpose may get lost along the way. As the development effort heats up, and as the customer and developers discover more about what is possible, the system could potentially wander away from the original goals as it undergoes construction. This is a bad thing unless there is some deliberate act by the client to change the goals. It may be necessary to appoint a person to be custodian of the goals, but it is probably sufficient to make the goals public and periodically remind the developers of them. *It should be mandatory to acknowledge the goals at every review session.*

Examples

We want to give immediate and complete response to customers who order our goods over the telephone.

We want to be able to forecast the weather.

Measurement

Any reasonable goal must be measurable. This is necessary if you are ever to test whether you have succeeded with the project. The measurement must quantify the *advantage* gained by the business through doing the project. If the project is worthwhile, there must be some solid business reason for doing it. For example, if the goal of the project is

We want to give immediate and complete response to customers who order our goods over the telephone.

you have to ask what advantage that goal brings to the organization. If immediate response will result in more satisfied customers, then the measurement must quantify that satisfaction. For example, you could measure the increase in repeat business (on the basis that a happy customer comes back for more), the increase in customer approval ratings from surveys, the increase in revenue from returning customers, and so on.

It is crucial to the rest of the development effort that the goal is firmly established, is reasonable, and is measured. It is usually the latter that makes the former possible.

2 The Client, the Customer, and Other Stakeholders

2a The Client

Content

This item gives the name of the client. It is permissible to have several names, but having more than three negates the point.

Motivation

The client has the final say on acceptance of the product, and thus must be satisfied with the product as delivered. You can think of the client as the person who makes the investment in the product. Where the product is being developed for in-house consumption, the roles of the client and the customer are often filled by the same person. If you cannot find a name for your client, then perhaps you should not be building the product.

Considerations

Sometimes, when building a package or a product for external users, the client is the marketing department. In this case, a person from the marketing department must be named as the client.

2b The Customer

Content

The person intended to buy the product. In the case of in-house development, the client and the customer are often the same person. In the case of development of a mass-market product, this section contains a description of the kind of person who is likely to buy the product.

Motivation

The customer is ultimately responsible for deciding whether to buy the product from the client. The correct requirements can be gathered only if you understand the customer and his aspirations when it comes to using your product.

2c Other Stakeholders

Content

The roles and (if possible) names of other people and organizations who are affected by the product, or whose input is needed to build the product.

Examples of stakeholders:

- Sponsor
- Testers
- Business analysts
- Technology experts
- System designers
- Marketing experts
- Legal experts
- Domain experts
- Usability experts
- Representatives of external associations

For a complete checklist, download the stakeholder analysis template at *www.volere.co.uk*.

For each type of stakeholder, provide the following information:

- Stakeholder identification (some combination of role/job title, person name, and organization name)
- Knowledge needed by the project
- The degree of involvement necessary for that stakeholder/knowledge combination
- The degree of influence for that stakeholder/knowledge combination
- Agreement on how to address conflicts between stakeholders who have an interest in the same knowledge

Motivation

Failure to recognize stakeholders results in missing requirements.

3 Users of the Product

3a The Hands-On Users of the Product

Content

A list of a special type of stakeholder—the potential users of the product. For each category of user, provide the following information:

- User name/category: Most likely the name of a user group, such as schoolchildren, road engineers, or project managers.
- User role: Summarizes the users' responsibilities.
- Subject matter experience: Summarizes the users' knowledge of the business. Rate as novice, journeyman, or master.
- Technological experience: Describes the users' experience with relevant technology. Rate as novice, journeyman, or master.
- Other user characteristics: Describe any characteristics of the users that have an effect on the requirements and eventual design of the product. For example:
  - Physical abilities/disabilities
  - Intellectual abilities/disabilities
  - Attitude toward job
  - Attitude toward technology
  - Education
  - Linguistic skills
  - Age group
  - Gender

Motivation

Users are human beings who interface with the product in some way. Use the characteristics of the users to define the usability requirements for the product. Users are also known as actors.

Examples

Users can come from wide variety of (sometimes unexpected) sources. Consider the possibility of your users being clerical staff, shop workers, managers, highly trained operators, the general public, casual users, passers-by, illiterate people, tradesmen, students, test engineers, foreigners, children, lawyers, remote users, people using the system over the telephone or an Internet connection, emergency workers, and so on.

3b   Priorities Assigned to Users

Content

Attach a priority to each category of user. This gives the importance and precedence of the user. Prioritize the users as follows:

- Key users: They are critical to the continued success of the product. Give greater importance to requirements generated by this category of user.
- Secondary users: They will use the product, but their opinion of it has no effect on its long-term success. Where there is a conflict between secondary users' requirements and those of key users, the key users take precedence.

- Unimportant users: This category of user is given the lowest priority. It includes infrequent, unauthorized, and unskilled users, as well as people who misuse the product.

The percentage of the type of user is intended to assess the amount of consideration given to each category of user.

Motivation

If some users are considered to be more important to the product or to the organization, then this preference should be stated because it should affect the way that you design the product. For instance, you need to know if there is a large customer group who has specifically asked for the product, and for which, if they do not get what they want, the results could be a significant loss of business.

Some users may be listed as having no impact on the product. These users will make use of the product, but have no vested interest in it. In other words, these users will not complain, nor will they contribute. Any special requirements from these users will have a lower design priority.

3c   User Participation

Content

Where appropriate, attach to the category of user a statement of the participation that you think will be necessary for those users to provide the requirements. Describe the contribution that you expect these users to provide—for example, business knowledge, interface prototyping, or usability requirements. If possible, assess the minimum amount of time that these users must spend for you to be able to determine the complete requirements.

Motivation

Many projects fail through lack of user participation, sometimes because the required degree of participation was not made clear. When people have to make a choice between getting their everyday work done and working on a new project, the everyday work usually takes priority. This requirement makes it clear, from the outset, that specified user resources must be allocated to the project.

3d   Maintenance Users and Service Technicians

Content

Maintenance users are a special type of hands-on users who have requirements that are specific to maintaining and changing the product.

Motivation

Many of these requirements will be discovered by considering the various types of maintenance requirements detailed in section 14. However, if we define the characteristics of the people who maintain the product, it will help to trigger requirements that might otherwise be missed.

4   Mandated Constraints

This section describes constraints on the eventual design of the product. They are the same as other requirements except that constraints are mandated, usually at the beginning of the project. Constraints have a description, rationale, and fit criterion, and generally are written in the same format as functional and nonfunctional requirements.

4a   Solution Constraints

Content

This specifies constraints on the way that the problem must be solved. Describe the mandated technology or solution. Include any appropriate version numbers. You should also explain the reason for using the technology.

Motivation

To identify constraints that guide the final product. Your client, customer, or user may have design preferences, or only certain solutions may be acceptable. If these constraints are not met, your solution is not acceptable.

Examples

Constraints are written using the same form as other atomic requirements (refer to the requirements shell for the attributes). It is important for each constraint to have a rationale and a fit criterion, as they help to expose false constraints (solutions masquerading as constraints). Also, you will usually find that a constraint affects the entire product rather than one or more product use cases.

Description: The product shall use the current two-way radio system to communicate with the drivers in their trucks.

Rationale: The client will not pay for a new radio system, nor are any other means of communication available to the drivers.

Fit Criterion: All signals generated by the product shall be audible and understandable by all drivers via their two-way radio system.

Description: The product shall operate using Windows XP.

Rationale: The client uses XP and does not wish to change.

Fit Criterion: The product shall be approved as XP compliant by the MS testing group.

Description: The product shall be a hand-held device.

Rationale: The product is to be marketed to hikers and mountain climbers.

Fit Criterion: The product shall weigh no more than 300 grams, no dimension shall be more than 15 centimeters, and there shall be no external power source.

Considerations

We want to define the boundaries within which we can solve the problem. Be careful, because anyone who has experience with or exposure to a piece of technology tends to see requirements in terms of that technology. This tendency leads people to impose solution constraints for the wrong reason, making it very easy for false constraints to creep into a specification. The solution constraints should only be those that are absolutely non-negotiable. In other words, however you solve this problem, you must use this particular technology. Any other solution would be unacceptable.

4b   Implementation Environment of the Current System

Content

This describes the technological and physical environment in which the product is to be installed. It includes automated, mechanical, organizational, and other devices, along with the nonhuman adjacent systems.

Motivation

To describe the technological environment into which the product must fit. The environment places design constraints on the product. This part of the specification provides enough information about the environment for the designers to make the product successfully interact with its surrounding technology.

The operational requirements are derived from this description.

Examples

Examples can be shown as a diagram, with some kind of icon to represent each separate device or person (processor). Draw arrows to identify the interfaces between the processors, and annotate them with their form and content.

Considerations

All component parts of the current system, regardless of their type, should be included in the description of the implementation environment.

If the product is to affect, or be important to, the current organization, then include an organization chart.

4c   Partner or Collaborative Applications

Content

This describes applications that are not part of the product but with which the product will collaborate. They can be external applications, commercial packages, or preexisting in-house applications.

Motivation

To provide information about design constraints caused by using partner applications. By describing or modeling these partner applications, you discover and highlight potential problems of integration.

Examples

This section can be completed by including written descriptions, models, or references to other specifications. The descriptions must include a full specification of all interfaces that have an effect on the product.

Considerations

Examine the work context model to determine whether any of the adjacent systems should be treated as partner applications. It might also be necessary to examine some of the details of the work to discover relevant partner applications.

4d   Off-the-Shelf Software

Content

This describes commercial, open source, or any other off-the-shelf software (OTS) that must be used to implement some of the requirements for the product. It could also apply to nonsoftware OTS components such as hardware or any other commercial product that is intended as part of the solution.

Motivation

To identify and describe existing commercial, free, open source, or other products to be incorporated into the eventual product. The characteristics, behavior, and interfaces of the package are design constraints.

Examples

This section can be completed by including written descriptions, models, or references to supplier's specifications.

Considerations

When gathering requirements, you may discover requirements that conflict with the behavior and characteristics of the OTS software. Keep in mind that the use of OTS software was mandated before the full extent of the requirements became known. In light of your discoveries, you must consider whether the OTS product is a viable choice. If the use of the OTS software is not negotiable, then the conflicting requirements must be discarded.

Note that your strategy for discovering requirements is affected by the decision to use OTS software. In this situation you investigate the work context in parallel with making comparisons with the capabilities of the OTS product. Depending on the comprehensibility of the OTS software, you might be able to discover the matches or mismatches without having to write each of the business requirements in atomic detail. The mismatches are the requirements that you will need to specify so that you can decide whether to satisfy them by either modifying the OTS software or modifying the business requirements.

Given the spate of lawsuits in the software arena, you should consider whether any legal implications might arise from your use of OTS. You can cover this in section 17, Legal Requirements.

4e Anticipated Workplace Environment

Content

This describes the workplace in which the users are to work and use the product. It should describe any features of the workplace that could have an effect on the design of the product, and the social and culture of the workplace.

Motivation

To identify characteristics of the workplace so that the product is designed to compensate for any difficulties.

Examples

The printer is a considerable distance from the user's desk. This constraint suggests that printed output should be deemphasized.

The workplace is noisy, so audible signals might not work.

The workplace is outside, so the product must be weather resistant, have displays that are visible in sunlight, and allow for the effect of wind on any paper output.

The product is to be used in a library; it must be extra quiet.

The product is a photocopier to be used by an environmentally conscious organization; it must work with recycled paper.

The user will be standing up or working in positions where he must hold the product. This suggests a hand-held product, but only a careful study of the users' work and workplace will provide the necessary input to identifying the operational requirements.

Considerations

The physical work environment constrains the way that work is done. The product should overcome whatever difficulties exist; however, you might consider a redesign of the workplace as an alternative to having the product compensate for it.

4f   Schedule Constraints

Content

Any known deadlines, or windows of opportunity, should be stated here.

Motivation

To identify critical times and dates that have an effect on product requirements. If the deadline is short, then the requirements must be kept to whatever can be built within the time allowed.

Examples

- To meet scheduled software releases.
- There may be other parts of the business or other software products that are dependent on this product.
- Windows of marketing opportunity.
- Scheduled changes to the business that will use your product. For example, the organization may be starting up a new factory and your product is needed before production can commence.

Considerations

State deadline limitations by giving the date and describing why it is critical. Also, identify prior dates where parts of your product need to be available for testing.

You should also ask questions about the impact of not meeting the deadline:

- What happens if we don't build the product by the end of the calendar year?
- What is the financial impact of not having the product by the beginning of the Christmas buying season?

4g   Budget Constraints

Content

The budget for the project, expressed in money or available resources.

Motivation

The requirements must not exceed the budget. This limitation may constrain the number of requirements that can be included in the product.

   The intention of this question is to determine whether the product is really wanted.

Considerations

Is it realistic to build a product within this budget? If the answer to this question is no, then either the client is not really committed to building the product or the client does not place enough value on the product. In either case you should consider whether it is worthwhile continuing.

5   Naming Conventions and Definitions

5a   Definitions of All Terms, Including Acronyms, Used in the Project

Content

A glossary containing the meanings of all names, acronyms, and abbreviations used within the requirements specification. Select names carefully to avoid giving a different, unintended meaning.

   This glossary reflects the terminology in current use within the work area. You might also build on the standard names used within your industry.

   For each term, write a succinct definition. The appropriate stakeholders must agree on this definition.

   Avoid abbreviations, as they introduce ambiguity, require additional translations, and could potentially lead to misinterpretation in the mind of anyone who is trying to understand your requirements. Ask your requirements analysts to replace all abbreviations with the correct term. This is easily done with word processors.

   Acronyms are acceptable if they are completely explained by a definition.

Motivation

Names are very important. They invoke meanings that, if carefully defined, can save hours of explanations. Attention to names at this stage of the project helps to highlight misunderstandings.

The glossary produced during requirements is used and extended throughout the project.

Examples

Truck: A vehicle used for spreading de-icing material on roads. "Truck" is not used to refer to goods-carrying vehicles.

BIS: Business Intelligence Service. The department run by Steven Peters to supply business intelligence for the rest of the organization.

Considerations

Make use of existing references and data dictionaries. Obviously, it is best to avoid renaming existing items unless they are so ambiguous that they cause confusion.

From the beginning of the project, emphasize the need to avoid homonyms and synonyms. Explain how they increase the cost of the project.

5b   Data Dictionary for Any Included Models

Content

Dictionary definitions of all information flows and stores used in models. Particular consideration should be given to defining the data attributes of all flows shown the context models (see sections 7 and 8).

This section should also contain any technical specifications for interfaces shown on the context models.

Motivation

The context diagram provides an accurate definition of the scope of the work being studied or the scope of the product to be built. This definition can be completely accurate only if the information flows bordering the scope have their attributes defined.

Examples

Road de-icing schedule = issue number + {road section identifier + treatment start time + critical start time + truck identifier} + depot identifier

As you progress through the requirements specification, define each of the elementary terms in detail.

Considerations

The dictionary provides a link between the requirements analysts and the implementers. The implementers add implementation details to the terms in the dictionary, defining how the data will be implemented. Also, implementers add terms that are present because of the chosen technology and that are independent of the business requirements.

6   Relevant Facts and Assumptions

6a   Facts

Content

Factors that have an effect on the product, but are not mandated requirements constraints. They could be business rules, organizational systems, or any other activities that have an effect on this product. Facts are things you want the reader of the specification to know.

Motivation

Relevant facts provide background information to the specification readers, and might contribute to requirements. They will have an effect on the eventual design of the product.

Examples

One ton of de-icing material will treat three miles of single-lane roadway.

The existing application is 10,000 lines of C code.

6b   Assumptions

Content

A list of the assumptions that the developers are making. These assumptions might be about the intended operational environment, but can be about anything that has an effect on the product. As part of managing expectations, assumptions also contain statements about what the product will *not* do.

Motivation

To make people declare the assumptions that they are making. Also, to make everyone on the project aware of assumptions that have already been made.

Examples

- Assumptions about new laws or political decisions.
- Assumptions about what your developers expect to be ready in time for them to use—for example, other parts of your products, the completion of other projects, software tools, or software components.
- Assumptions about the technological environment in which the product will operate. These assumptions should highlight areas of expected compatibility.
- The software components that will be available to the developers.
- Other products being developed at the same time as this one.
- The availability and capability of bought-in components.

- Dependencies on computer systems or people external to this project.
- The requirements that will specifically not be carried out by the product.

Considerations

We often make unconscious assumptions. It is necessary to talk to the members of the project team to discover any unconscious assumptions that they have made. Ask stakeholders (both technical and business-related) questions such as these:

- What software tools are you expecting to be available?
- Will there be any new software products?
- Are you expecting to use a current product in a new way?
- Are there any business changes you are assuming we will be able to deal with?

It is important to state these assumptions up front. You might also consider the probability of whether the assumption is correct and, where relevant, a list of alternatives if something that is assumed does not happen.

The assumptions are intended to be transient. That is, they should all be cleared by the time the specification is released—the assumption should have become either a requirement or a constraint. For example, if the assumption related to the capability of a product that is intended to be a partner product to yours, then the capability should have been proven satisfactory, and it becomes a constraint to use it. Conversely, if the bought-in product is not suitable, then it becomes a requirement for the project team to construct the needed capability.

7 The Scope of the Work

7a The Current Situation

Content

This is an analysis of the existing business processes, including the manual and automated processes that might be replaced or changed by the new product. Business analysts might already have done this investigation as part of the business case analysis for the project.

Motivation

If your project intends to make changes to an existing manual or automated system, you need to understand the effect of proposed changes. The study of the current situation provides the basis for understanding the effects of proposed changes and choosing the best alternatives.

7b   The Context of the Work

Content

The work context diagram identifies the work that you need to investigate to be able to build the product. Note that it includes more than the intended product. Unless we understand the work that the product will support, we have little chance of building a product that will fit cleanly into its environment.

The adjacent systems on the context diagram in Figure B.2 (e.g., Weather Forecasting Service) indicate other subject matter domains (systems, people, and organizations) that need to be understood. The

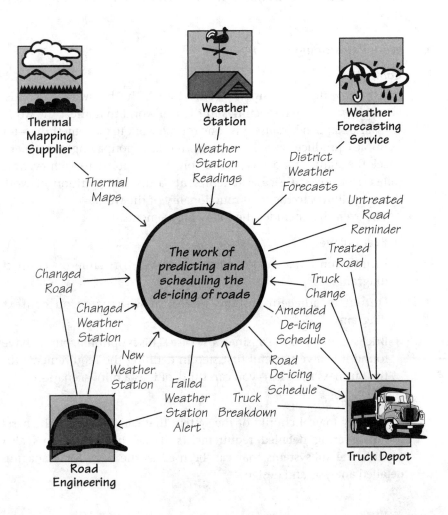

Figure B.2

This context diagram shows the scope of the work to be studied.

interfaces between the adjacent systems and the work context indicate why we are interested in the adjacent system. In the case of Weather Forecasting Service, we can say that we are interested in the details of when, how, where, who, what, and why it produces the District Weather Forecasts information.

Motivation

To clearly define the boundaries for the study of the work and requirements effort. Without this definition, we have little chance of building a product that will fit seamlessly into its environment.

Considerations

The names used on the context diagram should be consistent with the naming conventions and data dictionary definitions presented in section 5. Without these definitions, the context model lacks the required rigor, and it may be misunderstood. Relevant stakeholders must agree to the definitions of the interfaces shown on the context model.

7c   Work Partitioning

Content

A list showing all business events to which the work responds. Business events are happenings in the real world that affect the work. They also happen because it is time for the work to do something—for example, produce weekly reports, remind nonpaying customers, check the status of a device, and so on. The response to each event is called a business use case; it represents a discrete partition of work that contributes to the total functionality of the work.

The event list includes the following elements:

- Event name
- Input from adjacent systems (identical with name on context diagram)
- Output to adjacent systems (identical with name on context diagram)
- Brief summary of the business use case (This is optional, but we have found it is a very useful first step in defining the requirements for the business use case—you can think of it as a mini-scenario.)

Motivation

To identify logical chunks of the system that can be used as the basis for discovering detailed requirements. These business events also provide the subsystems that can be used as the basis for managing detailed analysis and design.

EVENT NAME	INPUT AND OUTPUT	SUMMARY
1. Weather Station transmits reading	Weather Station Readings (in)	Record the readings as belonging to the weather station.
2. Weather Service forecasts weather	District Weather Forecast (in)	Record the forecast.
3. Road engineers advise changed roads	Changed Road (in)	Record the new or changed road. Check that all appropriate weather stations are attached.
4. Road Engineering installs new Weather Station	New Weather Station (in)	Record the weather station and attach it to the appropriate roads.
5. Road Engineering changes Weather Station	Changed Weather Station (in)	Record the changes to the weather station.
6. Time to test Weather Stations	Failed Weather Station Alert (out)	Determine if any weather stations have not transmitted for two hours, and inform Road Engineering of any failures.
7. Truck Depot changes a truck	Truck Change (in)	Record the changes to the truck.
8. Time to detect icy roads	Road De-icing Schedule (out)	Predict the ice situation for the next two hours. Assign a truck to any roads that will freeze. Issue the schedule.
9. Truck treats a road	Treated Road (in)	Record the road as being in a safe condition for the next three hours.
10. Truck Depot reports problem with truck	Truck Breakdown (in) Amended Gritting Schedule (out)	Reassign available trucks to the previously assigned roads.
11. Time to monitor road treatment	Untreated Road Reminder (out)	Check that all scheduled roads have been treated in the assigned time, and issue reminders for any untreated roads.

Table B.1

Business Event List

Considerations

Attempting to list the business events is a way of testing the work context. This activity uncovers uncertainties and misunderstandings about the project and facilitates precise communications. When you do an event analysis, it will usually prompt you to make some changes to your work context diagram.

We suggest you gather requirements for discrete sections of the work. This requires you to partition the work, and we have found business events to be the most convenient, consistent, and natural way to break the work into manageable units.

8   The Scope of the Product

8a   Product Boundary

A use case diagram identifies the boundaries between the users (actors) and the product. You arrive at the product boundary by inspecting each business use case and determining, in conjunction with the appropriate stakeholders, which part of the business use case should be automated (or satisfied by some sort of product) and what part should be done by the user. This task must take into account the abilities of the actors (section 3), the constraints (section 4), the goals of the project (section 1), and your knowledge of both the work and the technology that can make the best contribution to the work.

The use case diagram (see Figure B.3) shows the actors outside the product boundary (the rectangle). The product use cases are the ellipses inside the boundary. The lines denote usage. Note that actors can be either automated or human.

Example

Derive the product use cases by deciding where the product boundary should be for each business use case. These decisions are based on your knowledge of the work and the requirements constraints.

8b   Product Use Case List

The use case diagram is a graphical way of summarizing the product use cases relevant to the product. If you have a large number of product use cases (we find 15–20 is a good limit), then it is better to make a list of the product use cases and model or describe each one individually.

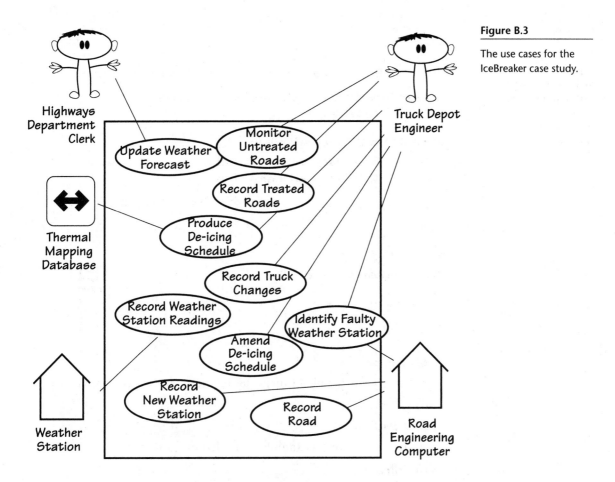

8c Individual Product Use Cases

This is where you keep details about the individual product use cases
on your list. You can include a scenario for each product use case on
your list.

9 Functional and Data Requirements

9a Functional Requirements

Content

A specification for each functional requirement. As with all types of
requirements, use the requirements shell. A full explanation is
included in this template's introductory material.

Figure B.4

A sample of a functional requirement using a snow card. Usually these requirements would be recorded in some electronic form using only textual field identifiers.

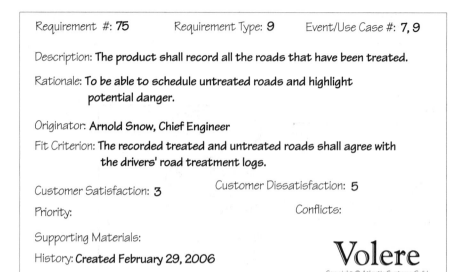

Requirement #: **75**   Requirement Type: **9**   Event/Use Case #: **7, 9**

Description: **The product shall record all the roads that have been treated.**

Rationale: **To be able to schedule untreated roads and highlight potential danger.**

Originator: **Arnold Snow, Chief Engineer**

Fit Criterion: **The recorded treated and untreated roads shall agree with the drivers' road treatment logs.**

Customer Satisfaction: **3**   Customer Dissatisfaction: **5**

Priority: Conflicts:

Supporting Materials:

History: **Created February 29, 2006**

Volere
Copyright © Atlantic Systems Guild

Motivation

To specify the detailed functional requirements for the activity of the product.

Examples

See Figure B.4 for an example of a filled in snow card.

Fit Criterion

Each functional requirement should have a fit criterion or a test case. In any event, the fit criterion is the benchmark to allow the tester to determine whether the implemented product has met the requirement.

Considerations

If you have produced an event/use case list (see sections 7b and 8a), then you can use it to help you trigger the functional requirements for each event/use case. If you have not produced an event/use case list, give each functional requirement a unique number and, to help with traceability, partition these requirements into event/use case–related groups later in the development process.

9b Data Requirements

Content

A specification of the essential subject matter, business objects, entities, and classes that are germane to the product. It might take the form of a first-cut class model, an object model, or a domain model. Alternatively, these requirements might be described by defining the terms in the dictionary described in section 5.

Motivation

To clarify the system's subject matter, thereby triggering recognition of requirements not yet considered.

Example

Figure B.5 is a model of the system's business subject matter using the Unified Modeling Language (UML) class model notation.

You can use any type of data or object model to capture this knowledge. The issue is to capture the meaning of the business subject matter and the connections between the individual parts, and to show that you are consistent within your project. If you have an established company standard notation, use that, as it will help you to reuse knowledge between projects.

Considerations

Are there any data or object models for similar or overlapping systems that might be a useful starting point? Is there a domain model for the subject matter dealt with by this system?

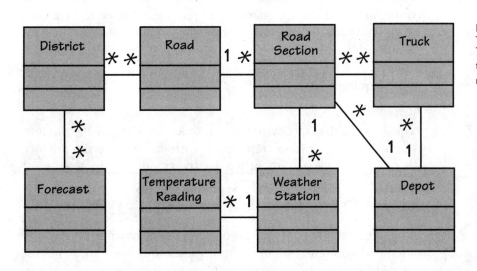

Figure B.5

The class model showing the stored data requirements.

10   Look and Feel Requirements

10a   Appearance Requirements

Content

The section contains requirements relating to the spirit of the product. Your client may have made particular demands for the product, such as corporate branding, colors to be used, and so on. This section captures the requirements for the appearance. Do not attempt to design it until the appearance requirements are known.

Motivation

To ensure that the appearance of the product conforms to the organization's expectations.

Examples

The product shall be attractive to a teenage audience.

The product shall comply with corporate branding standards.

Fit Criterion

A sampling of representative teenagers shall, without prompting or enticement, start using the product within four minutes of their first encounter with it.

The office of branding shall certify the product complies with the current standards.

Considerations

Even if you are using prototypes, it is important to understand the requirements for the appearance. The prototype is used to help elicit requirements; it should not be thought of as a substitute for the requirements.

10b   Style Requirements

Content

Requirements that specify the mood, style, or feeling of the product, which influences the way a potential customer will see the product. Also, the stakeholders' intentions for the amount of interaction the user is to have with the product.

In this section, you would also describe the appearance of the package if this is to be a manufactured product. The package may have some requirements as to its size, style, and consistency with other packages put out by your organization. Keep in mind the European laws on packaging, which require that the package not be significantly larger than the product it encloses.

The style requirements that you record here will guide the designers to create a product as envisioned by your client.

Motivation

Given the state of today's market and people's expectations, we cannot afford to build products that have the wrong style. Once the functional requirements are satisfied, it is often the appearance and style of products that determine whether they are successful. Your task in this section is to determine precisely how the product shall appear to its intended consumer.

Example

The product shall appear authoritative.

Fit Criterion

After their first encounter with the product, 70 percent of representative potential customers shall agree they can trust the product.

Considerations

The look and feel requirements specify your client's vision of the product's appearance. The requirements may at first seem to be rather vague (e.g., "conservative and professional appearance"), but these will be quantified by their fit criteria. The fit criteria give you the opportunity to extract from your client precisely what is meant, and give the designer precise instructions on what he is to accomplish.

11 Usability and Humanity Requirements

This section is concerned with requirements that make the product usable and ergonomically acceptable to its hands-on users.

11a Ease of Use Requirements

Content

This section describes your client's aspirations for how easy it is for the intended users of the product to operate it. The product's usability is derived from the abilities of the expected users of the product and the complexity of its functionality.

The usability requirements should cover properties such as these:

- Efficiency of use: How quickly or accurately the user can use the product.
- Ease of remembering: How much the casual user is expected to remember about using the product.

● Error rates: For some products it is crucial that the user commits very few, or no, errors.

● Overall satisfaction in using the product: This is especially important for commercial, interactive products that face a lot of competition. Web sites are a good example.

● Feedback: How much feedback the user needs to feel confident that the product is actually accurately doing what the user expects. The necessary degree of feedback will be higher for some products (e.g., safety-critical products) than for others.

Motivation

To guide the product's designers toward building a product that meets the expectations of its eventual users.

Examples

The product shall be easy for 11-year-old children to use.

The product shall help the user to avoid making mistakes.

The product shall make the users want to use it.

The product shall be used by people with no training, and possibly no understanding of English.

Fit Criterion

These examples may seem simplistic, but they do express the intention of the client. To completely specify what is meant by the requirement, you must add a measurement against which it can be tested—that is, a fit criterion. Here are the fit criteria for the preceding examples:

Eighty percent of a test panel of 11-year-old children shall be able to successfully complete [list of tasks] within [specified time].

One month's use of the product shall result in a total error rate of less than 1 percent.

An anonymous survey shall show that 75 percent of the intended users are regularly using the product after a three-week familiarization period.

Considerations

Refer to section 3, Users of the Product, to ensure that you have considered the usability requirements from the perspective of all the different types of users.

It may be necessary to have special consulting sessions with your users and your client to determine whether any special usability considerations must be built into the product.

You could also consider consulting a usability laboratory experienced in testing the usability of products that have a project situation (sections 1–7 of this template) similar to yours.

11b Personalization and Internationalization Requirements

Content

This section describes the way in which the product can be altered or configured to take into account the user's personal preferences or choice of language.

The personalization requirements should cover issues such as the following:

- Languages, spelling preferences, and language idioms
- Currencies, including the symbols and decimal conventions
- Personal configuration options

Motivation

To ensure that the product's users do not have to struggle with, or meekly accept, the builder's cultural conventions.

Examples

The product shall retain the buyer's buying preferences.

The product shall allow the user to select a chosen language.

Considerations

Consider the country and culture of the potential customers and users of your product. Any out-of-country users will welcome the opportunity to convert to their home spelling and expressions.

By allowing users to customize the way in which they use the product, you give them the opportunity to participate more closely with your organization as well as enjoy their own personal user experience.

You might also consider the configurability of the product. Configurability allows different users to have different functional variations of the product.

11c Learning Requirements

Content

Requirements specifying how easy it should be to learn to use the product. This learning curve ranges from zero time for products intended for placement in the public domain (e.g., a parking meter or a Web site) to a considerable amount of time for complex, highly technical products. (We know of one product where it was necessary for graduate engineers to spend 18 months in a training program before being qualified to use the product.)

Motivation

To quantify the amount of time that your client feels is allowable before a user can successfully use the product. This requirement guides designers to understand how users will learn the product. For example, designers may build elaborate interactive help facilities into the product, or the product may be packaged with a tutorial. Alternatively, the product may have to be constructed so that all of its functionality is apparent upon first encountering it.

Examples

The product shall be easy for an engineer to learn.

A clerk shall be able to be productive within a short time.

The product shall be able to be used by members of the public who will receive no training before using it.

The product shall be used by engineers who will attend five weeks of training before using the product.

Fit Criterion

An engineer shall produce a [specified result] within [specified time] of beginning to use the product, without needing to use the manual.

After receiving [number of hours] training a clerk shall be able to produce [quantity of specified outputs] per [unit of time].

[Agreed percentage] of a test panel shall successfully complete [specified task] within [specified time limit].

The engineers shall achieve [agreed percentage] pass rate from the final examination of the training.

Considerations

Refer to section 3, Users of the Product, to ensure that you have considered the ease of learning requirements from the perspective of all the different types of users.

11d Understandability and Politeness Requirements

This section is concerned with discovering requirements related to concepts and metaphors that are familiar to the intended end users.

Content

This specifies the requirement for the product to be understood by its users. While "usability" refers to ease of use, efficiency, and similar characteristics, "understandability" determines whether the users instinctively know what the product will do for them and how it fits into their view of the world. You can think of understandability as the product being polite to its users and not expecting them to know or learn things that have nothing to do with their business problem.

Motivation

To avoid forcing users to learn terms and concepts that are part of the product's internal construction and are not relevant to the users' world. To make the product more comprehensible and thus more likely to be adopted by its intended users.

Examples

The product shall use symbols and words that are naturally understandable by the user community.

The product shall hide the details of its construction from the user.

Considerations

Refer to section 3, Users of the Product, and consider the world from the point of view of each of the different types of users.

11e Accessibility Requirements

Content

The requirements for how easy it should be for people with common disabilities to access the product. These disabilities might be related to physical disability or visual, hearing, cognitive, or other abilities.

Motivation

In many countries it is required that some products be made available to the disabled. In any event, it is self-defeating to exclude this sizable community of potential customers.

Examples

The product shall be usable by partially sighted users.

The product shall conform to the Americans with Disabilities Act.

Considerations

Some users have disabilities other than the commonly described ones. In addition, some partial disabilities are fairly common. A simple, and not very consequential, example is that approximately 20 percent of males are red-green colorblind.

12 Performance Requirements

12a Speed and Latency Requirements

Content

Specifies the amount of time available to complete specified tasks. These requirements often refer to response times. They can also refer to the product's ability to operate at a speed suitable for the intended environment.

Motivation

Some products—usually real-time products—must be able to perform some of their functionality within a given time slot. Failure to do so may mean catastrophic failure (e.g., a ground-sensing radar in an airplane fails to detect an upcoming mountain) or the product will not cope with the required volume of use (e.g., an automated ticket-selling machine).

Examples

Any interface between a user and the automated system shall have a maximum response time of 2 seconds.

The response shall be fast enough to avoid interrupting the user's flow of thought.

The product shall poll the sensor every 10 seconds.

The product shall download the new status parameters within 5 minutes of a change.

Fit Criterion

Fit criteria are needed when the description of the requirement is not quantified. However, we find that most performance requirements are stated in quantified terms. The exception is the second requirement shown above, for which the suggested fit criterion is

The product shall respond in less than 1 second for 90 percent of the interrogations. No response shall take longer than 2.5 seconds.

Considerations

There is a wide variation in the importance of different types of speed requirements. If you are working on a missile guidance system, then speed is extremely important. By contrast, an inventory control report that is run once every six months has very little need for a lightning-fast response time.

Customize this section of the template to give examples of the speed requirements that are important within your environment.

12b Safety-Critical Requirements

Content

Quantification of the perceived risk of damage to people, property, and environment. Different countries have different standards, so the fit criteria must specify precisely which standards the product must meet.

Motivation

To understand and highlight the damage that could potentially occur when using the product within the expected operational environment.

Examples

The product shall not emit noxious gases that damage people's health.

The heat exchanger shall be shielded from human contact.

Fit Criterion

The product shall be certified to comply with the Health Department's standard E110-98. It is to be certified by qualified testing engineers.

No member of a test panel of [specified size] shall be able to touch the heat exchanger. The heat exchanger must also comply with safety standard [specify which one].

Considerations

The example requirements given here apply to some, but not all, products. It is not possible to give examples of every variation of safety-critical requirement. To make the template work in your environment, you should customize it by adding examples that are specific to your products.

Also, be aware that different countries have different safety standards and laws relating to safety. If you plan to sell your product internationally, you must be aware of these laws. A colleague has suggested that for electrical products, if you follow the German standards, the largest number of countries will be supported.

If you are building safety-critical systems, then the relevant safety-critical standards are already well specified. You will likely have safety experts on your staff. These experts are the best source of the relevant safety-critical requirements for your type of product. They will almost certainly have copious information that you can use.

Consult your legal department. Members of this department will be aware of the kinds of lawsuits that have resulted from product safety failure. This is probably the best starting place for generating relevant safety requirements.

12c Precision or Accuracy Requirements

Content

Quantification of the desired accuracy of the results produced by the product.

Motivation

To set the client's and users' expectations for the precision of the product.

Examples

All monetary amounts shall be accurate to two decimal places.

Accuracy of road temperature readings shall be within ±2°C.

Considerations

If you have done any detailed work on definitions, then some precision requirements might be adequately defined by definitions in section 5.

You might consider which units the product is intended to use. Readers will recall the spacecraft that crashed on Mars when coordinates were sent as metric data rather than imperial data.

The product might also need to keep accurate time, be synchronized with a time server, or work in UTC.

Also, be aware that some currencies have no decimal places, such as the Japanese yen.

12d Reliability and Availability Requirements

Content

This section quantifies the necessary reliability of the product. The reliability is usually expressed as the allowable time between failures, or the total allowable failure rate.

This section also quantifies the expected availability of the product.

Motivation

It is critical for some products not to fail too often. This section allows you to explore the possibility of failure and to specify realistic levels of service. It also gives you the opportunity to set the client's and users' expectations about the amount of time that the product will be available for use.

Examples

The product shall be available for use 24 hours per day, 365 days per year.

The product shall be available for use between the hours of 8:00 A.M. and 5:30 P.M.

The escalator shall run from 6 A.M. until 10 P.M. or the last flight arrives.

The product shall achieve 99 percent uptime.

Considerations

Consider carefully whether the real requirement for your product is that it is available for use or that it does not fail at any time.

Consider also the cost of reliability and availability, and whether it is justified for your product.

12e Robustness or Fault-Tolerance Requirements

Content

Robustness specifies the ability of the product to continue to function under abnormal circumstances.

Motivation

To ensure that the product is able to provide some or all of its services after or during some abnormal happening in its environment.

Examples

The product shall continue to operate in local mode whenever it loses its link to the central server.

The product shall provide 10 minutes of emergency operation should it become disconnected from the electricity source.

Considerations

Abnormal happenings can almost be considered normal. Today's products are so large and complex that there is a good chance that at any given time, one component will not be functioning correctly. Robustness requirements are intended to prevent total failure of the product.

You could also consider disaster recovery in this section. This plan describes the ability of the product to reestablish acceptable performance after faults or abnormal happenings.

12f Capacity Requirements

Content

This section specifies the volumes that the product must be able to deal with and the amount of data stored by the product.

Motivation

To ensure that the product is capable of processing the expected volumes.

Examples

The product shall cater for 300 simultaneous users within the period from 9:00 A.M. to 11:00 A.M. Maximum loading at other periods will be 150 simultaneous users.

During a launch period, the product shall cater for a maximum of 20 people to be in the inner chamber.

Fit Criterion

In this case, the requirement description is quantified, and thus can be tested.

12g Scalability or Extensibility Requirements

Content

This specifies the expected increases in size that the product must be able to handle. As a business grows (or is expected to grow), our software products must increase their capacities to cope with the new volumes.

Motivation

To ensure that the designers allow for future capacities.

Examples

The product shall be capable of processing the existing 100,000 customers. This number is expected to grow to 500,000 customers within three years.

The product shall be able to process 50,000 transactions per hour within two years of its launch.

12h Longevity Requirements

Content

This specifies the expected lifetime of the product.

Motivation

To ensure that the product is built based on an understanding of expected return on investment.

Examples

The product shall be expected to operate within the maximum maintenance budget for a minimum of five years.

13 Operational and Environmental Requirements

13a Expected Physical Environment

Content

This section specifies the physical environment in which the product will operate.

Motivation

To highlight conditions that might need special requirements, preparations, or training. These requirements ensure that the product is fit to be used in its intended environment.

Examples

The product shall be used by a worker, standing up, outside in cold, rainy conditions.

The product shall be used in noisy conditions with a lot of dust.

The product shall be able to fit in a pocket or purse.

The product shall be usable in dim light.

The product shall not be louder than the existing noise level in the environment.

Considerations

The work environment: Is the product to operate in some unusual environment? Does this lead to special requirements? Also see section 11, Usability and Humanity Requirements.

13b Requirements for Interfacing with Adjacent Systems

Content

This section describes the requirements to interface with partner applications and/or devices that the product needs to successfully operate.

Motivation

Requirements for the interfaces to other applications often remain undiscovered until implementation time. Avoid a high degree of rework by discovering these requirements early.

Examples

The products shall work on the last four releases of the five most popular browsers.

The new version of the spreadsheet must be able to access data from the previous two versions.

Our product must interface with the applications that run on the remote weather stations.

Fit Criterion

For each inter-application interface, specify the following elements:

- The data content
- The physical material content
- The medium that carries the interface
- The frequency
- The volume

13c Productization Requirements

Content

Any requirements that are necessary to make the product into a distributable or salable item. It is also appropriate to describe here the operations needed to install a software product successfully.

Motivation

To ensure that if work must be done to get the product out the door, then that work becomes part of the requirements. Also, to quantify the client's and users' expectations about the amount of time, money, and resources they will need to allocate to install the product.

Examples

The product shall be distributed as a ZIP file.

The product shall be able to be installed by an untrained user without recourse to separately printed instructions.

The product shall be of a size such that it can fit on one CD.

Considerations

Some products have special needs to turn them into a salable or usable product. You might consider that the product has to be protected such that only paid-up customers can access it.

Ask questions of your marketing department to discover unstated assumptions that have been made about the specified environment and the customers' expectations of how long installation will take and how much it will cost.

Most commercial products have some needs in this area.

13d   Release Requirements

Content

Specification of the intended release cycle for the product and the form that the release shall take.

Motivation

To make everyone aware of how often you intend to produce new releases of the product.

Examples

The maintenance releases will be offered to end users once a year.

Each release shall not cause previous features to fail.

Fit Criterion

Description of the type of maintenance plus the amount of effort budgeted for it.

Considerations

Do you have any existing contractual commitments or maintenance agreements that might be affected by the new product?

14   Maintainability and Support Requirements

14a   Maintenance Requirements

Content

A quantification of the time necessary to make specified changes to the product.

Motivation

To make everyone aware of the maintenance needs of the product.

Examples

New MIS reports must be available within one working week of the date when the requirements are agreed upon.

A new weather station must be able to be added to the system overnight.

Considerations

There may be special requirements for maintainability, such as that the product must be able to be maintained by its end users or by developers who are not the original developers. These requirements have an effect on the way that the product is developed. In addition, there may be requirements for documentation or training.

You might also consider writing testability requirements in this section.

14b Supportability Requirements

Content

This specifies the level of support that the product requires. Support is often provided via a help desk. If people will provide support for the product, that service is considered part of the product: Are there any requirements for that support? You might also build support into the product itself, in which case this section is the place to write those requirements.

Motivation

To ensure that the support aspect of the product is adequately specified.

Considerations

Consider the anticipated level of support, and what forms it might take. For example, a constraint might state that there is to be no printed manual. Alternatively, the product might need to be entirely self-supporting.

14c Adaptability Requirements

Content

Description of other platforms or environments to which the product must be ported.

Motivation

To quantify the client's and users' expectations about the platforms on which the product will be able to run.

Examples

The product is expected to run under Windows XP and Linux.

The product might eventually be sold in the Japanese market.

The product is designed to run in offices, but we intend to have a version running in restaurant kitchens.

Fit Criterion

- Specification of system software on which the product must operate.
- Specification of future environments in which the product is expected to operate.
- Time allowed to make the transition.

Considerations

Question your marketing department to discover unstated assumptions that have been made about the portability of the product.

15 Security Requirements

15a Access Requirements

Content

Specification of who has authorized access to the product (both functionality and data), under what circumstances that access is granted, and to which parts of the product access is allowed.

Motivation

To understand the expectations for confidentiality aspects of the system.

Examples

Only direct managers can see the personnel records of their staff.

Only holders of current security clearance can enter the building.

Fit Criterion

- System function name or system data name.
- User roles and/or names of people who have clearance.

Considerations

Is there any data that management considers to be sensitive? Is there any data that low-level users do not want management to have access to? Are there any processes that might cause damage or might be used for personal gain? Are there any people who should not have access to the system?

Avoid stating how you will design a solution to the security requirements. For instance, don't "design a password system." Your aim here is to identify the security requirement; the design will then come from this description.

Consider asking for help. Computer security is a highly specialized field, and one where improperly qualified people have no business. If your product has need of more than average security, we advise you to make use of a security consultant. Such consultants are not cheap, but the results of inadequate security can be even more expensive.

15b Integrity Requirements

Content

Specification of the required integrity of databases and other files, and of the product itself.

Motivation

To understand the expectations for the integrity of the product's data. To specify what the product will do to ensure its integrity in the case of an unwanted happening such as attack from the outside or unintentional misuse by an authorized user.

Examples

The product shall prevent incorrect data from being introduced.

The product shall protect itself from intentional abuse.

Considerations

Organizations are relying more and more on their stored data. If this data should be come corrupt or incorrect—or disappear—then it could be a fatal blow to the organization. For example, almost half of small businesses go bankrupt after a fire destroys their computer systems. Integrity requirements are aimed at preventing complete loss, as well as corruption, of data and processes.

15c Privacy Requirements

Content

Specification of what the product has to do to ensure the privacy of individuals about whom it stores information. The product must also ensure that all laws related to privacy of an individual's data are observed.

Motivation

To ensure that the product complies with the law, and to protect the individual privacy of your customers. Few people today look kindly on organizations that do not observe their privacy.

Examples

The product shall make its users aware of its information practices before collecting data from them.

The product shall notify customers of changes to its information policy.

The product shall reveal private information only in compliance with the organization's information policy.

The product shall protect private information in accordance with the relevant privacy laws and the organization's information policy.

Considerations

Privacy issues may well have legal implications, and you are advised to consult with your organization's legal department about the requirements to be written in this section.

Consider what notices you must issue to your customers before collecting their personal information. A notice might go so far as to warn customers that you intend to put a cookie in their computer. Also, do you have to do anything to keep customers aware that you hold their personal information?

Customers must always be in a position to give or withhold consent when their private data is collected or stored. Similarly, customers should be able to view any private data and, where appropriate, ask for correction of the data.

Also consider the integrity and security of private data—for example, when you are storing credit card information.

15d Audit Requirements

Content

Specification of what the product has to do (usually retain records) to permit the required audit checks.

Motivation

To build a system that complies with the appropriate audit rules.

Considerations

This section may have legal implications. You are advised to seek the approval of your organization's auditors regarding what you write here.

You should also consider whether the product should retain information on who has used it. The intention is to provide security such that a user may not later deny having used the product or participated in some form of transaction using the product.

15e Immunity Requirements

Content

The requirements for what the product has to do to protect itself from infection by unauthorized or undesirable software programs, such as viruses, worms, and Trojan horses, among others.

Motivation

To build a product that is as secure as possible from malicious interference.

Considerations

Each day brings more malevolence from the unknown, outside world. People buying software, or any other kind of product, expect that it can protect itself from outside interference.

16 Cultural and Political Requirements

16a Cultural Requirements

Content

This section contains requirements that are specific to the sociological factors that affect the acceptability of the product. If you are developing a product for foreign markets, then these requirements are particularly relevant.

Motivation

To bring out in the open requirements that are difficult to discover because they are outside the cultural experience of the developers.

Examples

The product shall not be offensive to religious or ethnic groups.

The product shall be able to distinguish between French, Italian, and British road-numbering systems.

The product shall keep a record of public holidays for all countries in the European Union and for all states in the United States.

Considerations

Question whether the product is intended for a culture other than the one with which you are familiar. Ask whether people in other countries or in other types of organizations will use the product. Do these people have different habits, holidays, superstitions, or cultural norms that do not apply to your own culture? Are there colors, icons, or words that have different meanings in another cultural environment?

16b Political Requirements

Content

This section contains requirements that are specific to the political factors that affect the acceptability of the product.

Motivation

To understand requirements that sometimes appear irrational.

Examples

> *The product shall be installed using only American-made components.*

> *The product shall make all functionality available to the CEO.*

Considerations

Did you intend to develop the product on a Macintosh, when the office manager has laid down an edict that only Windows machines are permitted?

Is a director also on the board of a company that manufactures products similar to the one that you intend to build?

Whether you agree with these political requirements has little bearing on the outcome. The reality is that the system has to comply with political requirements even if you can find a better, more efficient, or more economical solution. A few probing questions here may save some heartache later.

The political requirements might be purely concerned with the politics inside your organization. However, in other situations you may need to consider the politics inside your customers' organizations or the national politics of the country.

17 Legal Requirements

17a Compliance Requirements

Content

A statement specifying the legal requirements for this system.

Motivation

To comply with the law so as to avoid later delays, lawsuits, and legal fees.

Examples

> *Personal information shall be implemented so as to comply with the Data Protection Act.*

Fit Criterion

Lawyers' opinion that the product does not break any laws.

Considerations

Consider consulting lawyers to help identify the legal requirements.

- Are there any copyrights or other intellectual property that must be protected? Conversely, do any competitors have copyrights on which you might be in danger of infringing?

- Is it a requirement that developers have not seen competitors' code or even have worked for competitors?

- Do the Sarbanes-Oxley (SOX) Act, the Health Insurance Portability and Accountability Act (HIPAA), or the Gramm-Leach-Bliley Act have implications for your product? Check with your company lawyer.
- Might any pending legislation affect the development of this system?
- Are there any aspects of criminal law you should consider?
- Have you considered the tax laws that affect your product?
- Are there any labor laws (e.g., working hours) relevant to your product?

17b Standards Requirements

Content

A statement specifying applicable standards and referencing detailed standards descriptions. This does not refer to the law of the land—think of it as an internal law imposed by your company.

Motivation

To comply with standards so as to avoid later delays.

Example

> *The product shall comply with MilSpec standards.*
>
> *The product shall comply with insurance industry standards.*
>
> *The product shall be developed according to SSADM standard development steps.*

Fit Criterion

The appropriate standard-keeper certifies that the standard has been adhered to.

Considerations

It is not always apparent that there are applicable standards because their existence is often taken for granted. Consider the following:

- Do any industry bodies have applicable standards?
- Does the industry have a code of practice, watchdog, or ombudsman?
- Are there any special development steps for this type of product?

18 Open Issues

Issues that have been raised and do not yet have a conclusion.

Content

A statement of factors that are uncertain and might make significant difference to the product.

Motivation

To bring uncertainty out in the open and provide objective input to risk analysis.

Examples

Our investigation into whether the new version of the processor will be suitable for our application is not yet complete.

The government is planning to change the rules about who is responsible for gritting the motorways, but we do not know what those changes might be.

Considerations

Are there any issues that have come up from the requirements gathering that have not yet been resolved? Have you heard of any changes that might occur in the other organizations or systems on your context diagram? Are there any legislative changes that might affect your system? Are there any rumors about your hardware or software suppliers that might have an impact?

19 Off-the-Shelf Solutions

19a Ready-Made Products

Content

List of existing products that should be investigated as potential solutions. Reference any surveys that have been done on these products.

Motivation

To give consideration to whether a solution can be bought.

Considerations

Could you buy something that already exists or is about to become available? It may not be possible at this stage to make this determination with a lot of confidence, but any likely products should be listed here.

Also consider whether some products must not be used.

19b Reusable Components

Content

Description of the candidate components, either bought from outside or built by your company, that could be used by this project. List libraries that could be a source of components.

Motivation

Reuse rather than reinvention.

19c Products That Can Be Copied

Content

List of other similar products or parts of products that you can legally copy or easily modify.

Motivation

Reuse rather than reinvention.

Examples

> *Another electricity company has built a customer service system. Its hardware is different from ours, but we could buy its specification and cut our analysis effort by approximately 60 percent.*

Considerations

While a ready-made solution may not exist, perhaps something, in its essence, is similar enough that you could copy, and possibly modify, it to better effect than starting from scratch. This approach is potentially dangerous because it relies on the base system being of good quality.

This question should always be answered. The act of answering it will force you to look at other existing solutions to similar problems.

20 New Problems

20a Effects on the Current Environment

Content

A description of how the new product will affect the current implementation environment. This section should also cover things that the new product should *not* do.

Motivation

The intention is to discover early any potential conflicts that might otherwise not be realized until implementation time.

Examples

> *Any change to the scheduling system will affect the work of the engineers in the divisions and the truck drivers.*

Considerations

Is it possible that the new system might damage some existing system? Can people be displaced or otherwise affected by the new system?

These issues require a study of the current environment. A model highlighting the effects of the change is a good way to make this information widely understandable.

20b Effects on the Installed Systems

Content

Specification of the interfaces between new and existing systems.

Motivation

Very rarely is a new development intended to stand completely alone. Usually the new system must coexist with some older system. This question forces you to look carefully at the existing system, examining it for potential conflicts with the new development.

20c Potential User Problems

Content

Details of any adverse reaction that might be suffered by existing users.

Motivation

Sometimes existing users are using a product in such a way that they will suffer ill effects from the new system or feature. Identify any likely adverse user reactions, and determine whether we care about those reactions and what precautions we will take.

20d Limitations in the Anticipated Implementation Environment That May Inhibit the New Product

Content

Statement of any potential problems with the new automated technology or new ways of structuring the organization.

Motivation

The intention is to make early discovery of any potential conflicts that might otherwise not be realized until implementation time.

Examples

The planned new server is not powerful enough to cope with our projected growth pattern.

The size and weight of the new product do not fit into the physical environment.

The power capabilities will not satisfy the new product's projected consumption.

Considerations

This requires a study of the intended implementation environment.

20e Follow-Up Problems

Content

Identification of situations that we might not be able to cope with.

Motivation

To guard against situations where the product might fail.

Considerations

Will we create a demand for our product that we are not able to service? Will the new system cause us to run afoul of laws that do not currently apply? Will the existing hardware cope?

There are potentially hundreds of unwanted effects. It pays to answer this question very carefully.

21 Tasks

21a Project Planning

Content

Details of the life cycle and approach that will be used to deliver the product. A high-level process diagram showing the tasks and the interfaces between them is a good way to communicate this information.

Motivation

To specify the approach that will be taken to deliver the product so that everyone has the same expectations.

Considerations

Depending on the maturity level of your process, the new product will be developed using your standard approach. However, some circumstances are unique to a particular product and will necessitate changes to your life cycle. While these considerations are not product requirements, they are needed if the product is to be successfully developed.

If possible, attach an estimate of the time and resources needed for each task based on the requirements that you have specified. Attach your estimates to the events, use cases, and/or functions that you specified in sections 8 and 9.

Do not forget issues related to data conversion, user training, and cutover. These needs are usually ignored when projects set implementation dates.

21b   Planning of the Development Phases

Content
Specification of each phase of development and the components in the operating environment.

Motivation
To identify the phases necessary to implement the operating environment for the new system so that the implementation can be managed.

Fit Criterion
- Name of the phase.
- Required operational date.
- Operating environment components included.
- Functional requirements included.
- Nonfunctional requirements included.

Considerations
Identify which hardware and other devices are necessary for each phase of the new system. This list may not be known at the time of the requirements process, as these devices may be decided at design time.

22   Migration to the New Product

22a   Requirements for Migration to the New Product

Content
A list of the conversion activities. Timetable for implementation.

Motivation
To identify conversion tasks as input to the project planning process.

Considerations
- Will you use a phased implementation to install the new system? If so, describe which requirements will be implemented by each of the major phases.
- What kind of data conversion is necessary? Must special programs be written to transport data from an existing system to the new one? If so, describe the requirements for these programs here.

- What kind of manual backup is needed while the new system is installed?
- When are each of the major components to be put in place? When are the phases of the implementation to be released?
- Is there a need to run the new product in parallel with the existing product?
- Will we need additional or different staff?
- Is any special effort needed to decommission the old product?
- This section is the timetable for implementation of the new system.

22b   Data That Has to Be Modified or Translated for the New System

Content

List of data translation tasks.

Motivation

To discover missing tasks that will affect the size and boundaries of the project.

Fit Criterion

- Description of the current technology that holds the data.
- Description of the new technology that will hold the data.
- Description of the data translation tasks.
- Foreseeable problems.

Considerations

Every time you make an addition to your dictionary (see section 5), ask this question: Where is this data currently held, and will the new system affect that implementation?

23   Risks

All projects involve risk—namely, the risk that something will go wrong. Risk is not necessarily a bad thing, as no progress is made without taking some risk. However, there is a difference between unmanaged risk—say, shooting dice at a craps table—and managed risk, where the probabilities are well understood and contingency plans are made. Risk is only a bad thing if the risks are ignored and they become problems. Risk management entails assessing which risks are most likely to apply to the project, deciding a course of action if they become problems, and monitoring projects to give early warnings of risks becoming problems.

This section of your specification should contain a list of the most likely risks and the most serious risks for your project. For each risk, include the probability of that risk becoming a problem. Capers Jones's *Assessment and Control of Software Risks* (Prentice Hall, 1994) gives comprehensive lists of risks and their probabilities; you can use these lists as a starting point. For example, Jones cites the following risks as being the most serious:

- Inaccurate metrics
- Inadequate measurement
- Excessive schedule pressure
- Management malpractice
- Inaccurate cost estimating
- Silver bullet syndrome
- Creeping user requirements
- Low quality
- Low productivity
- Cancelled projects

Use your knowledge of the requirements as input to discover which risks are most relevant to your project.

It is also useful input to project management if you include the impact on the schedule, or the cost, if the risk does become a problem.

24 Costs

For details on how to estimate requirements effort and costs, refer to Appendix C, Function Point Counting: A Simplified Introduction.

The other cost of requirements is the amount of money or effort that you have to spend building them into a product. Once the requirements specification is complete, you can use one of the estimating methods to assess the cost, expressing the result as a monetary amount or time to build.

There is no best method to use when estimating. Keep in mind, however, that your estimates should be based on some tangible, countable artifact. If you are using this template, then, as a result of doing the work of requirements specification, you are producing many measurable deliverables. For example:

- Number of input and output flows on the work context
- Number of business events

- Number of product use cases
- Number of functional requirements
- Number of nonfunctional requirements
- Number of requirements constraints
- Number of function points

The more detailed the work you do on your requirements, the more accurate your deliverables will be. Your cost estimate is the amount of resources you estimate each type of deliverable will take to produce within your environment. You can create some very early cost estimates based on the work context. At that stage, your knowledge of the work will be general, and you should reflect this vagueness by making the cost estimate a range rather than a single figure.

As you increase your knowledge of the requirements, we suggest you try using function point counting—not because it is an inherently superior method, but because it is so widely accepted. So much is known about function point counting that it is possible to make easy comparisons with other products and other installations' productivity.

It is important that your client be told at this stage what the product is likely to cost. You usually express this amount as the total cost to complete the product, but you may also find it advantageous to point out the cost of the requirements effort as a whole, or the costs of individual requirements.

Whatever you do, do not leave the costs in the lap of hysterical optimism. Make sure that this section includes meaningful numbers based on tangible deliverables.

25   User Documentation and Training

25a   User Documentation Requirements

Content

List of the user documentation to be supplied as part of the product.

Motivation

To set expectations for the documentation and to identify who will be responsible for creating it.

Examples

- Technical specifications to accompany the product
- User manuals

- Service manuals (if not covered by the technical specification)
- Emergency procedure manuals (e.g., the card found in airplanes)
- Installation manuals

Considerations

Which documents do you need to deliver, and to whom? Bear in mind that the answer to this questions depends on your organizational procedures and roles.

For each document, consider these issues:

- The purpose of the document
- The people who will use the document
- Maintenance of the document

What level of documentation is expected? Will the users be involved in the production of the documentation? Who will be responsible for keeping the documentation up-to-date? What form will the documentation take?

25b Training Requirements

Content

A description of the training needed by users of the product.

Motivation

To set expectations for the training. To identify who is responsible for creating and providing that training.

Considerations

What training will be necessary? Who will design the training? Who will provide the training?

26 Waiting Room

Requirements that will not be part of the next release. These requirements might be included in future releases of the product.

Content

Any type of requirement.

Motivation

To allow requirements to be gathered, even though they cannot be part of the current development. To ensure that good ideas are not lost.

Considerations

The requirements-gathering process often throws up requirements that are beyond the sophistication of, or time allowed for, the current release of the product. This section holds these requirements in waiting. The intention is to avoid stifling the creativity of your users and clients, by using a repository to retain future requirements. You are also managing expectations by making it clear that you take these requirements seriously, although they will not be part of the agreed-upon product.

Many people use the waiting room as a way of planning future versions of the product. Each requirement in the waiting room is tagged with its intended version number. As a requirement progresses closer to implementation, then you can spend more time on it and add details such as the cost and benefit attached to that requirement.

You might also prioritize the contents of your waiting room. "Low-hanging fruit"—requirements that provide a high benefit at a low cost of implementation—are the highest-ranking candidates for the next release. You would also give a high waiting room rank to requirements for which there is a pent-up demand.

27 Ideas for Solutions

When you gather requirements, you focus on finding out what the real requirements are and try to avoid coming up with solutions. However, when creative people start to think about a problem, they always generate ideas about potential solutions. This section of the template is a place to put those ideas so that you do not forget them and so that you can separate them from the real business requirements.

Content

Any idea for a solution that you think is worth keeping for future consideration. This can take the form of rough notes, sketches, pointers to other documents, pointers to people, pointers to existing products, and so on. The aim is to capture, with the least amount of effort, an idea that you can return to later.

Motivation

To make sure that good ideas are not lost. To help you separate requirements from solutions.

Considerations

While you are gathering requirements, you will inevitably have solution ideas; this section offers a way to capture them. Bear in mind that this section will not necessarily be included in every document that you publish.

Function Point Counting: A Simplified Introduction

in which we look at a way to accurately measure the size or functionality of the work area, with a view toward using the measurement to estimate the requirements effort

Measuring the Work

Our discussion of function point counting is an appendix because it is, strictly speaking, outside the scope of the requirements analyst's normal responsibilities. That said, measuring the work area so as to estimate the size of the project definitely provides a benefit to any requirements analyst. So with the idea of making you interested in measuring, or making you interested in making your organization interested in measuring, here is a simplified (but not simplistic) introduction to counting function points.

The requirements activity is an investigation of a piece of work, with the potential to cause a change to that work, probably by automating some of it. The work in question can be automated, manual, scientific, commercial, embedded, a combination of the above, or anything else. The reason for measuring that work is to learn how "large" it is. The bigger the work (that is, the more functionality and data it contains), the longer it takes to study it. You would expect to spend more time studying an airline reservation system than you would studying a system for taking bar orders. Why? Because the airline reservation system contains more functionality. Naturally it takes longer to discover and understand that functionality, and to write the requirements for it.

Function points are a measure of the amount of functionality contained within a work area. They are a neutral measure of functionality, meaning that the type of work being done does not influence them. You can count the function points for air traffic control, car traffic control, or car cruise control. Once you know the function point count of a work area, you apply your metric to determine how long it takes to study that size of work area.

> *You cannot control what you cannot measure.*
>
> Source: Tom DeMarco

Over the years our industry has established that for most size metrics, a standard amount of work must be done to implement one unit of the metric. For example, if you use function points to determine the size of the product, then there are industry-standard figures of the number of hours (or the number of dollars) it takes to implement one function point. Thus, if you know the size of the work area, then it is a relatively straightforward matter to translate size into effort required to build the product.

For example, Capers Jones of Software Productivity Research gives us this rule of thumb:

$$\text{Effort in staff months} = (\text{function points} \div 150) \times \text{function points}^{0.4}$$

Thus, for a 1,000-function-point work area (this is a substantial, but not overly large area) the effort in person-hours is $(1,000 \div 150) \times 1,000^{0.4}$, which is 105.66 staff-months.

Jones's rule of thumb applies to the complete development effort, which includes the effort expended by everyone on the development side of the project. In the typical software project, about half the effort is spent debugging (most of which is correcting ill-gathered requirements), so it is safe to say that about one-third of Jones's number that would cover a thorough requirements effort.

On the one hand, this is a general guide; on the other hand, it is extremely useful. Using this rule of thumb, once you have counted the function points from your context model, you immediately have a fairly precise idea of the effort you need. Please take a moment to consider whether your current estimation process is accurate enough to persist with, or whether you should start to count function points.

The keyword here is "measure."

You can, of course, measure the size of your work area any way you and your organization think appropriate. The key word here is "measure." If you are not already using a measuring method, then we suggest you start with function point counting. While it is by no means the ultimate measuring method, it is widely used. Thus a lot is known about it, and a substantial body of information and statistics on function points is available.

READING

International Function Point Users Group. *IT Measurement: Practical Advice from the Experts.* Addison-Wesley, 2002.

Function points are not the only way to measure the size of a work area. You can use Mark II Function Points (a variation on standard function points), Capers Jones's Feature Points (another variation), Tom DeMarco's Bang, Barry Boehm's COCOMO, or any of dozens of measuring methods. However, at the requirements stage of development, function points are convenient and, given what you know of the product at this stage, probably the most appropriate measuring method to use.

If you do not already use another method and would like to get started with function points, then please join us for the rest of this appendix.

A Quick Primer on Counting Function Points

This appendix is a quick primer. It does not attempt to tell you everything there is to know about counting the size of a piece of work using function points. However, it is sufficient to get started, and could possibly make you better at estimating than many organizations are at the moment.

Function points are a measure of functionality. They are considered useful because of the following simple premises:

READING

Garmus, David, and David Herron. *Function Point Analysis: Measurement Practices for Successful Software Projects.* Addison-Wesley, 2001.

- The more functionality contained within the work, the more effort needed to study it and gather its requirements.
- The amount of functionality within the work is a direct result of the data it processes.
- The more data there is, and the more complex it is, the more functionality is needed to process it.
- Because data is more visible and measurable, it makes sense to measure the data and extrapolate the functionality from it.

As the development proceeds, your analysis models become more accurate, and thus your measuring can become more accurate along with them. Because you are still at the requirements stage, however, these guidelines are appropriate:

- Count function points quickly. Given the early stage of the project, good measurements now are more useful than perfect measurements later.
- Count the function points for the work in its entirety or treat each of the business use cases as a unit of work and count it separately.

Scope of the Work

You start counting function points by using what you already have. During the blastoff you built a context model of the work area. We discussed this model in Chapter 3, but for your convenience we reproduce it here as Figure C.1.

The context diagram shows the flows of data entering and leaving the work. Each flow that enters the work must be processed. The amount of functionality needed to process it depends on the amount of data carried by each occurrence of the flow. Thus one of the measurements used by function point counting is the number of data elements—you can also call these "attributes"—contained by the flow. Counting these elements is easier if you have already written a data dictionary entry for each flow. If not, the process is simple enough to do without this definition.

Figure C.1

The context model is one of the inputs to function point counting. It shows the flows of data entering and leaving the work area. Each flow triggers some functionality or is the product of some functionality. The amount of functionality is in proportion to the amount of data carried by the flow.

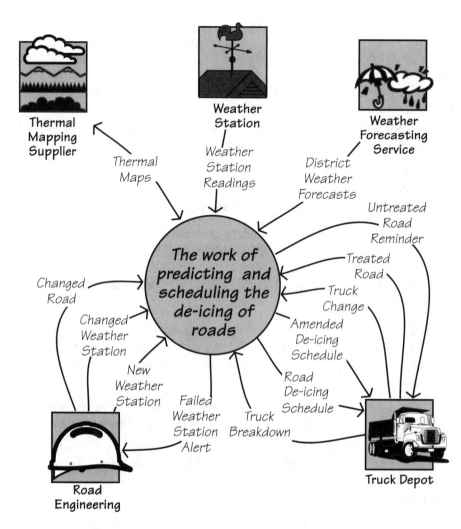

Data Stored by the Work

Another determinant of the needed functionality is the data to be stored by the work. Each database, file, or other storage medium for data requires some functionality to maintain it. Again, the amount of functionality depends on the amount of data (expressed as the number of data elements) and the complexity of the data (the number of records or tables the data is organized into). Quantifying these measures is easy enough if you have a class model of the data. We discussed this model in Chapter 14 when we were reviewing the specification; we reproduce it here as Figure C.2 for your convenience.

Each of the classes shown in the data model contains attributes—that is, the elementary items of data that together describe the class. There is a simple way

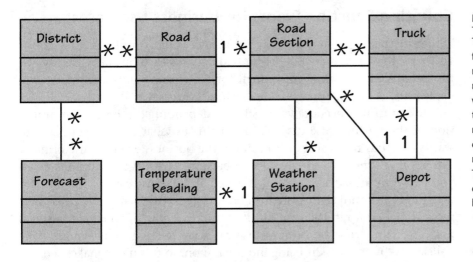

Figure C.2

The stored data model for the work area. The model includes a number of classes; the work stores data about the real-world artifacts represented by each class. Each class has a number of attributes. The function point counting procedure uses both of these numbers.

to distinguish between attributes and classes: Attributes have alphanumeric values, and classes do not.

If you look at both the context model in Figure C.1 and the class model in Figure C.2, you can imagine how the work uses the incoming data to process and maintain the stored data. These two models should be seen as two views of the same piece of work.

If you do not have a data model, we suggested alternative ways of determining and listing the classes in Chapter 14. At this stage, considering that speed is more important than hyperaccuracy, a list of classes will suffice.

Business Use Cases

With business use cases, you can again make use of what you already have to count the function points. In Chapter 4 Event-Driven Use Cases, we examined the idea of partitioning the work using business events. A business event is either a happening outside the work or a happening caused by the passage of time that triggers a response (we call it a business use case) from the work. Business use cases are not only a convenient way to gather requirements, but also a convenient way to count function points. Let's assume you have partitioned the work into business use cases, and show how they are measured.

Unfortunately, the UML use case diagram is of no help to us here, as it does not contain any information about the inputs, outputs, or stored data. Instead, we will use a data flow model of a business use case to illustrate how function points are counted. We hasten to add it is not necessary to draw these diagrams before counting function points; we use them in this appendix purely for illustrative purposes.

Counting Function Points for Business Use Cases

Earlier in this appendix, we noted that you could count function points either for the work as a whole or individually for each business use case. As the latter is usually more convenient for the requirements analyst, we will explain the counting process using business use cases.

The counting procedure varies slightly depending on the primary intention of the business use case. Think of this as what the adjacent system wants or needs that causes it to initiate the business event. If the primary intention is simply to supply data to be stored within the work (as when you pay your utility bill), then it is called an *input* use case. If the primary intention of the adjacent system when it triggers the business use case is to receive some output, then we call it, naturally enough, an *output* business use case. Time-triggered business use cases are referred to as *inquiries*. The data stored by the work is being inquired upon, so this name makes sense.

To measure the amount of functionality of a business use case—remember you are trying to figure out how long it will take to do the requirements analysis for the business use case—you count the data elements of the incoming and/or outgoing data flows as well as the number of classes referenced by the business use case. We will show how this is done for each of the types of business use case.

Counting Input Business Use Cases

One of the business events we mentioned in Chapter 4 is called "Weather station transmits reading." This is a simple enough event (see Figure C.3), and its primary intention is to update some internally stored data. Outputs from this kind of business use case, if any, are trivial and can safely be ignored. In the model of the business use case in Figure C.3, you see the incoming flow of data called Weather Station Reading and the functionality it triggers inside the work. As a result of this functionality, two classes of data are referenced. "Referenced" in this context can mean either the class is written to or read from—it does not matter which.

The model of the business use case shows all that is needed to count the function points.

Firstly, count the data elements or attributes that make up Weather Station Reading. This is easier if you have a data dictionary entry for this flow, but failing that, estimate the number. We could say it is likely to have an identifier for the weather station, the temperature, the moisture content of the road surface, the data, the time, and possibly one or two more elements. That makes seven attributes. Hold on to that number.

The business use case references two classes of data. Even without any detailed study of the work, it is easy enough to see that there is no need for any other stored data to be used by this business use case.

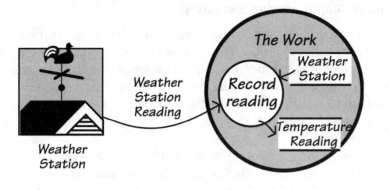

Figure C.3

Figure C.3 The primary intention of this input business use case is to alter internally stored data. It references two classes.

Next, convert those two numbers to function points. For that, use the information in Table C.1. The example business use case has seven attributes in the input flow and references two classes. The cell at the intersection of these counts gives a result of four function points.

Data Attributes of Input Flow

		1–4	5–15	16+
Classes Referenced	<2	3	3	4
	2	3	4	6
	>2	4	6	6

Table C.1

Function Point Counts for an Input Business Use Case: The correct function point counting terminology for these is "external input."

That's it for this business use case. The official function point counting practices include an additional step in which you assign a complexity measure and then use it to adjust the function point count. However, as few people bother with it and the increase in accuracy is marginal, we shall not discuss this step here.

The process outlined in this section is repeated for each of the input business use cases. These function point counts can then be aggregated to give the total count for the entire work, or you can use the counts to compare the relative expenses for analyzing each of the business use cases.

Of course, not all the business use cases are inputs.

Counting Output Business Use Cases

In an output business use case, the primary intention of the business use case is to achieve the output flow. That is, when the adjacent system triggers the business event, it wants the work to produce something. The oncoming data flow is a request for the output, and it contains whatever information is needed for the work to determine what is wanted. The work produces the significant output flow and, in so doing, makes some calculations, updates stored data, or both.

When measuring an output business use case, you count the data elements in the output flow—that is, the individual data items, or "attributes" of the flow. It would be helpful to have a data dictionary at this stage, but simply scrutinizing the flow leads you to make an educated guess about what it contains. For example, the Amended De-icing Schedule in Figure C.4 would be expected to contain the following data elements, plus maybe one or two others:

- Road
- Road section
- Truck identifier
- Starting time
- Latest possible time
- Distance to treat

Let's allow for some extras and say there are a total of eight data elements. It may seem a little cavalier to make guesses in this way, but when you look at Table C.2 you see the data elements in ranges of 1 to 5, 6 to 19, and 20 and higher. Thus your real need here is to determine, as best you can, which range the data element count for the output flow falls into.

Figure C.4

This is an output business use case. The primary goal of the adjacent system when initiating this business use case is to gain the output information.

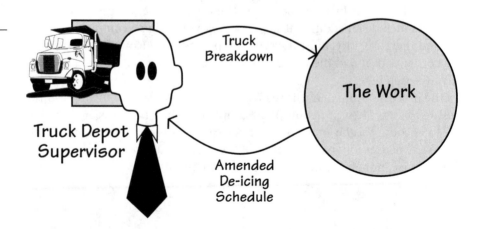

Data Attributes of Output Flow

		1–5	6–19	20+
Classes Referenced	<2	4	4	5
	2–3	4	5	7
	>3	5	7	7

Table C.2

Function Point Counts for an Output Business Use Case

The next step is to look at the stored data referenced by the business use case. In Figure C.3, we were kind enough to show the classes referenced by the business use case. We won't be so kind this time. However, go back to the class model in Figure C.2. Imagine the processing. You are rescheduling to cover for a broken-down truck. All that is needed is to find the roads and road sections allocated to the broken truck, find another truck attached to the same depot, and reallocate the roads and sections.

That's four classes: Road, Road Section, Truck, and Depot. Now refer to Table C.2. The number of attributes in the output flow is eight, and the number of classes referenced is four. The table shows seven function points for this combination.

These function points are added to the aggregate total, and you continue with the rest of the business use cases.

Counting Time-Triggered Business Use Cases

Time-triggered business use cases are almost always reports. They are produced when a predetermined time is reached—we report sales on the last day of the month; we send out invoices five days after the purchase—or because somebody wants to see a report or get some information from the work. The function-point-counting people know this kind of business use case as an *inquiry*. This is not a bad name, as the analysts start by making inquiries to the stored data.

The underlying assumption with this kind of business use case is it does not perform any significant calculations. If the processing involves more than just the simple retrieval of stored data, then it must be classified as an output business use case. That is, the stored data is updated and/or nontrivial calculations are involved. Your count must reflect this activity by allowing for its greater complexity.

The example shown in Figure C.5 is triggered by time. That is, every two hours the work sends a schedule to the Truck Depot showing which roads must be treated.

If the business use case shown in Figure C.5 were to produce an on-demand report, then it would be possible for someone at the Truck Depot to enter parameters to get the schedule he wanted. Unless nontrivial processing occurs

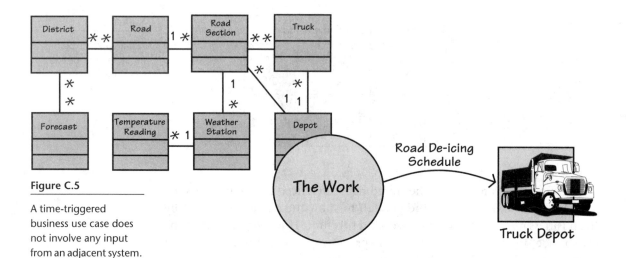

Figure C.5

A time-triggered business use case does not involve any input from an adjacent system. This kind of business use case is also called an *inquiry,* a name inspired by the fact that the stored data is simply inquired upon or retrieved (not modified) and no calculations are performed. In this instance, to produce the Road De-icing Schedule, the business use case needs to retrieve all of the stored data classes.

Table C.3

Function Point Count for an Inquiry (Time-Triggered Use Case)

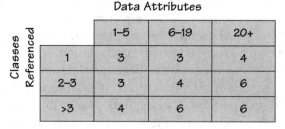

as a result and/or data stores are modified, this is still considered a time-triggered, or inquiry-type, business use case. For on-demand reports, you count the attributes in both the input parameter flow and the resultant output flow. However, if an attribute appears in both flows, it is counted only once.

To count the function points for the time-triggered business use case shown in Figure C.5, you use Table C.3. Our example business use case must reference all eight of the classes to make its predictions about ice formation. The amended schedule we saw previously had eight data attributes; the output here would have the same number.

Classes Referenced	Data Attributes		
	1–5	6–19	20+
1	3	3	4
2–3	3	4	6
>3	4	6	6

Note that these are *unduplicated* attributes. You are counting unique data attributes or elements, which you might also call *data element types.*

As shown in Table C.3, the combination of eight data attributes and more than three classes referenced yields six function points. Add the six function points to your aggregate total, and continue counting the other business use cases.

Counting the Stored Data

The data stored within the work area must be maintained. This upkeep naturally requires an amount of functionality, which is in turn counted by measuring the amount and complexity of the data. For this part of the count, you follow pretty much the same path as before—the difference is that you count only the stored data. Business use cases do not figure in this count at all.

Internal Stored Data

The first of the stored data to be counted is the data held inside the work area. Function-point-counting manuals refer to this information as *internal logical files;* they include the databases, flat files, paper files, or whatever else is part of your work area. Keep in mind that any files that are present for implementation reasons are not counted—for example, backups and manual files that are identical (or close) to automated files.

You use the class model of the data to count from. This time, for each entity, count its attributes. Skip any attributes that are present to serve purely technological reasons, but count foreign keys (pointers from one class to another). The count should be accurate enough to assign the class to one of the three columns shown in Table C.4.

Data Attributes

Classes Referenced		1–19	20–50	51+
	<2	7	7	10
	2–5	7	10	15
	>5	10	15	15

Table C.4

Function Point Counts for Internally Stored Data

The next count is *record elements*. These are either the class itself or subtypes of classes. That is, if the class has no subtypes, it is one unit of data and counts as one record element. Conversely, if there are subtypes, you must count them as record elements.

We do not have any subtypes in the IceBreaker class model, so let us invent some. Suppose that weather stations come in various types. One special type does not have a surface-moisture sensor. Consequently, predictions based on the data from this kind of weather station are made differently. Moreover, the work needs to keep special data relating to this kind of weather station. The stations also fail from time to time. When they do, the work needs to store special data relating to past predictions from this station.

Figure C.6

The *Weather Station* entity has two subtypes. The *Failed* subtype contains attributes about past predictions that are used in lieu of current readings. The *No moisture sensing* subtype has attributes that describe adjustments needed to compensate for this weather station's lack of a moisture sensor. These subtypes are necessary because their attributes do not apply to all weather stations.

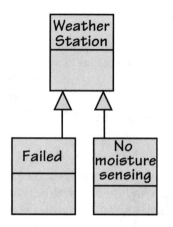

The result of these changes is that we have created two subtypes of the weather station class (also known as subclasses). Figure C.6 shows the resulting model.

In function point terms, the Weather Station entity counts for two record elements. You count only the subtypes, and not the parent entity. For the other entities in the class model, count them as having one record element.

The next task is to count the number of attributes in each class. This is not as arduous as it might at first seem. According to Table C.4, you need only know if there are between 1 and 19 attributes to the class, or between 20 and 50, or more than 51. Given these ranges and your desire to complete this count quickly, it is permissible to make some inspired guesses regarding the number of attributes for the entity.

Pick a class—say, Truck. How many attributes does the Truck class have? Or, as you could say here, does it have more than 19? Unlikely. So let us say that the Truck class has 19 or fewer attributes and no subclasses, so it counts as one record element. That means it needs seven function points' worth of functionality to support it.

You do the same thing for the remainder of the stored data. Most of the classes will also have a function point count of seven, as none of them should have more than 19 attributes. Weather Station is the only class to have subtypes (we gave it two hypothetical subtypes), but it would have fewer than 19 attributes, and so would account for seven function points. There are eight classes in the stored data model, so the aggregate count for the internal stored data is 56 function points.

Externally Stored Data

Most pieces of work make use of data that is stored and maintained outside of the work. For example, almost every project has to reference stored data that is owned by some other part of the organization or, in some cases, by another organization.

References to external stored data show up on the context diagram as interactions with *cooperative adjacent systems*. These adjacent systems receive requests for data and send back a response. The IceBreaker work, for example, uses thermal maps that are maintained by an outside body. When the scheduling business use case needs this data, it makes a request for the map of the appropriate district, and the thermal map supplier responds with the requested information. This interaction is shown in Figure C.7.

Although externally stored data does not have to be maintained by the work, the need for the data adds functionality to the work. Thus it, too, is counted. You make this count the same way as you did for the internal data. However, instead of building a data model, this time let's use educated guesses to size the data.

The stored data in this situation deals with the temperatures of roads. It gives the road-surface temperature for every meter of every road. However, even though the data is repetitive, you count it as a single iteration only.

No, don't even count. As you see in Table C.5, once again you merely need to guess whether the number of attributes is 19 or fewer, 20 to 50, or more than 50. The thermal mapping database would fall into the first column. Further educated guesswork would say there are fewer than two record elements—it could have been as many as five without making any difference to the count—and so this external data adds five function points to the functionality of the work.

You repeat this exercise for each of the classes in the externally stored data. For the IceBreaker work, there appears to be only one class in the database. This is a little unusual, but it can happen from time to time.

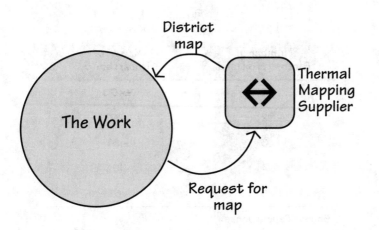

Figure C.7

The *Thermal Mapping Supplier* is an external system that maintains a database of the temperature differentials within areas. This data is too volatile for the IceBreaker work to maintain, so it elects to query this cooperative adjacent system whenever it needs the data.

Table C.5

Function Point Counts
for External Interface
Files

Data Attributes

		1–19	20–50	51+
Classes Referenced	<2	5	5	7
	2–5	5	7	10
	>5	7	10	10

A small aside: Figure C.7 shows the use of externally stored data. The flows to and from the adjacent system are *not* counted for function point purposes, because the adjacent system is a cooperative system. That is, it provides some service in collaboration with the work area. Thus the flow to the external system consists of the parameters needed to query the database, and the resultant data flow to the work consists of data as stored by the external database. For both flows, their attributes would be the same as the stored data and are not counted. For function point counting purposes, think about the use of the adjacent system's database only—in this case, it provides database access as if it belonged to the work area.

Adjust for What You Don't Know

You are counting function points during the requirements activity. You may not have all the data you need for a completely accurate function point count. In the preceding sections, we showed how you count function points using inputs, outputs, inquiries, internal files, and external files. However, even if you do not have all five of these parameters, you can still count function points. The count is simply adjusted according to how many of these parameters are available.

Table C.6

Uncertainty Ranges
Based on the Number of
Parameters Used in
Function Point Counting

Number of Parameters Used	Range of Uncertainty
1	±40%
2	±20%
3	±15%
4	±10%
5	±5%

Source: Capers Jones

Table C.6 gives the *range of uncertainty* depending on the number of parameters used in your count. For example, if you used only three parameters—say, the inputs, outputs, and inquiries (these are the easiest to use because they are the data flows on the context model)—then your function point count would be accurate within a range of ±15%.

What's Next After Counting Function Points?

The function point count for the requirements activity for the project is simply the aggregation of the counts for all the business use cases and the stored data. Now you must convert it to some indication of effort needed for the requirements activity. Earlier in this appendix, we introduced a rule of thumb used by Capers Jones. So many people use this rule that we believe it is worth trying on your project. Of course, data that comes from your own organization is preferable, but to get that data you have to count the function points for previous projects so that you come up with your own metric of hours (or money) needed per function point.

You can also get help. This appendix concludes by suggesting some resources that have useful information. As we said at the beginning, our aim is to give you a gentle introduction to counting function points, and to intrigue you enough to want to investigate the subject further.

A great deal of material is available on the Web, much of it for free. The following organizations are good places to start when you are looking for more information on function points as well as productivity metrics:

- The David Consulting Group (*www.davidconsultinggroup.com*)
- The Gartner Group (*www.gartner.com*)
- International Software Benchmarking Group (*www.isbsg.org.au*)
- International Function Point Users Group (*www.ifpug.org*)
- META Group (*www.metagroup.com*)
- Quality Plus Technologies (*www.qualityplustech.com*)
- Software Productivity Research (*www.spr.com*)
- United Kingdom Software Metrics Association (*www.uksma.co.uk/*)

Additionally, we recommend these resources:

Dekkers, *Carol. Demystifying Function Points: Clarifying Common Terminology. www.qualityplustech.com.*
This resource is used internally at IBM as one of its definition standards.

Dekkers, Carol. *Function Point Counting and CFPS Study Guides Volumes 1, 2, and 3*. Quality Plus, 2002. *www.qualityplustech.com*.
In addition to case studies, these study guides provide logistics and hints for the IFPUG Certified Function Point Specialist (CFPS) exam.

Fenton, Norman, and Shari Lawrence Pfleeger. *Software Metrics: A Rigorous and Practical Approach* (second edition). Thomson Computer Press, 1996.
This book describes several ways of measuring the software development process. The case studies by themselves—focusing on Hewlett-Packard, IBM, and the U.S. Department of Defense—are worth the price of the book.

Garmus, David, and David Herron. *Function Point Analysis: Measurement Practices for Successful Software Projects*. Addison-Wesley, 2001.
This book provides a thorough treatment of function point counting using the IFPUG rules.

International Function Point Users Group. *IT Measurement: Practical Advice from the Experts*. Addison-Wesley, 2002.

Pfleeger, Shari Lawrence. *Software Engineering: Theory and Practice* (second edition). Prentice Hall, 2001.
As the title suggests, this book is a more general text on software. However, the discussions of measurement are relevant to this chapter.

Putman, Lawrence, and Ware Myers. *Five Core Metrics: The Intelligence Behind Successful Software Management*. Dorset House, 2003.
Not function points, but some other very good ways and things to measure. The authors demonstrate how the five core metrics—time, effort, size, reliability, and process productivity—are used to control and adjust projects.

There's more to function point counting, of course, but our discussion here should suffice for the quick counts needed at requirements time.

Project Sociology Analysis Templates

in which we provide some help with finding the stakeholders for your project

This appendix contains templates that are designed to help you to do project sociology analysis. Its aim is threefold:

- To help you discover the relevant stakeholders for your project
- To help you identify gaps without stakeholder representation
- To help you agree on your decision-making structure

Stakeholder Map Template

Figure D.1 is a generic stakeholder map showing the potential classes of stakeholders. Use it as an aid for discovering your stakeholders. Refer to Chapter 3, Project Blastoff, for a discussion of each of the stakeholder classes.

Stakeholder Analysis Template

The template in Figure D.2 is a sample checklist you can use to identify and analyze your stakeholders. Note that the template's stakeholder classes correspond to those on the stakeholder map (Figure D.1). For each stakeholder class, we have suggested common roles that represent the class. Of course, you will want to modify this list to include role names that are appropriate for your organization. It will probably be more convenient for you to do so using a spreadsheet. A complete version of the template in the form of an Excel spreadsheet can be found at *www.volere.co.uk*.

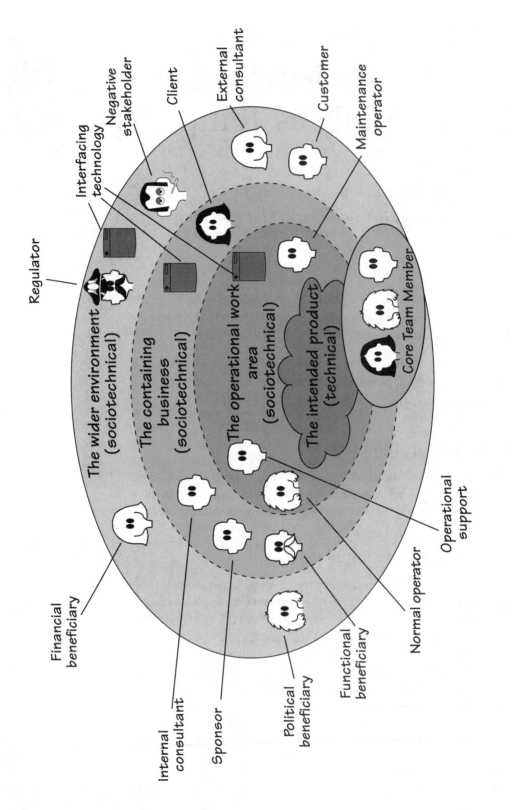

Figure D.1 This generic stakeholder map shows the various classes of stakeholders. Use it as an aid to identifying your stakeholders.

Figure D.2 Volere Stakeholder Analysis Template

Classes of Knowledge

Stakeholder Class (Class of stakeholders who share a particular stakeholding in the project)	Stakeholder Role (The job title, department, or organization that might indicate a role for this class of stakeholder)	Stakeholder Name (Or their representative)	Stakeholder Rationale (Consider benefits and impacts)	Necessary Involvement (When and how much time)	Goals	Business Constraints	Technical Constraints	Functionality	Look and Feel	Usability	Peformance	Safety	Operational Environment	Portability	Security	Cultural Acceptance	Legal	Maintenance	Estimates	Risk	Design Ideas
Operational Work Area Stakeholder Classes																					
Interfacing Technology																					
	Existing Software Systems																				
	Existing Hardware																				
	Existing Machines																				
Maintenance Operator																					
	Hardware Maintainer																				
	Software Maintainer																				
	Mechanical Part Maintainer																				
Normal Operator																					
	Operation Technical Users																				
	Operational Business Users																				
	Members of the Public																				
Operational Support																					
	Help Desk																				
	Coach/Mentor																				
	Trainer																				
	Installer																				

Figure D.2 Volere Stakeholder Analysis Template (continued)

Classes of Knowledge

Stakeholder Class (Class of stakeholders who share a particular stakeholding in the project)	Stakeholder Role (The job title, department, or organization that might indicate a role for this class of stakeholder)	Stakeholder Name (Or their representative)	Stakeholder Rationale (Consider benefits and impacts)	Necessary Involvement (When and how much time)	Goals	Business Constraints	Technical Constraints	Functionality	Look and Feel	Usability	Performance	Safety	Operational Environment	Portability	Security	Cultural Acceptance	Legal	Maintenance	Estimates	Risk	Design Ideas
Containing Business Stakeholder Classes																					
Client	Investment Manager																				
	Product Manager																				
	Strategic Program Manager																				
	Chief Executive																				
Functional Beneficiary	Manager of Operators																				
	Business Decision Maker																				
	Relative of Operator																				
	Product Manager																				
	Program Manager																				
	Another Department																				
	User of Reports																				
Interfacing Technology	Meta Manager																				
Internal Consultant	Business/Subject Expert																				
	Business Data Modeler																				
	Future Ideas Specialist																				
	Current Automation Specialist																				
	Usability Expert																				
	System Architect																				

Figure D.2 Volere Stakeholder Analysis Template (*continued*)

Classes of Knowledge

Stakeholder Class (Class of stakeholders who share a particular stakeholding in the project)	Stakeholder Role (The job title, department, or organization that might indicate a role for this class of stakeholder)	Stakeholder Name (Or their representative)	Stakeholder Rationale (Consider benefits and impacts)	Necessary Involvement (When and how much time)	Goals	Business Constraints	Technical Constraints	Functionality	Look and Feel	Usability	Performance	Safety	Operational Environment	Portability	Security	Cultural Acceptance	Legal	Maintenance	Estimates	Risk	Design Ideas
Internal Consultant (*continued*)	Marketing Specialist																				
	Sales Specialist																				
	Technology Expert																				
	Standards Specialist																				
	Testing Specialist																				
	Organizational Architect																				
	Aesthetics Specialist																				
	Graphics Specialist																				
Sponsor	Sponsor																				
	Project Champion																				
Wider Environment Stakeholder Classes																					
Customer	Department Manager																				
	Another Organization																				
	Member of the Public																				
Interfacing Technology	External Meta Manager																				
External Consultants	Auditors																				
	Focus Group																				

Figure D.2 Volere Stakeholder Analysis Template *(continued)*

Stakeholder Class (Class of stakeholders who share a particular stakeholding in the project)	Stakeholder Role (The job title, department, or organization that might indicate a role for this class of stakeholder)	Stakeholder Name (Or their representative)	Stakeholder Rationale (Consider benefits and impacts)	Necessary Involvement (When and how much time)	Goals	Business Constraints	Technical Constraints	Functionality	Look and Feel	Usability	Performance	Safety	Operational Environment	Portability	Security	Cultural Acceptance	Legal	Maintenance	Estimates	Risk	Design Ideas
External Consultants *(continued)*	Security Specialist																					
	Environmental Specialist																					
	Safety Specialist																					
	Outsourcee																					
	Cultural Specialist																					
	Legal Specialist																					
	Packaging Designer																					
	Manufacturer																					
	Negotiator																					
	Public Opinion																					
	COTS Supplier																					
	Inspector																					
Negative Stakeholders	Competitor																					
	Hacker																					
	Political Party																					
	Pressure Group																					
	Public Opinion																					
Core Project Team Stakeholder Classes																						
Core Team Members	Project Manager																					
	Business Analyst																					

Classes of Knowledge

Figure D.2 Volere Stakeholder Analysis Template *(continued)*

Classes of Knowledge

Stakeholder Class (Class of stakeholders who share a particular stakeholding in the project)	Stakeholder Role (The job title, department, or organization that might indicate a role for this class of stakeholder)	Stakeholder Name (Or their representative)	Stakeholder Rationale (Consider benefits and impacts)	Necessary Involvement (When and how much time)	Goals	Business Constraints	Technical Constraints	Functionality	Look and Feel	Usability	Performance	Safety	Operational Environment	Portability	Security	Cultural Acceptance	Legal	Maintenance	Estimates	Risk	Design Ideas
Core Team Members *(continued)*	Requirements Analyst																				
	System Analyst																				
	Tester																				
	Technical Writer																				
	Systems Architect																				
	Systems Designer																				

This template was produced as a result of collaborations between Suzanne Robertson of The Atlantic Systems Guild Ltd. and Chris Rupp of the Sophist Group, http://www.sophist.de and Ian Alexander of Scenario Plus, http://www.scenarioplus.org.uk/. Copyright © The Atlantic Systems Guild Ltd.

Glossary

Actor The person or automated system that interacts with a product use case. Actors are also known as users and end users.

Adjacent system A system (person, organization, computer system) that provides information to, or receives information from, the work that you are studying. You need to study the adjacent system to understand how it communicates as well as why it communicates with the work.

Agile Manifesto A set of principles that focuses on the delivery of working software to the customer, collaborative working practices, and the ability to respond rapidly to change.

Blastoff A technique for building the foundation for the requirements activity by establishing the scope-stakeholders-goals trinity and verifying the viability of the project.

Business event Something that happens to the business (usually called "the work") that makes it respond. Examples: "Customer pays an invoice," "Truck reports all roads have been treated," "Time to read electricity meters," "Surfer wants to search Web site."

Business use case The work's response to a business event. It includes the processes and the stored data needed to satisfy the request implicit in the business event. See also *Product use case*.

Client The person who pays for the development of the product, or who has organizational responsibility for the project. Also known as the sponsor.

Constraint A requirement, either organizational or technological, that restricts the way you produce the product. It may be a management edict on the way the product must be designed—"It must work on a 3G mobile phone"—or a budget that limits the extent of the product.

Context The subject matter, people, and organizations that affect the requirements for the product. The context of study, or the work context, identifies the business to be studied and the adjacent systems that interact with this work. The product context identifies the scope of the product and its interactions with users and other systems.

Customer   A person who buys the product.

Data flow   Data that moves from one process to another. Usually represented by a named arrow.

Design   The act of crafting a technological solution to fit the requirements, within the constraints.

Developer   Someone who contributes to the technological development of the product. Examples: designer, tester, programmer.

Event-driven use case   The work done by the product in response to a business event. Once the desired response to a business event is established, the requirements analyst and the designer determine how much of that response will be done by the automated product. The use case is a convenient way of identifying a user and a group of requirements that carry out a specific task for that user.

Fit criterion   A quantification or measurement of the requirement such that you are able to determine whether the delivered product satisfies (fits) the requirement.

Function point   A measure of the functionality of the work or a piece of software. Function points were first proposed by Allan Albrecht; today the method for counting function points is specified by the International Function Point User Group.

Functional requirement   Something that the product must do. Functional requirements are part of the fundamental processes of the product.

Nonfunctional requirement   A property or quality that the product must have, such as an appearance, speed, security, or accuracy property.

Product   That which you are about to build, and for which the requirements are written. In this book, "product" usually means a software product, but the requirements can be for any kind of product.

Product use case   The part of the business use case you decide to automate. You write the requirements for the product use case. See also *Business use case*.

Project goal   The reasons for doing the project, including a quantification of the expected benefit.

Prototype   A simulation of the product using either software prototyping tools, low-fidelity whiteboards, or paper mock-ups. The prototype is intended to make it easier for stakeholders to understand and describe their requirements.

Quality Gateway Application of a set of tests (e.g., relevance, ambiguity, viability, fit) to assure the quality of individual requirements before the requirements become part of the requirements specification.

Rationale The justification for a requirement. It is used to help understand a requirement, and sometimes reveals the real intention of the requirement.

Requirement Something that the product must do, or a property that the product must have, and that is needed or wanted by the stakeholders.

Requirements analyst The person who has responsibility for producing the requirements specification. The analyst does not necessarily do all of the requirements elicitation, but is responsible for coordinating the requirements effort. Depending on how roles are defined in an organization, this individual might be referred to as a business analyst, systems analyst, or requirements engineer.

Requirements pattern A cohesive collection of requirements that carry out some recognizable and potentially recurring functionality.

Requirements specification A complete collection of requirements knowledge for a specific project. The specification defines the product and may be used as a contract to build the product.

Requirements specification document A document that contains all or part of the requirements specification knowledge depending on who and why the knowledge is being communicated.

Requirements specification template A guide for gathering and organizing requirements knowledge. See Appendix B for an example.

Requirements tool A software tool capable of maintaining all or part of the requirements specification.

Retrospective A review designed to gather experience and provide input into improving the requirements process.

Scenario A breakdown of a business use case, or a product use case, into a series of stakeholder-recognizable steps. Scenarios are used for discovering and communicating work knowledge.

Sponsor See *Client.*

Stakeholder Any person who has an interest in the product and therefore has requirements for it, such as the client, a user, and someone who builds the product. Some stakeholders are remote, such as an auditor, a safety inspector, and the company lawyer.

System In the context of this book, a business system (not just the computer or the software system).

Systems analysis The craft of modeling the system's functions and data. Systems analysis can be done in several ways: data flow modeling, as defined by DeMarco; event response modeling, as per McMenamin and Palmer; use cases, as per Jacobson; or any of the many object-oriented methods, most of which use the Unified Modeling Language notation. See the Bibliography for references.

Technological requirement A requirement that is necessary only because of the chosen technology. It is not there to satisfy a business need.

Trawling techniques Techniques for discovering, eliciting, determining, and inventing requirements.

User The person or system that manipulates the product. Also known as an actor or end user.

Volere A set of principles, processes, templates, tools, and techniques developed to improve the discovery, communication, and management of requirements.

Work A business area of the organization that you have to understand. Also, the work the user is intended to do. The product is to become a part of this work.

Work context The extent of the business area under investigation, and the real world that surrounds it.

Bibliography

Alexander, Christopher. *Notes on the Synthesis of Form*. Harvard University Press, 1964.

Alexander, Christopher, et al. *A Pattern Language*. Oxford University Press, 1977.

Alexander, Ian, Neil Maiden, et al. *Scenarios, Stories, Use Cases Through the Systems Development Life-Cycle*. John Wiley & Sons, 2004.

Alexander, Ian, and Richard Stevens. *Writing Better Requirements*. Addison-Wesley, 2002.

Ambler, Scott. *The Elements of UML 2.0 Style*. Cambridge University Press, 2005.

Beck, Kent, with Cynthia Andres. *Extreme Programming Explained: Embrace Change*. Second edition. Addison-Wesley, 2004.

Beyer, Hugh, and Karen Holtzblatt. *Contextual Design: Defining Customer-Centered Systems*. Morgan Kauffmann, 1998.

Boehm, Barry. *Software Risk Management*. IEEE Computer Society Press, 1989.

Boehm, Barry, and Richard Turner. *Balancing Agility and Discipline: A Guide for the Perplexed*. Addison-Wesley, 2004.

Booch, Grady, James Rumbaugh, and Ivar Jacobsen. *Unified Modeling Language User Guide*. Second edition. Addison-Wesley, 2005.

Brooks, Fred. *No Silver Bullet: Essence and Accidents of Software Engineering* and *No Silver Bullet Refired*. *The Mythical Man-Month: Essays on Software Engineering*. 20th anniversary edition. Addison-Wesley, 1995

Buzan, Tony, with Barry Buzan. *The Ultimate Book of Mind Maps*. Harper Thorsons, 2006.

Carroll, John. *Scenario-Based Design*. John Wiley & Sons, 1995.

Checkland, Peter. *Systems Thinking, Systems Practice*. John Wiley & Sons, 1981.

Checkland, Peter, and J. Scholes. *Soft Systems Methodology in Action.* John Wiley & Sons, 1991.

Cockburn, Alistair. *Writing Effective Use Cases.* Addison-Wesley, 2001.

Cooper, Alan. *The Inmates Are Running the Asylum: Why High Tech Products Drive Us Crazy and How to Restore the Sanity.* Sams Publishing, 1999.

Davis, Alan. *Just Enough Requirements Management.* Dorset House, 2005.

DeMarco, Tom, and Tim Lister. *Peopleware. Productive Projects and Teams.* Second edition. Dorset House, 1999.

DeMarco, Tom, and Tim Lister. *Waltzing with Bears: Managing Risk on Software Projects.* Dorset House, 2003.

Fenton, Norman, and Shari Lawrence Pfleeger. *Software Metrics: A Rigorous and Practical Approach.* International Thomson Computer Press, 1997.

Ferdinandi, Patricia. *A Requirements Pattern: Succeeding in the Internet Economy.* Addison-Wesley, 2002.

Fowler, Martin. *UML Distilled: A Brief Guide to the Standard Object Modeling Language.* Third edition. Addison-Wesley, 2003.

Function Point Counting Practices Manual. International Function Point Users Group, Westerville, OH.

Garmus, David, and David Herron. *Function Point Analysis: Measurement Practices for Successful Software Projects.* Addison-Wesley, 2000.

Gause, Donald, and Gerald Weinberg. *Are Your Lights On? How to Figure Out What the Problem Really Is.* Dorset House, 1990.

Gause, Donald, and Gerald Weinberg. *Exploring Requirements: Quality Before Design.* Dorset House, 1989.

Gilb, Tom. *Competitive Engineering: A Handbook for Systems Engineering, Requirements Engineering, and Software Engineering Using Planguage.* Butterworth-Heinemann, 2005.

Gottesdiener, Ellen. *Requirements by Collaboration: Workshops for Defining Needs.* Addison-Wesley, 2002.

Hauser, John R., and Don Clausing. The House of Quality. *Harvard Business Review,* 1988.

Hay, David. *Data Model Patterns: Conventions of Thought.* Dorset House, 1995.

Highsmith, James. *Adaptive Software Development: A Collaborative Approach to Managing Complex Systems.* Dorset House, 2000.

Holtzblatt, Karen, Jessamyn Burns Wendell, and Shelley Wood. *Rapid Contextual Design: A How-to Guide to Key Techniques for User-Centered Design*. Morgan Kaufmann, 2004.

Hull, Elizabeth, Ken Jackson, and Jeremy Dick. *Requirements Engineering*. Second edition. Springer, 2005.

Jackson, Michael. *Problem Frames: Analyzing and Structuring Software Development Problems*. Addison-Wesley, 2001.

Jackson, Michael. *Software Requirements and Specifications: A Lexicon of Practice, Principles, and Prejudices*. Addison-Wesley, 1996.

Jacobson, Ivar, Magnus Christerson, Patrik Jonsson, and Gunnar Övergaard. *Object Oriented Software Engineering: A Use Case Driven Approach*. Addison-Wesley, 1992.

Jacobson, Ivar, Martin Griss, and Ralph Jonsson. *Software Reuse: Architecture Process and Organization for Business Success*. Addison-Wesley, 1997.

Jones, Capers. *Applied Software Measurement*. McGraw-Hill, 1991.

Jones, Capers. *Assessment and Control of Software Risks*. Prentice Hall, 1994.

Kerth, Norman. *Project Retrospectives*. Dorset House, 2001.

Kovitz, Benjamin. *Practical Software Requirements: A Manual of Content and Style*. Manning, 1999.

Kruchten, Philippe. *The Rational Unified Process: An Introduction*. Third edition. Addison-Wesley, 2004.

Lauesen, Soren. *Software Requirements: Styles and Techniques*. Addison-Wesley, 2002.

Lawrence-Pfleeger, Shari. *Software Engineering: Theory and Practice*. Prentice Hall, 1998.

Leffingwell, Dean, and Don Widrig. *Managing Software Requirements: A Use Case Approach*. Second edition. Addison-Wesley, 2003.

Maiden, Neil, and Suzanne Robertson. *Integrating Creativity into Requirements Processes: Experiences with an Air Traffic Management System*. International Conference on Software Engineering, May 2005.

McConnell, Steve. *Code Complete*. Second edition. Microsoft Press, 2004.

McMenamin, Steve, and John Palmer. *Essential Systems Analysis*. Yourdon Press, 1984.

Myers, Glenford, Corey Sandler, et al. *The Art of Software Testing*. Second edition. John Wiley & Sons, 2004.

Norman, Donald. *The Design of Everyday Things*. Basic Books, 2002.

Pardee, William J. *To Satisfy and Delight Your Customer*. Dorset House, 1996.

Pfleeger, Charles, and Shari Lawrence Pfleeger. *Security in Computing*. Third edition. Prentice Hall, 2002.

Pilone, Dan, and Neil Pitman. *UML 2.0 in a Nutshell*. O'Reilly, 2005.

Prieto-Diaz, Rubén, and Guillermo Arango. *Domain Analysis and Software Systems Modeling*. IEEE Computer Society Press, 1991.

Robertson, James, and Suzanne Robertson. *Complete Systems Analysis: The Workbook, the Textbook, the Answers*. Dorset House, 1998.

Robertson, Suzanne, and James Robertson. *Requirements-Led Project Management: Discovering David's Slingshot*. Addison-Wesley, 2005.

Rumbaugh, James, Ivar Jacobson, and Grady Booch. *Unified Modeling Language Reference Manual*. Second edition. Addison-Wesley, 2004.

Sommerville, Ian, and Pete Sawyer. *Requirements Engineering: A Good Practice Guide*. John Wiley & Sons, 1998.

Spolsky, Joel. *Joel on Software: And on Diverse and Occasionally Related Matters That Will Prove of Interest to Software Developers, Designers, and Managers, and to Those Who, Whether by Good Fortune or Ill Luck, Work with Them in Some Capacity*. Apress, 2004.

Tockey, Steve. *Return on Software: Maximizing the Return on Your Software Investment*. Addison-Wesley, 2004.

Weigers, Karl. *Software Requirements*. Second edition. Microsoft Press, 2003.

Weinberg, Jerry. *Quality Software Management. Volume 1: Systems Thinking. Volume 2: First-Order Measurement. Volume 3: Congruent Action. Volume 4: Anticipating Change*. Dorset House, 1992–1997.

Wiley, Bill. *Essential System Requirements: A Practical Guide to Event-Driven Methods*. Addison-Wesley, 2000.

Index

W

THIS BOOK IS SAFARI ENABLED

INCLUDES FREE 45-DAY ACCESS TO THE ONLINE EDITION

The Safari® Enabled icon on the cover of your favorite technology book means the book is available through Safari Bookshelf. When you buy this book, you get free access to the online edition for 45 days.

Safari Bookshelf is an electronic reference library that lets you easily search thousands of technical books, find code samples, download chapters, and access technical information whenever and wherever you need it.

TO GAIN 45-DAY SAFARI ENABLED ACCESS TO THIS BOOK:

- Go to **http://www.awprofessional.com/safarienabled**
- Complete the brief registration form
- Enter the coupon code found in the front of this book on the "Copyright" page

If you have difficulty registering on Safari Bookshelf or accessing the online edition, please e-mail customer-service@safaribooksonline.com.

Addison
Wesley

informIT

Register
Your Book

at www.awprofessional.com/register

You may be eligible to receive:

- Advance notice of forthcoming editions of the book
- Related book recommendations
- Chapter excerpts and supplements of forthcoming titles
- Information about special contests and promotions throughout the year
- Notices and reminders about author appearances, tradeshows, and online chats with special guests

Contact us

If you are interested in writing a book or reviewing manuscripts prior to publication, please write to us at:

Editorial Department
Addison-Wesley Professional
75 Arlington Street, Suite 300
Boston, MA 02116 USA
Email: AWPro@aw.com

Visit us on the Web: http://www.awprofessional.com

The type from
the template

List of events/
use cases that
need this
requirement

Requirement #: **Unique ID**   Requirement Type: Event/Use Case #:

Description: **A one-sentence statement of the intention of the requirement**

Ratonale: **A justification of the requirement**

Originator: **The person who raised this requirement**

Fit Criterion: **A measurement of the requirement such that it is possible
to test if the solution matches the original requirement**

Customer Satisfaction: Customer Dissatisfaction: Conflicts: **Other requirements
that cannot be
implemented if this**
Priority: **A rating of the customer value**

Supporting Materials: **Pointer to documents that
illustrate and explain this
requirement**   **one is**

History: **Creation,
changes**

Volere
Copyright @ Atlantic Systems Guild

Degree of stakeholder happiness if
this requirement is successfully implemented.
Scale from 1 = uninterested to
5 = extremely pleased.

Measure of stakeholder unhappiness
if this requirement is not part of the
final product.
Scale from 1 = hardly matters to
5 = extremely displeased.

PROJECT DRIVERS

1 The Purpose of the Project

1a   The user business or background of the
project effort
1b   Goals of the project

2 Client, Customer, and Other Stakeholders

2a   The client
2b   The customer
2c   Other stakeholders

3 Users of the Product

3a   The hands-on users of the product
3b   Priorities assigned to users
3c   User participation
3d   Maintenance users and service technicians

PROJECT CONSTRAINTS

4 Mandated Constraints

4a   Solution constraints
4b   Implementation environment of the
current system
4c   Partner or collaborative applications
4d   Off-the-shelf software
4e   Anticipated workplace environment
4f   Schedule constraints
4g   Budget constraints

5 Naming Conventions and Definitions

5a   Definitions of all terms, including
acronyms, used in the project
5b   Data dictionary for any included models